SIX PLAYS OF CHEKHOV

SIX PLAYS

OF

CHEKHOV

NEW ENGLISH VERSIONS

AND INTRODUCTION

By Robert W. Corrigan

FOREWORD BY HAROLD CLURMAN

Holt, Rinehart and Winston

NEW YORK · CHICAGO · SAN FRANCISCO
TORONTO · LONDON

Library of Congress Catalog Card Number: 62–13883

21569-0112

Printed in the United States of America

For

Esther Jane

With love and the hope

that she *does* get to Moscow!

CONTENTS

FOREWORD

by Harold Clurman

CHEKHOV becomes more wonderful to me with every new contact. An historian might well exclaim today, "To think that *The Sea Gull* was once considered an unintelligible play, and that even Stanislavsky failed at first to appreciate it." But I am not at all certain that I did on my initial encounter with the play—and that so much later than Stanislavsky!

It seems to me now that Chekhov is always new, always fresh and always moving. Yet there are still people who ask themselves what all the weeping is about in Chekhov, and others who find him untheatrical. There are those who think his plays glum; others insist that they are absurd. In his stimulating book *The Death of Tragedy*, George Steiner is on the verge of classifying Chekhov as one of the modern dramatists whose plays achieved the tragic dimension only to remind himself that Chekhov called these plays "comedies."

The truth is that none of these categories and definitions stand the test of our actual experience in the theatre because of Chekhov's *originality* which has very little to do with most academic tags.

Knowledge of Chekhov's major plays prove them perfect in craftsmanship and profoundly theatrical. This is not so if we think of theatre only as something spectacular or sensational and believe dramatic art limited to the Ibsen techniques. Chekhov's plays are consumately constructed, as Robert Corrigan takes pains to point out in his introduction, but their structure is of a special devising—which might be described as "seamless." One is not able to recognize the "mechanics" of workmanship. The plays unfold effortlessly as if what one were seeing (or reading) were simply the flow of everyday occurrences.

It is not this aspect of Chekhov's plays, however, which strikes me most forcibly as I read Corrigan's lucid, fluent, straightforward and eminently actable translations. It is the fact that these plays dwell in a realm beyond tragedy or comedy. They are deeply affecting even as they provoke laughter; they make us smile even as we feel our hearts ready to break.

I ask myself the secret of this dramatic miracle. The answer lies, I believe, in Chekhov's wisdom and humanity. He transcends the false opposition of optimism versus pessimism. Man is inadequate to his tasks, his promise, his ideals. His dignity lies in his never ending aspiration, which is also the source of his vulnerability. All Chekhov's characters are our kin because they are *real* people: one cannot label them. Even those who appear least amiable are rendered so understandable in relation to some need or desire we share with them that we cannot possibly hate them.

Everybody in Chekhov is willy-nilly made to speak from his heart, almost one might say from his unconscious. Without knowing it all the characters reveal themselves, though Chekhov never "explains" them, never removes the shadow of their mystery. (This is the mark of all genuine creation.) We are always made aware— no matter what foolishness is expressed or what reprehensible action is committed—what universal motive prompted the stupidity or the misdeed. For Chekhov accepts life. His is an attitude of tenderness—not forgiveness because there is after all nothing to forgive. The plays are wrought from a fabric of love.

The characters for the most part fail in their immediate aims; yet nearly all of them have some "premonition of happiness." Even in the depths of their wretchedness they feel they must go on, they must *"work,"* they must aspire. Chekhov never places himself above or beneath any living creature; he stands beside them.

The difference between Chekhov and the "sophisticates," the cynics, the prophets of doom, the preachers of hopelessness and futility may be gathered from his statement "He who desires nothing, hopes for nothing and is afraid of nothing cannot be an artist." This is not a mere credo, it reflects Chekhov's essential spirit, the very breath of his being. His humor is of the same stuff as his sorrow. His softness is his strength. His defeated (or frustrated) people are vibrant with life because they yearn to be fuller—more—than they are. There is neither scorn nor self-pity in Chekhov's view of the world. There is only the existence of man—and there is something truly classic in the lack of strain or hysteria, in the humility with which Chekhov confronts it. Chekhov speaks for himself when he has a character in *The Wood Demon* say "You must trust and believe in people. . . . or life becomes impossible."

Chekhov's work occupies a place among the peaks of world drama. I am grateful to Robert Corrigan for having made it easy for me to enjoy these inspiring plays once more.

INTRODUCTION

IN our times no playwright is more respected and less understood than Anton Chekhov. For most theatre people he is like Faulkner's Miss Emily—"a tradition, a duty, and a care; a sort of hereditary obligation." His plays are thought to be moody, complex, soulful, vague, and impossible to do successfully on the American stage. For the most part, readers and audiences have agreed with that critic who, on seeing the famous Cornell-Anderson-Gordon production of *The Three Sisters* in 1942, remarked that she "could not see much sense in three adults spending four acts in *not* going to Moscow when all the time they had the price of a railroad ticket." But since then conditions have changed, and today Chekhov's plays seem to have a startling and refreshing contemporaneity; they reflect as few plays do the spirit of our time. What accounts for this belated popularity? Why, a hundred years after he was born, do we think Chekhov has something significant to say to us today?

Part of the answer lies in the fact that all of his plays reflect the mood of spiritual discouragement which permeates the anxieties of the mid-twentieth century. In an age dominated by the fear of nuclear war, the tension of cold war diplomacy, and the insecurity of a defense economy, people wonder what, if anything, can be done to resolve the apparently insoluble problems of life. All of his life Chekhov, too, despaired of the fact that he was unable to answer life's important questions. "Life," he said, "is an insoluble problem." At the end of the first act of *The Sea Gull*, Dorn—one of the many doctors in Chekhov's plays—is trying to comfort the distraught and unhappy Masha, but all he can find to say is "But what can I do, my child? Tell me, what can I do? What?" This question, "What can I do?" runs like a leitmotiv through all of Chekhov's works. This is the clue to Chekhov's great modernity.

Chekhov more than any dramatist of the late nineteenth and early twentieth centuries was very conscious of the existential loneliness of the human condition. In fact, the central theme of all his plays is estrangement. He was conscious of man's helplessness before the overpowering forces of circumstance; he was aware of man's littleness, his insignificance in a gigantic and impersonal universe; he knew that no matter how closely men huddled together they could never really communicate. In short, he was aware of the fact that the very conditions of life doom man to failure and that there was nothing anyone could do about it. He knew the utter impossibility of finding an answer to the question "What can I do?"

In their ontological solitude, Chekhov's characters are like those helpless travelers described by Kafka in his *Notebooks:*

> We are in the situation of travelers in a train that has met with an accident in a tunnel, and this at a place where the light of the beginning can no longer be seen, and the light of the end is so very small a glimmer that the gaze must continually search for it and is always losing it again, and, furthermore, both the beginning and the end are not even certainties. Round about us, however, in the confusion of our senses, or in the supersensitiveness of our senses, we have nothing but monstrosities and a kaleidoscopic play of things that is either delightful or exhausting according to the mood and injury of each individual. What shall I do? or: Why should I do it? are not questions to be asked in such places.

The train of Chekhov's characters' lives has been wrecked too; there is no continuity upon which they can depend; everything seems ludicrous and absurd, painful and hopeless. Ivanov cannot extricate himself from the morass of his lassitude; nobody succeeds in finding love in *The Sea Gull*; no one achieves his goal in *Uncle*

Vanya; the sisters do not go to Moscow (and it would not have solved their problems if they had); and the cherry orchard is not saved. In short, there is nothing one can do in such a situation, and we notice that increasingly, as Chekhov matures, nothing is even attempted. Ivanov's and Treplev's suicides are at least solutions, albeit negative ones, to their problems. Uncle Vanya is incapable of even such a negative solution. In *The Three Sisters* the nearest attempt is Irina's and Tusenbach's decision to get married and at least try to make a new life. But even this fails, for despite man's best efforts, a meaningless and mocking fate will destroy him even before he begins. (And we must remember that the couple's approaching marriage was not anticipated joyfully, for Irina did not love Tusenbach.) Finally, in *The Cherry Orchard* nothing is attempted. The sending of Gaev to the auction is little more than an afterthought, a pitiful reminder that nothing can be done, for the cherry orchard—the symbol of their lives—is doomed, no matter who owns it, from the beginning.

But this is not the whole story. If it were, Chekhov's plays would be little more than unrelieved pictures of gloom, and this we know they are not. This is so because Chekhov, in spite of his realization that man was alone and doomed to failure in all of his attempts to find meaningful relationships and meaningful action, never abdicated his sense of responsibility for human life. Even though Chekhov knew there were no solutions, all his life he sought to find an answer, and his plays are a record of that quest. Thomas Mann, in his perceptive essay on Chekhov, in *Last Essays* (Knopf), was conscious of this when he wrote:

> One has to face the fact that man is a failure. His conscience, which belongs to the spirit, will probably never be brought into harmony with his nature, his reality, his social condition, and there will always be "honorable sleeplessness" for those who for some unfathomable reason feel responsible for human fate and life. If anyone ever suffered from this, it was Chekhov the artist. All his work was honorable sleeplessness, a search for the right, redeeming word in answer to the question: "What are we to do?" The word was difficult, if not impossible, to find.

This, I believe, was the central and creative tension in all of Chekhov's life and work. His own life was filled with the kind of experience that made him ever aware of the inevitability of failure and the absurdity of a man's attempts to triumph over his fate. All of his early years—and he did not have many years to live— were spent in an erosive struggle against poverty, and only shortly before he died did he achieve any kind of personal and financial independence. Finally, after years of hard work, he succeeded only to discover—before he could enjoy the fruits of his labor— that he was dying as a young man of tuberculosis. All of his life was a constant and quiet search for love, and he finally seemed to have found it in his marriage with the great actress Olga Knipper. But their happiness was at best sporadic—their careers kept them apart much of the time—and was never free of the engulfing shadow of his approaching death, a death which came less than three years after they were married. The same characteristic was true of his relationship with Stanislavsky and Danchenko at the Moscow Art Theatre. Without the encouragement and support of these two men, Chekhov very likely would never have succeeded as a playwright; in fact, it is doubtful that he would have written his last three plays. But his relationship with Stanislavsky was never a happy one and was a constant source of frustration to him, for Stanislavsky never understood what Chekhov was trying to do in the theatre and "ruined" his plays in production. Finally, his approaching death itself, which Chekhov as a physician was the first to diagnose, and the reality of which, because he was a physician, he could not escape in the mists of illusion, made the playwright ever aware of the loneliness and absurdity of his own existential nature. Death, and therefore, as we shall see, life also, was not an abstraction for Chekhov. He, like all men, was born to die; but unlike most of us, Chekhov lived his life with the full awareness of his unique, dying self.

Yes, Chekhov had good reason to know that life is loneliness, failure, and absurdity, but as I said earlier, that is not the whole story and this second aspect of his life is the source of strength for the other half of that creative tension which informs his plays. Chekhov countered the reality of his death with an equally powerful weapon—his own life. He met his dying life with honesty, reserve, integrity, and simplicity; and above all, as an artist, a doctor, and a man he had great sympathy for others and an abiding respect for the dignity of human life. Chekhov's career both as a dramatist and a physician took its nourishment from a single source: his great capacity to observe and cherish life; not life as an abstraction or as an ideal, but as a doomed phenomenon of which he was a part. His tolerance, sympathy, wisdom, and his hard-headed vision made it possible for him to achieve, as few writers do, an unflinching but generous perspective on life; a perspective which is a victory over our absurdities, but a victory won at the cost of humility, and won in a spirit of charity and enlightenment. Maxim Gorky, Chekhov's younger colleague, caught some of this when he wrote of Chekhov:

> I think that in Anton Chekhov's presence every one involuntarily felt in himself a desire to be simpler, more truthful, more one's self. . . . All his life Chekhov lived in his own soul; he was always himself, inwardly free, and he never troubled about what some people expected and others—coarser people—demanded of Anton Chekhov. . . . Beautifully simple himself, he loved everything simple, genuine, sincere, and he had a peculiar way of making other people simple.

And thus we find in his plays, as in his life, a regard for his characters' pathetic destinies, and a nobility in their attempts to change or overcome that destiny. Goethe once wrote: "It occurs to me that the hope of persisting, even after fate would seem to have led us back into the state of nonexistence, is the noblest of our sentiments." And this is the quality that informs Chekhov's characters. Vanya is a ridiculous, fumbling, grumbling, ineffectual, self-pitying man, and yet we take him and his plight seriously (we must or the play would collapse); we do, I think, because for all his weakness he never loses his sense of dignity. Tusenbach is a funny little man with his three names, his ugly appearance, his pampered childishness, and his ridiculous talk about the brickyards. He knows this, and he also knows that life has no meaning and will not change. But this does not keep him from making the effort, from asserting the validity of life in the face of death. In his last speech, when he knows he is going to be shot in the duel with Solyony, when he is fully aware that just as all his dreams are about to be realized he will be deprived of them, he is still able to say:

> Really, I feel fine. I feel as if I were seeing those pine trees and maples and birches for the first time in my life. They all seem to be looking at me, waiting for something. What beautiful trees— and when you think of it, how beautiful life ought to be when there are trees like these! *Shouts of "Halloo!" are heard.* I've got to go . . . Look at that tree, it's dead, but it goes on swaying in the wind with the others. And it seems to me that in the same way, if I die, I'll still have a part in life, one way or another. Good-bye, my darling . . . *Kisses her hands.*

We could continue this catalogue: the three sisters themselves, Nina, Lyubov, Gaev, in fact, just about every character Chekhov ever created. But the point is this: the creative tension of Chekhov's work springs from his recognition that in all men there is a great disparity between the facts of their animal existence and the aspiring ideals by which they attempt to live. But he accepted both, and he saw the life of a man as the meaningful and at the same time pathetic, ludicrous, and tragic attempt to bridge this gap. In Chekhov's plays this conflict is seen in his characters who embody both a terrible earnestness of purpose and an awkward and ridiculous acting out of that purpose. In his own life this conflict is reflected in the very act of writing itself. For Chekhov, as Thomas Mann has pointed out:

> Work, pursued relentlessly to the end with the awareness that one has no answers to the final questions, while one's conscience pricks one for throwing dust in the eye of the reader, remains a strange obligation in spite of all. It comes to this: One 'entertains a forlorn world by telling stories without ever being able to offer it the trace of a saving truth.' To poor Katya's question (in "A Tedious Tale"): 'What am I to do?' one can but answer: 'upon my honor and conscience, I don't know.' Nevertheless, one goes on working, telling

stories, giving form to truth, hoping darkly, sometimes almost confidently, that truth and serene form will avail to set free the human spirit and prepare mankind for a better, lovelier, worthier life.

One of the reasons that Chekhov's plays seem so difficult to audiences and critics alike is the fact that they are so different. Until recently, with the advent of the plays of Beckett, Ionesco, Adamov, Albee, and Pinter on our stages (Chekhov, I believe, is the legitimate father of the so-called "absurdist" movement in the theatre), we went to the theatre expecting to see a story about someone doing something, "character in action" is the way the critics put it. This story also usually involved some kind of "message" or "statement" about an aspect of human experience: Life can be good if we are honest with ourselves (*Pillars of Society*); life is always doomed because our irrational drives are at variance with our conscious aims (*Ghosts* and a host of other plays); one's marriage is doomed if as a husband you act and react like a soldier (*Othello*). In short, one of the things that we expect of a dramatic action is that it express some kind of completion to the statement: "Life is ———!"

Shortly before he died, Chekhov's wife asked him what he thought the meaning of life was. He replied: "You ask me what life is? It is like asking what a carrot is. A carrot is a carrot, and nothing more is known." Herein lies the basic secret, both in meaning and form, of Chekhov's drama. He did not believe that "life is something"; all of his plays are expressions of the proposition that "life is." This is what he meant in his often quoted and usually misinterpreted remark about what the nature of the theatre should be:

> A play ought to be written in which the people should come and go, dine, talk of the weather, or play cards, not because the author wants it but because that is what happens in real life. Life on the stage should be as it really is and the people, too, should be as they are and not stilted.

Such an idea of the theatre has tremendous implications for the drama, and we are just now becoming aware of them. First of all, it abolishes the traditional linear plot because Chekhov was not interested in presenting an action in any Aristotelian sense, but rather he was dramatizing a condition. Whenever one asks what the central action of a Chekhov play is, he comes a cropper. Is it Treplev's suicide? Vanya's attempted murder? The three sisters' attempt to go to Moscow? The sale of the cherry orchard? The answer in each case must be "no," for these are only small parts of the plays and everything that happens in the plays is not directly related to these events; "action" for Chekhov was an artificial concept. He was concerned with showing life as it is, and in life there is no central action, there are only people and the only thing that is basic to each individual is the ontological solitude of his being. As one of my students put it recently: "Chekhov's plays do not tell stories. What do stories have to do with life? To be about life, a story must either be myth, invention, or chronicle; it must have a protagonist or center. But then it becomes a personal narrative or history, either real or imaginary. Chekhov, on the other hand, is not interested in describing a personal history: he has no Oedipus, no Lear, no Macbeth. In showing us life as it is, he has no use for seeing particular men in particular world systems. Chekhov's subject matter is life itself, not 'the life of a great man named Othello,' or 'the life of a school teacher named Medvedenko.'" As a result, Chekhov sought to create in his plays a situation which would reveal the private drama that each man has inside himself and which is enacted every day in the random, apparently meaningless, and undramatic events of our common routine.

But because Chekhov is more concerned with the inner lives of his characters and is not interested in presenting an action, his plays seem lifeless, timeless, static. Such plays of "wrecked travelers" are bound to be the antithesis of an Aristotelian action. Like the characters in the novels of Kafka, Proust, and Joyce, the people in Chekhov's plays talk and plan a great deal, but they do nothing. In fact, part of each play's meaning derives from this disparity between language and action. And we notice that as he develops as a playwright, Chekhov increasingly seems to doubt

the possibility of meaningful action (even negative) at all. Ivanov,
Uncle George, and Treplev are able to commit suicide, but Uncle
Vanya fails in his attempt at murder; in *The Three Sisters* and
The Cherry Orchard nothing happens, and in the latter play not
even a gun is fired and no one dies. All of the traditional ingredi-
ents of dramatic action—love, murder, suicide, revenge—are present in the Chekhovian drama, but they are used differently, used
to serve different ends. They are not ends in themselves or plot
devices to further the action but are used as indirect means of
focussing our attention on the inner lives of the characters themselves.

Or again, we notice the quality of timelessness in the plays.
This is a strange effect, for all of the plays are structured within
a variation of an arrival-departure pattern and there is a great
specificity of time in each of the plays; we are conscious of dates,
ages, the passage of years, the time of day, the seasons. We know
that the cherry orchard is to be sold on August 22nd; Irina, Masha,
and Olga are respectively twenty, twenty-two, and twenty-eight at
the beginning of *The Three Sisters*, they are twenty-four, twenty-six,
and thirty-two at the end; the carnival party will be coming at
nine; and the daily routine of the Serebryakov estate with "tea at
eight, dinner at one, and supper in the evening" has been upset by
Professor's arrival. And yet, in spite of this frame of a time pattern,
we have no real sense of time passing. Chekhov for all his apparent
attention to temporal concerns has been interested only in revealing
more and more fully the continually shifting and changing state of
consciousness within each of the characters. And when the characters, if they do, come back momentarily to temporal reality, they
shout painfully as Vanya does:

> But, my God! Why are my thoughts so entangled? Why am I so old?
> Why won't she understand me? I despise all that rhetoric of hers, that
> indolent morality, that absurd talk about the destruction of the world.
> . . . *A pause.* Oh, how I have been deceived!

Or they sob with Irina:

> Where. . . . Where has it all gone? Where is it? Oh, God! I've
> forgotten. . . . I've forgotten everything . . . Everything's so con-

fused . . . I don't remember the Italian for "window" or for "ceiling" . . . Every day I'm forgetting more and more, and life's slipping by, and it will never, never return . . .

"Where has it all gone?" and in between these moments of painful discovery, they have not been concerned with time. Most of Chekhov's characters are like the three sisters, ageless and no age at all. Only those characters whose inner life Chekhov was not interested in revealing are conscious of time and change. The Natashas, Lopahins, and Yashas for the most part live only in the world of events and appointments to be kept; they make things happen, they are interested in time. Natasha asks what time it is; Lopahin is constantly looking at his watch. But most of the characters in Chekhov's world have no sense of time; as Kulygin points out to the three sisters, their clock "is seven minutes fast."

Further, Chekhov made it quite clear that what his characters do want in time is really nothing at all, only an illusion: Astrov's planting of forests, Nina's achievement on the stage, Serebryakov's articles, Irina's desire for work and dreams of true love, Vershinin's happiness in two or three hundred years, the trip to Moscow, finally the cherry orchard itself. If the orchard means so much to Lyubov, why does she do so little to save it? The fact is that Lyubov loves the orchard and at the same time does not care about it all. It is her life, but her life is meaningless. The orchard is at once the great cause, and nothing at all. All of Chekhov's characters finally arrive at that point where their most deep-felt needs are nothing, that existential nothingness which confronts Kafka's wrecked travelers. They want to be free of time; in fact, they wish to be free of life itself.

Finally, what it all boils down to is this: for Chekhov to show "life as it is," each of his characters must be defined by his solitude and estrangement from life and not by his participation in life. Each man's existence is ultimately solitary, and his unique self can only be known, if it ever can, only after all of his social contexts have been stripped away. And yet, although this may be true, no man can exist in the vacuum of self, albeit Chekhov's characters try to. Each of them attempts to build and then operate in his own little world, with no sense of social responsibility, totally unaware of the sufferings of others. Each character has his own thoughts and problems with which he is usually morbidly consumed. As a result, the people in Chekhov's plays never seem to hear or notice one another. Each has room only for himself and each acts in a social vacuum. And yet it is not always easy to keep the walls of these private worlds from breaking down. We notice that Chekhov generally sets his characters in restricted areas. The interiors are always closely confined rooms; the exteriors are usually attached to the house or are nearby. For this reason, if none other, Chekhov's characters are always in contact with each other and it is sometimes difficult to maintain a complete self-centeredness. As a result, each of his characters must have one or more protective escapes to which he can resort if too much is demanded of him. The plays are filled with escapes from social reality; for some it is drinking, for others, like Sonya, it is blind religious belief; for Vanya it is sleep; for Astrov it is beauty; for Gaev it is billiards and gum drops; for Andrey it is his violin, his books, his gambling; and for many it is work. No matter what the nature of the escape may be, they are all means whereby Chekhov's characters can return to their own little private worlds when outside demands become too great.

But Chekhov did not stop here. If he had, his characters would be little more than selfish and unattractive. And although we know this is true of them, we also know they are more than that. Chekhov's most profound insight was that in addition to knowing that each man is alone and that he seeks to maintain his solitude, he also knew that for each man solitude is unbearable. Man is aware that finally he is alone in the universe and that he is incapable of being alone. The essential drama of the human condition as it is expressed in Chekhov's plays lies in this tension between the uncertainty of each man's relationship to others and the uncertainty of his relationship to himself.

As we indicated earlier, Chekhov's plays are different from most plays we are accustomed to seeing or reading, and we suggested that this was because he was attempting to say something different and this required new dramatic forms and techniques. Therefore, we must now say something about certain dominant aspects of Chekhov's dramaturgy. From the very beginning we are faced with a difficult problem: it is impossible to use any of the usual procedures of dramatic criticism—narrating the plot line, describing the characters, thematic analysis—because the texture and density of a Chekhovian play defies such methods. To analyze these plays properly one would have to begin with the opening speech and then, making cross-relationships, work through the entire play until the final curtain in much the same manner one would give a critical reading of a poem. Such a procedure would not be to our purposes here; rather, I shall illustrate some of the major devices used by Chekhov to achieve his dramatic effects.

However, before we do this, we must discuss in greater detail the more general problem of form in a Chekhovian play. Earlier, we said that these plays were not imitations of an action in any Aristotelian sense. Chekhov was dramatizing a condition, and therefore he needed a dramatic form which, as Ionesco put it, "progressed not through a predetermined subject and plot, but through an increasingly intense and revealing series of emotional states." Such a drama must from the beginning then dispense with the traditional linear plot. The traditional plot is sequential; it starts at a certain moment in time and then moves through a series of events to a conclusion. Everything that occurs in this kind of play—each speech, every action, any symbols—is a part of the play's forward movement and is causally related to the sequence of events. It is this sequential nature of dramatic action, of which plot is the first form, that Aristotle was referring to when he said that tragedy is an imitation of an action "which has a beginning, a middle, and an end."

But as we said, Chekhov was not interested in "imitations of actions," he wanted to show "life as it is." Life as it is lacks the direction, the external causality, the cathartic effect of completed events. Like so many painters, composers, poets, novelists, and now, fifty years later, playwrights, Chekhov was aware that the crises which are so neatly resolved by the linear form of drama are not so neatly resolved in life. To be alive is to be in a continual state of crisis; in life as one crisis is resolved another is always beginning. He wanted his plays to express the paradox, the contradiction, and the incompleteness of experience; he wanted to suggest the raggedness, the confusion, the complexity of motivation, the "discontinuous continuity," and the basic ambiguity of all human behavior. Chekhov believed that the drama as he knew it could never express the "is-ness" of experience because it was under the destructive tyranny of a sequential and chronological structure. So in its place he invented a form which might be called, to use the terminology of the new criticism of poetry, a contextual or concentric action. (It is hardly fitting to use the word plot here, for, because of its usual connotations, it can only be misleading.) The structure of a Chekhovian play is epiphanic; its purpose is to reveal—literally, "to show forth"—the inner lives of his characters. In such a drama the plot has been twisted into a situation that is to reveal the psychic lives of the characters. There are many dramatic situations in a plot; here a single situation has been stretched to take the place of the plot. This inflation of the situation into the source of the dramatic action so that it replaces the plot is the vital secret of Chekhovian dramaturgy. To capture "the aimless, unclimactic multiplicity" of his characters' lives, Chekhov has created a form based on what Marvin Rosenberg has called "the tensions of context, rather than direction, of vertical depth, rather than horizontal movement." Chekhov takes a situation and then develops it concentrically, like a series of inscribed but tangential circles. For example, in *The Cherry Orchard* the situation at the beginning of the play is simply that Lyubov has arrived home because the cherry orchard is to be sold; at the end of the play the orchard has been sold and everyone leaves. Nothing happens really, the situation is single and static; but in the four acts in which the situation takes one—and the only one—forward step, Chekhov has revealed a great deal about the way "life is" for twelve people as they are related to that situation.

This is a new kind of drama and the devices which Chekhov used to create it and achieve meaning through it will appear by traditional standards to be untheatrical or, to use the language of his present-day followers, "anti-theatrical." And yet, as we pointed out earlier, Chekhov does use the techniques of the earlier realistic drama; only he uses them for different reasons and in different ways. It is quite proper, therefore, that his plays have been called "dramas of indirection."

Before examining the techniques of indirection, however, I should like to make one more point. In discussing the use of time in the plays, we noticed that there was a great specificity about time. This is but one example of the great specificity which informs Chekhov's drama, and this fact does much to account for the enduring quality of his art. The biggest danger that faces an artist when he is dealing with man's inner life is that in his presentation of that life he will of necessity become too private, too personal, too subjective, since such a life is the ultimate in subjectivity; but such subjectivity tends to cancel out all communication. If, as Chekhov maintains, all men are solitary and ultimately unknowable, how can the equally solitary reader or member of an audience enter into the private worlds that are being presented on the stage? How and why should they have relevance for us? Who really cares—except perhaps our psychiatrist—about the *psyche* of another, and even if we might care, how can we ever comprehend it? I believe Chekhov does much to overcome this problem—and it is a lesson that Beckett and Ionesco would do well to learn—by enclosing his subjective "actions" in an objective frame of specific external details. He was trying to capture the private inner lives of each of his characters, but he did it by means of those every-day events, objects, and expressions that as human beings, in all places and in all times, each of us shares. Chekhov was the great observer, and his plays are filled with the details of his observation. As a man Chekhov cared deeply for all of his fellow human beings; as an artist he always maintained complete objectivity. It is the fusion of these two characteristics that makes his plays great and, more important, makes them work as plays.

Keeping in mind, then, that all of Chekhov's plays are framed in great specificity of detail, what are some of the techniques of indirection which he employed to reveal the inner lives of his characters? The most obvious was his refusal to use the big scene, the stereotyped dramatic situation. There are no "obligatory" scenes or great denouements in a Chekhov play. Traditionally, such scenes were used to reveal through action the truth about a play's central characters. But for Chekhov, the truth is not dramatic in this way nor is it necessarily full of consequence; more likely, it is quite commonplace. We are accustomed to the "big" scenes and have come to expect them; when Chekhov refuses to give them to us we feel cheated. But Chekhov was not trying to fulfill our conditioned expectations and responses, he was showing "life as it is." We are moved by Othello's "Soft you; a word or two before you go" as his universe crashes down upon him, but in life our universes, if they do cave in, do not usually do so quite so dramatically; rather such times are hushed and of no great consequence to most people. So *The Sea Gull* ends with Dorn taking Trigorin aside and quietly telling him: "The fact is, Konstantin Gavrilovich has shot himself. . . ."

But the very muted and underplayed quality of the scene is precisely what gives it its effect. It may not be as theatrically exciting as Hedda Gabler's suicide, for instance, but it is much truer to life and in the long run its impact upon us is probably more lasting and horrible. Chekhov had a great distrust of the artificiality of the conventional big curtain scenes of the well-made play, and his work shows that he gradually discarded it altogether. In his early plays (*Platonov, Ivanov,* and *The Wood Demon* are for the most part structured according to the conventions of the well-made play) he uses the big curtain. For example in *Ivanov*, Act I ends with Anna's decision to follow her husband to the Lyebedevs', Act II ends with her discovery of Ivanov and Sasha in each other's arms, Act III with Ivanov's brutal revelation to his wife that she is soon to die, and Act IV with Ivanov's suicide. But Chekhov gradually came to see that such scenes were phony and while he was working on *The Wood Demon* he wrote:

> The demand is made that the hero and the heroine should be dramatically effective. But in life people do not shoot themselves, or hang themselves, or fall in love, or deliver themselves of clever sayings every minute. They spend most of their time eating, drinking, or running after women or men, or talking nonsense. It is therefore necessary that this should be shown on the stage.

The Sea Gull is the first play to manifest this change of attitude. The suicide is still there, but, as we have shown, it was used in a very different way. The only "dramatic" event in *Uncle Vanya* is Vanya's botched attempt to shoot Serebryakov near the end of the third act. In *The Three Sisters* Tusenbach is shot by Solyony in a duel, but his death is off-stage and the shot is muffled. Finally, in *The Cherry Orchard* none of the traditional dramatic events take place and even the sad departure of Lyubov and Gaev is undercut by the final appearance of the bumbling Feers. But more important than the gradual elimination of such theatrically effective scenes is the fact that when Chekhov uses them they are no longer ends in themselves but rather they serve as pointers to the more powerful, albeit less theatrical, drama that is taking place within the characters who are on the stage. By underplaying the big, exciting, dramatic events we are better able to see the drama and the complexity of the seemingly trivial, the inconsequential, and the simple that is the very tissue of the human situation. Chekhov had learned well the wisdom of *Hamlet*: "By indirections find directions out."

Chekhov's use of obligatory scenes, then, was ironic, and this leads us to another aspect of his dramaturgy. Throughout his life Chekhov constantly made the statement that "the truth about life is ironical," and since he was showing "life as it is," almost all of his dramatic devices were ironic. This is best seen in the disparity between what his characters say and what they do. Thus we find in all of his plays characters making brilliantly incisive remarks about themselves and other people, and yet they are said in such a way and are put in such an incongruous and ludicrous context that we do not stop to take them seriously when we hear them. The force of these statements is driven home cumulatively; we are suddenly aware as the play ends that the characters have done just the opposite in their actions to what they have expounded they should do in their dialogue. These flashes of self-revelation have been more than static, isolated, and disconnected statements of opinion; despite all their apparent ludicrousness, they have become ironically true. Thus, Yelena says to Sonya in the second act of *Uncle Vanya*: "You mustn't look at people that way. It isn't right. You must trust and believe in people, (*pause*) or life becomes impossible." Even at this point in the play we know that this is precisely what Yelena does not do. We tend to laugh at the incongruity of the situation; but as we leave the theatre our stomachs begin to squirm as the truth of her statement begins to sink in. Look at Yelena and one can see in dramatic terms just how impossible life can really become. But Chekhov has achieved his effect indirectly.

We find something similar in the third act of *The Cherry Orchard*, when Trofimov is telling Lyubov: "You mustn't worry, and above all you mustn't deceive yourself. For once in your life you must look the truth straight in the face." To be sure, Trofimov has spoken the truth about Madame Ranevsky, but it tells us very little about the Russian equivalent to our perpetual graduate student. After all, it is easy for almost anyone to make that observation about Lyubov (Lopahin has been telling her the same thing from the beginning of the first act); what is more important in the scene is how Trofimov reacts when Lyubov rebuffs him: "This is dreadful. . . . I can't stand it. I'm going. . . . *Goes out, but returns at once*. Everything's over between us!" By exaggerating (one of Chekhov's chief ironic techniques) his reaction, Chekhov points up the melodramatic quality of his exit and in so doing shows Trofimov as a comic butt. He underscores this by having Trofimov run out of the room and fall down the stairs in the midst of a chorus of laughter.

Or, to take a final example of this kind of ironic disparity between speech and action, let us look briefly at Treplev in *The Sea Gull*. Treplev is a typical adolescent writer—today we find his counterpart taking courses in creative writing and going to "writing workshops" in the summer. Treplev has lofty ideals, but he is a bad writer. (Chekhov makes this clear by contrasting him to Trigorin, who, although not great, is a good craftsman.) We learn of Treplev's ideals when he attacks the theatre:

> But in my opinion our theatre's in a rut. It's nothing but clichés and shopworn conventions. When the curtain opens on those three-walled "living rooms," and I see those famous and talented actors, those high priests of that sacred art, parade about in their costumes in front of the footlights showing the way people eat, drink, make love, and walk about; when I hear them try to squeeze a moral out of commonplace phrases and meaningless events—some cliché that everyone knows and is suitable for home consumption; when they give me a thousand variations of the same old thing over and over again. . . . I have to leave! . . . we need new forms, and if we can't have them, then it's better to have nothing at all!

Now all this may be true, but the fact that he says it does not make him a playwright. That Treplev is a bad writer is made very clear when his own play is produced:

> Men, lions, eagles, and partridges, horned deer, geese, spiders, and the silent fish of the deep, starfish and creatures which cannot be seen by the eye—all living things, all living things, all living things, having completed their cycle of sorrow, are now extinct. . . . I am alone. Once in a hundred years I open my lips to speak, and then my voice echoes mournfully in the void, unheard by all. . . . You, too, pale spirits do not hear me.

This is drivel (it seems to foreshadow the plays of the bad expressionists) and the disparity between what Treplev says about the theatre and what he writes for it is part of Chekhov's point. I think, as much as anything, it is Treplev's recognition of this fact that drives him to suicide. (But already I am aware that such analysis as this has falsified the significance of his death, for it tends to reduce the many interlocking meanings of the play to a single action.) We notice just before Nina's final appearance that the young writer is struggling over a description of moonlight:

> And the description of the moonlight is no good either. Trigorin's worked out his own techniques, so it comes easily for him . . . He'd just mention the neck of a broken bottle glittering in a mill stream and the black shadow of the mill wheel—and he's got a moonlight night. But for me it's the shimmering light, the silent twinkling of the stars, and the distant sounds of a piano, dying away in the still, fragrant air . . . It's terrible!

We know from a letter written by Chekhov to his brother Alexander in 1886 that the playwright approves of the "Trigorin method," for in that letter he uses word for word the example of the moonlit night that appears in Konstantin's speech. And, finally, as Nina leaves him, she not only confesses that she still loves Trigorin but she also goes out the door reciting the lines of Treplev's ill-fated play. The final truth about Konstantin Treplev is very sad and pathetic, but it has been revealed to us indirectly by the ironic devices of Chekhov's method.

We have already indicated that Chekhov often achieves his irony by the use of an undercutting speech. Such a device does much to give the plays their comic quality (we shall discuss the nature of Chekhov's comedy presently), but it also is a means whereby Chekhov can reveal some truth about the inner lives of his characters. For instance, in the first act of *Uncle Vanya*, Vanya has been arguing with his mother and he is finally shut up. An awkward pause follows, and to relieve the tension of this pause Yelena remarks: "What a fine day! Not too hot." Vanya self-pityingly replies: "Yes, a fine day to hang oneself!" This line is immediately followed by Marina's coming in to look for the chickens. She says: "Here chick, chick, here chick." In her world, in which she is doing her job, this is a perfectly logical line; however, coming as it does immediately after Vanya's ironic self-dramatizing, it is not only immensely funny but it acts as a commentary on Vanya's line. The result is a kind of grotesque humor which makes us laugh with a lump in our throat. It is funny until we realize the total implications of our laughter.

We find much the same thing in the opening act of *The Cherry Orchard*. Lyubov has just arrived and she is gushing about her "dear, beautiful nursery," Gaev is talking about efficiency, and exactly at this point Charlotta, in a conversation with Pishchik, announces that "my dog eats nuts, too." In short, all this talk is just so much gabble. Or to take a final example, in the opening scene of *The Three Sisters* Olga and Irina are talking about how wonderful it would be to go back to Moscow. Tusenbach, Chebutykin, and Solyony are carrying on their own conversation in the adjoining room; we catch only snatches of their talk, but notice how Chekhov uses it:

> OLGA I wanted so much to go home again. Go home to Moscow!
> CHEBUTYKIN, *sarcastically to* SOLYONY. A small chance of that!
> TUSENBACH, *also to* SOLYONY. Of course, it's nonsense.

A few lines later the dialogue goes as follows:

> IRINA Go to Moscow! Sell the house, leave everything here, and go back to Moscow.
> OLGA Yes, to go back to Moscow! As soon as possible.
> CHEBUTYKIN *and* TUSENBACH *laugh.*

No more need be said; from the beginning of the play the sisters' talk of returning to Moscow is an idle dream, but it has been shown to us by the ironical device of the undercutting speech.

I should like to point out one more ironic device. It is a commonplace that Chekhov's characters are addicted to making speeches. Gaev makes a speech to the bookcase; Trofimov is constantly carrying on about the "brave new world" that is approaching; Vershinin and Tusenbach, when they have nothing better to do, philosophize; Vanya is continually making speeches; and so on. But, beginning with Stanislavsky, many interpreters of Chekhov have missed the point of this speechifying. T. S. Eliot was very perceptive on this point when he wrote in his essay "Rhetoric and Poetic Drama":

> Speechmaking in a play can serve useful dramatic ends. Genuine rhetoric is a device of great effect when it occurs in situations where a character in a play *sees himself* in a dramatic light. In plays of realism we often find parts which are never allowed to be consciously dramatic, for fear, perhaps, of their appearing less real. But in actual life, in many of those situations in actual life which we enjoy consciously and keenly, we are at times aware of ourselves in this way, and these moments are of very great usefulness to dramatic verse. They are valuable because they give us a new clue to the character, for we discover the angle from which he views himself.

"We discover the angle from which he views himself"—not the way we see him, or the other characters see him, or the playwright sees him. Thus by contrasting the way the characters see themselves with what they do and with the way the other characters view them, Chekhov, again by indirection, is able to reveal the way life really is.

A few words should probably be said about Chekhov's use of symbols. It has often been noted that the modern drama, beginning with Ibsen, has been increasingly dependent upon nonverbal symbolism and the imagery of inanimate objects (what Cocteau refers to as "poetry of the theatre") to achieve emotional depth within theatrical conventions which are, for the most part, committed only to external reality. Ibsen, beginning with *A Doll's House* and *Ghosts,* and most explicitly in *The Wild Duck,* used symbols to give a metaphoric meaning that a predominantly naturalistic theatre denied him. Chekhov also used this kind of symbolism, but in a fashion different from his contemporaries (or, indeed, those that followed him). Unlike Ibsen's "ghosts," Chekhov's symbols are never abstractions, nor are they simply analogous to the play's action; they are always concrete, they are a part of the life of the people in his plays; in a word, they are organic to the texture and meaning of the play. Nor, like the "wild duck," are they bizarre superimpositions on the action. (I believe the wild duck symbolism works, but the Ekdal attic stretches conventions of naturalistic verisimilitude almost to the breaking point. What is more crucial, one has the feeling that the wild duck metaphor existed prior to the writing of the play, as a kind of symbolic framework, and that Ibsen then created an action to fit the frame.) There are big, almost all-inclusive symbols—the sea gull, Astrov's forests, Moscow, the cherry orchard—in a Chekhovian play, and these symbols do give meaning and depth to large segments of the plays of which they are a part. But these extending symbols are effective because they grow out of the action and are not imposed upon it, and, more important, because they rest upon the less noticeable but more significant symbolic underpinning of the whole play. For example, Moscow is the symbol of the three sisters' dream of happiness. This we know is an illusion and their belief in this illusion shows how out of touch with reality they are. And yet the play is filled with less obvious symbols that make it clear that everyone in the play—with the exception of Natasha—has to some degree lost touch with reality. These lesser symbols support the over-arching Moscow symbol and, what is more, give it its organic quality. To point out but one instance, as the play opens Irina is celebrating her birthday (more exactly the anniversary of her baptism) and old Dr. Chebutykin, who perhaps more than all the others has lost touch with reality, with great ceremony brings Irina her present—a silver samovar. Everyone gasps, and with protestations of "you shouldn't have done it" and "it costs too much money," the incident is dropped as quickly as possible. The point is that in Russia a silver samovar is the traditional gift of a husband to his wife on their silver wedding anniversary. Nothing could have more effectively nor more completely shown just how out of touch with reality the doctor had become; nor, we might add, have revealed the lifetime of pain and disappointment that was the result of Irina's mother's decision to marry Brigadier General Prozorov rather than young Dr. Chebutykin.

In *Uncle Vanya* we notice how Chekhov uses a symbol to achieve another effect. Several of the plays have references to the watchman's rattle or stick. In nineteenth century Russia the watchman would go about the estate clacking his sticks—much as our present-day nightwatchmen make the rounds with clock and key; the purpose of this was both to frighten any prowlers that might be about and to let the members of the household know that they were being protected. But Chekhov did not include this effect for verisimilitude alone; he also used it as a thematic symbol.* Such is the use of the watchman at the end of the second act of *Uncle Vanya*: Yelena and Sonya have just had an honest talk with each other and because of it they are capable of feeling. The windows are open, it has been raining, and everything is clean and refreshed. Yelena thinks she can play the piano again; as Sonya goes to get permission, the watchman's rattle is heard; Yelena has to shut the window—the source of refreshment—and Serebryakov says "no." Their whole life of feeling has been so protected by the "watchmen" of their lives that they have no feelings left.

There are countless examples such as these in the plays. All of Chekhov's symbols have this same kind of organic quality; they deepen and enhance the play's meaning, but more importantly they too serve as a means of pointing, indirectly, to that inner drama which is at the heart of each of the plays.

There is one more aspect of Chekhov's art which I should like to discuss: the tendency on the part of his characters to aestheticize life. All of the people in Chekhov's plays are shown to be either consciously or unconsciously aware of their own inadequacies as people. They realize that in one way or another they have failed as human beings, and they therefore attempt to make their lives

---

* Chekhov did not believe in verisimilitude for its own sake. He was constantly quarreling with Stanislavsky over just this point. The famous director was always trying to introduce realistic touches—the croaking of frogs, the barking of dogs, crying children—that served no organic function in the play. When Stanislavsky defended his actions by saying that such effects did occur in real life, Chekhov replied: "Quite true, but the stage demands a certain amount of convention. You have no fourth wall, for instance. Besides, the stage is art; the stage reflects the quintessence of life. Nothing superfluous should be introduced on the stage."

like the more perfect world of art. This desire to identify with art manifests itself in various ways. The most obvious is the tendency on the part of several of the characters to identify with great artists of the past or with great heroes from literature. Serebryakov as he suffers from the pains of old age and a life of retirement (not to mention the probable realization that his life and work as a scholar may have been as meaningless as Vanya says it was), identifies with Turgenev, when he says at the opening of the second act of *Uncle Vanya*: "They say Turgenev got heart trouble from gout. I'm afraid I'm getting it too." In *The Three Sisters*, Solyony is constantly insulting and antagonizing people because he feels inferior to them. In a quiet moment with Tusen-bach, whom he later kills, he confesses: "When I'm alone with someone I'm all right, I'm just like everybody else. When I'm in a group of people, I get depressed and shy, and . . . I talk all sorts of nonsense." This shy captain wears the mask of Lermontov—he is always quoting the Russian Byron; he has been in several duels; and he will brook no rivals in love. Vanya, unable to stand the final disillusionment of his life's work, shouts: "My life's ruined! I'm gifted, I'm intelligent, I'm courageous. . . . If I'd had a normal life, I might have become a Schopenhauer, a Dostoyevsky. . . ." Finally, in *The Sea Gull*, Treplev, out of the despair of his mother's rejection, identifies himself with Hamlet.

This aestheticizing tendency is also seen in the way Chekhov's characters are more conscious of *how* they say things than what they say. In the third act of *The Cherry Orchard*, Epihodov says to Varya: "I wish you'd express yourself more delicately." He does not care what is said so long as it is said beautifully. Or, in *The Three Sisters*, Vershinin has just made one of his typical speeches about how beautiful life will be in two or three hundred years, and Irina, oblivious to the meaning of what he has said, says with a sigh: "Really, someone should have written all that down."

The desire for beautiful expression is directly related to the many quotations and literary allusions which we find in the plays. There are quotations from Shakespeare, Pushkin, Krylon, Lermon-tov, and Gogol, to name but a few, and allusions to Ostrovsky,

Balzac, Batyushkov, and Turgenev. Chekhov's characters are always quoting and talking—in short, finding comfort in words. They are attempting to give a meaning to their otherwise empty and meaningless lives through words by giving their words artistic form.

Finally, and most profoundly, the aestheticizing of life is carried to its limit by those characters who seek to make their own lives into works of art. Consider Astrov's remarks about Yelena in the second act of *Uncle Vanya*:

> In a human being, everything ought to be beautiful: face and dress, soul and thoughts. She is very beautiful, there's no denying it, but, after all, all she does is eat, sleep, go for walks, fascinate us by her beauty and—nothing more. She has no duties, other people work for her.

Later, he says to Sonya:

> I am old, tired, unimportant; my feelings are dead. I could never care for any one again. I don't love anyone, and I don't think I shall ever love anyone. The only thing that appeals to me is beauty. I just can't remain indifferent to it. If, for example, Yelena wanted to, she could turn my head in a day.

Finally, he forces the affair with Yelena; his outburst is not one of physical passion but a reaction to her beauty which culminates in his asking her to keep a tryst in a beautiful forest arbor. We are reminded of Hedda Gabler's request that Lövborg shoot himself beautifuly—through the head. Thus the man who has failed, who is incapable of loving anyone, attempts to substitute an erotic picture of idyllic love for a mature and demanding relationship. It is a relationship that is symbolized by the "autumn roses" Vanya brings to Yelena; such roses—like all the love affairs in Chekhov's plays—are very beautiful, but they discolor and disintegrate the moment they are touched.

This tendency is most fully developed in Trofimov in *The Cherry Orchard*. Like Astrov, he has become a walking vegetable, an emotional turnip. He loves life and the beauties of nature, but he hates anything animal or physical. Thus his whole relationship with Anya is vegetative. He wants to look at her, but even the slightest trace of physical desire is repulsive. "We are above love," he says. He cannot accept the responsibility of human animal existence and must escape into the ideal world of art which is bloodless but extremely beautiful. This, then, is but another of the dramatic processes of indirection which Chekhov employs to reveal the absorbing drama of "life as it is," as opposed to the tendency toward statement which is so prevalent in the modern theatre.

Finally, something must be said about Chekhov and comedy. Critics are continually telling us that Chekhov is funny, and also we know that both *The Sea Gull* and *The Cherry Orchard* were called comedies by their author, and that he conceived none of his plays (despite Stanislavsky's interpretations) as tragedies. But Chekhov's plays are so unlike most of the comedies we know that we are not sure we should trust even the author's assurances that they are. Perhaps a better way of understanding what is meant when Chekhov is referred to as a comic writer is to recall that he was writing a drama that was to show "life as it is." Another way of describing "life as it is" is expressed in Santayana's statement, "Everything in Nature is lyrical in its ideal essence, tragic in its fate, and comic in its existence." This provides a very important insight into the form of Chekhovian drama, and it also accounts for the complex overtones that are present in the plays, for Chekhov's characters respond to all three of Santayana's levels with an especial intensity. They are comedians by necessity, smitten with a tragic sense of life, lyrically in love with the ideal in a world poorly equipped to satisfy such aspirations.

The essential quality of the "is-ness" of life is, as we said earlier, its absurdity, its futility. Some would argue that this is tragic, perhaps the most tragic condition of all, but as Dorothy Sayers has wisely pointed out: "The whole tragedy of futility is that it never succeeds in achieving tragedy. In its blackest moments it is inevitably doomed to the comic gesture." Thus, when man comes to see his existence as absurd, that it is governed by the irrational, the inexplicable, and the nonsensical, he moves into the realm of the comic. For comedy presupposes such a world, a world being made and turned upside down. As Gautier put it, "Comedy is the logic of the absurd," and thus it can admit the disorderly and the improbable into the realm of art. Chekhov was aware that the fragmentary, schizoid life that each of us lives is an existential comedy. His plays suggest that man lives in the midst of so many irreconcilable forces—both within and without—that the only way life can be given form in art is in comedy. But it is a special kind of comedy, a grotesque kind of comedy, which makes us, as I said earlier, laugh with a lump in our throats. This is so because for all of its awareness of the absurdity of experience, it is also extremely conscious of the suffering, struggle, and failure of experience. Christopher Fry wrote in his essay "On Comedy" (*Tulane Drama Review*, Vol. 4, Spring, 1960):

> I know that when I set about writing a comedy the idea presents itself to me first of all as tragedy. The characters press on to the theme with all their divisions and perplexities heavy about them; they are already entered for the race to doom, and good and evil are an infernal tangle skinning the fingers that try to unravel them. If the characters were not qualified for tragedy there would be no comedy, and to some extent I have to cross the one before I can light the other. In a century less flayed and quivering we might reach it more directly; but not now unless every word we write is going to mock us.

Chekhov, I think, would have seen the applicability of Fry's remarks to the plays in this volume, for they too contain such a vision of life, a vision that may be summed up by the closing prayer of Joyce's *Finnegans Wake*:

> Loud, heap miseries upon us yet entwine
> Our arts with laughters low. In the name
> Of the former and of the latter and of
> Their holocaust, All men.

And yet, somehow, I am not content to stop here. Traditionally, we think of tragedy as a form which celebrates man's capacity to suffer and aspire even though he is doomed to destruction by the inexorable workings of fate. Comedy, on the other hand, celebrates man's capacity to endure. It is *terribly* conscious of the resilience of the human spirit. Fry, in the essay just quoted, distinguished the two forms in this way:

> The difference between tragedy and comedy is the difference between experience and intuition. In the experience we strive against every condition of our animal life: against death, against the frustration of ambition, against the instability of human love. In the intuition we trust the arduous eccentricities we are born to, and see the oddness of a creature who has never got acclimatized to being created.

Perhaps this explains the mysterious quality of affirmation that we sense in Chekhov's plays. There have been many playwrights in the modern theatre who were conscious of the doomed nature of human experience, but I know of none who accepted this fact and still had such trust in the enduring qualities of those "arduous eccentricities we are born to" as did Anton Chekhov.

A NOTE ON THE VERSIONS IN THIS VOLUME

"If life begins on the other side of despair, the translator's life begins on the other side of impossibility."

ERIC BENTLEY

In the theatre one writes or translates only for actors—never for readers. Even the most cursory glance at the history of the theatre shows that whenever playwrights cease writing for actors the theatre loses its vitality and loses its literature too. Certainly Shakespeare provides us with our strongest evidence on this point, but Aeschylus, Sophocles, Euripides, Molière, or Anton Chekhov would do just as well. Shakespeare is the greatest *dramatist* in the English language and his plays are great works of literature, but he was not writing literature; he was primarily writing for actors, and, as we know, he was writing for specific actors. And this, I believe, is one of the chief sources for his plays' enduring vitality. Furthermore, I would even maintain that Shakespeare would never have created some of the scenes he did if he had not known the actors who were to play them. The same thing was true of the theatre in Greece in the fifth century, in France in the seventeenth, and in Russia at the end of the nineteenth. Sophocles had his Burbage, Molière was his own Will Kemp, and Chekhov had Stanislavsky and the company of the Moscow Art Theatre.

It is for this reason that the first law in translating for the theatre is that everything must be speakable. It is necessary at all times for the translator to hear the actor speaking in his mind's ear. He must be conscious of the gestures of the voice that speaks —the rhythm, the cadence, the interval. He must also be conscious of the look, the feel, and the movement of the actor while he is speaking. He must, in short, render what might be called the whole gesture of the scene. To do this it is important to know what words do and mean, but it is more important to know what they cannot do at these crucial moments when the actor needs to use a vocal or physical gesture. Only in this way can the translator hear the words in such a way that they play upon each other in harmony, in conflict, and in pattern—and hence as dramatic.

Chekhov was very much aware of this when he was writing his own plays. He insisted on hearing his script read by the actors before making his final revisions, and he refused to have his plays published until he could incorporate the changes made in them during the rehearsal period. In 1889 when the editor Plescheyev wanted to publish *The Wood Demon,* Chekhov wrote to him: "I never consider a play ready for publication until it has been revised during rehearsals. Wait, please. It is not too late yet. When the play has been revised at the rehearsals, I shall take advantage of your kind offer without waiting for an invitation."

In addition to being playable it is imperative that an English version of a foreign play be rendered into good English. I do not wish to get involved in the controversy of literal as opposed to free translations, but obviously the translator must not feel he has to have a word for word correspondence. I am in complete accord with Eric Bentley on this point when he writes: "Accuracy must not be bought at the expense of bad English. Since we cannot have everything, we would rather surrender accuracy than style. This, I think, is the first principle of translating, though it is not yet accepted in academic circles. The clinching argument in favor of this principle is that, finally, bad English cannot be accurate translation—unless the original is in bad German, bad French, or what have you."

Finally, the language used in any version of a Chekhov play must be simple. Earlier in my introduction I tried to show that in a Chekhovian play the dramatic action is enclosed in a very simple and seemingly inconsequential frame. The surfaces of life are apparently reproduced with all their natural and familiar inanity. There is very little that is dramatic in the events themselves. What makes these episodes powerful theatre is the way they are combined, the sequences, the underlying associations and complications, the contrasts and ironies. It is in this way, we said, that the profound meanings are created. But if this is true of Chekhov's dramaturgy, it must be equally true of the speech. It is easy, natural, simple. Therefore the inner meanings and profundities of the plays will only be achieved in English by capturing this interaction of surface simplicities, and not through complex or vague lines, nor through what Stark Young called a "muggy, symbolic, swing-on-to-your-atmosphere sort of tone." These, then, were the governing principles that I followed in making the English versions of Chekhov's plays that appear in this volume.

Finally, a word should be said about the absence of Chekhov's first full-length play, *Platonov*, from this volume. This play was never published during Chekhov's lifetime and he did several versions of it. The most reliable of the existing manuscripts is three times the length of any other Chekhov play and, more important, the ending of the play is lost—in fact, it is not definitely known whether Chekhov ever finished the play. All these facts add up to this: any published version of *Platonov*—and there have been at least three to my knowledge—is not the play Chekhov wrote but an adaptation. Of necessity any adaptor would have to cut and then piece together the original manuscript, and then, on top of that, would have to devise his own ending for the play. I am not saying that such an adaptation is without value—the existing ones shed a great deal of light on Chekhov's development as a playwright; such an adaptation, however, is outside the purpose of this volume.

Robert W. Corrigan

Pittsburgh, 1962

SIX PLAYS OF CHEKHOV

IVANOV

CAST

NIKOLAI ALEXEYEVICH IVANOV, *a landowner*

ANNA PETROVNA (before her marriage, Sarah Abramson), *his wife*

MATVYEY SEMYONICH SHABYELSKY, *his maternal uncle*

PAVEL KERYLOVICH LEBEDEV, *Chairman of the County Council*

ZINAIDA SAVESHNA, *his wife*

SASHA, *their daughter*

YEVGENY KONSTANTINOVICH LVOV, *a young doctor*

MARFA YEGOROVNA BABAKINA, *a young widow and daughter of a wealthy merchant*

DIMITRI NEKITOVICH KOSICH, *a tax official*

MIHAIL MIHAILOVICH BORKIN, *manager of Ivanov's estate*

AVDOTYA NAZAROVNA, *an old woman*

YEGORS, *a friend of the Lebedevs'*

FIRST GUEST

SECOND GUEST

THIRD GUEST

FOURTH GUEST

PYOTR, *Ivanov's servant*

GAVRILA, *Lebedev's servant*

VISITORS

*The action of the play takes place
in one of the provinces of Central Russia.*

ACT I

The garden of IVANOV's *estate. On the left, the front of the house with a terrace. One window is open. In front of the terrace a large semicircular lawn from which paths lead into other parts of the garden. On the right are several garden chairs and tables. A lamp on one of the tables is lit. It is evening. As the curtain rises, the sound of a cello and piano duet can be heard.* IVANOV *is sitting at the table, reading a book.* BORKIN *in riding boots and carrying a gun enters the garden; he is slightly drunk. On seeing* IVANOV, *he approaches him on tiptoe and, when almost next to him, aims the gun at his face.*

IVANOV *sees* BORKIN, *starts and jumps up.* For God's sake, Misha, what are you doing? Don't frighten me like that. . . . I'm upset enough as it is without more of your stupid jokes. . . . *Sits down.* You've frightened me, and now you're very pleased with yourself.

BORKIN *laughs heartily.* Calm down! . . . I'm sorry. *Sits down beside him.* I won't do it again, really I won't. *Takes off his cap.* God, it's hot. You won't believe me, but I've walked fifteen miles in less than three hours. . . . I'm worn out. . . . Just feel my heart, see how it's pounding.

IVANOV *continues reading.* Sure, but later on. . . .

BORKIN No, feel it now. *Takes* IVANOV's *hand and puts it to his chest.* Do you hear that? It must be heart trouble. I might die suddenly at any moment. Tell me, would you be sorry if I died?

IVANOV Don't bother me, I'm reading . . . later . . .

BORKIN No seriously, Nikolai Alexeyevich, would you be sorry if I died suddenly? Would you really be sorry?

IVANOV Leave me alone!

BORKIN Just tell me, would you be sorry?

IVANOV I'm sorry that you smell of vodka. It's disgusting, Misha.

BORKIN *laughs.* Do I smell of vodka? How amazing! . . . Not that there's really anything so amazing about it. I just happened to meet one of the judges at Plesniky, and I have to admit we did have eight drinks together. They say that drinking is good for you, is that true? Well, tell me, is it?

IVANOV This is too much. . . . Listen, Misha, you're going too far . . .

BORKIN Well, well . . . I'm sorry! By all means, my friend, stay where you are. I won't bother you. *Gets up and walks off.* The kind of people there are around here—you can't even talk to them. *Returns.* Oh, by the way, I'd almost forgotten . . . You'd better give me eighty-two roubles.

IVANOV What for?

BORKIN I have to pay the workmen tomorrow.

IVANOV I haven't got it.

BORKIN Thanks a lot! *Mimics him.* I haven't got it! . . . The workmen have to be paid, don't they?

IVANOV I don't know. I haven't got any money. They'll just have to wait until the first of the month, when I get my salary.

BORKIN Oh, what's the use of trying to talk business with people like you? . . . Don't you understand, the workmen aren't coming to get paid on the first of the month, they're coming tomorrow morning!

IVANOV Well, there's nothing I can do about it. Why do you always bother me? And just when I'm busy reading or writing, or . . .

BORKIN What I want to know is, are the workmen going to be paid or not? Oh, what's the use of talking to you! . . . *Waves his hand.* What kind of landowner are you, anyway? You and your scientific farming. You've got a thousand acres of land and not a cent to your name. It's like owning a wine cellar without a corkscrew! I'll just have to sell some horses tomorrow. . . . Oh, you don't think I will? . . . Well, I sold the oats before we cut it! And you just wait, I think I'll sell the rye tomorrow, too! *Walks up and down the stage.* You needn't think I'm going to stand on ceremony with you—or do you? Well, I shan't, I'm not that sort of man.

SHABYELSKY, *off-stage through the window.* It's impossible to play with you. . . . You've got an ear like a fish.

ANNA, *appearing at the window.* Who is it? Is that you, Misha? What are you jumping up and down like that for?

BORKIN If you had to deal with your "*cher Nicolàs,*" you'd jump up and down, too!

ANNA Oh, Misha, will you have them bring some hay down to the croquet lawn?

BORKIN *waves his hand.* Don't bother me, please.

ANNA Such manners! . . . That tone of voice isn't becoming at all. If you want women to like you, you must never be angry or obstinate. *To her husband.* Nikolai, let's go and play some croquet!

IVANOV It's not good for you to be in the fresh air, my dear. You'd better go in. *Shouts.* Uncle, will you shut the window? *The window is shut.*

BORKIN And another thing, you've only got two more days before you'll have to pay Lebedev the interest on the mortgage.

IVANOV I know. I'll go over there today and ask him to wait . . . Looks at his watch.

BORKIN When are you going?

IVANOV Pretty soon.

BORKIN, *eagerly.* Wait a minute! . . . isn't it Sasha's birthday today? . . . And I almost forgot! What a memory! *Skips about.* I'm going to a birthday party! I'm going to a birthday party! *Chants.* I'm going to a birthday party! First, I'll have a swim, and then I'll chew some mint to get rid of the smell of this vodka—and then I'll be ready to start the day all over again. My dear Nikolai Alexeyevich, you're the joy of my life. Why if it weren't for your always being so gloomy and depressed you and I could do great things together. God knows, I'd do anything for your sake. Do you want me to marry Marfoosha Babakina? I'd give you half the dowry—no, not half—you could have it all!

IVANOV Will you please stop all this nonsense!

BORKIN No, I mean it. Do you want me to marry Marfoosha? We'll share the dowry . . . But why do I suggest this? You don't understand, do you? *Mimics him.* "Will you please stop all this nonsense!" You're a good man and you're intelligent but you haven't got oomph—you know—no drive. If you'd only get me mad enough to hit somebody, make the sparks fly. . . . You're just neurotic, a weakling. Why, if you were a normal man, you'd be making a million a year. Take me, for instance. If I had twenty-three hundred roubles right now, I'd have twenty thousand in two weeks. You don't believe me? You think that's nonsense, too? Well, it's not. You give me twenty-three hundred roubles, and inside of two weeks I'll show you twenty thousand. On the other side of the river, just across from us, Ovsianov is selling a strip of land for twenty-three hundred roubles. If we buy it, then both banks will be ours, and if both the banks are ours—do you see what I mean—we'd have the right to build a dam. Well, that's true, isn't it? Then we tell everybody that we're going to build a mill, and when people down the river hear that we plan to dam the river they'll make a fuss. All right, we'll say, if you don't want the dam, you'll have to pay us not to build it. See what I mean? We'd get five thousand from the factory, for sure—and probably three from Korolkov . . . and the monastery would pay five, too . . .

IVANOV That's dishonest, Misha. Keep your rotten schemes to yourself, or I'll lose my temper.

BORKIN, *sitting down at the table.* Oh, well! . . . I knew it! You'll never do anything, and you won't let me do anything either.

Enter SHABYELSKY *and* LVOV.

SHABYELSKY, *coming out of the house with* LVOV. Dostors are no better than lawyers; the only difference is that lawyers only rob you, while doctors rob you and kill you, too. I'm not speaking of present company, you understand. *Sits down on one of the seats.* Frauds and swindlers, that's what they are. You might find an exception to the rule in Utopia, but . . . I've spent more than twenty thousand on doctors and hospital bills, and I haven't met a doctor yet who wasn't a swindler.

BORKIN, *to* IVANOV. You won't do anything, and won't let me either. That's why we're broke.

SHABYELSKY As I say, I'm not speaking of present company. There may be one or two exceptions, but anyway . . . *Yawns.*

IVANOV, *closing his book.* Well, what's the news, Doctor?

LVOV, *glancing back at the window.* No change from the morning: she should go to the Crimea at once. *Walks up and down the stage.*

SHABYELSKY *bursts out laughing.* To the Crimea! . . . We should be doctors, Misha! Then, if some Madame Angot or Ophelia got bored and started sneezing, all we'd have to do is write out a prescription based on the latest findings of medical research. Let's see—first, a young doctor, and then a trip to the Crimea, and when she gets there—a handsome Tartar guide . . .

IVANOV, *to the* COUNT. Oh, stop it, will you? *To* LVOV. To go to the Crimea takes money. Even if I could get the money—you know she absolutely refuses to go.

LVOV Yes, I know she does. *Pause.*

BORKIN Listen, Doctor, is Anna Petrovna really so sick that she must go to the Crimea?

LVOV *glances back at the window.* Yes, she's got tuberculosis.

BORKIN Hm! . . . that's not good . . . I've had a feeling for some time that from the look on her face she wouldn't last long.

LVOV Please, not so loud . . . they can hear you in the house. *Pause.*

BORKIN *sighs.* Such is life . . . It's like a flower that blooms gaily in a meadow, and then along comes a goat and eats it up, and—it's all over. . . .

SHABYELSKY All this is just nonsense! Nonsense, I say . . . *Yawns.* You're just a fraud. *Pause.*

BORKIN Well, gentlemen, I've been trying to tell Nikolai Alexeyevich how to make money; again I've got a great idea, but, as usual, the seed's fallen on barren ground. You can't tell him anything. Just look at him—bored, depressed, gloomy, miserable. . . .

SHABYELSKY *rises and stretches himself.* You're so smart, you've got all sorts of schemes, and you're always telling everybody what they ought to do—but you've never taught me anything, never once! . . . Come on, smartie, give me some advice!

BORKIN *rises.* I can think of a dozen things. Why, if I were you, I'd have twenty thousand roubles in a week. *Walks off.*

SHABYELSKY, *following him.* What do you mean? How?

BORKIN There's nothing to explain. It's all very simple. *Returns.* Nikolai Alexeyevich, give me a rouble! IVANOV *silently hands him the money.* "Merci." *To the* COUNT. You've still got plenty of trumps in your hand.

SHABYELSKY, *following him.* Well, what are they?

BORKIN If I were in your place, I'd have thirty thousand in a week, maybe more.

BORKIN *and* COUNT *go out.*

IVANOV, *after a pause.* Useless people, useless talk, and being forced to answer all those stupid questions. . . . Doctor, this has made me so tired I'm almost ill. I've gotten so irritable and rude lately that I don't even recognize myself. I've always got a headache, I can't sleep, there are noises in my ears. And there's simply

nowhere to go where I can find any peace . . . simply nowhere . . .

LVOV I want to talk very seriously with you, Nikolai Alexeyevich.

IVANOV What about?

LVOV It's about Anna Petrovna. *Sits down.* You're right, she
refuses to go to the Crimea, but she would go if you'd go with
her.

IVANOV, *after a moment's thought.* It would take a lot of money
for us both to go. Besides, I couldn't get away for that long. I've
already taken one vacation.

LVOV All right, then, that's out. The next point is this. The
most effective cure for tuberculosis is absolute rest and peace of
mind. But your wife doesn't get a minute's rest. She's constantly
worried about your relationship. I'm very much concerned about
this, so you must forgive me if I speak frankly. The way you treat
her is beginning to kill her. *Pause.* Nikolai Alexeyevich, I don't
want to think that of you! . . .

IVANOV Well, it's true I know . . . I feel terribly guilty about
it, but my mind's so confused . . . I'm in a kind of stupor . . .
paralyzed . . . I can't understand myself. I don't understand other
people. *Glances at the window.* Someone might hear us, let's take
a walk. *They rise.* My friend, I'd like to tell you the whole story
from beginning to end, but it's so long and complicated that it
would take me all night. *They start walking off.* Anya is a remarkable and exceptional woman. She gave up her religion, her parents,
and her money for me; and if I'd asked for a hundred more sacri-
fices, she would consent to every one of them without batting an
eye. As for me—well, there's nothing remarkable about me, and
I haven't given her anything. However, it's a long story . . . The
point is, Doctor, that . . . *Hesitates.* that, to put it briefly, I was
passionately in love with her when we were married and I
promised I'd love her forever. And now, after five years, she's still
in love with me, but I . . . *Makes a helpless gesture with his
hands.* And when you tell me that she's going to die soon, I don't
feel any love or even pity but a kind of emptiness, a kind of
fatigue . . . To an outsider it must seem horrible; I don't know
myself what's happening to me . . .

ironic juxta.

They walk off. Enter SHABYELSKY.

SHABYELSKY *laughs loudly as he comes in.* Why, he's not a fraud after all, he's a genius! They ought to put up a monument in his honor. He's a perfect example of the rottenness in our world today: the lawyer, the doctor, the businessman, the banker. *Sits down on the bottom step of the terrace*. The amazing thing is, that he never went to college. Why he'd be the perfect scoundrel if he'd had a little more education. "You could make twenty thousand in a week. You've still got the ace of trumps in your hand . . . your title of Count." *Laughs uproariously*. "Why, any girl with a dowry would marry you." . . . ANNA PETROVNA *opens the window and looks down*. "Would you like me to fix it up with Marfoosha?" he says. Who in the blazes is this Marfoosha, anyway? Oh, of course, it's that Balabalkina woman . . . Babakalkina . . . the one that looks like a laundress.

ANNA Is that you, Count?

SHABYELSKY What do you want? ANNA *laughs. With a Jewish accent*. Vy do you laff?

ANNA I was thinking of something you said at dinner, do you remember? How did it go? Something about a repentant thief, and a horse. . . .

SHABYELSKY A repentant thief, a sick horse that's gotten better, and a baptized Jew . . . are all worth the same in the end.

ANNA *laughs*. You can't even tell a joke without being bitter. You really are a malicious person. *Seriously*. All joking apart, Count, you really aren't a very agreeable person you know. Living with you is so depressing and upsetting. You're always grumbling and complaining; and to listen to you everyone is a scoundrel. Be honest with me, Count, have you ever said a good word for anybody?

SHABYELSKY What is this, the Inquisition?

ANNA We've been living here together five years now, and I've never once heard you speak of anyone without sneering. What have they done to you? Do you really think you're better than everybody else?

SHABYELSKY Not at all. I'm as much of a scoundrel as everybody else. . . . Just a useless old man. I'm always running myself down. Who am I? What am I? Once I was rich and free and happy, but now . . . I'm just a parasite, the object of charity, a useless buffoon. I show my indignation and contempt for them, and they laugh at me; I laugh, and they shake their heads sadly and say: "The old guy's off his rocker." But most of the time they don't even hear me, or notice me for that matter. . . .

ANNA, *quietly.* It's screeching again. . . .

SHABYELSKY What's screeching?

ANNA The owl. It screeches every night.

SHABYELSKY Let it screech. Things can't get any worse than they are already. *Stretches himself.* Oh, my dear Sarah, if I'd only won a hundred thousand or so—you know what I'd do? You'd never see me again. I'd get out of this hole, and all your damned charity, and you'd never see me again till Judgment Day.

ANNA And what would you have done if you'd won the money?

SHABYELSKY, *after a moment's thought.* Well, first of all, I'd have gone to Moscow and listened to the gypsies sing. Then . . . then I'd go to Paris. I'd rent a house and go to church every day. . . .

ANNA And what else?

SHABYELSKY I'd spend my days sitting beside my wife's grave, thinking. I'd have sat there until I died. You see, my wife's buried in Paris. *Pause.*

Doesn't listen

ANNA How terribly depressing! Let's play another duet, or do something?

SHABYELSKY All right, go and get the music ready.

ANNA *moves away from the window. Enter* IVANOV *and* LVOV *at the end of the garden.*

IVANOV *comes down the avenue with* LVOV. My good fellow, you just graduated from medical school last year, you're young and full of energy, while I'm thirty-five. I have a right to give you advice. Don't marry Jewesses, or neurotics, or blue stockings, but choose a nice ordinary girl, a girl who doesn't sparkle, and talk a lot. Just try to make your life as quiet as possible; the duller and more monotonous the background the better. Don't try to fight the masses single-handed, don't tilt with windmills, don't knock your head against brick walls. . . . And, for God's sake, forget scientific farming, new methods of education for the peasants, and fervent speeches . . . Shut yourself up in your shell and do as best you can the job God gave you . . . That's the only honest and healthy way to live as a human being. As for my own life— how tiring it's been! So full of mistakes, injustice, inconsistency! *Seeing the* COUNT, *with irritation.* What are you always hanging around for, Uncle? You never give me a chance to talk to anyone!

SHABYELSKY, *in a tearful voice.* Isn't there any place a poor old man can go? *Jumps up and goes into the house.*

IVANOV *shouts after him.* I'm sorry, I'm sorry! *To* LVOV. Now I've hurt his feelings. What did I do that for? Really, my nerves are so on edge. I've got to do something about it. I must. . . .

LVOV, *excitedly.* Nikolai Alexeyevich, I've listened to everything you've said, and . . . now I'm going to speak frankly, without beating around the bush. In everything you say, even in the tone of your voice, there's only heartless egoism and pitiless cruelty. . . . Here's the closest person in the world to you, dying because of you; her days are numbered, and yet you feel so little affection for her that you can go about giving advice and analyzing your feelings . . . I can't express it very well, I'm not good at making speeches, but . . . Really, you disgust me!

IVANOV Perhaps I do. . . . It's easy for an outsider. Probably you can see through me, and no doubt I'm very much to blame. *Listens.* It sounds as if the horses are ready. I must go and get ready. *Walks toward the house, then stops.* You don't like me, Doctor, and you don't conceal it. Your sincerity does you credit . . . *Enters the house.*

LVOV, *alone.* Damn it . . . I missed the chance again! Why didn't I say what I meant to say. He always upsets me. Every time I open my mouth something inside me *Points to his chest.* begins to suffocate me and turns over inside me, and my tongue seems to get stuck in my mouth. How I hate this Tartuffe, this pompous impostor! I hate him with all my heart. . . . Look at him! Getting ready to go out! . . . His poor wife's only pleasure in life is to have him near her; he's her whole life and she begs him to spend just one evening with her, just one, but he . . . oh, he can't! He finds his home too dull, no new faces here. Just one evening at home and he'd have to shoot himself in despair. Poor fellow . . . he needs new fields for his villainous schemes, I know. . . . Oh, I know why you go to the Lebedevs' every night! I know!

SHABYELSKY, *coming out of the house with* IVANOV *and* ANNA. Look here, Nikolai, this is too much! You go out every night and leave us here alone. We go to bed at eight o'clock out of sheer boredom. It's a miserable existence. Why can you go out if we can't? Why?

ANNA Leave him alone, Count! Let him go if he wants to. . . .

IVANOV, *to his wife.* My dear, you know you're sick. That's why you can't go out. The doctor, here, has said that with your cough you mustn't go out at night. Didn't you, Doctor? You're no child, Anyushka, you must be reasonable. . . . *To the* COUNT. And what would you do over there?

SHABYELSKY I'd go to Hell, if only I could get away from here! I'm bored. I'm going crazy with boredom! Everybody's tired of me. You leave me at home to entertain Anya, but I've almost nagged her to death!

ANNA Leave him alone, Count, please. Let him go if he enjoys it there.

IVANOV What do you mean, Anya? You know I don't go there for my own pleasure. I've got to talk to Lebedev about the mortgage.

ANNA I don't know why you feel you need to justify yourself. Go ahead. No one's trying to stop you.

IVANOV Please, let's not be angry with one another. It's really so unnecessary.

SHABYELSKY, *in a tearful voice.* Nikolai, my dear boy, please take me with you! It might be pleasant to see all those fools and scoundrels. Please, you know I haven't been out since Easter.

IVANOV, *irritated.* All right then, come along! How tiresome you all are!

SHABYELSKY Yes? Oh, thank you, thank you! . . . *Takes his arm gaily and leads him aside.* May I wear your straw hat?

IVANOV Yes, but hurry up, please. *The* COUNT *runs into the house.* How tired I am of you all! However . . . God, what am I saying? I know I'm acting abominably talking to you this way, Anya. It's never happened before. Well, good-bye, Anya, I'll be back by one.

ANNA Kolya, darling, please stay home tonight!

IVANOV, *agitated.* My darling, my love, my poor unhappy girl, please don't try to stop me from going out at night. I know it's cruel and selfish of me, but you must let me be selfish. I can't stand it here. As soon as the sun goes down I'm overcome with despair and it torments me. Don't ask me why. I don't know myself. Honestly, I don't. I'm depressed here, so I go to the Lebedevs' and it's even worse there, so I come home, and I'm still depressed, and it goes on and on like that all night long . . . It's just too much . . .

ANNA Kolya . . . please stay? We can talk the way we used to. . . . We can have supper together, then read. . . . The old grumbler and I can play some duets for you. . . . *Puts her arms round him.* Please stay! . . . *Pause.* I don't understand you anymore. This has been going on for a whole year. Why have you changed?

IVANOV I don't know, I don't know. . . .

ANNA And why don't you want me to go with you when you go out at night?

IVANOV Oh, I suppose I might as well tell you if you really want to know. It's cruel to say this, but I hope you'll understand. When I get depressed like I am now, I . . . I begin to stop loving you. Then I want to run away from you, then I have to get out of here, that's all.

ANNA Depression! Oh, I understand, I understand. . . . Listen, my darling! Why don't you sing and laugh and get angry, like you used to do? Stay here, and we'll laugh and drink together, and your depression will be gone in no time. Would you like me to sing something? Or should we go in your study and sit in the twilight, like we used to, and you can tell me about your depression. . . . Your eyes look so sad! I'll look into them and cry, and we'll both feel better. . . . *Laughs and weeps.* Or—can't we? How does the song go, Kolya? "The flowers return in the spring but lost happiness never returns." . . . No? Well, go then, go. . . .

IVAN Pray for me, Anya! *Starts off, then stops and thinks.* No, I can't do it! *Goes out.*

ANNA Yes, go! . . . *Sits down at the table.*

LVOV, *walking about the stage.* Anna Petrovna, you must obey the rule: you must go in as soon as the sun goes down. The damp evening air is bad for you.

ANNA Yes, sir.

LVOV What do you mean, "Yes, sir." I'm being very serious.

ANNA But I don't want to be serious. *Coughs.*

LVOV You see—you're coughing already.

Enter SHABYELSKY.

SHABYELSKY *comes out of the house wearing a hat and an over-*

coat. Where's Nikolai? Are the horses ready? *Walks quickly up to* ANNA *and kisses her hand.* Good night, my darling. *Makes a grimace.* Gewalt! *In Jewish accent.* I beg your pardon. *Goes out quickly.*

LVOV What an idiot!

Pause. The distant sound of an accordion is heard.

ANNA How sad and lonely it is! . . . You see, the coachmen and the cooks are dancing, while I . . . I'm all alone . . . Yevgeny Konstantinovich, what are you so nervous about? Come here, sit down! . . .

LVOV I can't sit still. *Pause.*

ANNA They're playing the "Starling" in the kitchen. *Sings.* "Starling, starling, where are you? . . . On the mountain drinking dew." *Pause.* Are your father and mother living, Doctor?

LVOV My father's dead, but my mother's alive.

ANNA Do you miss your mother very much?

LVOV I haven't time to miss anybody.

ANNA *laughs.* "The flowers return in the spring, but lost happiness never returns" . . . I wish I could remember who told me that. It must have been Nikolai. *Listens.* The owl's screeching again!

LVOV Well, let it screech!

ANNA You know, Doctor, I'm beginning to think that Fate's cheated me. Lots of people who are probably no better than me are happy, and yet they haven't had to pay for their happiness. But I've paid for every minute of mine . . . And what a price I've paid! Why should I have to pay so much? My dear friend, you've always been very kind to me, so gentle, so afraid to tell me the truth—but do you think I don't know what's the matter with me? I know perfectly well. However, let's not talk about it . . . *With a Jewish accent.* I beg your pardon! Can you tell funny stories?

LVOV No, I can't.

ANNA Nikolai can. . . . But, you know, I can't understand the unfairness of people: why don't they respond to love with love, why must they answer truth with lies? How much longer are my father and mother going to go on hating me? They live fifty miles away, and I can feel their hatred day and night, even when I'm asleep. And I don't understand Nikolai's depression. He says it's only at night that he doesn't love me, when he feels depressed. I understand that, but suppose he's stopped loving me altogether? Of course, that's impossible but—if he has? No, no, I mustn't even think about it. *Sings.* "Starling, starling, where are you?" *Starts.* What frightening thoughts I have! You aren't married, Doctor, and there are lots of things you can't understand . . .

LVOV You say you don't understand. *Sits down beside her.* No, I'm the one who doesn't understand—I don't understand you! Tell me this, how did it happen that you, an intelligent, honest, yes, saintly woman, allowed yourself to be so horribly deceived? Why are you here? What have you got in common with that cold, heartless . . . but let's leave your husband out of it—what have you in common with these useless, vulgar people? Oh, my God! . . . That eternal grumbler, the crazy old Count—and that scoundrel, that outrageous impostor Misha with his disgusting face! Tell me, why? How did you get here?

ANNA *laughs.* He used to talk just like that . . . Exactly like that. . . . But he's got bigger eyes than you, and when he was excited they used to glow like burning coals . . . Go on, go on.

LVOV *gets up and waves his hand.* What's the use! You'd better go in.

ANNA You're saying all sorts of things about Nikolai. Do you really understand him? How can you get to know a man in six months? He's a remarkable man, Doctor, and I regret you didn't know him two or three years ago. He's depressed now, he's silent and he doesn't do anything, but before . . . Oh, he was wonderful! I fell in love with him at first sight. *Laughs.* I gave one look at him, and I was caught like a mouse in a trap! He said: Come with me—and I did. I cut every tie that bound me to my old life, just like one cuts dead leaves from a plant—and I went. . . . *Pause.* But things are different now . . . Now he goes off to the Lebedevs' to amuse himself with other women, and I . . . sit here in the garden and listen to the owl screeching . . . *A watchman can be heard.* Doctor, do you have any brothers and sisters?

LVOV No, I haven't. ANNA *sobs.* What is it? What's the matter?

ANNA I can't stand it, Doctor, I must go . . .

LVOV Where?

ANNA To him . . . I'm going . . . Get the horses, will you? *Runs into the house.*

LVOV I absolutely refuse to treat anybody under these conditions! Not only don't they pay me, but they upset me, too. No, I'm finished. I've had enough! *Goes into the house.*

Curtain

ACT II

A drawing room in the LEBEDEVS' *house; in the center a door leading to the garden, also doors right and left. The room is furnished with expensive antique furniture, which is covered with linen dust covers. Pictures on the walls; the room is lighted by chandeliers.* ZINAIDA *is on a sofa; on either side of her sit elderly ladies in armchairs; the young people sit on chairs. In the back, by the door leading into the garden, several guests are playing cards; among them are* KOSICH, AVDOTYA NAZAROVNA *and* YEGORS. GAVRILA *stands by the door on the right; the* MAID *is passing a tray of cookies and other pastries. Throughout the act, guests pass in and out from the garden and through the door on the right.* BABAKINA *enters through the door on the right and approaches* ZINAIDA.

ZINAIDA, *joyfully.* Darling, Marfa Yegorovna!

BABAKINA How are you, Zinaida Saveshna? Congratulations on your daughter's birthday! *They embrace.* I hope she'll . . .

ZINAIDA Thank you, my dear, I'm so glad you could come. . . . How are you?

BABAKINA Fine, thank you. *Sitting down beside her.* Good evening, you young people! . . .

The GUESTS *rise and bow.*

FIRST GUEST, *laughing.* "Young people" . . . as if you were so old!

BABAKINA, *with a sigh.* I can't pretend any longer! You young people make me feel so old.

FIRST GUEST *laughs deferentially.* That's a lot of nonsense . . . You may be a widow, but you're still prettier than any of the girls.

GAVRILA *brings* BABAKINA *tea.*

ZINAIDA, *to* GAVRILA. Really, Gavrila, why do you serve the tea like that? Go and bring some preserves. Gooseberry, or something . . .

BABAKINA Please don't bother, I don't care for any, thanks. . . . *Pause.*

FIRST GUEST On your way did you come through Mushkme?

BABAKINA No, through Spask. That road's better.

FIRST GUEST You're right, I'd forgotten.

KOSICH Two spades.

YEGORS Pass.

AVDOTYA Pass.

BABAKINA Zinaida, did you know lottery tickets are going up again? Can you imagine it: tickets for the first draw are now two hundred and seventy, and for the second they're nearly two hundred and fifty. It's never happened before. . . .

ZINAIDA, *with a sigh.* Well, if you've a lot of tickets you're in luck.

BABAKINA Not really, my dear. Even though the price is high, they aren't a good investment. The insurance alone. . . .

ZINAIDA Perhaps, but all the same you never can tell. *Sighs.* God is good . . .

THIRD GUEST In my opinion, ladies, right now there aren't *any* good investments. Blue-chip stocks bring in practically nothing, and speculation is very risky. As I see it, today the investor is in a more dangerous position than those who. . . .

BABAKINA *sighs.* That's probably true!

The FIRST GUEST *yawns.*

BABAKINA Do you think it's very polite to yawn in the presence of ladies?

FIRST GUEST I beg your pardon, I didn't mean to . . .

ZINAIDA *gets up and goes out through the door on the right; a long silence follows.*

YEGORS Two hearts.

AVDOTYA Pass.

KOSICH Pass.

BABAKINA, *aside.* Lord, how boring this is! It's enough to kill you!

ZINAIDA, *coming out of the door on the right with* LEBEDEV, *in a subdued voice.* What's the idea—sitting out there by yourself? What do you think you are, a prima donna or something? Now come in here and be with your guests! *She takes her former seat.*

LEBEDEV *yawns.* Oh, what a life! We certainly pay for our sins! *Seeing* BABAKINA. But look, there's our little sunbeam . . . *Greets her.* How are you, my dear?

BABAKINA Very well, thank you.

LEBEDEV That's wonderful! Splendid! *Sits down in an armchair.* Well, well. . . . Gavrila!

GAVRILA *brings him a small glass of vodka and a glass of water; he drinks the vodka first, then the water.*

FIRST GUEST Good health to you! . . .

LEBEDEV Health, indeed! I'm lucky to stay alive. *To his wife.* Where's our little girl, my dear?

KOSICH, *tearfully.* Now you just tell me, why haven't we taken a single trick? *Jumps up.* Why the devil did we lose?

AVDOTYA *also jumps up, angrily.* Because, my friend—you don't know how to play. Why do you, anyway? You haven't any right to lead somebody else's suit. So you held back your ace and got stuck with it!

Both leave the table and come to the group.

KOSICH, *tearfully.* Just listen to this, my friends. . . . I had the ace, king, queen, jack, and eight of diamonds, the ace and a little spade, and one little heart, just one, you understand . . . And what does she do? She can't even make a little slam. I opened with no trump. . . .

AVDOTYA, *interrupting.* I was the one who opened with no trump! You bid two no. . . .

KOSICH This is impossible! . . . Just let me. . . . You had . . . I had . . . You had . . . *To* LEBEDEV. Here, you decide it, Pavel Kerylich! I had the ace, king, queen, jack and eight of diamonds. . . .

LEBEDEV, *stopping his ears.* For God's sake, will you please stop it! . . . Please!

AVDOTYA *shouts.* I began the no trump!

KOSICH, *fiercely.* I'll be damned if I'll ever play with that old bag again! *Goes rapidly out into the garden.*

AVDOTYA Ugh! He makes my blood boil! Old bag, am I? You're the old bag!

BABAKINA Well, you're not the sweetest person in the world, Auntie dear.

AVDOTYA, *seeing* BABAKINA, *throws up her hands.* Well, if it isn't my precious Marfa Yegorovna! . . . I must be blind as a bat. Here, you been here all this time and I didn't see you . . . my sweet. *Kisses her shoulder and sits down beside her.* How wonderful it is to see you. Here, let me look at you. I can't hurt you just by looking at you, can I? I haven't got an evil eye!

LEBEDEV She's off again! . . . Why don't you find her a husband instead of talking so much?

AVDOTYA Just see if I don't! I'll have her married if it's the last thing I do. And that goes for Sasha, too. You just see if I don't. Before I'm dead and buried, I say . . . *Sighs.* The trouble is . . . where do you find husbands these days? Here they are, our future husbands, all huddled together like a bunch of drowned rats! . . .

THIRD GUEST That's a rather unfortunate comparison, I must say. As I see it, if our modern young men prefer to remain single, it's not their fault, but the existing social conditions. You see. . . .

LEBEDEV That's enough! Please don't start philosophizing! I can't stand it.

Enter SASHA.

SASHA *comes in and walks up to her father.* Isn't it a beautiful evening. How can you stand sitting in here in this stuffy room?

ZINAIDA Sashenka, don't you see that Marfa's here?

SASHA Oh, I'm terribly sorry. *Goes up to* BABAKINA *and greets her.*

BABAKINA My, how snobbish you've gotten lately, Sanechka. . . . You haven't been to see me in so long. *They embrace.* Congratulations, darling! . . .

SASHA Thank you. *Sits down beside her father.*

LEBEDEV Yes, Avdotya Nazarovna, it's no easy job finding a good husband these days. And it's not just husbands—it's hard to find a good man period. Most of our young men, if they'll forgive me, are so insipid that . . . they haven't any blood, they're like a well-done steak. What a bunch! They don't know what a good conversation is; they can't dance and they don't know how to drink.

AVDOTYA Oh, they know how to drink; they're past-masters at it, as long as you've got some liquor around.

LEBEDEV Oh, anybody can drink that way . . . even a horse knows how to drink . . . But they don't know the art of drinking! Why in my day, we'd study and work all day long, and then at night we'd be off. We'd dance till dawn, and flirt with the girls, and we'd drink, too. *Rubs his chin.* And we'd tell stories and talk about ideas until our tongues were dragging . . . But the men today . . . *Waves his hand.* Well, I just don't understand them. They're no good to man or beast. Why, in the whole county there's one man who's worth his salt, and he's married, *Sighs.* and it seems that he's beginning to be like all the rest . . .

BABAKINA Who's that?

LEBEDEV Nikolai Ivanov.

BABAKINA Yes, he's a fine man— *With a grimace.* Only he's so unhappy.

ZINAIDA That's true, but what do you expect? *Sighs.* He made a terrible mistake, poor man! He married a Jewess, and, of course, he figured that her parents would give them a fortune; but it didn't turn out that way . . . The day she married him, her parents disowned her. They say, in fact, that they've even put a curse on her. So he didn't get any money, after all. He regrets it now, all right, but it's too late.

SASHA Mama, that's not true.

BABAKINA, *with animation.* How can you say that, Sasha? Everyone knows it. If he didn't want her money, why would he marry a Jew? God knows there are enough attractive Russian girls. He made a mistake, that's all! *Getting excited.* And my, does she have to take it from him now. It's amazing. Sometimes he comes home and looks right at her and says, "Your parents swindled me! Get out of my house!" But where can she go? Her father and mother won't take her back. She might get a job as a maid somewhere, but she doesn't have any training. So he torments her until even the Count stands up for her. Why, if it weren't for the Count, she'd have been tormented to her grave by now. . . .

AVDOTYA They say he locks her up in a cellar and stuffs her with garlic. She keeps on eating it until she reeks . . . *Laughter.*

SASHA Papa, you know that isn't true!

LEBEDEV What difference does it make, Sasha, let them chatter if they enjoy it. *Shouts.* Gavrila! GAVRILA *brings him vodka and water.*

ZINAIDA Yes, the poor man's almost ruined. His finances are in terrible shape. Why, if it weren't for Borkin, he and his Jewess wouldn't even have anything to eat. *Sighs.* And what a problem he's been to us. God knows it's been difficult. Why do you know that he's owed us over nine thousand for more than three years?

BABAKINA, *horrified*. Nine thousand!

ZINAIDA Yes . . . My dear husband lent him the money. He doesn't know a good risk from a bad one. Oh, I don't mind the principal so much, but I wish he'd pay the interest.

SASHA, *passionately*. Mother, you've discussed all this a thousand times already!

ZINAIDA What difference does it make to you? Don't tell me you're defending him?

SASHA, *rising*. But how can you have the heart to talk that way about a man who hasn't done you any harm? Tell me, what harm has he done you?

THIRD GUEST Let me say just one thing, Alexandra Pavlovna, I respect Nikolai Alexeyevich, and I've always felt it a privilege to know him—though, just between us, he is quite an adventurer.

SASHA If that's your opinion, I congratulate you.

THIRD GUEST To prove it I'll tell you something that Borkin told me. Two years ago when there was a cattle epidemic, he bought a herd of cows, insured them. . . .

ZINAIDA Yes, yes, yes! I remember hearing that.

THIRD GUEST He insured them, and, do you know, then he infected them so he could get the insurance money.

SASHA Oh, that's sheer nonsense! No one ever bought any cattle or then infected them! It was all Borkin's idea, and everywhere he went he boasted about it. When Ivanov found it out, he didn't forgive Borkin for two weeks. Ivanov's only fault is weakness of character. He trusts people too much! That's why he hasn't fired Borkin long ago! He's been robbed blind! Anyone who wanted to could take advantage of his generosity.

LEBEDEV Sasha, don't get so excited about it. Calm down.

SASHA But why does everybody talk such nonsense? Anyway, I'm getting tired of it. All anybody wants to talk about is Ivanov, Ivanov, Ivanov! *Goes towards the door, then returns*. You amaze me! *To the young guests*. I'm simply amazed at your patience. How can you sit there like that? Aren't you bored? Why even the air in here is stuffy! Well, say something, try to entertain the girls, but for heaven's sake, do something! Can't you do anything else but talk about Ivanov, can't you laugh, or sing, or dance, or something? . . .

LEBEDEV, *laughing*. That's right, tell them off, Sasha! Give them the devil!

SASHA Look, will you do me just one favor. If you don't want to dance, or sing, or laugh—if all that bores you, all right. But for once in your life, and I know it will be hard, will you try to make a tremendous effort and think of something witty and original to say that will amuse us? It doesn't matter if it's rude or malicious, so long as it's funny. Or else, you might think of something that you could do as a group. Nothing spectacular, just a little bit daring, so we could admire you for once in our lives! You do want us to like you, don't you? . . . Then why don't you do something about it? Oh, what a sad bunch you are, all of you—it's enough to make one cry, just looking at you! I've told you a thousand times, and I'll go on telling you, too—you're a sad bunch!

Enter IVANOV *and* SHABYELSKY.

SHABYELSKY *comes in with* IVANOV *through the door on the right*. Who's making a speech here? You, Sasha? *Laughs loudly and shakes hands with her*. Many happy returns, my dear, may you live as long as possible and never be born again.

ZINAIDA, *joyfully*. Nikolai Alexeyevich, Count!

LEBEDEV Well! Who's this . . . It's not you, Count! *Goes to meet him*.

SHABYELSKY, *seeing* ZINAIDA *and* BABAKINA *and stretching his arms towards them*. Two gold mines on the same sofa! . . . What a beautiful sight! *Greets them; to* ZINAIDA. How are you, Zuzu? *To* BABAKINA. And you, my sweet?

ZINAIDA It's so good to see you, Count. You come so seldom these days. *Shouts*. Gavrila, bring some tea! Won't you sit down. *Gets up and goes out through the door on the right, then returns immediately, looking extremely preoccupied*. SASHA *takes her former seat*. IVANOV *greets everybody in silence*.

LEBEDEV, *to* SHABYELSKY. Where've you been? What's up? This is a real surprise! *Embraces him*. Oh, Count, you old rascal, you! Decent people don't act the way you do, thank God. *Leads him to the front of the stage by his arm*. Why haven't you been to see us? Are you angry or something?

SHABYELSKY How am I to get here, on a broomstick? I haven't got any horses, and Nikolai won't bring me with him. He says I have to stay at home with Sarah and keep her company. Send your horses for me, and I'll be glad to come. . . .

LEBEDEV *waves his hand.* Easy to say! Zuzu would sooner die than lend her horses. My dear friend, my good old friend! You mean more to me—are nearer and dearer to me—than anyone else in the world. You and I are the only ones left now from the good old days! "In you I love my former griefs, And all the days of my youth that's lost" . . . I'll stop joking, but sometimes I feel almost as if I were going to cry. *Embraces the* COUNT.

SHABYELSKY Let's stop it now! You know, you smell like a wine cellar. . . .

LEBEDEV You can't imagine how I miss my old friends! Sometimes I get so lonely and bored, I could hang myself just for something to do. *Quietly.* Zuzu's driven anybody that's the least bit interesting away by being so stingy. Nothing left but well-dressed bums. Look at them, the numbskulls. But come along now—let's have some tea. . . .

GAVRILA *brings the* COUNT *some tea.*

ZINAIDA, *preoccupied, to* GAVRILA. Really, why do you serve the tea that way? Bring some preserves. Gooseberry, or something.

SHABYELSKY, *laughing loudly, to* IVANOV. Didn't I tell you? *To* LEBEDEV. I made a bet with him on the way over that the first thing Zuzu would do when we got here, would be to offer us some gooseberry jam.

ZINAIDA You haven't changed have you, Count? It still amuses you to laugh at people.

LEBEDEV She made twenty jars of it this year, so how else do you expect her to get rid of it?

SHABYELSKY *sits down beside the table.* But you're still making money, Zuzu? I suppose you've got a million or so by now, eh?

ZINAIDA, *with a sigh.* To an outsider it may seem that we're rich, but where do they think the money comes from? It's nothing but gossip!

SHABYELSKY But we know, don't we! We know what a poor hand you are at this game . . . *To* LEBEDEV. Pasha, tell me honestly, have you saved a million?

LEBEDEV I don't know. You'll have to ask Zuzu.

SHABYELSKY, *to* BABAKINA. And pretty soon our plump little pigeon here will have a million, too! She gets prettier and plumper every day, no, every hour . . . That's what a lot of money does to a woman!

BABAKINA Thank you very much, your Excellency, but I don't like your little jokes.

SHABYELSKY Oh, come now, my little gold mine, this isn't a joke. It's simply a cry from the heart that I can't contain. Really, I love you and Zuzu more than all the world. *Gaily.* Such rapture! . . . Such bliss! Just to look at the two of you, and I'm ecstatic!

ZINAIDA You haven't changed. *To* YEGORS. Yegorushka, blow out the candles. There's no need to keep them burnng if you're not playing any more. YEGORS *starts, then blows out the candles and sits down. To* IVANOV. And how's your wife, Nikolai Alexeyevich?

IVANOV Not at all well. Today the doctor told me that it's definitely T.B. . . .

ZINAIDA Really? How sad! . . . *Sighs.* And we're all so fond of her . . .

SHABYELSKY That's just a lot of nonsense! . . . She hasn't got T.B. at all. Just because that quack of a doctor says so, doesn't mean she has it. Aesculapius wants to come to the house, so he invents T.B. Fortunately for him, her husband's not jealous! IVANOV *makes an impatient move.* As for Sarah, I don't trust a single thing she does. All my life I've never trusted doctors, or lawyers, or women. It's nonsense, I tell you. He's a quack!

LEBEDEV You're an amazing man, Matvyey! You never stop playing the misanthrope just like a child with a new toy. You're a man like any other, but to hear you talk one would think you'd got a frog in your throat, or a cold in the head.

SHABYELSKY Well, you don't expect me to go around kissing every fraud and impostor I meet, do you?

LEBEDEV But where are these impostors and frauds?

SHABYELSKY Well, present company excepted, of course, but . . .

LEBEDEV There's you "but" . . . You're just playing your role again.

SHABYELSKY My role? . . . It's lucky for you that you don't know what the world's really like.

LEBEDEV I don't know what life's all about, eh? Well I'll tell you: I just sit about and wait for the moment when I can kick the bucket. That's the meaning of life! You, and I, brother, are too old to think about the meaning of life. *Shouts*. Gavrila!

SHABYELSKY You've had enough already. Just look at the color of your nose!

LEBEDEV Never mind, my friend. I'm not getting married today.

ZINAIDA Doctor Lvov hasn't been here for a long time. He seems to have forgotten us.

SASHA He's my favorite aversion—that paragon of honesty! He can't ask for a glass of water, or smoke a cigarette without letting you know how wonderfully honest he is. Walking or talking, it's written all over his forehead: "I'm an honest man!" Lord, how he bores me!

SHABYELSKY He's a narrow-minded, conceited fraud! *Mimics*. "Make way for honest labor!" Just like a parrot! He honestly thinks he's another St. Francis! And anyone who doesn't shout as loud as he does is a scoundrel! And he has such insight! If a peasant is prosperous and lives like a human being, it means he's a thief. If I wear a velvet coat and am dressed by a valet, I'm a scoundrel and the valet is my slave. He's so honest the world isn't big enough to hold him. And he gets so nervous, he actually frightens me sometimes. He really does . . . I feel at any moment he may, out of a sense of duty, hit me in the face and call me a scoundrel.

IVANOV Yes, he is pretty hard to take, but still I like him. He's very sincere.

SHABYELSKY Oh, yes, his sincerity is fine! Last night he came up to me, and for no reason at all, said, "Count, I find you most distasteful!" Thank you very much! And believe me, it isn't just because he doesn't know better; there's a purpose behind it. His voice trembles, his eyes are red, his knees shake . . . The hell with his confounded sincerity! I may be repulsive to him, it may be true, and I'll even admit it, but he doesn't have to say so to my face. I'm a worthless old man, but he might have had the decency to respect my grey hairs . . . It's such a meaningless, ruthless kind of honesty!

LEBEDEV Now, now, you were young once yourself, you should try to understand.

SHABYELSKY Yes, I was young once, and foolish, too, and I've thought of myself as another Chatsky, too—exposing scoundrels and impostors for what they were. But never in all my life did I call a thief a thief to his face, or talk about a rope in the house of a condemned man. I was brought up with manners. But your fat-headed fraud would be on the top of the world—if Fate would give him a chance—and would think he was struggling with life's greatest problems, if he could slap my face publicly in the name of basic principles and human ideals.

LEBEDEV All young men are like that. I had an uncle once, who followed Hegel . . . he would fill his house with guests, and after a drink or two he'd get up on a chair and begin: "You ignoramuses! You're the powers of darkness! The dawn of a new life is approaching . . ." and so on. And he'd keep right on preaching to them . . .

SASHA And what did the guests do?

LEBEDEV Nothing. They just listened and went on drinking. Once I challenged him to a duel . . . my own uncle. It was over a discussion of Francis Bacon. It seems to me, although you know my memory's slipping—I was sitting there where Matvyey is sitting now, and my uncle and Gerasim Nilich, were standing over there where Nikolai is . . . Well, Gerasim Nilich asked a question . . .

Enter BORKIN. *He comes skipping and singing into the room through the door on the right. He is overly dressed and carries a package. There is a murmur of welcome.*

YOUNG LADIES Mihail Mihailovich!

LEBEDEV It's Misha, I can tell . . .

SHABYELSKY The life of the party!

BORKIN Here I am everybody! *Runs up to* SASHA. Most noble signorina, may I congratulate the whole world on the birth of such an exquisite flower as you? . . . As a token of my inestimable admiration, may I present you *Hands her the package.* with these fireworks and Roman candles which I made myself, especially for this occasion? May they brighten the night just as you brighten the shadows of this dark world. *Bows theatrically.*

SASHA Thank you.

LEBEDEV, *laughing loudly, to* IVANOV. Why don't you get rid of this Judas?

BORKIN, *to* LEBEDEV. Pavel Kerilich, my compliments! *To* IVANOV. My patron . . . *Sings.* "Nicolàs voilà," hi-ho, hi-ho! *Goes round greeting everybody.* The most honorable Zinaida Saveshna. . . .

The divine Marfa Yegorovna. . . . Most worthy Avdotya Nazarovna. . . . Your Excellency . . .

SHABYELSKY, *laughing loudly.* The life of the party! . . . As
soon as he arrives, everything seems more alive. D'you notice it?

BORKIN Ohhh, I'm tired. I've said "hello" to everybody, haven't
I? Well, what's the latest news? Isn't there some tidbit, something
spicy? *Earnestly, to* ZINAIDA. Just listen to this, my dear . . . As
I was on my way over here . . . *To* GAVRILA. Gavrila, bring me
some tea, but no gooseberry jam! *To* ZINAIDA. As I was on my
way over here, I saw some peasants stripping the bark off your
willow trees down by the river. Why don't you lease those trees?

LEBEDEV, *to* IVANOV. Why don't you get rid of this Judas?

ZINAIDA, *amazed.* Why, of course! That's true! I never thought
of it!

BORKIN, *moving his arms as if doing physical exercises.* I just
have to have my exercise . . . Now, isn't there some game we
could play? Marfa Yegorovna, I feel wonderful . . . quite exalted!
Sings. "Again I stand before you". . .

ZINAIDA By all means, let's do something—everybody's bored.

BORKIN Really, what's the matter with everybody? You all sit
around solemn as a jury! Let's do something! What will it be?
Forfeits, dancing, or fireworks? . . .

YOUNG LADIES, *clapping.* Firewords, fireworks! *They run into the
garden.*

SASHA, *to* IVANOV. Why are you so depressed today?

IVANOV Oh, I've got a headache, Sasha—besides, I'm just depressed.

SASHA Come in here.

*They go out through the door on the right; all the others go out
into the garden except* ZINAIDA *and* LEBEDEV.

ZINAIDA That's what I like to see—now, there's a young man
for you. He hasn't been here a minute and he's made everybody
happy. *Turns down the large lamp.* As long as they're out in the
garden there's no point in wasting good candles. *Blows out the
candles.*

LEBEDEV, *following her.* Zuzu, we ought to give our guests something to eat . . .

ZINAIDA Just look at all these candles . . . no wonder people
think we're rich. *Blows them out.*

Zinaida — stingy

LEBEDEV, *following her.* Zuzu, why, you should give them something to eat. . . . They're young, they must be hungry by now, poor things . . . Zuzu . . .

ZINAIDA The Count didn't finish his tea. What a waste of sugar! . . . *Goes out through the door on the left.*

LEBEDEV Oh, I give up! *Goes out into the garden.*

SASHA, *entering with* IVANOV *through the door on the right.* Everyone's gone into the garden.

IVANOV So, that's how things are, Sasha. I used to work hard and think a lot, and I never felt tired. Now, I don't do anything and think about nothing, and I'm always exhausted. My conscience tortures me night and day, and I have terrible feelings of guilt, but I don't know what for. And, then, there's Anya's T.B., and the debts, and this constant gossiping, meaningless chatter, and backbiting, and then there's that stupid Borkin. . . . My home has become unbearable to me, and living there is worse than torture. Frankly, Sasha, the very presence of my wife who loves me dearly has become unbearable. You're an old friend, and I can be honest with you—I come over here just to amuse myself, but I'm bored here, too, and already I'm anxious to get home again. Please, forgive me, I'll just leave quietly.

SASHA Nikolai Alexeyevich, I understand your problems. You're unhappy because you're lonely. You need someone to love, someone who understands you. Love is your only hope!

IVANOV Is it really, Sasha! Can you imagine a worn out old fossil like me getting involved in a new love affair! God protect me from that! No, my dear, romance isn't the answer. Let me tell you something—and I'm being completely honest with you; I can stand all these things! Anxiety, depression, bankruptcy, the loss of my wife, premature old age, loneliness, but I just can't bear the contempt I have for myself. The shame that I, a strong, healthy man, have somehow become a kind of Hamlet, a Manfred, just about kills me! Oh, I know there are fools who are flattered when you call them a Hamlet, but to me it's an insult! It wounds my pride, I'm oppressed with shame, and I suffer . . .

SASHA, *jokingly, through tears.* Nikolai Alexeyevich, let's run away to America together.

IVANOV I haven't got enough energy to walk to that door, and you want to go to America! *They go towards the garden exit.*

Really, Sasha dear, it must be terrible living here. When I look at the kind of people around you, I'm really frightened for you. Whom could you marry here? Your only hope will be if some visiting lieutenant or student takes you away. . . . ZINAIDA *enters through the door on the left with a jar of preserves.* Excuse me a minute, Sasha. I'll be right out . . . SASHA *goes out into the garden.* Zinaida Saveshna, I want to ask you a favor. . . .

ZINAIDA What is it, Nikolai Alexeyevich?

IVANOV *hesitates.* Well . . . you see . . . as you probably know, the interest on my mortgage is due the day after tomorrow, and I was wondering if I could have a little more time, or if you would add the interest to the principle. . . . Well, you see, I can't pay it. I haven't any money.

ZINAIDA, *alarmed.* But, Nikolai Alexeyevich, how can I? What kind of business is that? No, please don't mention it. For goodness sake, please don't torment an unfortunate old woman like that. . . .

IVANOV I'm sorry, forgive me . . . *Goes out into the garden.*

ZINAIDA Oh, my, how he frightened me! . . . Why, I'm trembling all over . . . all over. *Goes out through the door on the right.*

KOSICH *enters through the door on the left and walks across the stage.* I had the ace, king, queen, jack and eight of diamonds, the ace and a little spade . . . a singleton in hearts, and she, damn her, wouldn't go to slam. . . . *Goes out.*

Enter AVDOTYA NAZAROVNA *and the* FIRST GUEST.

AVDOTYA *enters with the* FIRST GUEST *from the garden.* I'd like to get my claws into her, the old miser. I'd tear her to pieces! Do you think it's funny? Why, I've been here since five o'clock, and she hasn't even offered me a bit of stale herring! What a house! . . .

FIRST GUEST I'm so bored that I could beat my head against the wall! Lord, what queer people they are! Pretty soon I'll start howling like a wolf and snapping at people from sheer boredom and hunger.

AVDOTYA Why, I'll tear her to pieces!

FIRST GUEST I think I'll have one more drink, and go! Even your talk about finding me a beautiful woman couldn't keep me here now. How the hell can a man think of love when he hasn't had a drink since dinner?

Lvov = "honesty"

AVDOTYA Let's go and see if we can find something . . .

FIRST GUEST Sh-sh! Be quiet! I think there's some brandy in the sideboard in the dining room. We'll find Yegors. Sh-sh!

They go out through the door on the left. ANNA PETROVNA *and* LVOV *enter through the door on the right.*

ANNA Don't worry, they'll be glad to see us. Hmmmm, no one's here, they must be in the garden.

LVOV I wish you'd tell me why you've brought me into this den of wolves. This is no place for us. Honest people can't even breathe here!

ANNA Now you listen to me, "Mister, I'm an honest man!" It's very rude to take a lady out and do nothing but talk about how honest you are! You may be honest, but you're frightfully boring. Never tell a woman how good you are; let her find out for herself. When Nikolai was your age, he sang songs and told us wonderful stories, and yet we all knew what kind of man he was.

LVOV Don't talk to me about your Nikolai, I know all about him!

ANNA You're a good man, Doctor, but you don't understand people at all. Now, let's go into the garden. He never used to say, "I'm honest. I can't breathe in this place." He never talked about "wolves" and "dens." He wasn't concerned with animals, and when he was upset about something, all he'd say was, "Oh, how unjust I've been today!" or "Anya, I'm sorry for that man!" That's what *he'd* say, but you . . . *They go out.*

Enter AVDOTYA NAZAROVNA *and* FIRST GUEST.

FIRST GUEST, *entering through the door on the left.* If there isn't any in the dining room, there must be some in the kitchen. Let's find Yegors, he's probably in the drawing room. *Go out through the door on the right.* BABAKINA *and* BORKIN *run in from the garden, laughing;* SHABYELSKY *trots in after them, also laughing and rubbing his hands.*

BABAKINA Oh, I'm so bored! *Laughs loudly.* This is deadly! They just sit there as if they'd swallowed a poker. Why, my bones are frozen stiff with boredom. *Jumps about.* Let's do something! BORKIN *seizes her by the waist and kisses her cheek.*

SHABYELSKY *laughs and snaps his fingers.* Well, I'll be damned! *Cackling.* Isn't that something . . .

BABAKINA Let go of me, keep your hands off, you beast! What will the Count think? Let me go!

BORKIN My angel, my sweet! *Kisses her.* Lend me twenty-three hundred roubles!

BABAKINA Most certainly not. . . . All this playing is fine, but when it comes to money . . . forget it! No! . . . Now, please let go of my hands! . . .

SHABYELSKY, *trotting around them.* What a beautiful flower! . . . Isn't she beautiful!

BORKIN, *seriously.* All right, that's enough. Let's get to the point in a businesslike way. Now, I want you to tell me honestly, no beating about the bush, just yes or no. *Points to the* COUNT. He needs money, at least three thousand a year. You need a husband. Do you want to be a Countess?

SHABYELSKY, *laughing loudly.* What a cynic!

BORKIN Do you want to be a Countess? Yes or no?

BABAKINA, *upset.* You're making all this up, Misha. And besides, you don't do things like this, in such a hurry. . . . If the Count wants to marry me he can ask me himself, and . . . and anyway I don't understand what this is all about . . . it's so sudden I mean . . .

BORKIN Now, don't try to pretend! . . . It's a simple matter of business. . . . Yes, or no?

SHABYELSKY, *laughing and rubbing his hands.* Well, I'll be damned! I'd better do something. My precious one. *Kisses* BABAKINA's *cheek.* You charmer! . . . You little duck! . . .

BABAKINA Wait! Stop it! You've got me all upset. . . . Go away, go! . . . No, don't go yet! . . .

BORKIN Quickly! Yes, or no? We can't stand around here all night . . .

BABAKINA Count, why don't you come and visit me for a few days . . . We could have a good time, it's not like this place. Come tomorrow. *To* BORKIN. Or is this all a joke?

BORKIN, *angrily.* How could I joke about something like this?

BABAKINA Stop, wait a minute. . . . Oh, I feel faint! I feel faint! A Countess . . . I'm going to faint. . . . I'm falling . . .

BORKIN *and the* COUNT, *laughing, take her by the arms and kiss her on the cheeks as they lead her out through the door on the right.* IVANOV *and* SASHA *run in from the garden.*

IVANOV, *clutching his head in despair.* It can't be true! Please don't, Sasha, don't. Oh, it can't be!

SASHA, *with abandon.* I'm madly in love with you . . . You're my joy, my life, my happiness, the meaning to everything! To me —you are everything. . . .

IVANOV But why, why? My God, I don't understand . . . Sasha, please don't say it . . .

SASHA Since I was a little girl you've been the only joy in my whole life. I loved you, I loved you body and soul, more than I loved myself, and now . . . Oh, I love you, Nikolai Alexeyevich . . . I'll go anywhere with you, to the end of the world . . . but please, let's go soon, otherwise I'll die . . .

IVANOV *bursts into happy laughter.* What is this? Can it mean the beginning of a new life for me? Can it, Sasha? Oh, my happiness! . . . *Draws her to himself.* My youth, my joy! ANNA PETROVNA *enters from the garden and, seeing her husband and* SASHA, *stops as if rooted to the spot.* Yes—I'll live again! Yes, and I'll work! *They kiss. After kissing,* IVANOV *and* SASHA *look round and see* ANNA PETROVNA. *Horrified.* Sarah!

Curtain.

ACT III

IVANOV's *study. It is noon. There is a desk with papers, books, packages, knickknacks, and revolvers lying in disorder on it; also a lamp, water carafe, a plate of salt herring, bread, and pickles. On the walls hang maps, pictures, guns, sickles, riding crops, etc.* SHABYELSKY *and* LEBEDEV *are sitting by the desk.* BORKIN *is astride a chair in the middle of the stage.* PYOTR *is standing by the door.*

LEBEDEV The policy of France is definite and clear-cut . . . They know what they want—to skin the Germans alive, and that's all. But the Germans are playing a different tune. France isn't their only problem . . .

SHABYELSKY Nonsense! In my opinion, the Germans are cowards, and so are the French. They shake their fists at one another, but,

Good imagery - luxury v stinginess of Lebedev's house

take my word for it, they'll never go beyond that. They won't fight.

BORKIN Why should they? What's the use of all these congresses and arms races and all the money that's wasted? You know what I'd do? I'd catch all the dogs in the country, inject them with Pasteur's serum, and then let them loose on each other. All our enemies would go mad in a month.

LEBEDEV, *laughing.* He's got a small head, but it holds great ideas . . . millions of them, like fish in the sea.

SHABYELSKY Yes, he's a real genius!

LEBEDEV God bless you, Misha, anyway, you make us laugh! *Stops laughing.* But what's all this, gentlemen, here we are talking about France and Germany and never a word about vodka! *"Repetatur." Fills three glasses.* Here's to you! *They drink and eat.* This is the best herring.

SHABYELSKY Yes, and these pickles are good too. Scientists have been trying to invent something better than pickles since the world began, and they've never succeeded. *To* PYOTR. Pyotr, go and bring us some more pickles, and four onion rolls, too. Make sure they're hot. PYOTR *goes out.*

LEBEDEV Caviar is good with vodka, too. Only you have to know how to serve it. It takes skill . . . First, you take a quarter pound of pressed caviar, two green onions, a little olive oil, and mix it all up and then, you squeeze just a little lemon juice on top . . . h-h-h-um-um! The smell alone'll drive you crazy.

BORKIN Guinea hens are good, too, but you've got to cook them right. First you clean them, then roll them in bread crumbs and fry them until they're brown, so that they crackle as you eat them. . . . Crunch, crunch. . . .

SHABYELSKY Yesterday we had white mushrooms at Babakina's. They were very good.

LEBEDEV Really!

SHABYELSKY Only they were prepared in a special way—with lots of onion and bay leaf and all sorts of spices. When they took the top off the pan, the bouquet was intoxicating.

LEBEDEV What do you say! *"Repetatur,"* gentlemen! *They drink.* Your health . . . *Looks at his watch.* It doesn't look like Nikolai's going to get here. It's time for me to go. You say you've had mushrooms at Babakina's, we never have them at our house. By the way, what's going on? How come you go to Marfoosha's so often?

SHABYELSKY, *pointing at* BORKIN *with a movement of his head.* It's his idea—he wants me to marry her. . . .

LEBEDEV Marry her? At your age?

SHABYELSKY I'm sixty-two.

LEBEDEV A perfect age to get married. And Marfoosha's the perfect woman for you.

BORKIN It's not Marfoosha, it's her money . . .

LEBEDEV Her money? I suppose you'd like the moon, too?

BORKIN You won't talk about the moon after he gets married and stuffs his pockets. Then you'll be licking your chops with envy.

SHABYELSKY He really means it. Our great genius is certain that I'm going to take his advice and marry her.

BORKIN Well, isn't that right? Have you changed your mind?

SHABYELSKY What do you mean? Are you mad? When was it ever made up? . . .

BORKIN Thanks a lot! Much obliged to you. Thanks for letting me down. First you say you'll marry her, then you say you won't . . . only the devil knows which it is. But you gave me your word of honor! So you aren't going to marry her, is that it?

SHABYELSKY *shrugs his shoulders.* He's really serious. . . . What an amazing fellow!

BORKIN, *indignantly.* In that case, what did you get her all upset for? Now that she's got her heart set on being Countess, she can't sleep or eat. . . . How can you joke about things like that? Do you call that honorable?

SHABYELSKY *snaps his fingers.* All right then—supposing I play this disgusting trick? Eh? Just to spite them! All right, I'll do it. On my honor, I'll do it. That'll be some joke!

Enter LVOV.

LEBEDEV Aesculapius—our most humble respects . . . *He shakes* LVOV'*s hand and sings.* "Doctor, doctor, save me, pray, I'm scared to death of dying today."

LVOV Isn't Ivanov back yet?

LEBEDEV No, I've been waiting for him for more than an hour myself. LVOV *paces the stage impatiently.* How's Anna Petrovna today?

LVOV   Very bad.

LEBEDEV *sighs.* May I go and see her?

LVOV   No, please don't. She's asleep. *Pause.*

LEBEDEV   She's a wonderful woman . . . *Sighs.* When she fainted at our house on Sasha's birthday, I could tell from her face that she didn't have long to live, poor thing. I can't understand why she fainted though. I ran into the room, and there she was on the floor, white as a ghost, with Nikolai on his knees beside her, and Sasha was standing there crying. Sasha and I went around for a week in a daze.

SHABYELSKY, *to* LVOV. Tell me, you high priest of Science, what scholar discovered that frequent visits from a young doctor help cure ladies suffering from chest ailments? It's a remarkable discovery! Remarkable indeed! What kind of treatment is it? Allopathic or homeopathic? LVOV *starts to answer him, then, with an impatient gesture, goes out.* What a look that was!

LEBEDEV   What's bothering you, Count? Why do you try to offend him?

SHABYELSKY, *with irritation.* Well, why does he tell such lies? She's got T.B., there's no hope, she's going to die . . . It's nonsense, I say! I can't stand that.

LEBEDEV   But why do you think he's lying?

SHABYELSKY *gets up and walks to and fro.* A living being doesn't just die suddenly for no reason at all! Let's drop the subject!

KOSICH *runs in, out of breath.* Is Nikolai Alexeyevich here? How d'you do? *Quickly shakes hands all round.* Is he here?

BORKIN   No, he isn't!

KOSICH *sits down, then jumps up.* In that case, I've got to go. *Drinks a glass of vodka and quickly eats a snack.* I must go. Business. . . . I'm absolutely exhausted. . . . Can hardly stand on my feet . . .

LEBEDEV   Where've you been?

KOSICH   Barabanov's. We just finished playing cards . . . played all night long. I lost everything I had . . . That Barabanov is a real shark. *Tearfully.* Just listen to this: I had a heart . . . *He turns to* BORKIN, *who jumps away from him.* He bids diamonds, I go hearts, and he goes diamonds . . . Well, I didn't get a trick. *To* LEBEDEV. We played four clubs. I had the ace, queen, and six in my hand, and the ace, ten and three of spades . . .

LEBEDEV *stops his ears.* Spare me, for God's sake, will you!

KOSICH, *to the* COUNT. But you understand—the ace, queen and six of clubs; the ace, ten and three of spades . . .

SHABYELSKY, *pushing him away.* Get out of here. I don't want to hear any more. . . .

KOSICH And suddenly, my luck went bad. He trumped my ace of spades the first round!

SHABYELSKY, *snatching up a revolver from the desk.* Get out, or I'll shoot! . . .

KOSICH, *waving his hand.* What's wrong . . . Can't I even open my mouth? It's like living in the wilds of Australia: no common interests, no public spirit . . . Everyone all wrapped up in himself . . . Well, I've got to go . . . it's time. *Snatches up his cap.* My time's valuable. *Shakes hands with* LEBEDEV. Pass!

Laughter. KOSICH *goes out and collides with* AVDOTYA NAZAROVNA *in the doorway.*

AVDOTYA *gives a shriek.* Damn you, you nearly knocked me down!

ALL TOGETHER She's here again! *All laugh.*

AVDOTYA Oh, there you are! I've been looking all over the house for you. And how are these nice people today? Eating well? *Shakes hands.*

LEBEDEV What brings you here?

AVDOTYA I'm here on business . . . *To the* COUNT. Concerning you, your Excellency. *Bows.* She sends her regards and hopes you're feeling well . . . And she told me—the sweet little thing—to tell you that if you don't come to see her tonight, she'll cry her eyes out. "Take him aside and whisper into his ear," that's what she said. But why do that? We're all friends here. Anyway, we're not stealing chickens; why, this is a real love affair, and we're arranging things lawfully and with mutual consent . . . Oh, no, I never touch it, old sinner that I am, well, I suppose just this once . . . All right, I'll have one.

LEBEDEV So'll I. *Pours it out.* You know, old girl, you do pretty well! Why, I've known you for the last thirty years, and you were an old woman when I met you.

AVDOTYA Well, I've lost count of the years. I've buried two husbands, and I'd have married a third, but no one would take me without a dowry. I've had eight children. *Takes her glass.* Well, we've begun a good work, may it end as well as it's begun. They'll be happy, and we'll rejoice in their happiness. The best of luck to them. *She drinks.* Whew! This vodka's strong!

SHABYELSKY, *laughing loudly, to* LEBEDEV. The amazing thing is, they think I'll do it . . . It's amazing! *Rises.* But what if I did? You know, Pasha, just out of spite . . . For something to do.

LEBEDEV Such nonsense! We'd better just get ready to kick the bucket. As for Marfoosha's money, forget it! We've had our day.

SHABYELSKY By God, I'll do it! Honest, I will!

Enter IVANOV *and* LVOV.

LVOV I've got to see you . . . just five minutes.

LEBEDEV Nikolai! *Goes to meet* IVANOV *and embraces him.* How are you, my friend? I've been waiting for more than an hour.

AVDOTYA *bows.* How d'you do, sir?

IVANOV, *bitterly.* So you've turned the library into a bar again, have you? I've asked you all a thousand times not to do it. . . . *Walks up to the table.* See, you've spilled vodka over my things . . . crumbs . . . pickles . . . It's disgusting!

LEBEDEV It was my fault, Nikolai, my fault . . . Now if you'll forgive me, I've got to talk with you, my friend, about a very important matter.

BORKIN So do I.

LVOV Nikolai Alexeyevich, may I have a word with you?

IVANOV *points at* LEBEDEV. He wants to talk with me. Will you wait; I'll see you afterwards . . . *To* LEBEDEV. Well, what is it?

LEBEDEV, *to the others.* If you don't mind, I'd like to speak to him privately. Please.

The COUNT *goes out with* AVDOTYA, BORKIN *follows, then* LVOV.

IVANOV Pasha, you can drink as much as you like, it's your weakness, but please keep it away from my uncle. He never used to drink, and it's bad for him.

LEBEDEV, *alarmed.* Oh, my boy, I didn't know . . . I didn't even notice. . . .

IVANOV If that old baby died—I'd be the one to blame, not you . . . Now, what is it you want to see me about? *Pause.*

LEBEDEV You see, Nikolai . . . The fact is, I don't know how to begin, how to put it so it isn't so brutal . . . Nikolai, I'm ashamed, I know I'm blushing and my tongue's tied, but, please,

please try to put yourself in my place. Understand that I'm not the boss, but a slave. Please forgive me . . .

IVANOV What is it?

LEBEDEV My wife's sent me. . . . Do me a favor, be a good friend, pay her the interest! Believe me, she's been nagging me to death. For God's sake, pay it and get the thing settled!

IVANOV Pasha, you know I haven't any money.

LEBEDEV I know, I know, but what am I to do? She won't wait. If she sues you, how could Sasha and I ever look you in the face again?

IVANOV I'm terribly ashamed, Pasha, and I wish I could just sink through the floor, but . . . but where can I get the money? Tell me: where? All I can do is wait until fall, when we sell the corn.

LEBEDEV *shouts.* But she won't wait! *Pause.*

IVANOV I admit you're in an awkward position, and it isn't very pleasant; but mine's even worse. *Walks up and down, deep in thought.* I can't think of anything . . . I haven't anything left to sell . . .

LEBEDEV Why don't you go and ask Mulbach for the sixteen thousand he owes you? IVANOV *shakes his head despairingly.* I'll tell you what I'll do, Nikolai . . . I know you'll be angry, but . . . do it as a favor to an old drunkard! Just between friends . . . I am your friend, you know. . . . We're both college graduates, both liberals . . . we share the same ideas, have the same interests . . . why, we even went to the same university, oh, Moscow our alma mater . . . *He takes out his wallet.* Here, I've got some money, nobody at home knows about it. Take it as a loan . . . *Takes out the money and puts it on the table.* Forget your pride and take it . . . this is between friends . . . I'd take it from you, honestly I would . . . *Pause.* There it is, eleven hundred roubles. Go and see her right away and give it to her and say, "Take the money, Zinaida Saveshna, and I hope you choke on it!" But remember, don't let her know you got it from me! If you do, I'll really get it from old gooseberry jam. *Stares at* IVANOV. All right, forget it! *Quickly picks up the money from the table and puts it in his pocket.* Really, I was only joking . . . Forgive me, for God's sake! *Pause.* I didn't mean to insult you! IVANOV *waves his hand.*

Things aren't very good, are they? . . . *Sighs*. You're having your troubles, a streak of bad luck. You know, my friend, a man is like a samovar. He can't always stand cooly on the shelf, every once in a while some hot coals are put into him and "fizz". . . . It's a bad analogy, I know, but it's the best I can think of . . . *Sighs*. Misfortune tempers the soul, so I don't worry about you, Nikolai. Everything will turn out all right. But it does annoy me that other people talk about you as they do. It makes me angry! Where does all this gossip get started anyway. Why the whole countryside's buzzing. They say you'll be arrested; that you're a murderer, a monster, and a thief . . .

IVANOV Forget it, I don't care! . . . Anyway, I've got a headache.

LEBEDEV It's all because you think too much.

IVANOV I never think.

LEBEDEV Forget the whole thing, Nikolai, but do come and see us. Sasha's very fond of you, she understands and appreciates you. She's a fine, honest girl, Nikolai. She doesn't take after her father or mother at all. Sometimes I look at her, and I can't believe that such a treasure could belong to an old drunkard like me. Come along and see her—it'll cheer you up. She's good and sincere. . . . *Pause.*

IVANOV Pasha, please leave me alone . . .

LEBEDEV I understand, I understand. . . . *Hurriedly looks at his watch.* Yes, I understand. *Embraces* IVANOV. Good-bye. I've got to get over to the opening of the new school. *Walks to the door, then stops.* And she's smart, too. . . . Why, yesterday she and I were talking about gossip, *He laughs.* and she said, "Father, fireflies shine so birds can find them at night, and good people shine so gossipers and slanderers can destroy them." Pretty good, isn't it? Another George Sand.

IVANOV Pasha! *Stops him.* What's the matter with me?

LEBEDEV I've wanted to ask you the same thing, but I didn't think I should. I don't know, my friend. Sometimes I think you've had too many problems, but then I know you're not the kind that would let trouble get you down. So it must be something else, Nikolai, but just what it is—I can't imagine.

IVANOV I can't either . . . unless it's, but no . . . that's not it! *Pause.* What I was going to say is this. I used to have a workman, called Semyon, do you remember him? Well, once during threshing, he was trying to show the girls how strong he was, so he lifted two sacks of rye on to his back, and strained himself. Soon after that he died. Well, I think I've done the same thing. First in high school, then at the university, then the farm, the schools for the peasants, one project after another . . . I had different ideas than other people had! I married differently, I took risks, I was passionately involved with everything I did, I threw my money about right and left. I've experienced more happiness and more pain than anyone I know. I, too, tried to take on too heavy a load and I couldn't take it. At twenty we're all heroes, ready for anything, but at thirty we're worn out, useless men. How do you explain such weariness? However, I may be wrong. . . . You'd better go now, Pasha, I must be boring you to death.

LEBEDEV, *eagerly.* Maybe, you got out on the wrong side of the bed this morning.

IVANOV That's stupid, Pasha . . . and stale, too. Go on, good-bye!

LEBEDEV That's true, it's stupid. Of course. I'm going at once . . . *Goes out.*

IVANOV, *alone.* I'm a worthless, pitiful, contemptible man. Only a wretched, old drunkard like Pasha can still love and respect me. Oh, God, how I hate myself! I hate my voice, my hands, my thoughts, my clothes, every step I take. It's ridiculous and disgusting; only a few months ago I was strong and healthy, full of energy, enthusiasm, and high spirits . . . I used to be able to do an honest day's work, could express myself so that even the dullest nitwit would understand and be moved; when I saw pain I could weep, when I saw evil I was indignant. I knew what inspiration was then, I knew the beauty and creativity of those silent nights when I'd sit at my desk—sometimes working, sometimes just sitting there dreaming and thinking—from dusk until dawn. I believed then; I looked into the future as trustfully as a child looks into its mother's eyes . . . But now, oh, my God! I'm tired, I have no hope; I waste my days and nights. I can't seem to think or do anything. The estate's going to ruin, the forests are being cut down. *Weeps.* My land looks at me reproachfully, like an orphan looks at a stranger. I expect nothing, I regret nothing, but my soul trembles with fear at the thought of each new day . . . And then when I think about Sarah! I promised I'd love her forever, I told her how happy we'd be, and I painted a picture of the future that was brighter than anything she'd ever dreamed of! She believed me, and for the past five years she's been sinking under the weight of self-sacrifice, wearing herself out in her struggles with her conscience, and yet—not once did she ever reproach me—with a word or even a glance . . . And what happens? I stop loving her. . . . How? Why? What for? I can't understand it. Now she's suffering, she's probably going to die . . . and I . . . I, like a contemptible coward, run away from her pale face, her sunken chest, her pleading eyes . . . Oh, God. I hate myself! I'm so ashamed. *Pause.* And sweet little Sasha is touched by my troubles. She says she loves me—me, almost an old man—and I get carried away; I forget everything else and am caught up in the music of the thought. Pretty soon I'm shouting: "A new life! Happiness!" But the next day I don't any more believe in this new life and happiness than I believe that I'm happy now. . . . What's the matter with me then? Why have I fallen into these depths of despair? Why am I so weak-willed? Why this nervousness? If my poor wife does anything to wound my pride, if the servants annoy me, or if my gun doesn't go off, I lose my temper, become violent, and don't act like myself at all . . . *Pause.* I don't understand it, I don't, I don't! . . . I feel like putting a bullet through my head! . . .

LVOV *comes in.* I must talk to you, Nikolai Alexeyevich.

IVANOV If we keep on talking like this every day, Doctor, it will be more than either one of us can stand.

LVOV Will you listen to me?

IVANOV Oh, I listen to you. I do every day, don't I? But I still don't know what you want me to do.

LVOV I've made it clear enough, and only someone as cruel as you wouldn't understand me.

IVANOV I know, my wife is going to die. I know. It's my fault. I know you're an honest man. What else can I say?

LVOV The sight of human cruelty is more than I can stand! A woman is dying. She has a father and a mother whom she loves and whom she longs to see before she dies. They know that she's dying soon and that she still loves them, but—and this is what's so cruel—they won't see her, they won't forgive her, they flaunt their zealousness to all the world. And you, the man for whom she's sacrificed everything—her home, her happiness, her wealth —what do you do? Every day, without a qualm, you go to the Lebedevs'. And everybody knows why!

IVANOV I haven't been there in two weeks . . .

LVOV, *without listening to him.* You have to be blunt with people like you—there's no other way; so I'm going to call a spade a spade. And if you don't like it, don't listen. You want her to die, so you can be free; all right, but why can't you wait? Do you think you'd lose that girl and her money if you'd let your wife die naturally instead of bringing it on faster with your heartless cruelty? Well? You're such an impostor . . . yes a regular Tartuffe—that whether it was one year or even two, you could seduce the girl and get her money just as you have now. So what's the hurry? Why is it so important that you kill your wife off now? Why not next month? or next year!

IVANOV Why are you torturing me like this? . . . What kind of a doctor are you that you think I'll keep control forever? It's all I can do not to answer your insults.

LVOV Stop that! You're not deceiving me, so let's stop pretending!

IVANOV You're very clever, aren't you? Well, just listen to me. You think it's the easiest thing in the world to figure me out. Well, admit it? It's simple isn't it? I married Anya for her money, but I didn't get the money. I was tricked, so now I'm destroying her, so I can marry someone else for her money. . . . That's right, isn't it? How easy it all is! A man is such a simple, uncomplicated machine. . . . No, Doctor, we all have too many wheels and gears for us to be judged by first impressions or by a few external traits. I don't know you, you don't know me, and we don't know ourselves. Isn't it possible to be a good doctor—and at the same time not understand people? You'll have to admit that, unless you're blind.

LVOV But do you really think that you're so mysterious and I'm so stupid that I can't tell the difference between good and evil?

IVANOV It's obvious that we'll never agree. So, for the last time, without beating around the bush, what do you want me to do? *Angrily.* And anyway, who do you think you are, the prosecuting attorney, or my wife's doctor?

LVOV I'm a doctor, and as a doctor, I demand that you treat your
wife differently. You're killing her!

IVANOV But what am I supposed to do? Just tell me that. If you
know me so well—better than I know myself—then tell me, what
should I do?

LVOV Well, first, don't carry on your affair so openly.

IVANOV Oh, my God! Do you mean to say that you think you
understand yourself? *Drinks water.* Get out of here! I'll admit I'm
guilty—yes, a thousand times; but I'll answer to God for that . . .
but no one has given you the right to torture me like this every
day.

LVOV And what right have you to insult my sense of justice?
You've ruined my soul. Until I came out here, I could accept
people who were stupid, insane, over-emotional, but I never imagined that anyone could be intentionally evil . . . I used to love
and respect people, but since I've known you . . .

IVANOV I know all about it.

LVOV You do, do you? *He sees* SASHA *who has just come in
wearing a riding habit.* Well, then I hope we understand each
other. I certainly see things clearly now . . . perfectly! *Shrugs his
shoulders and walks out.*

IVANOV, *alarmed.* Sasha—what are you doing here?

SASHA How are you? You didn't expect me, did you? Why
haven't you been to see us?

IVANOV Sasha, for God's sake, this is dangerous! And think what
it might do to my wife.

SASHA She won't see me. I came in through the back door. I'll
go in a minute. I'm so anxious about you; are you well? Why
haven't you been to see us?

IVANOV My wife's upset enough as it is, she's dying, and you
come here! Sasha, Sasha, how could you be so thoughtless?

SASHA But I had to! You haven't been to see us for two weeks,
you didn't answer my letters. I've been so worried about you.
I imagined you here suffering dreadfully, perhaps you were sick,
maybe even dead . . . I haven't slept a single night. I'll go in a
minute . . . But please tell me, are you all right?

IVANOV No, I'm not! I'm worn out, and nobody lets me alone
. . . I can't stand it any longer. And now you! It just isn't right,

Sasha. Somehow it's perverted and morbid. Am I as guilty as all that. Am I, Sasha?

SASHA Why talk that way? There's no need to be so gloomy. You're not guilty. You? What for?

IVANOV I don't know, I don't know. . . .

SASHA That's no answer. A sinner must know what he's guilty of. Have you been forging checks or what?

IVANOV Oh, don't be silly.

SASHA Are you to blame because you've stopped loving your wife? Perhaps, but no one's master of his feelings; you didn't want to stop loving her. Are you to blame because she saw me telling you I loved you? No, you didn't want her to see it.

IVANOV, *interrupting.* Keep it up . . . Fallen in love, fallen out of love, not master of my feelings—they're nothing but clichés . . . it's all very sentimental, but it doesn't help a bit . . .

SASHA Oh, it's impossible to talk with you. *Looks at the pictures on the walls.* How well that dog's painted! Was it done from life?

IVANOV Yes, from life. And this romance of ours is the same old story. "A man loses heart, everything crumples around him and his world collapses. Suddenly, a girl appears. She's beautiful, brave, spirited, and she offers him a helping hand." It's very lovely, but things like that only happen in novels. In real life . . .

SASHA It happens in real life, too!

IVANOV I see you don't know life very well. My sufferings seem noble to you, you think you've discovered another Hamlet . . . but this neurotic state should be laughed at, and that's all! People ought to die laughing at this role I'm playing; but not you— oh, what a fuss you make! My Guardian Angel! You're going to be noble and save me! . . . Oh, how I hate myself today! Something's got to give or I'll break . . . I'll break something!

SASHA That's it, that's it, that's just what you need. Let yourself go, break something, start shouting. . . . You're angry with me, it was foolish of me to come here. All right, then, get mad at me—shout, stamp your feet. Well? Go ahead. *Pause.* Well?

IVANOV You silly little girl.

SASHA Wonderful! Finally a smile! Please, do me a favor, smile again!

IVANOV *laughs*. You know, every time you start reforming me, your face becomes so naïve; your eyes get bigger and bigger, as if you were looking at a falling star. Wait, there's something on your shoulder . . . *He brushes some dust off her shoulder with his hand.* A man who's naïve is a fool. But women somehow contrive to be naïve in such a way that it's charming and natural, and helpful . . . and not silly as it really is. . . . And then there's that strange way you have of ignoring a man as long as he's well and happy, and on top of the world. But as soon as he starts sliding downhill, crying like poor Lazarus, you grab onto him. Is it really worse to be the wife of a strong, independent man than to nurse a whimpering invalid?

SASHA Yes, it is.

IVANOV But why? *Laughs loudly.* It's a good thing Darwin can't hear you, or he'd give you the devil! It's people like you that are ruining the human race. Thanks to you, soon the world will be filled with neurotics and invalids.

SASHA There are so many things men don't understand. Any girl would rather love a failure than a success, because she wants her love to accomplish something. . . . Do you understand what I'm saying? She wants to participate. A man has his work, so for him love is secondary. Love for him, is having a chat with his wife at the end of the day, taking a walk in the garden, spending a few pleasant hours with her forgetting his problems, crying a bit at her grave—that's all. But for us—love is everything; it's our whole life! I love you, and that means that I dream of how I can make you happy, how I'd follow you to the ends of the earth . . . If you went up the highest mountain, I'd follow you, or if you fell into the deepest pit, I'd follow you. For instance, nothing could make me happier than staying up all night helping you with your work, or watching over you all night so that no one woke you up, or just walking with you for miles, a thousand miles! . . . I remember once about three years ago you came to our house after you'd been threshing all day. You were covered with dust and exhausted, and you asked for a glass of water. I went to get it for you, but when I came back you were sound asleep on the sofa. You slept there almost all day, and I guarded the door, so no one would bother you. How happy I was! The more a woman can do for a man, the more she loves him—the more she feels her love.

IVANOV A love that accomplishes something . . . My dear . . . that's a little girl's dream, a fairy tale . . . although, that's probably the way it ought to be . . . *Shrugs his shoulders.* I don't know! *Gaily.* Honestly, Sasha, I'm a good man. You know that! Oh, I know I talk too much, but I've never said anything derogatory about women. I've never said so-and-so is immoral. I've always been grateful to women and that's all. My dear girl, you are very good, and I'm a ridiculous old fool—I just upset people and complain from morning till night. *He laughs and then goes to her.* But now, Sasha, you must go! We've been forgetting ourselves. . . .

SASHA Yes, it's time I went. Good-bye! I'm afraid that honest doctor of yours will tell Anna Petrovna about my being here—because he's so honest. Now listen to me: go to your wife now and stay with her, stay and stay and stay; if it's for a year—then stay a year. If it's ten years—stay ten years. This you must do, it's your duty. It will be painful, but you must do it; ask her forgiveness, weep—this is what you ought to do, and the main thing is to do what is right. But the main thing is—don't forget your work!

IVANOV Suddenly, I have this crazy feeling again—as if the whole world were turned upside down.

SASHA God bless you, Nikolai! You must forget about me completely. I'll be happy if you just send me a note every two weeks or so. As for me, I'll write to you.

BORKIN *pokes his head through the door.*

BORKIN Nikolai Alexeyevich, may I come in? *Sees* SASHA. I beg your pardon. I didn't see you . . . *Comes in.* "Bonjour!" *Bows.*

SASHA, *embarrassed.* How do you do?

BORKIN You get prettier every day.

SASHA, *to* IVANOV. Well, I must be going, Nikolai Alexeyevich. Good-bye. *Goes out.*

BORKIN What a beautiful sight! I came on prosaic business, and I found poetry. . . . *Sings.* "You come to me as a beautiful bird". . . . IVANOV *paces nervously back and forth.* BORKIN *sits down.* You know, Nikolai, she's got something you don't find in most women, doesn't she? Something strange and mysterious . . . *Sighs.* As a matter of fact, she's the richest girl in the county, but her mother's such a shrew that no one wants to marry her. After she dies Sasha will get it all, but until then she'll only get ten thousand, and some old dishes. And Mama will expect gratitude even for that. *Rummages through his pockets.* Cigarette? *Offers his cigarette case.* They're very good.

IVANOV *walks up to* BORKIN, *almost speechless with rage.* Get out of this house right now and don't you dare set foot in it again! Get out! Now! BORKIN *half rises and drops his cigarette.* Right now!

BORKIN Nikolai, what's the matter? Why are you angry?

IVANOV Why? Where did you get those cigarettes? Do you think I don't know where you take the old man every day and what for?

BORKIN *shrugs his shoulders.* Why worry about that?

IVANOV What kind of a scoundrel are you? Why you've disgraced me everywhere with your crooked schemes. You and I have nothing in common, so get out of this house, right now! *Paces back and forth.*

BORKIN I know you're saying all this because you're upset about something, so I won't be angry with you. Go ahead, insult me as much as you like. . . . *Picks up the cigarette.* As for your depression, I think it's time you got over it. After all you're not a child any more . . .

IVANOV What did I tell you? *Trembling.* Are you trying to mock me? *Enter* ANNA PETROVNA.

BORKIN Well, here's Anna Petrovna. . . . I'll go. *Goes out.* IVANOV *stops beside his desk and stands with his head down.*

ANNA, *after a pause.* Why was she just here? *Pause.* So that's what you are! Now I understand you! Finally I see how dishonorable, how degraded you really are . . . Do you remember how you told me once that you loved me. Well, it was a lie! But, I believed you and I left my parents, gave up my faith and followed you . . . All that talk about beauty and truth, your noble aspirations . . . nothing but lies, and I believed every word. . . .

IVANOV Anya, I have never lied to you . . .

ANNA I've lived with you for five years, I've been unhappy and sick, but I've loved you and never left you for a minute. . . . You've been my idol. . . . And you? All this time you've had the gall to deceive me . . .

IVANOV Anya, don't say what isn't so. I've made mistakes, true enough, but I've never told a lie in my life. . . . You can't accuse me of that. . . .

ANNA Oh, I see it all now. You married me expecting my parents would forgive me and give us the money . . . You thought that. . . .

IVANOV Good God! Anya, don't torture me like this, I can't stand it! *Weeps.*

ANNA Be quiet! Then when you found that there wouldn't be any money, you started a new game. . . . Now I remember everything, now I understand. *Weeps.* You've never loved me, or been faithful to me. . . . Never! . . .

IVANOV Sarah, that is a lie! . . . Say anything you want, but don't insult me with a lie . . .

ANNA Dishonorable and degraded. . . . You owe Lebedev money, and so to avoid paying it back, you're trying to seduce his daughter, to deceive her just as you deceived me. It's true isn't it?

IVANOV, *suffocating.* For God's sake, stop! I don't know what I might do if you keep it up! I'm choking with rage, and I . . . I might insult you . . .

ANNA You scoundrel, you've always deceived me, and not just me alone . . . You've blamed all your crimes on Borkin, but now I know who's guilty . . .

IVANOV Sarah, stop this, and leave right now, or I'll lose control and say something terrible! Go before I . . . I . . . *Shouts.* Shut up, you Jew!

ANNA I won't . . . You've deceived me for too long to shut up.

IVANOV So you won't be quiet! *Struggles with himself.* For God's sake . . .

ANNA Go on, get out of here and deceive Sasha, too.

IVANOV All right, you might just as well know the truth . . . you're going to die soon. The doctor told me that you're dying . . .

ANNA *sits down, her voice failing her.* When did he say that? *Pause.*

IVANOV, *clutching his head with his hands.* Oh, God, what have I done? What have I done?

Curtain.

About a year passes between the third and fourth acts.

ACT IV

Drawing room at the LEBEDEVS'. *There is an arch center stage separating the drawing room from the ballroom; there are doors right and left. Antique bronze and family portraits are on the walls. Everything is arranged for a reception. There is a piano with a violin on top of it and a cello beside it. During the entire act visitors in evening clothes walk through the ballroom.*

LVOV *comes in, looks at his watch.* It's nearly five. The ceremony will begin in a minute. First the blessing, and then off to the church So this is the triumph of virtue and justice. Not being able to rob Sarah, he killed her, and found another victim. He'll play the game with her, too, until he's robbed her, and then he'll put her out of the way just like Sarah. The same sordid story all over again. *Pause.* He's in seventh heaven now, he thinks he's going to live to a contented old age, and die with a clear conscience. . . . Oh, no you won't, Ivanov! I'll show the world what you're really like! When I tear off your damned mask, and everyone knows what a scoundrel you are, you'll be thrown out of your seventh heaven head first into a pit so deep that even the devil himself couldn't pull you out! I'm an honest man; so, it's my duty to show people the truth, to open their eyes. I'll do my duty, and then, tomorrow—I'll get out of this damn place! *Thinking.* But how'll I do it; it would be a waste of breath to explain everything to Lebedev. I could get in an argument and challenge Ivanov to a duel? God, I'm as nervous as a child and can't seem to think very clearly. What shall I do? Challenge him to a duel?

KOSICH *enters, happily to* LVOV. Yesterday I bid a small slam in clubs and made a grand slam. Only that damned Barabanov spoiled the whole game for me again. We were playing—I bid a no trump, he passes. Two no trump, he passes. I go to three clubs . . . then three diamonds . . . and then believe it or not—I bid slam. But he never indicated that he had the ace. If the idiot had, I'd have bid a grand slam in no trump . . .

LVOV Excuse me, I don't play cards, and so it's impossible for me to share your enthusiasm. Is the ceremony about to begin?

KOSICH Soon, I think. They're trying to revive Zuzu. She's crying her heart out . . . she's so upset about losing the dowry.

LVOV What about her daughter?

KOSICH Oh, no, only the dowry. And on top of it, it annoys her that he's marrying her daughter, because that means he won't have to pay his debt. You can't very well sue your son-in-law.

BABAKINA, *all dressed up, walks pompously across the stage past* LVOV *and* KOSICH. KOSICH *bursts out laughing behind his hand; she looks around.* Idiot! KOSICH *hits her in the ribs and laughs loudly.* You boor! *Goes out.*

KOSICH, *laughing loudly.* She's really gone crazy! She was like any other woman until she began having delusions about being a countess. Now she's impossible! *Mimics her.* You boor!

LVOV, *agitated.* Listen, tell me honestly, what do you think of Ivanov?

KOSICH He's no good . . . a lousy card player. Why, last year at Easter we began to play: I, the Count, Borkin and Ivanov. I started to deal. . . .

LVOV, *interrupting him.* Is he a good man?

KOSICH Ivanov? Oh, he's a good one all right. A clever schemer! He knows all the tricks of the trade. He and the Count are exactly alike. They can smell money a mile off. He missed on the Jewess, so now he's trying to get ahold of Zuzu's money bags. I'll bet you he'll ruin her in less than a year. And you watch, the Count will do the same thing to Babakina. They'll take the money and live happily ever after. Doctor, what's wrong with you today? You look like a ghost.

LVOV Oh, it's nothing. I drank too much yesterday.

LEBEDEV *comes in with* SASHA. We can talk here. *To* LVOV *and* KOSICH. Go into the ballroom, gentlemen, and talk with the young ladies. We want to talk privately.

KOSICH *snaps his fingers in admiration as he passes* SASHA. What a picture! A queen of trumps!

LEBEDEV All right, caveman, get going! LVOV *and* KOSICH *go out.* Sit down, Sasha, that's it . . . *Sits down and glances round.* Now listen very carefully to me and with proper respect. The fact is that your mother's asked me to give you a message . . . Do you understand? I'm not speaking for myself, but on orders from your mother.

SASHA Hurry up, Father!

LEBEDEV You're to have fifteen thousand roubles as a dowry. And we don't want any argument about it later. Wait, be quiet! That's only the beginning, wait for the rest. You'll have fifteen thousand, however, since Nikolai Alexeyevich owes your mother nine thousand, she's deducted that from your dowry. . . . Then, besides that . . .

SASHA Why do you tell me?

LEBEDEV Your mother told me to.

SASHA Well, leave me alone! If you had any respect for me or yourself, you wouldn't think of talking to me like this. I don't want your money. I haven't asked for it, and I never shall!

LEBEDEV What are you getting mad at me for? The rats in Gogol at least sniffed before they ran away—but you jump on me without even waiting to hear what I'm going to say, you independent minx!

SASHA Leave me alone and don't insult me with all your calculations and disgusting talk about money.

LEBEDEV, *flying into a temper.* Bah! You're just like your mother! The two of you will drive me to suicide or murder! One shouts all day long, nagging and screeching at me, while she counts her money, and you, you're so clever and humane, and emancipated that you can't even understand your own father. The hell with it! I insult you! Don't you know that before I came in to insult you, I was being torn to pieces in there? *Points to the door.* You don't understand! This is too much, I must be losing my mind! . . . I'll go! *Goes to the door, then stops.* I don't like this business at all . . . I don't like anything about it!

SASHA What don't you like?

LEBEDEV Everything!

SASHA What do you mean, everything?

LEBEDEV Do you think I'm going to sit down and tell you all about it? I don't like anything about it, that's all! And I don't like this marriage at all! *Approaches* SASHA *and continues affectionately.* Forgive me, Sasha, please—I'm sure your marriage is a wise thing, that you're not misguided and honestly love him and aren't marrying him for the wrong reasons. But there's something wrong about it, it's not the real thing! It isn't like other marriages. You're young and fresh, and as pure as the morning dew, and he's . . . he's a widower, and he's been around a lot, and he's worn out. I don't understand him at all, God help him! *Kisses his daughter*. Sasha, forgive me, but there's something wrong about the whole thing. There's so much talk. First Sarah died and then suddenly he wanted to marry you. . . . *Quickly*. But I'm just being an old woman. . . . I'm beginning to sound like an old maid. Don't listen to me or anybody else, just listen to your own heart.

SASHA Father, I've had the same feeling myself . . . Nothing's quite as it should be, something's wrong. If you only knew how depressed I am; it's almost unbearable. And yet it embarrasses me to say anything and I'm afraid to confess that I feel that way. Oh, Papa, say something that will cheer me up, please . . . tell me what to do!

LEBEDEV What's the matter, Sasha? What is it?

SASHA I'm so frightened. I've never been so frightened before in my whole life. I don't feel like I know him at all and sometimes I don't think I ever will. All the time we've been engaged, he's never smiled once, he's never looked right into my eyes. He's always complaining, and saying he's sorry, and hinting that he's guilty of something, and he's always so nervous. . . . I'm tired of it. There are even moments when I think that I don't love him enough. And now when he comes to see us, or talks to me, I begin to get bored. What does it all mean, Papa, what does it mean? I'm so afraid!

LEBEDEV My darling, my only child, listen to me! Give him up!

SASHA, *alarmed*. No! No! Don't say that!

LEBEDEV I mean it, Sasha! Oh, I know there'll be a scandal and all the neighbors will gossip, but it's certainly better to go through that than to ruin your whole life.

SASHA Don't say that, Father, don't! I'm not listening. One just has to get over such gloomy thoughts. He's a good, unhappy, misunderstood man; I will love him, learn to understand him, and put him on his feet again. I'll do my duty! That's settled!

LEBEDEV That's not your duty, that's madness!

SASHA That's enough. I've confessed something to you which I didn't even want to admit to myself. Now, let's forget it, and don't tell anybody!

LEBEDEV I'm really confused. Either I've gotten too old or you're too brilliant, but I'll be damned if I understand this business at all.

SHABYELSKY, *coming in.* The hell with everybody, including myself! It's disgusting!

LEBEDEV What is it?

SHABYELSKY Honestly, I mean it; I'm going to have to do something so horrible and so low that everyone will be disgusted; myself included. No matter what it costs, I'll do it. Honestly, I will! I've told Borkin to go ahead and announce my engagement. *Laughs.* Everyone else is a scoundrel, so I'll be one, too.

LEBEDEV Oh, I'm sick of all this! Listen, Matvyey, if you keep on talking like this, you'll end up in the bughouse, if you'll pardon the expression.

SHABYELSKY And how's the bughouse worse than anywhere else? Do me a favor and take me there right away. Please do! Everyone's so wicked and useless and petty-minded and stupid, and I disgust myself so much that I don't believe a word I say. . . .

LEBEDEV Let me give you some advice, my friend. Put a candle in your mouth, light it, and blow fire at people. Or even better, get your hat and go home. This is a wedding and everyone wants to have a good time, and you go around croaking like a frog. Really, I mean it. . . . SHABYELSKY *leans on the piano and begins to cry.* Good Lord! . . . Matvyey! . . . Count! . . . What's the matter? Matyusha? My dear friend . . . my oldest friend . . . Did I hurt you? Please forgive me! You must forgive me. I didn't mean to hurt you. . . . Forgive an old drunkard. . . . Here's some water. . . .

SHABYELSKY I don't want it. *Raises his head.*

LEBEDEV Why are you crying?

SHABYELSKY It's nothing . . . just nothing . . .

LEBEDEV No, Matyusha, tell me the truth . . . What is it? What's happened?

SHABYELSKY I just happened to see this cello, and . . . I remembered the sweet little Jewess! . . .

LEBEDEV Yes! What a time to think of her! May she rest in peace. But really, this isn't the time to think of her. . . .

SHABYELSKY We used to play duets together. . . . She was a beautiful woman, a wonderful woman! . . . SASHA *sobs.*

LEBEDEV What, now you? . . . Stop it! Good God, now they're both howling, while I . . . I . . . Why don't you go somewhere else where the guests won't see you?

SHABYELSKY Pasha, when the sun's shining you can feel cheerful even in a cemetery. And when there's hope, you can be happy even in old age. But I haven't got any hope, not any at all!

LEBEDEV Yes, it's true, you are in a bad way. . . . You haven't got any children, or money, or work . . . But, what can you do about it? *To* SASHA. Now, why are you crying?

SHABYELSKY Pasha, give me some money. I'll pay you back in the next world. I'll go to Paris and see my wife's grave. I've given away a lot of money in my life. I've given away half my fortune, so I've a right to ask for a little bit now. Anyway, you're my friend . . .

LEBEDEV, *bewildered.* My dear friend, I haven't got any money! Well, all right, all right! That is, I can't promise anything, but you understand . . . of course, of course! *Aside.* This is too much!

BABAKINA *comes in.* And where did my suitor go? Count, how dare you leave me alone? Oh, you naughty man you! *Taps the* COUNT *on the hand with her fan.*

SHABYELSKY, *impatiently.* Leave me alone! I can't stand you!

BABAKINA, *upset.* What? What did you say?

SHABYELSKY I said, leave me alone!

BABAKINA *falls into an armchair.* Oh! *Weeps.*

ZINAIDA *comes in, weeping.* Someone's just come . . . It must be one of the attendants. It's time for the ceremony to start . . . *Sobs.*

SASHA, *imploringly.* Mother!

LEBEDEV Well, now everyone's bawling. A regular quartet! Will you please stop it, we've had enough rain lately! Matvyei! . . . Marfa Yegorovna! . . . If you keep this up, I . . . I'll start crying, too . . . *Cries.* Oh, God!

ZINAIDA If you don't need your mother any more, if you're determined to disobey her . . . well, have your own way. . . . I'll give you my blessing . . .

IVANOV *comes in, wearing a tail-coat and gloves.*

LEBEDEV This is more than I can take. What do you want?

IVANOV Excuse me, everybody . . . but if you don't mind, I'd like a few words alone with Sasha.

LEBEDEV It's not right for the groom to see the bride before the wedding! You should be at the church!

IVANOV Pasha, please . . .

LEBEDEV *shrugs his shoulders, then he,* ZINAIDA, *the* COUNT *and* BABAKINA *go out.*

SASHA, *sternly.* What do you want?

IVANOV I'm so angry I'm ready to explode, but I'll try to stay calm. Listen. Just now, as I was getting dressed for the wedding, I looked at myself in a mirror, and I saw how grey my hair was. Sasha, let's forget all this! Let's stop this senseless comedy before it's too late . . . You're young and pure, you've got your whole life ahead of you, and I . . .

SASHA I've heard all this before . . . a thousand times, and I'm tired of it! Now go to the church, and don't keep people waiting any longer!

IVANOV I'll go home in a minute, and then you explain to your family that there won't be any wedding. Say anything you want. It's time we came to our senses. I've been playing Hamlet and you've been playing a noble-minded young girl—but we couldn't keep this little charade up for very long.

SASHA, *losing her temper.* What are you talking like this for? I refuse to listen to you.

IVANOV But I'm talking to you, and I'll keep right on talking.

SASHA What do you mean, coming here like this? And all your complaining is absolutely ridiculous.

IVANOV No, I'm not complaining any more That it's ridiculous I'll admit. You're ridiculous and I'm a thousand times more ridiculous. The whole world ought to laugh at me. I looked at myself in the mirror a little while ago and my conscience revealed the truth to me. I laughed at myself and nearly went mad with shame. *Laughs.* Melancholy! Noble grief! Uncontrollable sorrow! Only one thing's missing—I don't write poetry. Should I whine and complain and mope around, and make everyone miserable? No, I won't! Oh, to realize that your strength and energy are gone forever, that you're useless and decayed, that you're a coward and that you're stuck in the mire of a most loathsome melancholy. Should I confess all this when I can see the sun shining and the ants carrying their burdens with a sense of self-contentment—No, I won't! Do you think I can stand having some people think I'm a fraud and others feeling sorry for me as they offer me a helping hand, and others, and these are the worst of all, listening reverently to my sighs, looking at me as if I were some newly discovered Mohammed, and expecting me to reveal the secret of the universe? . . . No, thank God, I still have some pride and conscience left! On my way over here, I laughed at myself, and it seemed to me that the birds and the flowers were laughing at me, too. . . .

SASHA This isn't anger, it's madness!

IVANOV You think so? No, I'm not mad. I'm seeing things clearly for the first time and my mind is as clear as your conscience. We love each other, but we'll never be married! It's all right for me to rant and rave as much as I like, but I don't have the right to ruin other people's lives! I poisoned the last year of my wife's life with my bitterness. Since we've been engaged, you've forgotten how to laugh and you've become five years older. And what about your poor father? Everything in his life used to be simple and clear-cut; and now, thanks to me, he doesn't understand anything. It doesn't matter whether I go to a meeting, or hunting, or visiting—wherever I go, I bring depression, boredom, and discontent with me. Wait a minute, don't interrupt me! I'm being very blunt about this, but you must try to understand. The bitterness of it is choking me, and I can't speak any other way. I've never lied and I never used to complain about my lot in life. And yet, somehow, without even noticing it, I've become a complainer, I find fault in everybody and everything, and I curse my fate. And as a result, everyone who listens to me is infected with this same disgust for life, and they begin to find fault with it too. What a fine way to look at life! As if I were doing the world a favor by being alive! That's fine!

SASHA But wait a minute! If what you say is true, then it follows that you're sick of all this complaining and that the time has come to begin a new life! That's wonderful!

IVANOV What's so wonderful about it! What new life is there for me? I'm beyond saving, and it's about time we both understood that. A new life!

SASHA Nikolai, snap out of it! What proof do you have that you can't be saved? Why all the cynicism? No, I won't listen to you and I won't talk any more, either . . . Now, go to the church!

IVANOV I'm lost!

SASHA Don't shout like that, the guests will hear you.

IVANOV If an intelligent, educated, healthy man for no good reason starts complaining about life, if he starts rolling downhill, he'll keep right on till he hits the bottom—there's no hope for him! Well, what hope have I? I can't drink because liquor makes me sick; I can't write bad poetry, I can't rationalize the boredom in my soul as something noble and lofty. Boredom is boredom, weakness is weakness—you can't call them anything else. I'm finished, finished . . . And there's no point in talking about it any more! *Glances around.* Someone may come in! Listen, if you really love me, then help me, now. Forget me and forget this marriage! Right now!

SASHA Oh, Nikolai, if you only knew how you're torturing me! How much more am I supposed to endure? You're a kind, intelligent person, so consider this for a minute: is it fair to burden me with these problems? Every day there is some problem, each one more difficult than the one before . . . I want a love that's alive! This isn't alive; our love's become a kind of martyrdom!

IVANOV When you're my wife the problems won't be any easier, they'll be worse, so forget the whole thing now! Try to understand! You're not doing this because you love me, but because of the obstinacy of your honest nature. You decided you were going to save me—no matter what the obstacles—and it made you feel good to be doing such a noble thing. But you're willing to stop now, and only the falsest kinds of feeling keep you from it. Won't you understand!

SASHA What crazy logic that is! How can I give you up? How can I? You haven't got a mother, or a sister, or friends. . . . You're ruined, your estate's gone, everyone despises you. . . .

IVANOV I was a fool to come here. I should have done what I meant to do. . . .

Enter LEBEDEV.

SASHA *runs towards her father.* Father, for God's sake help me; he's come running in here like a lunatic, and starts torturing me! He insists that the marriage must be called off because he doesn't want to ruin me. Tell him I don't want his generosity, and that I know what I'm doing!

LEBEDEV I don't understand . . . What generosity?

IVANOV There's not going to be any wedding.

SASHA Yes, there will! Papa, tell him that there will be a wedding!

LEBEDEV Wait, wait! Why don't you want there to be a wedding?

IVANOV I've explained it all to her, but she refuses to understand.

LEBEDEV No, not to her, explain it to me, and explain it so I can understand it. Oh, Nikolai Alexeyevich, may God be your judge! You've brought so much commotion into our lives that I feel as if I were living in a museum of nightmares. I see everything and I don't understand it . . . It's too much for me . . . Well, what do you want me to do. I'm an old man, you know. Should I challenge you to a duel?

IVANOV There's no need for any duel. All you have to do is keep your head on your shoulders and be able to understand a few simple words.

SASHA *paces the stage in agitation.* This is terrible, terrible! He's just acting childish!

LEBEDEV I guess all you can do is put up with it. Now, you listen to me, Nikolai! You think you're acting wisely and discreetly, according to all the rules of psychology—but I think this whole unfortunate business is scandalous. Now listen to an old man for the last time. This is all I want to tell you, so just relax. Look at things simply like everybody else! In this world everything's really quite simple. The ceiling is white, your shoes are black, sugar is sweet. You love Sasha, she loves you. If you love her—stay with her, if you don't love her—go, we won't blame you for it. It's really as simple as that! You're both healthy, intelligent and good young people, and you're well fed and clothed, thank God . . . What more do you want? You don't have any money; well, that doesn't really matter. You can't buy happiness . . . Oh, I understand . . . your estate's mortgaged, and you can't pay the interest, but I—I'm her father, I understand . . . her mother can do as she likes. If she won't give you any money, well, then she won't. Sasha says she doesn't want a dowry. As for all your principles, Schopenhauer . . . that's all nonsense . . . Now, I've got ten thousand in the bank. *Looks round.* Nobody knows I've got it. It was my grandmother's. That'll be for the two of you. You may have it, but on one condition—you must give your uncle a couple of thousand . . .

Visitors begin to assemble in the ballroom.

IVANOV Pasha, there's no use discussing it any more. I'm acting as I must . . . as my conscience tells me.

SASHA And I'm acting as mine tells me. You can say anything you like, but I refuse to let you go. I'm going to get mother to settle this. *Goes out.*

LEBEDEV I'm completely confused . . .

IVANOV Listen, my friend . . . I'm not going to try and explain myself to you. I'm not going to say I'm rotten, healthy or neurotic. You wouldn't know what I was talking about. I used to be young, eager, sincere, and intelligent. I used to love and hate and believe in a way that most people couldn't even imagine; I could do the work of ten men, and I had more dreams than any ten men, too; I wasn't afraid to tilt with windmills, to butt my head against a brick wall. . . . Without knowing my strength or any weakness, without even thinking, without knowing anything about life, I carried a load that was too much for me, and I broke under the strain. Oh, I did everything in extremes: I drank too much, I worked too hard, I was always excited, there were no limits to my energy. Well, what else could you expect? There are so few of us and so much to do, so much! And see how cruelly fate—that fate which I fought against so bravely—see how it's revenged itself on me. I'm worn out, broken. At thirty-five I'm an old man. I go about with a heavy head and a lazy mind, weary, useless, and discouraged—without faith, or love, or purpose in life; I wander like a shadow among my friends, and I don't know who I am, or why I'm alive, or what I want out of life. Love is nonsense, and so is love-making; work and play are both wastes of time; and the most passionate of speeches are insipid and just a lot of words. So wherever I go, I bring nothing but sadness, weariness, boredom, discontent, disgust with life. I'm ruined, completely and hopelessly ruined! Before you stands a man who at thirty-five is tired, disillusioned, and broken by the trivia of existence—ashamed of his failure and mocking his weakness . . . Oh, how my pride rebels against it all. I'm choked with anger! *Staggering.* You see I'm staggering . . . I haven't any more strength. Where's Matvyey? Tell him to take me home.

VOICES IN THE BALLROOM The best man's here!

SHABYELSKY, *coming in.* Here I am. Had to borrow this old coat, haven't any gloves. . . . So everybody jokes about it, and some of them even gave me scornful looks. Such disgusting people!

BORKIN *enters quickly, carrying a bouquet; he wears dress clothes.*

Oh, where is he? *To* IVANOV. There you are! They've been waiting for you all this time at the church and you're still here, philosophizing. What a fool you are! You make me laugh! Don't you know you're supposed to go to the church with me and not with the bride? Then I'm supposed to come back from the church and get her. Don't you understand that? Sometimes you make me laugh.

LVOV *comes in, to* IVANOV. Oh, so here you are! *Loudly.* Nikolai Alexeyevich Ivanov, I want to announce to all the world that you are a worthless scoundrel!

IVANOV, *coldly*. Thank you very much.

General astonishment.

BORKIN, *to* LVOV. Sir, how contemptible can you be? I challenge you to a duel!

LVOV Monsieur Borkin, I am disgraced to have to speak to you; I would never fight with you. As for Monsieur Ivanov, he can have satisfaction from me whenever he wishes.

SHABYELSKY Then, sir, I'll fight you!

SASHA, *to* LVOV. Why did you do that? What did you insult him for? My friends, please let him tell me why he insulted Nikolai!

LVOV Alexandra Pavlovna, I have not insulted him without good reasons. I came here as an honest man to tell you the truth, and I beg you to listen to me.

SASHA Well, what are you going to say? That you're an honest man? The whole world knows it! But, tell me, do you understand yourself? You came here just now—as an honest man—and insulted him so horribly that you nearly killed me. Before that you followed him like a shadow and interfered with his life. But, of course, you were convinced that this was your duty, you were an honest man. You meddled with his private life, you maligned him and found fault with him whenever you could; you sent me and all my friends anonymous letters—oh, but you were being such an honest man. Yes, Doctor, you were so honest you couldn't even spare his dying wife, you couldn't spare her even a moment's peace with your suspicions. And no matter what violent, or cruel, or mean things you ever do, you'll always think of yourself as a totally honest and noble person!

IVANOV, *laughing*. This isn't a wedding, it's a congressional debate! Bravo, bravo!

sasha, *to* lvov. So just think that over: do you see what kind of a person you are, or don't you? Stupid, heartless people! *Takes* ivanov's *hand.* Let's leave here, Nikolai! Father, come along!

ivanov Go? Where do you want me to go? Wait, I'll put an end to all this! I feel that my youth has been reawakened—the old Ivanov has spoken! *Takes out a revolver.*

sasha *shrieks.* I know what he's going to do! Nikolai, for God's sake!

ivanov I've been going downhill long enough, now the time has come for me to stop! This is enough! Get out of my way! Thank you, Sasha!

sasha *shrieks.* Nikolai, for God's sake! Stop him!

ivanov Leave me alone! *Rushes off the stage and shoots himself.*

Curtain.

THE WOOD DEMON

CAST

ALEXANDER VLADIMIROVICH SEREBRYAKOV, *a retired professor*

YELENA ANDREYEVNA, *his wife, aged twenty-seven*

SOFIA ALEXANDROVNA (SONYA), *the professor's daughter, by his first marriage, aged twenty*

MARYA VASSILYEVNA VOYNITSKAYA, *widow of a privy councillor, mother of George, and the professor's first wife*

GEORGE PETROVICH VOYNITSKY, *her son* 47 yrs old loves Yelena

LEONID STEPANOVICH ZHELTOUKHIN, *a wealthy young man, who has studied Technology at the University*

YULIA STEPANOVNA (JULIA), *his sister, aged eighteen*

IVAN IVANOVICH ORLOVSKY, *a landowner*

FYODOR IVANOVICH ORLOVSKY, *his son* 35 yrs old

MIHAIL LVOVICH KHROUSCHOV (THE WOOD DEMON) *a landowner, who is also a doctor*

ILYA ILYICH DYADIN

VASSILY, *Zheltoukhin's man-servant*

SEMYON, *a laborer employed at Dyadin's flour mill*

ACT I

The garden terrace of the manor house on the ZHELTOUKHIN *estate. In front of the house there are two tables. The large table is set for lunch and on the smaller one there are hors d'oeuvres. It is a little after two o'clock in the afternoon.* ZHELTOUKHIN *and* JULIA *come out of the house.*

JULIA You ought to wear your grey suit. It looks better.

ZHELTOUKHIN What difference does it make?

JULIA Oh, Lennie, why are you such a bore sometimes? Now please don't be like this on your birthday. *Laying her head on his chest.* And no scenes, do you promise?

ZHELTOUKHIN Stop blubbering, will you!

JULIA, *through tears.* Lennie!

ZHELTOUKHIN Why don't you do what I ask you to do, instead of giving me all those tearful kisses and soulful sisterly looks and those silly damn presents which are absolutely useless? And why didn't you write to the Serebryakovs?

JULIA But, Lennie, I did write!

ZHELTOUKHIN To whom?

JULIA I wrote to Sonya. I asked her to be sure to come today at one o'clock. Honestly, I did!

ZHELTOUKHIN And yet here it is past two, and they haven't come. Oh, what difference does it make. I don't care! So, I'm humiliated. So, she doesn't give a damn about me. I know I'm not handsome and I'm boring, and there's nothing romantic about me. If she were to marry me it would only be for my money.

JULIA Not handsome! . . . Oh, you're wrong.

ZHELTOUKHIN Oh, stop it! Do you think I'm blind? My beard's all wrong, it grows from the neck. . . . And look at this damn moustache . . . and my nose. . . .

JULIA Why do you press your cheek like that?

ZHELTOUKHIN My eye aches.

JULIA Oh, it's swollen. Here, let me kiss it, and it will go away.

ZHELTOUKHIN Don't be silly!

Enter ORLOVSKY *and* VOYNITSKY.

ORLOVSKY Sweetheart, when are we going to eat? It's after two!

JULIA I know, Godfather, but the Serebryakovs haven't come yet!

ORLOVSKY Well, how much longer do we have to wait? I'm hungry, my sweet, and George wants his lunch too.

ZHELTOUKHIN, *to* VOYNITSKY. Are they coming?

VOYNITSKY Well, when I left, Yelena Andreyevna was dressing.

ZHELTOUKHIN Then they are coming?

VOYNITSKY You can never be sure. Our great General may suddenly dream up an attack of the gout, or something like that—and they won't come.

ZHELTOUKHIN In that case let's eat. What's the use of waiting? *Shouting.* Ilya Ilyich! Sergey Nikodymich!

Enter DYADIN *and two or three guests.*

ZHELTOUKHIN Please help yourselves. *Standing round the small table.* The Serebryakovs haven't come yet. Fyodor Ivanovich isn't here; and the Wood Demon isn't either . . . People just don't care about us, they've forgotton us.

JULIA Godfather, will you have some vodka?

ORLOVSKY Just a touch. That's fine . . . thank you.

DYADIN, *adjusting the napkin round his neck.* How wonderfully you arrange everything, Yulia Stepanovna! Whether I drive through the fields, or take a walk under the shady trees in your orchard, or look at this table—everywhere I see the mighty power of your bewitching little hand. Here's to your health!

JULIA We all have our problems, Ilya Ilyich! Why last night, for instance, Nazarka forgot to bring in the young turkeys, and this morning five of them died.

DYADIN How horrible! Such things shouldn't happen. Turkeys are such delicate birds.

VOYNITSKY, *to* DYADIN. Waffles, cut me some ham!

DYADIN Gladly, my friend. It's a glorious ham. One of the wonders of the Arabian nights. *Cutting.* And Georgie, I'm cutting it according to all the rules of art. Why even Beethoven or Shakespeare couldn't do it better. Only the knife isn't very sharp. *Sharpening the knife on another knife.*

ZHELTOUKHIN, *shuddering.* H-s-s-s! . . . Cut it out, Waffles! I can't stand it!

ORLOVSKY How is everyone, George Petrovich? How are you all getting along?

VOYNITSKY We aren't.

ORLOVSKY Haven't you any news for us?

VOYNITSKY No, it's all old. I'm the same as ever, no . . . worse, for I've become lazy. I do nothing any more but grumble like an old crow. My mother, the old magpie, is still babbling about the emancipation of women, with one eye on her grave and the other on her learned books, in which she is forever rummaging in the hopes of finding the dawn of a new life.

ORLOVSKY And how's Alexander?

VOYNITSKY The professor has, unfortunately, not yet been eaten up by the moths. As usual, he sits in his study from morning till night. . . .

> Straining our mind, wrinkling our brow,
> We write, write, write,
> With no respite
> Or hope of praise in the future or now.

Oh, poor unfortunate paper! Sonya, as usual, reads the latest novels and keeps a diary.

ORLOVSKY My dear fellow. . . .

VOYNITSKY With my powers of observation I ought to write a novel. Just think of the plot: the life of a retired professor, as stale as a piece of mildewed bread, racked with gout, headaches, and rheumatism, his heart bursting with jealousy and envy—as jealous as Othello—living on the estate of his first wife, although he hates it, because he can't afford to live in town. He's always whining about his hard fate, although as a matter of fact, he's extraordinarily lucky.

ORLOVSKY Oh, come now!

VOYNITSKY What do you mean, "oh, come now!" Think of his luck! I won't even go into the fact that he's only the son of a common, ordinary parson, who went to college, and somehow managed to get his degree and a chair at the University. I'll not even mention that he's become the son-in-law of a senator and is called "your excellency." Forget all that. But let me tell you this: he's been writing about art for twenty-five years, and he doesn't know the first thing about it. For twenty-five years he has been hashing over the thoughts of other men on realism, naturalism, and all the other nonsensical "isms"; for twenty-five years he has been reading and writing things that intelligent men have always known and that are stupid and boring to those who don't care; for twenty-five years he has been pouring water from one glass into another. And yet look at his success! His fame! Why? By what right?

ORLOVSKY, *laughing aloud*. You know, I believe you envy him.

VOYNITSKY Yes, I do! Look at the success he's had with women! Don Juan himself was no luckier. His first wife, my sister, was beautiful, gentle, as pure as the blue sky, generous, with more suitors than the number of all his pupils put together and she loved him as only creatures of angelic purity can love those who are as pure and beautiful as they are themselves. My mother—his mother-in-law—adores him to this day, and he still inspires her with a kind of worshipful awe. And now, his second wife is, as you can plainly see, a great beauty, and she's intelligent too; and yet she married him in his old age and surrendered to him all the glory of her beauty and freedom. What for? Why? And she's so gifted, such an artist! How wonderfully she plays the piano!

ORLOVSKY They really are a very gifted family, aren't they?

ZHELTOUKHIN Indeed they are. Sofia Alexandrovna, for instance, has a remarkable voice. A wonderful soprano! I've never heard anything like it even in Petersburg. But, you know, she strains on the highest notes. It's a great pity. Give me those high notes! Give me those high notes! Oh, if she had those notes, she would be absolutely perfect, do you know . . . But forgive me, gentlemen, I must have a word with Julia . . . *Taking* JULIA *aside.* Send one of the servants to their house. Send a note telling them that if they can't come now, be sure to come for dinner. . . . *In a lower voice.* But don't write anything silly, I don't want to be disgraced, and for heaven's sake, spell things right . . . "Drive" is spelled "i-v-e" . . . *Aloud and tenderly.* Please, my dear!

JULIA Certainly. *Going out.*

DYADIN They say that Yelena Alexandrovna, whom I have not yet had the pleasure and honor of meeting, has not only a beautiful face, but a beautiful soul as well.

ORLOVSKY That's right, she's a marvelous woman.

ZHELTOUKHIN Is she faithful to him?

VOYNITSKY Unfortunately, she is.

ZHELTOUKHIN Why unfortunately?

VOYNITSKY Because such fidelity is false and unnatural. Oh, it sounds very good, but there is no rhyme nor reason to it. It's immoral for a woman to deceive and endure an old husband whom she hates. But for her to stifle her pathetic youth, those intense longings within her heart—her feelings . . . that's not immoral! It's all nonsense.

DYADIN, *in a tearful voice.* Georgie, don't talk like that. Really, please don't. . . . It makes me terribly upset. . . . Gentlemen, I have no great talent and cannot speak with eloquence, but allow me to speak out without elegant phrases, as my conscience prompts me. . . . Gentlemen, well, really, you know anyone who is unfaithful to one's wife or husband is a disloyal person and will betray his country, too!

VOYNITSKY Oh, Waffles, dry up!

DYADIN No, allow me, Georgie! . . . Ivan Ivanovich, Lennie, and all of you my dear friends, please consider the vicissitudes of my fate. It is not a secret that my wife ran away with a lover the day after our wedding, because of my . . . ah . . . rather unprepossessing appearance.

VOYNITSKY Do you blame her?

DYADIN But listen, gentlemen! Since then I have never failed to do my duty. I love her and am true to her to this day. I help her all I can and I've given my fortune to educate the children she had by her lover. I've done my duty and I'm proud of it. Yes, I am proud. I've lost my happiness, but I've kept my pride. And she? Her youth's gone, her beauty has faded according to the laws of nature, and her lover—may he rest in peace—is dead. What does she have left? *Sitting down.* I'm speaking seriously, and you laugh. . . .

ORLOVSKY You're a kind man, Ilya, and have a noble spirit, but you talk too much and you wave your hands. . . .

FYODOR IVANOVICH *comes out of the house. He is dressed in a sleeveless overcoat made of the finest cloth; high boots; his chest covered with ribbons, medals, and a solid gold chain with trinkets. He has expensive rings on his fingers.*

FYODOR Well, here you are! How are you all?

ORLOVSKY, *joyously.* Fyodor, my boy!

FYODOR, *to* ZHELTOUKHIN. Happy birthday . . . how old is

it? . . . *Greeting the whole company*. Father! Waffles! Everybody having a good time?

ZHELTOUKHIN Where have you been? How come you're so late?

FYODOR Whew, it's hot! I need a drink.

ORLOVSKY, *with an admiring look at him*. My friend, look at that beard. My, what a handsome lad. Look at him: isn't he handsome?

FYODOR Here's to the birthday-boy! *Drinking*. Aren't the Sere-bryakovs here?

ZHELTOUKHIN They haven't come yet.

FYODOR Hmm, I see! . . . And where's Julia?

ZHELTOUKHIN I don't know where she is. It's time she brought out the cake. Excuse me, I'll get her. *Going out*.

ORLOVSKY Our Lennie certainly is in a good humor today. So sulky!

VOYNITSKY He's a beast!

ORLOVSKY His nerves must be upset, he can't help it. . . .

VOYNITSKY He's so conceited, that's why he has bad nerves. If I were to praise this herring, he'd be all hurt because I wasn't talking about him. Quiet, here he comes.

Enter JULIA *and* ZHELTOUKHIN.

JULIA Fyodor, dear, how are you? *Kissing one another*. Do have something to eat. *To* ORLOVSKY. Look, Godfather, what I'm giving Lennie for his birthday. *Showing a little shoehorn to serve as a watch-stand*.

ORLOVSKY Aren't you a sweet girl, such a fine shoe! Isn't that nice!

JULIA The gold ribbon alone cost eight and a half roubles, and look at the borders with all the tiny little pearls. And here it says: "Leonid Zheltoukhin." "A present to him I love." . . .

DYADIN Let me see! How delightful!

FYODOR That's enough, now Julia, tell them to bring some champagne!

JULIA But Fyodor dear, that's for tonight!

FYODOR Why, tonight? Tell them to bring it at once, or I'll leave. Where do you keep it? I'll get it myself.

JULIA Fyodor, you always upset things. *To* VASSILY. Vassily, here's the key! Get the champagne. It's in the pantry by the bag of raisins in the corner. Be careful you don't break anything!

FYODOR Vassily, bring three bottles!

JULIA A fine husband you'll make, Fyodor . . . *Serving out the cake to the company.* Have some more, please, gentlemen. . . . Dinner won't be until six. . . . You'll never amount to anything, Fyodor . . . You're beyond hope.

FYODOR Now, you're beginning to preach at me.

VOYNITSKY I think someone is coming . . . Do you hear?

ZHELTOUKHIN Why, yes. . . . It's the Serebryakovs. . . . At last!

VASSILY *announces the* SEREBRYAKOVS.

JULIA, *crying out.* Sonya dear! *Running out.*

VOYNITSKY, *singing.* "Let's meet them! Come on, let's go" . . . *Going out.*

ZHELTOUKHIN How tactless some people are! He's having an affair with the professor's wife and can't keep quiet about it.

FYODOR Who?

ZHELTOUKHIN George, of course. He was singing her praises so much just before you came—well, it's downright indecent.

FYODOR How do you know she's his mistress?

ZHELTOUKHIN I'm not blind! . . . Besides, everybody's talking about it.

FYODOR Nonsense. She's nobody's mistress . . . yet. But she will be soon—mine. Mine, do you understand. Mine!

SEREBRYAKOV, MARYA VASSILYEVNA, VOYNITSKY, *with* YELENA ANDREYEVNA *on his arm,* SONYA *and* JULIA.

JULIA, *kissing* SONYA. Sonya, darling!

ORLOVSKY, *going to meet them.* Good to see you, Alexander, how are you, my friend? *Embracing one another.* You're well? Quite well?

SEREBRYAKOV And how are you, my dear friend? You look fine! I am very glad to see you. How long have you been back?

ORLOVSKY I returned on Friday. *To* MARYA VASSILYEVNA. Marya Vassilyevna! How are you, Your Excellency? *Kissing her hand.*

MARYA My dear! . . . *Kissing him on the head.*

SONYA Godfather!

ORLOVSKY Sonechka, my darling! *Kissing her.* My little canary bird! . . .

SONYA As usual, your face is radiant, kindly, and good! . . .

ORLOVSKY And you've grown taller, and prettier, my sweet! . . .

SONYA How have you been? Well, I hope.

ORLOVSKY Very well! Couldn't be better.

SONYA I'm so glad, Godfather. *To* FYODOR. Oh, I didn't see our elephant. *Embracing one another.* You're so sunburned and hairy . . . just like a spider!

JULIA Really, Sonya!

ORLOVSKY, *to* SEREBRYAKOV. Well, how've you been?

SEREBRYAKOV So so . . . and you?

ORLOVSKY Couldn't be better. I'm alive and enjoying myself. I gave my estate to my son, my daughters are married to good men, and now I'm free as the air.

DYADIN, *to* SEREBRYAKOV. It pleased Your Excellency to arrive a little late and the cake has gotten cold. Allow me to introduce myself. I am Ilya Ilyich Dyadin, or Waffles, as some people call me because of my pock-marked face.

SEREBRYAKOV Glad to meet you.

DYADIN Madam! Mademoiselle! *Bowing to* YELENA *and to* SONYA. These people are all my friends, Your Excellency. Once I had a large fortune, but for personal reasons, or, as people in intellectual circles put it, for reasons for which the editor accepts no responsibility, I gave my share to my brother, who, on a certain unfortunate occasion, owed the government seventy thousand roubles of its own money. I now exploit nature's stormy elements. I make the stormy waves turn the wheels of a flour mill, which I rent from my good friend, the Wood Demon.

VOYNITSKY Waffles, dry up!

DYADIN I've always had great respect *Bowing down to the ground.* for the great men of science, who adorn our country's horizon. Forgive my audacity, but I should like very much to pay Your Excellency a visit and to talk about the ultimate deductions of science.

SEREBRYAKOV By all means, I'll be delighted to see you.

SONYA Where did you spend the winter, Godfather? You just seemed to disappear.

ORLOVSKY I was in Gmunden, my sweet, then to Paris, Nice . . . oh, and in London too . . .

SONYA How wonderful! What a lucky man!

ORLOVSKY Why don't you join me when I go again in the fall?

SONYA, *singing.* "Tempt me not without need" . . .

FYODOR Don't sing at the table, or your husband's wife will be a scatterbrain.

DYADIN I wish I could take a picture of this table "*à vol d'oiseau*." What a fascinating bouquet! Such a combination of grace, beauty, profound learning, popu . . .

FYODOR What a fascinating speech! Cut it out, will you! You sound as though someone were rubbing your back with sand-paper . . .

Laughter.

ORLOVSKY, *to* SONYA. And you, my darling, you're not married yet . . .

VOYNITSKY Good Lord, whom could she marry? Humboldt is dead. Edison is in America, Schopenhauer's dead too. . . . The other day I found her diary on her desk: this size! I opened it and read: "No, I shall never fall in love. . . . Love is the egotistical attraction of my ego to an object of the opposite sex." . . . And you ought to see what else is there! Transcendental, culminating point of the integrating principle . . . ugh! And what good will all this do them?

SONYA Some people have to be ironical, Uncle George, but you shouldn't be.

VOYNITSKY What are you so angry about?

SONYA If you say another word, one of us will have to go home. Either you or I. . . .

ORLOVSKY, *laughing aloud.* What a character!

VOYNITSKY Yes, a character indeed, I must say . . . *To* SONYA. Give me your hand! Please do! *Kissing her hand.* Peace! Are we friends again . . . I promise I won't do it again.

KHROUSCHOV, *coming out of the house.* I wish I were a painter! What a wonderful group!

ORLOVSKY, *joyously.* My dear godson!

KHROUSCHOV Congratulations to Lennie. How are you, Julia? You look splendid today! Godfather! *Kissing* ORLOVSKY. And Sophia Alexandrovna! . . . *Greeting the rest of the company.*

ZHELTOUKHIN How come you're so late! Where have you been?

KHROUSCHOV At a patient's.

JULIA Oh, and the cake's cold.

KHROUSCHOV It doesn't matter, Julia, I'll eat it cold. Where do you want me to sit?

SONYA Sit here . . . *Pointing to a seat beside her.*

KHROUSCHOV The weather's wonderful and I'm starved . . . Yes, thanks. First some vodka . . . *Drinking.* To Lennie! And now a little cake. . . . Julia, give it a kiss, it'll taste better . . . *She kisses it. "Merci!"* How are you, godfather? I haven't seen you for a long time.

ORLOVSKY Yes, it's been a long time. I've been abroad.

KHROUSCHOV I heard about it . . . and envied you. And how are you, Fyodor?

FYODOR All right, your prayers support us, like pillars. . . .

KHROUSCHOV How are your affairs?

FYODOR I can't complain. I'm having a good time. Only, you know my friend, there's so much running back and forth. It's really disgusting! First to the Caucasus, and then back here again— always on the move, until I'm just worn out. You know, I've got two estates there!

KHROUSCHOV Yes, I know.

FYODOR I'm busy colonizing and catching tarantulas and scorpions. Business is going all right, but as for "my surging passions, we won't talk about that!" Things haven't changed there.

KHROUSCHOV You're in love, of course?

FYODOR Let's drink to that, Wood Demon. . . . *Drinking.* Gentlemen, never fall in love with a married woman! On my honor, I'd rather be shot in the arm, or even the leg—and I have—than be in love with a married woman. . . . It's more bother than it's . . .

SONYA Is it hopeless?

FYODOR Hopeless! I should say not. In this world nothing's hopeless. There isn't a man in the world who needs to be unhappy in love. Unhappy in love—all that sighing and moaning is just a lot of nonsense. All you have to do is want something enough. If I don't want my gun to misfire, it doesn't. If I want a certain woman to love me, she'll fall in love with me. And that, my dear Sonya, is the way it is. Once I make up my mind about a woman, she's got as much chance of escaping as flying to the moon.

SONYA What a terror, you are!

FYODOR She won't get away from me! Why I don't have to say more than three words to her and she's in my power. All I have to say to her is, "Madam, whenever you look out of a window think of me. I want you to." And so she thinks of me a thousand times a day. And that's not all, I bombard her with letters every day. . . .

YELENA Letters aren't a very reliable method are they? She may get them, but how do you know she reads them?

FYODOR So that's what you think. Well, in my thirty-five years I've never met the woman yet who'd have the courage not to open a letter addressed to her.

ORLOVSKY, *looking admiringly at him.* You see! What a boy! That's my son! I used to be like that. Just like it! Only difference was I wasn't in the war; but I drank and threw money about—Yes, a chip off the old block!

FYODOR Misha, I really do love her, I'm madly in love with her. . . . If she'd agree, I'd give her everything I've got. . . . I'd carry her off to the Caucasus, to the mountains, and we'd live like singing birds. . . . Why, Yelena Andreyevna, I'd guard her, like a faithful dog, and she would be to me as the marshal of nobility sings: "Thou wilt be the queen of the universe, my dearest love." Oh, she doesn't know how happy she could be!

KHROUSCHOV And who's this lucky woman?

FYODOR If you know too much, you'll get old to soon. . . . But enough of this. Let's sing a different song. I remember, about ten years ago—when Lennie was still at school—we were celebrating his birthday as we are now. I rode home—Sonya on my right arm, and Julia on my left, and they both held on to my beard. Now, let's drink to those dear friends of my youth, to Sonya and Julia!

DYADIN, *laughing aloud.* That's fascinating! Just fascinating!

FYODOR Once after the war, I was having a drink with a Turkish Pasha in Trebisond. . . . And all at once he asked me. . . .

DYADIN, *interrupting.* Let's drink a toast to more amicable relationships. "*Vivat*" friendship! Here's to you!

FYODOR Wait! Stop it! Stop it! Sonya, listen to me! I want to make a bet, damn it! I am putting three hundred roubles here on the table! After lunch let's go and play croquet, and I'll bet you that in one turn I can get through all the hoops and back to the starting post.

SONYA You're on! Only I haven't got three hundred roubles.

FYODOR If you lose, you are to sing to me forty times.

SONYA Agreed.

DYADIN That is fascinating! Just fascinating! [repet.

YELENA, *looking at the sky*. What kind of bird is that?

ZHELTOUKHIN A hawk.

FYODOR Ladies and Gentlemen, let's drink to the health of the hawk!

SONYA *laughs aloud*.

ORLOVSKY Now you've got her started! What's the matter?

KHROUSCHOV *laughs aloud*.

ORLOVSKY What are you laughing about?

MARYA Sophia! It is not right to carry on that way.

KHROUSCHOV Oh, I am so sorry! . . . I'll stop in a minute. . . .

ORLOVSKY But what's all this laughing without any reason.

VOYNITSKY Those two, all you've got to do is snap your fingers, and they burst out laughing. Sonya! *Snapping his fingers*. Look, see! . . .

KHROUSCHOV Stop it! *Looking at his watch*. Well, I have eaten and had a drink, and now I've to go. It's time I went.

SONYA Where to?

KHROUSCHOV To see a patient. I'm getting to hate my practice as much as an unloved wife, or a long winter. . . .

SEREBRYAKOV But, what do you mean, my good man, medicine is your profession, your work, so to say . . .

VOYNITSKY, *ironically*. He's got another profession. He digs peat on his estate.

SEREBRYAKOV What?

VOYNITSKY Peat! A mining engineer has calculated with absolute certainty that there is peat on his land worth seven hundred and twenty thousand roubles. It's no joke.

KHROUSCHOV I don't dig peat for the money.

VOYNITSKY Why do you dig it then?

KHROUSCHOV So you don't cut down the forests.

VOYNITSKY Why not cut them? To hear you talk, one would think that forests only existed for young lovers.

KHROUSCHOV I never said anything of the sort.

VOYNITSKY Everything I've heard you say so far in defense of the forests is old hat and silly. I'm sorry, but I've got good reasons for saying this—why I've heard your speeches so many times I know them by heart. For instance . . . *Raising his voice and gesticulating, as though imitating* KHROUSCHOV. You, men, are destroying the forests, but they beautify the earth, and so teach man to understand the beautiful, and instill in him a feeling of respect and awe. Forests temper the severity of the climate. In countries where the climate is warmer, less energy is wasted on the struggle with nature and that is why man there is more gentle and loving; the people there are beautiful, supple, and sensitive; their speech is refined and their movements graceful. Art and learning flourish among them, their philosophy is not so depressing, and they treat women with refinement and nobility. And so on and so on. All this is charming but not convincing, and so, I hope you'll permit me, my friend, to go on burning wood in my fireplaces and building my barns with wood.

KHROUSCHOV Of course, I don't object to your cutting wood when you have to, but why destroy the forests? The woods of Russia are trembling under the blows of the axe; the homes of the wild animals and birds have been destroyed; the rivers are drying up, and many beautiful landscapes are gone forever. And why? Because men are too lazy and stupid to bend over and pick up their fuel from the ground. *Pointing to the trees.* Who but a senseless savage could burn so much beauty in his fireplace and destroy what he cannot create himself? Man has reason and creative powers so that he may increase that which has been given to him. Until now, however, he has not created, he has only destroyed. The forests are disappearing, the rivers are drying up, the game is being destroyed, the climate is spoiled, and the earth becomes poorer and more ugly every day. *To* VOYNITSKY. Oh, I see the irony in your eyes; you don't take me seriously and think everything I'm saying is old-fashioned. But when I cross those peasant forests which I have saved from the axe, or when I hear the rustling of the young trees, which I have planted with my own hands, I feel as if I had had some small share in improving the climate, and that if mankind is happy a thousand years from now, I shall have been partly responsible in my small way for its happiness. When I plant a young birch tree and see it budding and swaying in the wind, my heart swells with pride and I realize that, thanks to me, there is one more life added to this earth.

FYODOR, *interrupting.* Your health, Wood Demon!

VOYNITSKY All this is very fine, but if you considered it from a scientific point of view, instead of as a piece of romantic fiction. . . .

SONYA Uncle George! You don't know what you're talking about. Do keep quiet!

KHROUSCHOV Yes, George Petrovich, please let's not discuss it any further.

VOYNITSKY Whatever you say!

MARYA Oh! Oh!

SONYA What is it, Grandmother?

MARYA, *to* SEREBRYAKOV. I forgot to tell you, Alexander. . . . I must be losing my memory. . . . I had a letter today from Paul Alexeyevich in Kharkov. . . . He asked to be remembered to you. . . .

SEREBRYAKOV Thank you, I am very glad.

MARYA And he sent me his latest article and asked me to show it to you.

SEREBRYAKOV Is it interesting?

MARYA Yes, but it's so strange. He refutes the very theories he defended seven years ago. Isn't that so typical of our time? Never have people betrayed their convictions so easily as they do now. It's appalling!

VOYNITSKY Oh, there's nothing so appalling about it. Have some fish, Mother.

MARYA But I have something to say. I want to talk.

VOYNITSKY But that's all we've been doing for the last fifty years. Just talk about new trends and schools; it's time we quit all this nonsense.

MARYA It seems that you never want to listen to what I have to say. If you will pardon me, George, you have changed so much during this past year that I hardly know you. You used to be a man of strong convictions and had such an illuminating personality. . . .

VOYNITSKY Oh, yes! I had an illuminating personality which illuminated no one. Permit me to get up. I had an illuminating personality. You couldn't say anything more cruel. Here I am forty-seven years old. Until last year I tried, as you still do, to blind my eyes with meaningless pedantry to the truths of life. Yes, I did it on purpose, to avoid seeing life as it really is . . . and I thought I was doing the right thing. But now . . . oh, if you only knew! If you knew how I lie awake at night, heartsick and angry, thinking how stupidly I wasted my time when I might have been taking from life everything which is now denied me because I am old.

SEREBRYAKOV Look here, George! You seem to blame your former convictions for something. . . .

SONYA Please, father! This is so dreary!

SEREBRYAKOV Look here! You talk as if your former convictions were somehow to blame. It's not your convictions, but yourself who is at fault. You forgot that convictions without deeds are dead. You ought to have been at work.

VOYNITSKY Work? Not everyone is capable of being a writing machine.

SEREBRYAKOV What do you mean by that?

VOYNITSKY Nothing. Let's forget it. We're not at home now.

MARYA I am completely losing my memory. . . . I forgot to remind you, Alexander, to take your medicine before lunch; I brought it with me, but forgot to remind you.

SEREBRYAKOV You don't have to.

MARYA But you're not well, Alexander! In fact, you're very ill!

SEREBRYAKOV Why make a fuss about it? Old, ill, old, ill . . . that's the only thing I hear! *To* ZHELTOUKHIN. Leonid Stepanovich, allow me to get up and go into the house. It is rather hot here and the mosquitoes are bothering me.

ZHELTOUKHIN By all means. Anyway, we've finished lunch.

SEREBRYAKOV Thank you. *Going into the house;* MARYA *following him.*

JULIA, *to her brother.* You'd better go with the professor! This is so embarrassing!

ZHELTOUKHIN, *to her.* Damn him! *Going out.*

DYADIN Julia Stepanovna, allow me to thank you from the bottom of my soul. *Kissing her hand.*

JULIA Don't mention it, Ilya Ilyich! You've eaten so little . . . *The company getting up and thanking her.* Don't mention it! You've all eaten so little!

FYODOR What are we going to do now? Let's play croquet and settle our bet . . . and then?

JULIA And then we shall have dinner.

FYODOR And then?

KHROUSCHOV And then you'll come to my place. I'll arrange a fishing party on the lake for this evening.

FYODOR Wonderful!

DYADIN This is fascinating! Just fascinating!

SONYA Well, it's settled then. We'll play croquet and settle our bet. . . . Then Julia will give us an early dinner, and about seven we'll drive over to the Wood . . . I mean to Mr. Khrouschov's. Splendid! Come on, Julia, let's get the balls. *Going with* JULIA *into the house.*

FYODOR Vassily, carry the wine to the lawn! We will drink to the conquerors. Come along, Father, and join us in the game.

ORLOVSKY After a while, my boy, I'd better stay with the professor for a few minutes. All of this is a bit awkward and one must keep up appearances. You play my ball for a while, I'll come presently. . . . *Going into the house.*

DYADIN I'm going to listen to the most learned Alexander Vladimirovich. In anticipation of the high delight, which . . .

VOYNITSKY You're a bore, Waffles! Go on!

DYADIN I am going. *Going into the house.*

FYODOR, *walking into the garden, singing.* "Thou wilt be the queen of the universe, my dearest love" . . . *Going out.*

KHROUSCHOV I'll leave quietly. *To* VOYNITSKY. George Petrovich, I beg of you, please let's never talk of forests or medicine again. I don't know why, but when you start talking about these things, for the rest of the day I feel as if I had eaten my dinner out of rusty pots. Good-bye, now. *Going out.*

VOYNITSKY How narrow-minded he is! Everyone says stupid things, but I don't like it when it is done with pathos.

YELENA George, you've been behaving impossibly again. What sense was there in arguing with Marya Vassilyevna and Alexander, and calling him a "writing machine." How petty and small it all is!

VOYNITSKY But suppose I hate him?

YELENA You hate Alexander without reason; he's like everyone else. . . .

SONYA *and* JULIA *pass into the garden with balls and mallets for croquet.*

VOYNITSKY If you could only see your face, your every movement and gesture! . . . You're too lazy to live! How boring your life must be.

YELENA Yes, it is tedious, and dreary, too! *After a pause.* All of you abuse my husband before my eyes as if I weren't even here. And you look at me with compassion thinking: "Poor woman, she's married to an old man." Everyone would like me to leave Alexander. Oh, but how well I understand your sympathy and compassion! As the Wood Demon said just now, see how thoughtlessly you destroy the forests, so that soon there will be nothing left on earth. In just the same way you recklessly destroy human beings, and soon, thanks to you, loyalty and purity and self-sacrifice will have vanished along with the woods. Why can't you look with calm indifference at a woman unless she belongs to you. Because. . . . The Wood Demon is right. You are all possessed by a demon of destruction. You spare neither forests, nor birds, nor women, nor one another.

VOYNITSKY Would you mind stopping all this philosophizing. I don't like it.

YELENA Tell Fyodor that I'm sick and tired of his impudence. It's revolting. To stare at me and talk in the presence of everybody about his love for some married woman—how terribly witty!

Voices in the garden. Bravo! Bravo!

But how nice the Wood Demon is! He comes here quite often, but I'm shy and have never talked to him, as I should have liked to; he doesn't like me, and thinks I'm disagreeable and proud. Do you know, George, why you and I are such friends? I think it's because we're both dull and tiresome people. Yes, tiresome people. Don't look at me that way, I don't like it.

VOYNITSKY How can I look at you in any other way since I love you? You are my happiness, my life, my youth! . . . I know that the chances of your loving me in return are *nil*. But I ask nothing of you, only let me look at you, listen to you . . .

SEREBRYAKOV, *in the window.* Yelena dear, where are you?

YELENA I'm here.

SEREBRYAKOV Come in and stay with us awhile, dear. . . . *Disappearing.*

YELENA *goes into the house.*

VOYNITSKY, *following her.* Let me tell you of my love; don't drive me away, I have no other happiness.

Curtain.

ACT II

The dining room of the SEREBRYAKOVS' *house. It is night. The click of the Watchman's rattle is heard from the garden.* SEREBRYAKOV *sits dozing in an armchair by an open window and* YELENA, *likewise half asleep, is seated beside him.*

SEREBRYAKOV, *awaking.* Who's there! Is that you, Sonya?

YELENA It's me. . . .

SEREBRYAKOV Oh, it's you, Lenotchka! . . . This pain is unbearable!

YELENA Your blanket's on the floor. . . . *Wrapping it round his legs.* I'll shut the window.

SEREBRYAKOV No, leave it open; I'm suffocating as it is. . . . I'd just dropped off to sleep and I dreamt that my left leg belonged to someone else, and the pain was so agonizing I woke up. I don't believe this is gout; it's more like rheumatism. What time is it?

YELENA Twenty after one. *A pause.*

SEREBRYAKOV In the morning will you bring me Batushkov's essays from the library?

YELENA What?

SEREBRYAKOV Bring me Batushkov's essays in the morning. I remember seeing the book there somewhere. Oh, why do I find it so hard to breathe?

YELENA You're tired. You haven't slept for two nights now.

SEREBRYAKOV They say that Turgenev's got heart trouble from gout. I'm getting it, too. Damn this terrible old age! Ever since I've grown old I've been hateful to myself. And the rest of you must think I'm a pretty disgusting spectacle.

YELENA You talk as if we were to blame for your old age.

SEREBRYAKOV I'm more hateful to you than to all the others.

YELENA Don't be silly! *Moving away and sitting down at some distance.*

SEREBRYAKOV You're right, of course. I'm no fool; I understand. You're young and healthy and beautiful. You long for life, and I am an old man, almost a corpse. Oh, I know it. And, of course, it is foolish of me still to be alive. But wait a bit, I'll set you free soon.

YELENA Alexander, this is exhausting me! If I deserve any reward for these sleepless nights, I only ask that you be quiet! For God's sake, be quiet!

SEREBRYAKOV It seems that everybody is exhausted, thanks to me. Everybody is miserable and depressed; everyone's youth is wasting away; I am the only one enjoying life in peace and contentment. Oh, yes, of course!

YELENA Be quiet! I tell you, you're wearing me out!

SEREBRYAKOV Why, of course. I'm wearing everybody out.

YELENA, *crying*. This is unbearable! Please, just tell me what you want me to do.

SEREBRYAKOV Nothing.

YELENA Then please be quiet.

SEREBRYAKOV It's funny that everybody listens to George and his old fool of a mother, but the moment I open my mouth, you all begin to feel abused. You can't even bear the sound of my voice. Suppose I am hateful, suppose I am a selfish and egocentric tyrant, haven't I the right to be at my age? Haven't I deserved it? My life has been hard. Orlovsky and I were undergraduates together. Ask him. He had a good time and ran around with gypsy women, while I lived in a cheap, dirty room. I worked night and day, like an ox. I starved and worried because I was living at someone else's expense. Then I went to Heidelberg to the university, but I saw nothing of Heidelberg. I went to Paris, but I saw nothing of Paris—all I did was sit in my room and work. And when I became professor I served scholarship with faith and truth. I always have, and I still am. So, haven't I, I ask you, the right to be respected, the right to be pampered and cared for. . . .

YELENA No one's disputing your rights. *The window is flapping in the wind. The wind's rising. I'll shut the window. Shutting it.* It's going to rain in a few minutes. . . . Your rights have never been questioned by anybody.

A pause. Outside the night Watchman clicks his rattle and sings a song.

SEREBRYAKOV I've spent my life working for the cause of learning. I'm accustomed to my study, the library and the lecture hall and to the regard and admiration of my colleagues. And now, I suddenly find myself in this wilderness, in this vault, condemned to see the same stupid people from morning till night and to listen to their trivial conversation. I want to live! I long for success and fame and the tension of an active world, and here I am in exile! Oh, it's terrible to spend every moment grieving for a past that is lost, to witness the success of others and to sit here with nothing to do but fear death! I can't stand it! It's more than I can endure. And you, you won't even forgive me for being old.

YELENA Wait a while! Be patient! In five or six years I'll be old, too.

Enter SONYA.

SONYA I wonder why the doctor hasn't come yet. I told Stepan that if the doctor at Zemstvo couldn't come, to drive over and get the Wood Demon.

SEREBRYAKOV Oh, what do I care about your Wood Demon? He knows as much about medicine as I do about astronomy.

SONYA We can't send for famous specialists to come here to cure your gout, can we?

SEREBRYAKOV I refuse to talk to that madman.

SONYA Do whatever you please. *Sitting down.* It makes no difference to me.

SEREBRYAKOV What time is it?

YELENA Nearly two.

SEREBRYAKOV It's stifling in here. . . . Sonya, hand me that medicine there on the table.

SONYA, *handing him the medicine.* Here you are.

SEREBRYAKOV, *irritably.* No, not that one. It's no use asking for anything!

SONYA Please, don't be cross with me! Some people may enjoy it, but spare me, if you please, because I don't like it.

SEREBRYAKOV That girl's impossible. What are you so upset about?

SONYA And why do you always sound so gloomy! Some people might think you were unhappy. But I don't know anyone luckier than you are.

SEREBRYAKOV Why, of course! I am very, very happy.

SONYA Certainly, you're happy. . . . And if you've gout, you know perfectly well that the attack will pass by the morning. So why complain and make such a fuss about it?

Enter VOYNITSKY *in a dressing gown, with a candle.*

VOYNITSKY A storm's on it's way. *A flash of lightning.* Sonya, you and Yelena had better go and get some sleep. I'll relieve you.

SEREBRYAKOV, *frightened.* No, no, don't leave me alone with him! Oh, please don't. He'll begin lecturing me again.

VOYNITSKY But they need some rest! They haven't slept for two nights now.

SEREBRYAKOV All right, let them go to bed, but please, you go away, too. Thank you. I beg of you, please go away. In the name of our former friendship, don't refuse me. We'll talk some other time.

VOYNITSKY Our former friendship! . . . That's news to me.

YELENA Shh, please be quiet, George!

SEREBRYAKOV My dear, don't leave me alone with him! He'll begin his infernal lecturing.

VOYNITSKY This is absurd.

KHROUSCHOV'S *voice, behind the scene.* They're in the dining room? Here, take this, and please take care of my horse.

VOYNITSKY The doctor's here.

Enter KHROUSCHOV.

KHROUSCHOV What weather! It's terrible! The rain followed me all the way, and I just missed it. Well, how is everyone tonight?

SEREBRYAKOV I'm sorry we bothered you. Really, I don't need anything.

KHROUSCHOV It's quite all right! Now, what's ailing you, Alexander Vladimirovich? The idea of your getting sick. You know that's against the rules.

SEREBRYAKOV Why do doctors always speak to their patients in such a condescending tone?

KHROUSCHOV, *laughing.* Well, you shouldn't be so observant. . . . *In a gentle voice.* Now let's come and lie down on your bed. You can't be comfortable here and in bed you'll be warmer. So come along . . . I'll examine you there . . . and everything will be all right.

YELENA Do as the doctor says, Alexander.

KHROUSCHOV If you find it hard to walk, we can move you in your chair.

SEREBRYAKOV I can manage. . . . I'll walk . . . *Getting up.* Only they shouldn't have bothered you. KHROUSCHOV *and* SONYA *supporting him under the arm.* Besides, I don't believe in . . . in pharmacy. Why do you help me? . . . I can walk by myself. *Going out with* KHROUSCHOV *and* SONYA.

YELENA He so completely exhausts me, that I can hardly stand up.

VOYNITSKY He has exhausted you and I have exhausted myself. I haven't had a bit of sleep for three nights now.

YELENA There's something wrong in this house. Your mother hates everything, but her pamphlets and the professor. The professor is irritable; he doesn't trust me and he's afraid of you. Sonya is cross with her father and hasn't spoken to me; you hate my husband and openly sneer at your mother. I'm irritated and bored to death. Why, I've nearly burst into tears at least twenty times today. I can't figure out what's wrong; it's as if we are all at war with each other. But what's the sense of it?

VOYNITSKY Why don't you stop all your speculating?

YELENA There's something wrong in this house, that's why! You are a cultured and intelligent man, George. Certainly you must understand that the world is not destroyed by murderers and criminals, but by hate and malice and by all this spiteful gossiping and petty wrangling that goes on among our intellectuals. You must help me make peace. I can't do it alone.

VOYNITSKY, *seizing her hand.* My darling! First, help me to make peace with myself!

YELENA Let go! *Taking away her hand.* Go away!

VOYNITSKY The rain will soon be over, and all nature will awake refreshed. Only I am not refreshed by the storm. Night and day I am haunted by the thought that my life has been hopelessly wasted and is lost forever. My past doesn't count because I frittered it away on trifles, and the present is so grotesque in its senselessness. What shall I do with my life and my love? What's going to become of them? This glorious passion in my heart will be lost as a ray of sunlight is lost in a dark chasm, and my life will be lost with it.

YELENA When you speak to me of your love, I feel numb and don't know what to say. Forgive me, I have nothing to say. *Starting to go.* Good night!

VOYNITSKY, *barring her way.* If you only knew how it tortures me to think that beside me in this house is another life that is being

Voynitsky → escapes → drunk

wasted and is lost forever—yours! What are you waiting for? What accursed philosophy, what damn theory, stands in your way? Try and understand. The highest morality does not consist in putting fetters on your youth and in trying to suppress your thirst for life.

YELENA, *looking fixedly at him*. George, you're drunk!

VOYNITSKY Perhaps . . . perhaps.

YELENA Is Fyodor here?

VOYNITSKY He's spending the night. Perhaps I'm drunk . . . yes, perhaps I am; nothing's impossible.

YELENA Have you been drinking together? What for?

VOYNITSKY Because in that way at least I experience a semblance of life. Let me do that, Yelena!

YELENA You never used to drink, and you never used to talk so much. Go to bed! You bore me. And tell your friend Fyodor that if he won't stop pestering me, I'll see to it he stops. Now, please go!

VOYNITSKY, *kissing her hand*. My darling! . . . My wonderful one!

Enter KHROUSCHOV.

KHROUSCHOV Your husband is asking for you.

YELENA, *taking her hand away from* VOYNITSKY. Thank you, I'm coming. *Going out*.

KHROUSCHOV, *to* VOYNITSKY. Nothing is sacred to you! You and the dear lady who has just gone out ought to remember that her husband was once the husband of your own sister, and that a young girl lives under the same roof with you! The whole county is talking about your affair. Such a disgrace! *Going out to the patient*.

VOYNITSKY, *alone*. She's gone! *A pause*. It was ten years ago that I first met her at my sister's house. She was seventeen and I thirty-seven. Why didn't I fall in love with her then and propose to her? It would have been so easy . . . then! And if I had, she would now be my wife. Yes, tonight's thunderstorm would have awakened us both. But I would have held her in my arms and whispered: "Don't be afraid! I'm here." Oh, bewitching dream, so sweet that I smile when I think of it. *He laughs*. But, my God! Why are my thoughts so entangled? Why am I so old? Why won't she understand me? I despise all that rhetoric of hers, that indolent morality, that absurd talk about the destruction of the world. *A pause.* What's wrong with me? Oh, how I envy Fyodor with his women and good times, and even the Wood Demon with all his stupid talk of trees. They're sincere and open . . . free from this damn, poisonous irony.

Enter FYODOR IVANOVICH, *wrapped in a blanket.*

FYODOR, *in the doorway.* Are you alone? No women around? *Entering.* The storm woke me. It was a wonderful rain. What time is it?

VOYNITSKY The devil only knows.

FYODOR I thought I heard Yelena's voice.

VOYNITSKY She was here a moment ago.

FYODOR What a magnificent woman! *Looking at the bottles of medicine on the table.* What's this? Peppermint pills? *Tasting.* Yes, a magnificent woman! . . . What's wrong with the professor? Is he sick?

VOYNITSKY He's very sick.

FYODOR I can't understand such an existence. They say the ancient Greeks used to throw their sickly children off the cliffs of Mont Blanc. They ought to throw his kind off too.

VOYNITSKY, *irritably.* It wasn't Mont Blanc, but the Tarpeian rock. What a fool you are!

FYODOR Well, if it's a rock. . . . What difference does it make? What's the matter with you tonight? You seem so gloomy. Is it because you feel sorry for the professor?

VOYNITSKY Leave me alone. *A pause.*

FYODOR Or perhaps you're in love with the professor's wife? Why, that's it. . . . Sigh for her. . . . Only listen to me: If I ever find out that even a fraction of the rumors that are floating about the county are true, I'll throw *you* off the Tarpeian rock. And I'm not kidding.

VOYNITSKY She's my friend!

FYODOR Already?

VOYNITSKY What do you mean by "already"?

FYODOR A woman can be a man's friend only after having first been his acquaintance and then his mistress . . . then she becomes his friend.

VOYNITSKY What a coarse philosophy!

FYODOR Let's drink to it. Come on, I've still got a bottle of chartreuse. We'll drink it and when dawn comes we'll go over to my place. All right? *Seeing* SONYA *enter.* I beg your pardon, I haven't got a tie on! *Runs out.*

SONYA Uncle George, you and Fyodor have been drinking champagne again and driving about in a troika. The bright birds singing together! It's all very well for Fyodor, he's always been like that. But why must you follow his example? It's wrong at your age.

VOYNITSKY Age has nothing to do with it. If there isn't any reality, then you must create illusions. That's better than nothing.

SONYA But the hay hasn't been brought in, and Guerasim said today that it would rot because of all this rain. And here you waste your time living in illusions. *Frightened.* Uncle, there are tears in your eyes!

VOYNITSKY Tears? No . . . nonsense! . . . You looked at me then just as your dead mother used to. Oh, my darling . . . *Eagerly kissing her hands and face.* My sister . . . my sweet sister! . . . Where are you now? Oh, if you only knew; if you only knew!

SONYA If she only knew what, Uncle?

VOYNITSKY It's very sad, so useless . . . *Enter* KHROUSCHOV. But never mind . . . I'll tell you later. . . . Now, I'd better go. . . . *Going out.*

KHROUSCHOV Your father refuses to listen to anything I say. I tell him he has gout, and he insists it's rheumatism; I tell him to lie down, and he sits up. *Taking his hat.* My nerves can't take it.

SONYA He's been spoiled. Put down your hat and wait till the rain stops. Won't you have something to eat?

KHROUSCHOV Yes, I think I will.

SONYA I like to eat at night. I'm sure we'll find something in the sideboard . . . *Rummaging there.* He doesn't need a doctor. What he needs is a dozen ladies standing around him gazing into his eyes and sighing, "Professor, Professor!" Here's some cheese. . . .

KHROUSCHOV You shouldn't talk about your father that way. I agree, he's a difficult person; but compared to the others, well, all the Uncle Georges and Orlovskys aren't worth his little finger.

SONYA Here's a bottle of something. . . . I'm not speaking of my father, but of the great man. I love my father, but I'm sick of

great men with their Chinese ceremonies. . . . *They sit down.*
What a downpour! *A flash.* Oh!

KHROUSCHOV The storm's passing. It's only rained a little bit
here. . . .

SONYA, *pouring out.* Here you are!

KHROUSCHOV May you live to be a hundred! *Drinking.*

SONYA You're angry because we bothered you tonight?

KHROUSCHOV Not at all. In fact, if you hadn't called me, I'd be
sleeping now, and seeing you like this is much pleasanter than seeing you in my dreams.

SONYA Why do you look so annoyed then?

KHROUSCHOV Because I am annoyed. We're alone here, so I can
speak frankly. Oh, Sonya, how I'd love to take you away from here
this very minute. I couldn't bear to live in this house, and I can't
help but feel it's poisoning you. There is your father, completely
absorbed in his books, and in his gout; then there's your Uncle
George; and finally your stepmother. . . .

SONYA What about her?

KHROUSCHOV There are some things I just can't say. I just can't.
But there's so much I don't understand about people. In a human
being everything ought to be beautiful: the face, clothes, the soul,
the thoughts. . . . Oh, I've seen lots of beautiful faces and pretty
clothes, and I've been carried away by them; but as for the soul
and thoughts, my God! A beautiful dress sometimes covers a soul
so black that no amount of make-up will ever be able to hide it.
. . . Forgive me, I'm very upset. . . . But you are very dear to
me. . . .

SONYA, *dropping a knife.* I've dropped it . . .

KHROUSCHOV, *picking it up.* That's all right. . . . *After a pause.*
Have you ever noticed when you cross a dense forest in the middle
of the night and see a small light shining ahead in the distance,
how you forget your weariness and the darkness and the sharp
branches that lash your face? . . . As you know, I work from
morning till night, winter and summer, and I fight with those who
don't understand me. At times I suffer a great deal . . . But at
last I've found my light. . . . I can't say that I love you more than
all the world. Love to me is not everything in life . . . love is a
reward. But my darling, there's no greater reward than that for
one who works and struggles and suffers . . .

SONYA, *in agitation.* I'm sorry . . . Can I ask you something, Mihail?

KHROUSCHOV What? Ask it quickly. . . .

SONYA Well, you come to our house a lot, and sometimes I go with you to yours. Admit it, don't you feel guilty about it?

KHROUSCHOV What do you mean?

SONYA I mean, don't your liberal feelings ever conflict with your being close friends with us. I've been to the Institute, Yelena is an aristocrat, we dress fashionably; and you're a liberal. . . .

KHROUSCHOV But . . . why . . . talk about that now? This isn't the time for that.

SONYA But you dig peat and plant trees . . . and it's all very strange . . . To come right to the point, you're a socialist. . . .

KHROUSCHOV Liberal, socialist! . . . Sonya, how can you be serious about it? Why even your voice is trembling!

SONYA But I am serious. Very serious.

KHROUSCHOV But you can't be, you can't. . . .

SONYA I promise you I am. Suppose I had a sister and you fell in love with her and married her. You'd never forgive yourself and you'd be ashamed in front of the doctors at Zemstvo. You'd feel ashamed for having married an aristocrat, who dressed in the latest fashions and didn't know how to work. I know you would, I can see it in your eyes. So all these forests of yours, the peat, the embroidered shirts, they're nothing but a facade, an act. To be frank, it's all a lie!

KHROUSCHOV Why? Why have you insulted me? . . . But I guess I am a fool; it serves me right. I shouldn't have intruded where I wasn't welcome! Good-bye. *Going to the door.*

SONYA Forgive me. . . . I was blunt, I apologize.

KHROUSCHOV, *returning.* If you only knew how oppressive it is here! Everyone here is suspicious. They look at a man and try to make him into a socialist, a psychopath, a phrase-monger, anything you like, but a human being. "Oh, he's a psychopath!" and they're satisfied. "He's a phrase-monger," and they're as happy as if they'd discovered America. And when people don't understand me and don't know what label to use, they don't blame themselves, but me, and so they say, "He's peculiar, neurotic!" You're not even twenty, but you are already like your father and your Uncle George—old and stuffy, and I wouldn't be the least surprised if you were to call me in to cure your gout. One can't live like that! Whoever I am, look straight into my eyes, candidly, without reservations, without reforms; above all try to see me as a human being; otherwise there will never be any satisfaction in your relationships with other people. Good-bye! And remember what I've said: with cunning, suspicious eyes like yours, you will never be able to love! . . .

SONYA That's not true!

KHROUSCHOV It is true!

SONYA It's not true! Since you're so smart . . . I love you! I love you, and it hurts me. Now leave me alone! Go away, I beg you . . . don't come to our house . . . don't come. . . .

KHROUSCHOV Allow me then! *Going out.*

SONYA, *alone.* I've made him angry. God forbid that I should ever have a temper like his! *After a pause.* He speaks very well, but who can guarantee that it is not just talk? All he thinks about are forests, and planting trees. . . . That's all very well, but it is quite possible that all this is neurotic . . . *Covering her face with her hands.* I can't figure it out! *Crying.* He's studied medicine and yet his chief interests are outside medicine. . . . It's all so strange, so strange . . . Oh, God, help me!

Enter YELENA ANDREYEVNA.

YELENA, *opening the windows.* The storm's over! What a refreshing breeze! *After a pause.* Where's the Wood Demon?

SONYA He's gone.

YELENA Sonya!

SONYA Yes?

YELENA How much longer are you going to be annoyed with me? We've done nothing to hurt each other. Why should we be enemies? It's time we stopped. . . .

SONYA I feel this too . . . *Embracing her.* Oh, let's be friends again!

YELENA With all my heart! *Both are strongly moved.*

SONYA Has father gone to bed?

YELENA No, he's sitting up in the drawing room . . . You know, it's strange . . . I guess only the Lord knows what's kept us apart all these weeks. *Looking at the table.* What's all this?

SONYA The Wood Demon just had some supper.

YELENA Here's some wine . . . Let's drink to our friendship.

SONYA Yes, let's.

YELENA From the same glass . . . *Pouring out wine.* It's much better that way. Now, we are friends, aren't we?

SONYA Friends! *They drink and embrace.* I've wanted us to be friends for so long, but I felt shy . . . *Crying.*

YELENA Why are you crying then?

SONYA I don't know. *Pause.* Let's forget it.

YELENA There, there don't cry. *She cries.* Silly! Now I'm crying too. *Pause.* You're angry with me because you think I married your father for his money, but you mustn't believe all the gossip you hear. I swear to you I married him for love. I was fascinated by his fame and his learning. I know now it wasn't real love, although it seemed real enough at the time. I'm innocent, and yet ever since my marriage your searching suspicious eyes have been accusing me of an imaginary crime.

SONYA Peace! Come, let's forget the past. This is the second time today that I've heard that I have cunning, suspicious eyes.

YELENA You mustn't look at people that way. It isn't right. You must trust and believe in people . . . or life becomes impossible.

SONYA "A frightened crow fears the bush." I've been disillusioned so many times.

YELENA In whom? Your father is a good, honest man, he works hard. Today you belittled him for being happy. If he was happy—absorbed in his work, he wasn't aware of it. I've never tried to hurt either your father or you. Uncle George is a good, honest, but unhappy and dissatisfied man . . . Whom, then, can't you trust? *After a pause.*

SONYA Tell me, truthfully, as a friend . . . Are you happy?

YELENA Truthfully, no.

SONYA I knew that. One more question: Would you like your husband to be young?

YELENA What a child you are! Of course, I would. *Laughing.* Go on, ask me something else.

SONYA Do you like the Wood Demon?

YELENA Yes, very much.

SONYA, *laughing.* I have a silly look on my face . . . don't I? He's just left, and his voice still rings in my ears; I can hear the sound of his footsteps; I can see his face in the dark window. Oh, I want so to tell you all that I have in my heart! But I can't, I'm ashamed. Come to my room and I'll tell you there. Oh, what a silly person you must think I am. Tell me . . . Is he really a nice man?

YELENA Very, very nice. . . .

SONYA His forests and his peat—they seem so strange to me. . . . I don't know what to make of them.

YELENA It isn't a matter of forests, dear. He's a man of genius. Do you realize what that means? It means he is a man of great courage, one with deep insights and clear and far-reaching vision. He plants a tree or digs up some peat and his mind swings a thousand years into the future and he envisions the happiness of all mankind. Such people are rare and should be loved. God bless you. You're both good, honest, courageous people. So he's wild at times; you're sensible and clear-headed . . . you'll get along beautifully together. *Getting up.* As for me, I'm worthless—an empty and quite pathetic woman. I've always been worthless; in music, in love, in my husband's house . . . in fact, in everything. If I dared even for a moment to consider . . . Oh, Sonya, I am really very, very unhapy. *Walking excitedly back and forth.* I can never achieve happiness in this world. Never. Why do you laugh?

SONYA, *laughing and putting her hands over her face.* I am so happy! So very happy!

YELENA, *wringing her hands.* And how unhappy I am!

SONYA I am happy . . . happy.

YELENA How I should like some music now. I believe I could play again.

SONYA, *embracing her.* Oh, do, do! I couldn't possibly go to sleep now. Do play.

YELENA Yes, I will. Your father's still awake. Music annoys him when he's ill, but if he says I may, then I shall play a little. Go . . . go and ask him, Sonya.

SONYA I'll be right back. *Going out.*

The sound of the nightwatchman's rattle comes from the garden.

YELENA I haven't played for a long time. And now I shall sit and play and cry like a child . . . *Going to the window.* Yefim, is that you out there?

THE WATCHMAN'S *voice.* Ye-s!

YELENA Don't make so much noise. Your master is ill.

THE WATCHMAN's *voice.* I'm going! *Whistling.* Nigger! Jack! Nigger!

After a pause.

SONYA, *returning.* He says "no"!

Curtain.

ACT III

The drawing room of the SEREBRYAKOVS' *house. There are three doors: one to the right, one to the left, and one in the middle. It is early afternoon. Off-stage* YELENA *can be heard playing Lensky's aria before the duel from the opera* Eugene Onegin. ORLOVSKY, VOYNITSKY, *and* FYODOR IVANOVICH (*the latter dressed in a Circassian uniform with a hussar's hat in his hand*) *are seated.*

VOYNITSKY, *listening to the music.* Yelena's playing my favorite aria . . . *The music comes to an end.* Yes . . . it's a beautiful piece. . . . I've never been so bored in my life . . .

FYODOR You've never really been bored, my friend. Why when I was in Serbia that was the real thing! It was hot and stuffy and dirty and I was hung over . . . Once I remember sitting in a dirty little shed . . . Captain Kashkinazi was there, too . . . We'd talked about everything there was to talk about, there was nothing to do, no place to go, we didn't want a drink— It was so bad you wanted to hang yourself just for excitement. We just sat there, looking at each other . . . He at me, I at him; he at me, I at him . . . We look at each other and don't know why we're doing it. . . . An hour goes by, then another, and still we keep on looking. All of a sudden he jumps up for no reason and draws his sabre and comes after me . . . I draw—for he'd have killed me!—and it started: chic-chac, chic-chac, chic-chac, and finally after great difficulty, we were separated. I didn't get hurt, but to this very day Captain Kashkinazi has a scar on his face. That's what can happen when you're really bored.

ORLOVSKY Yes, I guess such things happen.

Enter SONYA.

SONYA, *aside*. I don't know what to do with myself! *Walking and laughing*.

ORLOVSKY Sweetheart, where are you going? Why don't you sit down with us for a bit?

SONYA Fedya, come here . . . *Taking* FYODOR *aside*. Come here. . . .

FYODOR What do you want? What are you so happy about?

SONYA Promise me that you will do what I ask you?

FYODOR Tell me, first.

SONYA Go over to the . . . Wood Demon's.

FYODOR What for?

SONYA Just because . . . just drive over and see him . . . ask him why he hasn't been here for the last two weeks.

FYODOR She's blushing! Shame on you! Look everybody, Sonya's in love!

ALL Sonya's in love!

SONYA *covers her face and runs away*.

FYODOR She's flitting about from room to room like a shadow, and doesn't know what to do with herself. She's in love with the Wood Demon.

ORLOVSKY She's a delightful girl . . . I wish, Fyodor, that you'd marry her. You won't find another girl like her. But that's the way it goes . . . But it would certainly be wonderful for me. Then I could come and see you and your wife, and the family by the fireside, and the samovar humming on the table.

FYODOR I'm not very good about these things, father; but if I ever was crazy enough to get married, I'd marry Julia. At least she's small. If you're going to make a mistake, make it a small one. And she's a good housekeeper, too. *Clapping his forehead*. Now I've got an idea!

ORLOVSKY What's that?

FYODOR Let's have some champagne!

VOYNITSKY It's too early, and besides it's too hot for champagne . . . wait a while . . .

ORLOVSKY, *admiringly*. What a boy! He wants champagne at this hour.

Enter YELENA, *walking across the stage.*

VOYNITSKY Look at her. Roaming up and down out of sheer idleness and boredom. A beautiful picture, I must say.

YELENA Stop it, George! I'm surprised it doesn't bore you playing the same note from morning till night.

VOYNITSKY, *barring her way.* A talented artist! But do you look like an artist? Apathetic, indolent, lazy . . . You're so virtuous that I can't stand to look at you . . .

YELENA Don't look then . . . let me go. . . .

VOYNITSKY Why are you pining away? *In a lively tone.* Come, darling, my sweet one, be sensible! A mermaid's blood runs in your veins, why don't you act like one?

YELENA Leave me alone!

VOYNITSKY Let yourself go for once in your life; fall head over heels in love with some other water sprite. . . .

FYODOR And plunge headlong into a bottomless quarry with him and leave the almighty professor and the rest of us amazed and waving our hands!

VOYNITSKY Be a mermaid and love while you may!

YELENA There's no need for you to tell me how to live. I'd know, without your telling me, how I'd live if I could. Oh, to be free as a bird, to fly away from all your drowsy faces and your monotonous mumblings and forget that you've even existed at all! Oh, to forget oneself and what one is . . . But I am a coward; I am afraid, and tortured by my conscience. I know that if I were to be unfaithful, every other wife would do the same thing and leave her husband, too. But then God would punish me. If it weren't for my conscience, I'd show you how free my life could be. *She goes out.*

ORLOVSKY My, but she's beautiful.

VOYNITSKY I believe I'll soon begin to despise that woman! She's shy like a little girl, and philosophizes like an old deacon, wrapped up in virtue! She makes my blood boil.

ORLOVSKY Stop it now . . . By the way, where's the professor?

VOYNITSKY In his study, where else? You'll find him writing away as usual.

ORLOVSKY He wrote me and asked me to come here to talk over some business. What's it about?

VOYNITSKY He doesn't have any business. He writes junk, grumbles and is jealous, that's all.

ZHELTOUKHIN *and* JULIA *enter by the door on the right.*

ZHELTOUKHIN Hello everybody! *Greeting them.*

JULIA How are you, godfather! *Kissing Orlovsky.* Hello, Fedya! *Kissing him.* And you, too, George Petrovich! *Kissing him.*

ZHELTOUKHIN Is Alexander Vladimirovich here?

ORLOVSKY Yes. He's in his study.

ZHELTOUKHIN Will you excuse me, then? He wrote saying he wanted to see me on some business matter . . . *Going out.*

JULIA George Petrovich, did the barley you asked for come yesterday?

VOYNITSKY Yes, it did. Thanks. How much do we owe you? We also owe you for something in the spring. I don't remember what . . . but we've got to settle our accounts. It messes things up, and I like to get the bills paid.

JULIA In the spring we sent you eight bushels of corn, two heifers, a calf, and some butter.

VOYNITSKY How much does it all come to?

JULIA I can't tell you right off without a counting board.

VOYNITSKY Here, I'll get you one, if you need it . . . *Goes out and returns with a counting board.*

ORLOVSKY Sweet, is your brother well?

JULIA Yes, thank God he is, godfather. Oh, where did you get such a pretty tie?

ORLOVSKY In town, at Kirpichov's.

JULIA It's so pretty! I'll buy one like it for Lennie.

VOYNITSKY Here's the counting board.

JULIA *sits down and raps the beads on the counting board.*

ORLOVSKY The good Lord's certainly given Lennie a fine manager! Imagine, a slip of a thing like that working away. Just look at her!

FYODOR Yes, and all he does is lie around pressing his cheek. How lazy can you get?

JULIA Now you've got me all mixed up.

VOYNITSKY Come on, let's go into another room. It's dull in here anyway. . . . *Yawning.*

ORLOVSKY Whatever you say . . . I don't mind.

They go out by the left door.

JULIA, *alone; after a pause.* Fedya all dressed up in a Circassian uniform . . . That's what happens when parents aren't strict enough with their children. He's the handsomest man in the county, he's witty and rich, and yet not a bit of good. . . . He's hopeless! *Rapping on the counting board.*

Enter SONYA.

SONYA So you're here, Julia dear? I didn't know . . .

JULIA, *kissing her.* Sonya!

SONYA What are you doing? Counting? What a fine manager you are—the mere sight of you makes me envious! Why don't you get married?

JULIA Well, one or two men have been mentioned, but I wasn't interested in them. A real suitor wouldn't want to marry me! *Sighing.* No!

SONYA But why?

JULIA I'm uneducated; I didn't even finish high school.

SONYA But why not?

JULIA It was too hard for me. SONYA *laughs.* Why are you laughing?

SONYA I feel so strange inside . . . Oh, Julia, I'm so happy today I'm almost bored by my own happiness. . . . I don't know what to do with myself. . . . Let's talk of something . . . Have you ever been in love? JULIA *affirmatively nods her head.* Yes? Is he interesting? JULIA *whispers in her ear.* Fyodor?

JULIA, *affirmatively nodding her head.* And you?

SONYA Yes . . . only not with Fyodor. *Laughing.* Go on, tell me more. . . .

JULIA I've wanted to talk with you for a long time, Sonya.

SONYA Well, go ahead.

JULIA I want to be honest . . . You see . . . I've always liked you . . . I've got lots of friends, but you're my best one. If you were to say to me, Julia, give me ten horses, or two hundred sheep, I'd do it with pleasure . . . I'd do anything for you . . .

SONYA What are you blushing for?

JULIA I'm embarrassed . . . I . . . I really like you very much. Of all my friends you're the very best . . . You're not proud . . . What a pretty dress you're wearing!

SONYA We'll talk about the dress later . . . Go on. . . .

JULIA, *getting up.* I don't know how to be sophisticated. . . . I'm proposing to you . . . Make me happy . . . I mean . . . I mean . . . I mean . . . marry Lennie. *Covering her face.*

SONYA, *getting up.* We'd better not talk about it, Julia dear . . . *Enter* YELENA.

YELENA There's no place you can go in this house. The Orlovskys and George are everywhere; no matter what room I go into, they're there. It's so exasperating. What are they doing here? Why don't they go somewhere else?

JULIA, *through tears.* How do you do, Yelena Andreyevna? *Making to kiss her.*

YELENA How do you do, Julia dear! Forgive me, I don't like continuous kissing. Sonya, what's your father doing? *A pause.* Sonya, why don't you answer me? I ask you: what's your father doing? *A pause.* Sonya, why don't you answer me? I asked you what your father was doing. *A pause.* Why don't you answer me, Sonya?

SONYA You want to know? Come here . . . *Taking her aside.* Well, I'll tell you . . . My heart is too pure today and I can't talk to you and go on pretending. Here, take this! *Handing her a letter.* I found it in the garden. Julia, let's go! *Going out with* JULIA *by the left door.*

YELENA, *alone.* What's this? A letter from George to me! But why should I be blamed for it? Oh, how cruel of her! . . . How mean! Her heart is so pure that she can't talk to me . . . My God, how could she insult me like that! I'm getting . . . I'm going to faint!

FYODOR, *coming out by the left door and crossing the stage.* Why are you always startled when you see me? *A pause.* H'm! . . . *Taking the letter from her hands and tearing it to pieces.* Throw this away. You must think only of me. *A pause.*

YELENA What's the meaning of that?

FYODOR It means that if I have my eye on a woman, it's no use her trying to escape from my grasp.

YELENA Not at all, it simply means that you're an insolent fool.

FYODOR Tonight at half-past seven you'll wait for me on the little bridge in the garden . . . Do you understand? . . . I've nothing more to say to you . . . And so, my angel, until seven-thirty! *Trying to take her arm.* YELENA *gives him a slap on the face.* Isn't that a little too much!

YELENA Go away!

FYODOR As you wish . . . *Walking away and returning.* I am touched . . . Let's talk it over peacefully. . . . You see . . . I've experienced everything in the world; I've even had goldfish soup. But I've never flown in a balloon, nor carried off the wife of a learned professor. . . .

YELENA Please, go!

FYODOR In a minute. . . . I've experienced everything . . . And that's made me so insolent that I never know what I'll do next. I mean, I am telling you all this because I want you to know that if you ever need a friend or a faithful dog, you've only to turn to me . . . I am touched. . . .

YELENA I don't want any dogs. . . . So, please go!

FYODOR As you wish. *With feeling.* Nevertheless, I am touched . . . deeply touched. . . . Yes . . . *Irresolutely going out.*

YELENA, *alone.* My head aches . . . Every night I have nightmares that something terrible is going to happen. . . . But what a dreadful place this is! The young people were born here and grew up together, and they're so close and always kissing one another; soon, I think, they'll have devoured one another. . . . The forests are being saved by the Wood Demon, but there's no one to save human beings. *She goes to the left door, but on noticing* ZHELTOUKHIN *and* JULIA *coming in by that door, she goes out by the middle door.*

JULIA How unfortunate we are, Lennie. I'm so unhappy.

ZHELTOUKHIN But who gave you the right to talk to her? You've spoiled everything for me! She'll think that I can't speak for myself, and . . . it's so common! I've told you a thousand times to forget the whole affair. Nothing but humiliation and all these hints. Oh, it's vile . . . The old man must have guessed that I'm in love with her, and already he's taking advantage of my feelings! He wants me to buy this estate from him.

JULIA How much does he want for it?

ZHELTOUKHIN Sh-sh! . . . They're coming. . . .

Enter by the left door: SEREBRYAKOV, ORLOVSKY, *and* MARYA VASSILYEVNA, *the latter reading a pamphlet as she comes in.*

ORLOVSKY I'm not feeling too well, myself. The last two days my head and my whole body have been aching. . . .

SEREBRYAKOV Where are the others? I don't like this house. It is a labyrinth. Twenty-six huge rooms. People are all over the place and you can never find anyone. *Ringing.* Ask George Petrovich and Yelena to come here.

ZHELTOUKHIN Julia, you're not doing anything; go and find George and Yelena. JULIA *goes out.*

SEREBRYAKOV After all, one can become reconciled to being an invalid, but not to this absurd way of life you have here in the country. I feel as if I had been cast off from this earth and dumped onto a strange planet.

ORLOVSKY Well, it depends on how you look at it. . . .

MARYA, *reading.* Will somebody give me a pencil. . . . Here's another contradiction. I'll have to make a note of it.

ORLOVSKY Here you are, Your Excellency! *Handing her a pencil and kissing her hand.*

Enter VOYNITSKY.

VOYNITSKY You wanted to see me?

SEREBRYAKOV Yes, George.

VOYNITSKY What do you want?

SEREBRYAKOV Now . . . why are you so upset? *A pause.* If it's anything I've done, I beg your forgiveness.

VOYNITSKY Forget that high and mighty tone . . . Let's get to the point . . . What do you want?

Enter YELENA.

SEREBRYAKOV Here's Lenotchka, too. . . . Sit down, ladies and gentlemen. *A pause.* I have asked you here, my friends, to announce that the Inspector-General is coming. . . . But all joking aside, this is an important matter. I have invited you here, gentlemen, to ask you for your aid and advice, and realizing your unbounded kindness, I believe I can count on both. I'm a scholar and bound to my library, and I'm not familiar with practical affairs. I am unable, I find, to dispense with the help of well-informed people such as you, Ivan, and you, Leonid, and you, George. The truth is, *"manet omnes una nox,"* that is to say, our lives rest in the hands of God, and as I am old and ill, I realize that the time has come for me to dispose of my property in the interests of my family. My life is nearly finished, and I'm not thinking of myself, but I must consider my young wife and daughter. To continue living in the country is impossible for them.

YELENA It's all the same to me.

SEREBRYAKOV We were just not meant for country life. And yet, we cannot afford to live in town on the income from this estate. The day before yesterday I sold some of the woods for timber for four thousand roubles, but that is an expedient which we can't resort to every year. We must work out some method of guaranteeing ourselves a permanent and . . . a more or less fixed annual income. With this object in view, a plan has occurred to me which I now have the honor of proposing to you for your consideration. I shall give you only a rough outline of it, omitting all the bothersome and trivial details. Our estate does not yield, on an average, more than two percent on the investment. I propose to sell it. If then we invest our capital in bonds and other suitable securities, it will bring us four to five percent and we should probably have a surplus of several thousand roubles, with which we could buy a small house in Finland. . . .

VOYNITSKY Wait a minute, I don't believe I heard you quite right . . . Repeat what you've just said . . .

SEREBRYAKOV I said we would invest the money in bonds and with the surplus buy a house in Finland . . .

VOYNITSKY No, not Finland. . . . You said something else . . .

SEREBRYAKOV I propose to sell this estate.

VOYNITSKY Yes, that was it. . . . So you are going to sell the estate . . . Splendid! That's a fine idea! . . . And what do you propose to do with my mother and myself?

SEREBRYAKOV That will be taken care of in due course. After all, we can't do everything at once, can we?

VOYNITSKY Wait a minute! It's clear that up to now I've never had an ounce of sense in my head. I've always been stupid enough to think that the estate belonged to Sonya. My late father bought it as a wedding gift for my sister, and as our laws were made for Russians and not for Turks, I foolishly imagined that my sister's estate would pass on to her child.

SEREBRYAKOV Why, of course, it belongs to Sonya. Has anyone denied it? I don't wish to sell it without Sonya's consent; on the contrary, what I'm doing is for her welfare.

voynitsky This is absolutely crazy! Either I've gone insane or . . . or . . .

marya George, don't contradict the professor! He knows better than we do what's right and what's wrong.

voynitsky Give me some water . . . *Drinking*. Go on! Say anything you like.

serebryakov I can't understand why you are so upset! I don't pretend that my plan is ideal, and if you all object to it, I shall not insist.

Enter dyadin, *wearing a frock-coat, white gloves and a broad-brimmed top hat.*

dyadin Good afternoon, ladies and gentlemen. I'm sorry to come in without being announced. I know I shouldn't have done it, and I hope you'll excuse me, but there wasn't a single servant in the hall.

serebryakov, *embarrassed*. It's good to see you . . . Please come in . . .

dyadin, *bowing ceremoniously*. Your Excellency, ladies and gentlemen, my intrusion into your domains has a double aim. I've come, first of all, to pay my humble respects to you, sir. Secondly, since we're having such beautiful weather, I should like to invite you all to visit me. I live in a water-mill which I rent from our mutual friend the Wood Demon. It's a secluded and poetic spot where at night you can hear the splashing of the water nymphs and during the day. . . .

voynitsky Wait a minute, Waffles, we're discussing business. Wait a little . . . later . . . *To* serebryakov. Here, ask him what he thinks; this estate was purchased from his uncle.

serebryakov Ah! Why should I ask questions? What good would it do?

voynitsky The estate was bought for ninety-five thousand roubles. My father paid seventy thousand and left a mortgage of twenty-five thousand. Now listen . . . This estate could never have been bought if I had not renounced my share of the inheritance in favor of my sister, whom I dearly loved. And what's more, I worked like a slave for ten years and paid off the mortgage.

serebryakov What do you want me to do, then?

voynitsky Thanks entirely to my personal efforts, the estate is now free from debt and in good condition; and now . . . as I am getting old, you propose to kick me out!

SEREBRYAKOV I don't understand what you're talking about!

VOYNITSKY For twenty-five years I have managed this estate. I have sent you the proceeds from it regularly like an honest servant, and in all those years you have never once even thanked me! No, not once, neither in my youth nor now. You gave me a meager salary of five hundred roubles a year . . . a beggar's pittance, and you have never once thought of adding a rouble to it.

SEREBRYAKOV How should I know about such things, George? I'm not a practical man and I don't understand such matters. You could have increased it as much as you liked!

VOYNITSKY Yes, why didn't I steal? Don't you all despise me for not stealing? It would have been only fair, and I wouldn't be a poor man now.

MARYA, *sternly.* George!

DYADIN, *in agitation.* Don't, George . . . don't . . . This is so upsetting. . . . Why spoil such a pleasant relationship? *Embracing him.* Please stop.

VOYNITSKY For twenty-five years I've been sitting here with my mother buried like a mole. Every thought and hope we had was yours and yours alone. All day long we talked with pride of you and your work; and we spoke your name with respect . . . yes, almost with reverence. We wasted our evenings reading your books and articles, which I now detest from the bottom of my heart.

DYADIN Don't, George, don't! . . . Please!

SEREBRYAKOV What in God's name do you want, anyhow?

VOYNITSKY We used to consider you a superman, a kind of demigod, but now the scales have fallen from my eyes and I see you as you are! You write about art without knowing a thing about it. Why, those books of yours which I used to think were so wonderful aren't worth a copper kopeck!

SEREBRYAKOV Can't anyone stop him? I'm leaving here immediately!

YELENA George, I demand that you stop this! Do you hear?

VOYNITSKY I refuse! *Barring* SEREBRYAKOV's *way.* Wait! I haven't finished yet! You have ruined my life! I have never really lived!

Thanks to you, my best years have gone for nothing. They have been ruined! I hate you!

DYADIN I can't stand it! . . . I can't! . . . I'm going . . . *Going out in violent agitation by the door on the right.*

SEREBRYAKOV What do you want from me? What right do you have to speak to me like that? If the estate is yours, take it. I don't want it!

ZHELTOUKHIN, *aside* Now the fat's in the fire! . . . I'm getting out of here. *Going out.*

YELENA If you don't stop, I'll go away from this hell right now. *Crying out.* I can't stand it any longer!

VOYNITSKY A life ruined! I'm gifted, I'm intelligent, courageous. . . . If I'd a normal life, I might have been a Schopenhauer, a Dostoevsky. . . . I'm talking nonsense! I am going insane! . . . Mother, I'm in despair! Oh, mother!

MARYA Do as Alexander tells you!

VOYNITSKY Mother! What am I to do? Never mind, don't tell me! I know myself what I must do! *To* SEREBRYAKOV. You will remember me! *Going out the middle door;* MARYA VASSILYEVNA *following after him.*

SEREBRYAKOV This is too much! What does it all mean? Take that madman out of here.

ORLOVSKY He'll be all right, Alexander; let him calm down a bit. Don't get so upset.

SEREBRYAKOV I can't live under the same roof with him! He's always there *Pointing to the middle door.* almost beside me . . . Let him move into the village, or into one of the wings; or I'll move myself. But I cannot stay in the same house with him.

YELENA, *to her husband.* If anything like this happens again, I'll leave this house!

SEREBRYAKOV Don't try to frighten me, please!

YELENA I'm not trying to frighten you, but you all seem to have agreed to make my life pure hell . . . I'll leave this place, I tell you!

SEREBRYAKOV Everybody knows perfectly well that you are young and I am old, and that you're doing me a great favor by living here. . . .

YELENA Go on! . . . Go on! . . .

ORLOVSKY Why, why, why! . . . My dear friends!

Enter KHROUSCHOV *hurriedly.*

KHROUSCHOV, *in agitation.* I'm glad I found you, Alexander Vladimirovich . . . Excuse me for interrupting. . . . But that isn't the point. How could you do it?

SEREBRYAKOV What do you mean?

KHROUSCHOV Forgive me, I'm upset . . . I've been riding very fast . . . Alexander Vladimirovich, I hear that you've just sold your wood to Kirpichov for timber. If it is true, and not just gossip, then I beg you, don't do it.

YELENA Mihail Lvovich, my husband isn't in the mood now to talk about business. Won't you come with me into the garden?

KHROUSCHOV But I must settle it now!

YELENA As you please . . . I can't do any more . . . *Going out.*

KHROUSCHOV Let me go over to Kirpichov and tell him that you've changed your mind . . . Please? To destroy a thousand trees for the sake of two or three thousand roubles, for women's rags, whims, luxury . . . To destroy them so that posterity should curse our savagery! If you, a scholar, a famous man can do such a thing, then others below you will do it, too. This is terrible!

ORLOVSKY Misha, let's talk about it later!

SEREBRYAKOV Come, let's go in, Ivan Ivanich; will there never be any peace here.

KHROUSCHOV, *barring* SEREBRYAKOV's *way.* Wait a minute. Look, professor . . . In three months' time I'll have the money and I'll buy it myself.

ORLOVSKY Forgive me, Misha, I know this is upsetting . . . You're a man of ideas . . . and we respect you for it, *Bowing.* but why make such a fuss?

KHROUSCHOV, *flaring up.* My dear godfather, there are too many good-natured men on earth, and I've always been suspicious of this! They're good-natured because they're indifferent!

ORLOVSKY Have you come here to quarrel, my boy? Don't! An idea is an idea, but you need a heart, too. *Pointing to the heart.* Without that, all your forests and peat aren't worth a kopeck . . . Please don't be offended, but you're still so young . . . oh, how very green!

SEREBRYAKOV, *sharply.* And next time, please don't bother to come unless you're invited; and please no more of your psychopathic pranks! Everyone here seems determined to try my patience, well, you've succeeded . . . Now, please leave me alone! All these forests of yours and the peat are nothing more than the delirium of a psychopath—there, if you must have it, is my opinion! Come, Ivan Ivanich! *Going out.*

ORLOVSKY, *following after him.* Alexander, that was going too far, why be so harsh? *Going out.*

KHROUSCHOV, *alone, after a pause.* Delirium, psychopath! . . . According to the scholar I'm mad. . . . I bow to your authority, Excellency, and I'm going home immediately to shave my head . . . No! It is the earth, that let's you go on living, which is mad! *Going hurriedly towards the right door;* SONYA, *who has stood listening outside all through the last scene, coming in by the left door.*

SONYA, *running after him.* Stop! . . . I heard everything . . . Say something! . . . Quickly . . . for I can't stand it much longer and will do it myself!

KHROUSCHOV Sophia Alexandrovna, I've already said all that I can say. I begged your father to spare the trees. I know I'm right, but he insulted me, and called me a madman . . . I mad!

SONYA Please, please! . . .

KHROUSCHOV No, those who hide a cruel heart behind their learning, those who pass off their lack of compassion as profound wisdom, no, they aren't mad. And those unfaithful women who marry old men so they can have elegant clothes bought with money gained by cutting down forests, no; they aren't mad either!

SONYA Listen to me, listen! . . . *Grasping his hands.* Let me say . . .

KHROUSCHOV Let's put an end to all this. I am a stranger to you, and I know what you think, and I've nothing more to say. Good-bye. I'm sorry that after our close friendship, which meant a great deal to me, I shall only have the memory of your father's gout and your arguments about my liberal views. . . . But I don't feel it's my fault . . .

SONYA, *crying, covering her face, and hurriedly walking out by the left door.* I've been fool enough to fall in love here and I hope this will be a lesson to me! I'm getting out of this cesspool! *Going to the right door;* YELENA *coming in by the left door.*

YELENA You're here! Wait just a minute . . . Ivan Ivanich

has just told me that my husband insulted you . . . You must forgive him, he's very upset today and just didn't understand . . . As for myself, I believe in you, Mihail Lvovich! I sincerely respect you, and I sympathize with you. With a pure heart I offer you my friendship! *Holding out both hands.*

KHROUSCHOV, *with aversion.* Get away from me! . . . I despise your friendship! *Going out.*

YELENA, *alone, groaning.* Why? Why?

A shot is heard behind the scene. Marya Vassilyevna *comes out by the middle door, staggers, cries out and falls unconscious to the ground.* SONYA *comes in and runs out the middle door.*

SEREBRYAKOV, ORLOVSKY, ZHELTOUKHIN, *coming in.* What's the matter?

SONYA *is heard crying out; she returns and cries,* Uncle George has shot himself!

She, ORLOVSKY, SEREBRYAKOV *and* ZHELTOUKHIN *run out through the middle door.*

YELENA, *moaning.* Why? Why?

DYADIN *appears at the door on the right.*

DYADIN, *in the doorway.* What's the matter?

YELENA, *to* DYADIN. Take me away from here! Throw me off a cliff, kill me, but don't make me stay here! Quickly, I beg you!

Goes out with DYADIN.

Curtain.

ACT IV

The forest and the house by the mill which DYADIN *rents from* KHROUSCHOV. YELENA ANDREYEVNA *and* DYADIN *sitting on a bench under the window.*

YELENA Ilya, will you drive over to the post office again tomorrow?

DYADIN Certainly, I will.

YELENA I'll wait another three days and if I don't get an answer from my brother, I'll borrow the money from you and go to Moscow. I just can't stay here any longer.

DYADIN Of course . . . *A pause.* I don't want to seem to be giving you advice, but all your letters and telegrams, and my trips to the post office every day, well, if you'll forgive me, they don't mean a thing. No matter what your brother says, you'll go back to your husband.

YELENA I will not go back . . . I've got to think it over, Ilya Ilyich. I don't love my husband. I was very fond of the young people, but they were unjust to me all along. Why should I go back there? You will say it is my duty—I know that perfectly well, but, I repeat, I've got to think it over. . . . *A pause.*

DYADIN I know! . . . The greatest Russian poet Lomonosov ran away from home to find his fortune in Moscow. This was a courageous act . . . But why did *you* run away? Your happiness, if we're honest about it, is nowhere to be found . . . It's in the nature of things that the canary should sit in its cage and look on at the happiness of others; and this will never change.

YELENA Perhaps I'm not a canary, but a free sparrow!

DYADIN A bird is judged by its flight, my friend . . . During these last two weeks anyone else would have been in ten towns, and nobody could have kept up with her. But you've only run as far as the mill, and even that's been too much. No, you'll stay here a little longer, and you'll go home to your husband. *Listening.* I hear someone coming. *Getting up.*

YELENA I'll go in.

DYADIN I won't bother you any more . . . I'll just go down to the mill and take a little nap . . . I was up before dawn this morning.

YELENA After you've had your nap, we'll have some tea together. *Going into the house.*

DYADIN, *alone.* What a story all this would make: an unattractive man carries off the young wife of a famous professor. How delightful! *Going away.*

SEMYON, *carrying buckets, and* JULIA *coming in.*

JULIA Hello, Semyon! Is Ilya at home?

SEMYON Yes, he's down at the mill.

JULIA Will you call him for me?

SEMYON Yes, certainly. *Going away.*

JULIA, *alone.* He's probably asleep! . . . *Sitting down on the bench under the window and sighing deeply.* Some sleep, others sit, and I work all day long, always running . . . *With a still deeper sigh.* What's the use. Goodness, Waffles is a silly man. All the pigs running loose. It'll serve him right if they eat up the corn . . .

Enter DYADIN.

DYADIN, *putting on his coat.* Here you are, Julia Stepanovna! Excuse my appearance . . . I was just relaxing for a bit in the embraces of Morpheus.

JULIA How are you?

DYADIN Excuse me for not asking you in . . . but the place is all messed up. Perhaps you'd like to come down to the mill? . . .

JULIA This is fine right here. I've come to ask if it would be all right for us all to come out here for a picnic?

DYADIN Why, I'd be delighted!

JULIA I came ahead . . . the rest will be here soon. If you'd be good enough to have a table brought out and the samovar . . . and if you'll tell Semyon to get the food out of the carriage.

DYADIN Of course. *A pause.* Well, how is everyone?

JULIA Not very good, Ilya Ilyich. . . . This whole business has upset me so, and, of course, you know that the professor and Sonya are staying with us.

DYADIN Yes, I'd heard that.

JULIA Since George's suicide, they've been afraid to stay in that house. During the day it isn't so bad, but at night they sit huddled together in one room until daybreak. They're terrified that George's ghost will apear in the dark . . .

DYADIN Superstition! . . . And do they talk about Yelena Andreyevna?

JULIA Of course, they do. *A pause.* She just vanished!

DYADIN Yes, like in a novel; she just disappeared.

JULIA And now nobody knows where she is . . . Maybe she ran away, or perhaps, in despair, she. . . .

DYADIN God is merciful, Julia Stepanovna! Everything will be all right.

Enter KHROUSCHOV *with a portfolio and drawing case.*

KHROUSCHOV Hello! Anybody here? Semyon!

DYADIN Here we are.

KHROUSCHOV Oh! . . . How do you do, Julia.

JULIA Hello, Mihail Lvovich!

KHROUSCHOV I've come out here to work again, Ilya Ilyich. I can't seem to stay at home. Will you ask them to bring my easel out under this tree. And bring some lanterns, too. It'll be dark soon.

DYADIN, *going out*. I'll be glad to take care of it.

KHROUSCHOV How is everything, Julia?

JULIA So-so . . . *A pause*.

KHROUSCHOV I hear the Serebryakovs are staying with you?

JULIA Yes.

KHROUSCHOV H'm! . . . And what's Lennie doing?

JULIA He just sits at home with Sonechka . . .

KHROUSCHOV Oh, I see! *A pause*. Why doesn't he marry her?

JULIA That's a good question. *A sigh*. He's well educated, and she's from a good family . . . I've always wanted them—

KHROUSCHOV She's a fool!

JULIA Don't talk like that.

KHROUSCHOV And Lennie's not very bright either. All of your people are extra special. Your home's a veritable citadel of learning.

JULIA Have you had your lunch yet?

KHROUSCHOV Why do you ask that?

JULIA You're so irritable.

Enter DYADIN *and* SEMYON; *both carrying a table*.

DYADIN You've picked an ideal spot to work in, Misha. It's an oasis! You can imagine that you're surrounded with palm trees, and Julia here is a doe, and you—a lion, and I—a tiger! . . .

KHROUSCHOV You're a gentle soul, Ilya Ilyich, but an odd one! What with your silly words, shuffling feet, and stooped shoulders! . . . Why if a stranger were to see you, he wouldn't know what to make of you.

DYADIN That's my destiny . . . A fatal predestination.

KHROUSCHOV At it again . . . fatal predestination! Cut it out, will you? *Fixing a chart on the table*. By the way, I'll be spending the night.

DYADIN Delighted . . . Poor Misha, you are angry, while my heart's filled with inexpressible joy! As though a bird were singing in my heart.

KHROUSCHOV Well, rejoice then. *A pause*. There may be a bird

in your heart, but there's a frog in mine. Just one catastrophe after
another. First, Shimansky's sold his forest for timber. Then Yelena
Andreyevna runs away from her husband, and nobody knows
where she is. And I feel that I'm getting more stupid and narrow-
minded every day . . . Oh, and did you know George left a diary.
First Orlovsky had it, and then I read it . . . a dozen times. . . .

JULIA Yes, we read it, too.

KHROUSCHOV The affair between George and Yelena, which was
talked about all over the countryside, turns out to be nothing but
the most abominable kind of slander. I believed it and spread it
along with the others; I hated, despised, and insulted her.

DYADIN That wasn't right.

KHROUSCHOV Oh, I'm a fine person. I first heard it from your
brother, Julia. And I believed him, and I've never respected him.
And I didn't believe that woman who was proving her loyalty
before my very eyes. I'm as stupid as the rest of you; I'd rather
believe evil than good.

DYADIN, *to* JULIA. Let's take a walk down to the mill, my dear.
And let Mr. Crosspatch work here . . . You go to work, Misha,
my friend. *Going out with* JULIA.

KHROUSCHOV, *alone; mixing the colors in a saucer.* One night I
saw him with her hand next to his face. That night he wrote all
about it in his diary: how I came in, what I said. And he called
me a fool and narrow-minded . . . *A pause.* And then he blamed
Sonya for having fallen in love with me . . . She's never loved
me . . . Oh, now I've smudged it . . . *Rubbing the paper with
a knife.* Even if there's some truth in it, I mustn't think of it . . .
It all began foolishly, and it's bound to end that way . . . SEMYON
and the laborers bringing in a large table. What's that for?

SEMYON Ilya Ilyich told us to bring it out. Company's coming
from the Zheltoukhin estate for a picnic.

KHROUSCHOV I see. Well, that means no more work. I might as
well pack up my things and go home.

Enter ZHELTOUKHIN *with* SONYA *on his arm.*

ZHELTOUKHIN, *singing.* "Unwillingly I come by hidden forces
drawn."

KHROUSCHOV Who's that? Oh? *Hastily packing his case of instru-
ments.*

ZHELTOUKHIN Let me ask you one more thing, Sophia . . . Remember when you had lunch at our house on my birthday, did you laugh at the way I looked?

SONYA Lennie, how can you say such a thing? I don't know why I was laughing.

ZHELTOUKHIN, *having noticed* KHROUSCHOV. Oh, you're here, too! How are you?

KHROUSCHOV Hello.

ZHELTOUKHIN I see you're working. That's fine! . . . Where's Waffles?

KHROUSCHOV Down there. . . .

ZHELTOUKHIN Where's that?

KHROUSCHOV I thought I made myself clear . . . At the mill.

ZHELTOUKHIN Oh, well I'd better go and see him. *Walking away and whistling.* "Unwillingly I come by hidden forces drawn." *Going out.*

SONYA Hello.

KHROUSCHOV Hello.

SONYA What are you drawing?

KHROUSCHOV Oh, nothing.

SONYA Is it a plan?

KHROUSCHOV No, it's a map showing all the forests in our district. I've marked it out. *After a pause.* See, the green indicates where there were forests in our grandfathers' time; and this brighter green shows where forests have been cut down during the last twenty-five years; and the blue tells where there still are forests . . . intact. . . . Yes . . . *A pause.* Well, and how are you? Are you happy?

SONYA Now isn't the time to think of happiness.

KHROUSCHOV What else should we think about?

SONYA Our present unhappiness was caused by the fact that we were thinking too much of our own happiness. . . .

KHROUSCHOV So!

After a pause.

SONYA There's no evil without some good in it. Our sorrow has taught me that we must forget our own happiness and think only of the happiness of others. Our lives should be a continual act of self-sacrifice . . .

KHROUSCHOV Yes . . . *After a pause.* Marya Vassilyevna's son has shot himself, but she still goes on searching for contradictions in her books. A great misfortune has come to you, and you're consoling your vanity with thoughts of sacrifice . . . No one has any compassion for others. We're all doing the wrong thing and everything's being destroyed. I'll leave here in a minute and won't bother the two of you . . . Why are you crying? I didn't mean to make you cry.

SONYA Never mind, never mind . . . *Wiping away her tears.* *Enter* JULIA, DYADIN, *and* ZHELTOUKHIN.

SEREBRYAKOV's *voice.* Hallo! Where are you all?

SONYA, *crying out.* Here we are, father!

DYADIN They're bringing the samovar! Isn't this delightful! *He and* JULIA *arranging things on the table.*

Enter SEREBRYAKOV *and* ORLOVSKY.

SONYA Over here, father!

SEREBRYAKOV Oh, there you are.

ZHELTOUKHIN, *aloud.* Gentlemen, court's in session! Waffles, open up the liquor.

KHROUSCHOV, *to* SEREBRYAKOV. Professor, I ask you to forgive me and let bygones be bygones. *Holding out his hand.*

SEREBRYAKOV By all means. Certainly. You must forgive me, too. The next day I thought the whole thing through, and I was really very upset . . . Let's be friends. *Taking his arm and going to the table.*

ORLOVSKY You two should've done that a long time ago. A bad peace is better than a good quarrel.

DYADIN Your Excellency, I am delighted that it's pleased you to honor my oasis with your presence. Absolutely delighted!

SEREBRYAKOV Thank you, my dear sir. It is indeed a fine place. A real oasis!

ORLOVSKY Do you love nature, Alexander?

SEREBRYAKOV Very much. *A pause.* Gentlemen, the best thing for us to do is to keep talking. One must look misfortune straight in the face. I'm happier than any of you, because I'm suffering the greatest misfortune.

JULIA We won't have any sugar with our tea, just jam.

DYADIN, *bustling about among the company.* How pleasant everything is! How pleasant!

SEREBRYAKOV Lately, Mihail Lvovich, I have passed through so much that I believe I could write a treatise for the benefit of all

Great juxtaposition undercutting
of speeches in this scene (picnic at
mill) hodge podge

mankind on the art of living. We can live an age and learn an age, but it is misfortunes that teach us.

DYADIN He who remembers the evil past will lose an eye. But God is merciful; and all's well that ends well.

SONYA *starting*.

ZHELTOUKHIN What made you jump?

SONYA I heard someone crying.

DYADIN It's probably the peasants fishing down at the river. *Pause*.

ZHELTOUKHIN Didn't we agree to go on as if nothing had happened? . . . And yet . . . there's a strange kind of tension. . . .

DYADIN I've always had a great respect for scholarship, Your Excellency, and, if I may say so, my feelings for it have a certain family connection. My brother's wife's brother, Konstantin Garrilich Novossyolov, perhaps you've heard of him, was an M.A.

SEREBRYAKOV I didn't know him personally, but I know the name. *A pause*.

JULIA Tomorrow it will be exactly fifteen days since George died.

KHROUSCHOV Julia, let's not talk about it.

SEREBRYAKOV Yes, we must be courageous! *A pause*.

ZHELTOUKHIN There's still a strange kind of tension. . . .

SEREBRYAKOV Nature abhors a vacuum. Two of my closest relations have been taken from me. But to fill this gap, I've been given two new friends. I drink your health, Leonid Stepanovich!

ZHELTOUKHIN Thank you, Alexander Vladimirovich! Allow me in turn to drink to the continued fruitfulness of your scholarship. "Sow the seeds of wisdom, of goodness, of eternity! Sow the seeds! And the Russian folk will give you their hearty gratitude!"

SEREBRYAKOV Such a compliment means a great deal to me. I wish from the bottom of my heart that the time may soon come when our friendship has even more intimate bonds.

Enter FYODOR.

FYODOR Here's where you are! A picnic!

ORLOVSKY Hello, my boy.

FYODOR How are you? *Embracing* SONYA *and* JULIA.

ORLOVSKY I haven't seen you for two weeks. Where've you been? What've you been doing?

Fyodor – playboy, vain

FYODOR I just came from Lennie's; they told me you were all over here.

ORLOVSKY Where have you been?

FYODOR I haven't been to bed in three days. Last night I lost five thousand at cards. You know, drinking, gambling, the usual thing.

ORLOVSKY What a boy! You must still be a little high.

FYODOR Not at all. Julia, some tea, please! Just lemon. Too bad about George, wasn't it. To put a bullet through his head for no reason at all. And with a French revolver, too! He ought have at least used a Russian one.

KHROUSCHOV Will you please be quiet! How low can you get?

FYODOR Oh, I'm a beast all right, but a pedigree one! *Stroking his beard.* Why this beard alone . . . Yes, I'm a beast, and a fool, and a rascal, and yet I just have to will it and the finest girl in the world would marry me. Sonya, marry me . . . *To* KHROUSCHOV. Oh, I'm so sorry. . . . Forgive me . . .

KHROUSCHOV Stop playing the fool.

JULIA You're a lost soul, Fedya! There isn't a bigger drunkard and spendthrift in the whole district. The mere sight of you breaks my heart.

FYODOR Stop your whining and come here and sit next to me . . . That's right. I'll come and visit you for two weeks . . . I really need a rest. *Kissing her.*

JULIA You ought to be ashamed of yourself. You should be a comfort to your father in his old age, and you only disgrace him.

FYODOR I promise you, I'll give up drinking! *Pouring out a drink.*

JULIA But why are you drinking then?

FYODOR Just one little one. *Drinking.* Wood Demon, here. I give you a team of horses and my gun. I'm going to Julia's for the next two weeks.

KHROUSCHOV It would do you more good to be sent into active service.

JULIA Here, drink some tea!

DYADIN And have some crackers.

ORLOVSKY, *to* SEREBRYAKOV. You know, Alexander, until I was forty I led the same kind of life as Fyodor here. One day I began counting how many women I'd made unhappy and when I got

Does Orlovsky have the answer? No!

to seventy I stopped counting. But when I reached forty something happened to me. I couldn't find any peace of mind. I tried everything—reading, work, travel—but nothing helped. Then one day I went to visit my old friend, Dimitri Palovich. After lunch, so as not to fall asleep, we began shooting at a target in the back yard. There were lots of people there. You were there, too, Waffles, do you remember?

DYADIN Oh yes, I was there . . . I remember.

ORLOVSKY Suddenly, I couldn't stand it any longer. I started to weep, and then I staggered, and suddenly cried out at the top of my voice: "My friends, forgive me, for the love of Christ!" And at that very moment I felt my heart become pure, and gentle, and warm; and from that time on, there's never been a happier man than I in the whole world. You should do the same thing, Alexander.

SEREBRYAKOV What! *A glow appears in the sky.*

ORLOVSKY Do the same as I did. Capitulate. Surrender.

SEREBRYAKOV Here's an example of our national philosophy. You advise me to ask forgiveness. But why? It's I who should be asked to forgive.

SONYA But, father, it is *our* fault.

SEREBRYAKOV Is it? You're all, I gather, thinking of my attitude toward my wife. But do you really think that I'm to blame for what's happened? Why, that's ridiculous. She's forgotten her duty and left me at a time when I needed her.

KHROUSCHOV Alexander Vladimirovich, listen to me . . . For twenty-five years you've been a professor and have served scholarship; I plant forests and practice medicine—but what's the point of it, if we hurt those for whom we are working? We say that we are serving humanity, but at the same time we inhumanly destroy one another. For instance, did you or I do anything to save George? Where's your wife, whom we all insulted? Where's your peace of mind, where's your daughter's peace of mind? Everything's been destroyed, ruined. You call me a Wood Demon, but there's a demon in all of you. You're all wandering lost in a dark forest, you're all groping to find a way in life. We know just enough and feel just enough to ruin our own lives and the lives of others. YELENA *comes out of the house and sits down on the bench under the window.* I thought I was a man of ideas, a humane person, but at the same time I refused to forgive people their slightest mistakes. I listened to gossip and believed it, and gossiped just like everyone else. When your wife offered me her friendship in good faith, I self-righteously rebuffed her, saying: "Get away from me. I despise your friendship!" That's the kind of person I am. There's a demon in me; I'm narrow-minded, and stupid, and blind. But you, professor, aren't exactly an eagle yourself. Yet the whole countryside, all the women, think of me as a hero, as a great liberal; and you, you're famous all over Russia. But if people really think I'm a hero and really think you're famous, then all it means is that there aren't any heroes; that there aren't any truly creative men, that there isn't anyone who can lead us out of the dark forest, that there isn't anyone who can repair the damage we have done. It means that there are no real eagles who deserve to be famous.

SEREBRYAKOV I'm sorry, but I didn't come here to debate with you or to justify my reputation . . .

ZHELTOUKHIN Don't you think, Misha, we should change the subject?

KHROUSCHOV In a minute; anyway I'm going to leave. Yes, I'm narrow-minded, but you, professor, you're no eagle. George was unimaginative, too, since he couldn't find anything better to do than put a bullet through his head. You're all narrow-minded, and as for the women. . . .

YELENA, *interrupting*. As for the women, they aren't any better. *Advancing toward the table*. I left my husband, but do you think I used my freedom? Don't worry . . . I'll come back . . . *Sitting down at the table*. I have come back.

General consternation.

DYADIN, *laughing aloud*. That is delightful! The debate is over, and now, gentlemen, let me say a word. Your Excellency, it was I who carried off your wife, as once upon a time a certain Paris carried off the fair Helen. There may not be any pock-marked Parises, but there are more things in heaven and earth, Horatio, than are dreamt of in your philosophy!

KHROUSCHOV I don't understand what's going on—why it's Yelena Andreyevna!

YELENA I've been here with Ilya Ilyich for the last two weeks.

Why do you all look at me so strangely? Why doesn't anybody say something? I was by the window and heard everything. *Embracing Sonya.* Oh, let's be friends, Sonya.

DYADIN, *rubbing his hands.* This is delightful!

YELENA, *to* KHROUSCHOV. Mihail Lvovich! *Holding out her hand.* He who remembers the evil past will lose an eye. Hello, Fyodor Ivanich! . . . and Julia, my dear! . . .

ORLOVSKY The beautiful professor's wife has returned . . . She's come back to us again.

YELENA I missed you all so much. Hello, Alexander! *Holding out her hand to her husband; the latter turning his face away.* Alexander!

SEREBRYAKOV You've forgotten your duty.

YELENA Alexander!

SEREBRYAKOV I don't deny that I'm very glad to see you and I'm perfectly willing to talk to you . . . at home, that is . . . not here . . .

ORLOVSKY But my friend! *A pause.*

YELENA I see. So it means, Alexander, that our problem has been solved by not being solved at all. If that's the way it's to be, fair enough. I'm an episodic creature and my happiness doesn't really matter, it's the woman's happiness . . . Sitting at home, eating, drinking, sleeping, and listening to your husband talk on and on about his gout, his rights, and his fame. Why do you all cover your eyes? Are you embarrassed? Come, let's have a drink. What difference does it make?

DYADIN Everything always turns out right in the end.

FYODOR, *coming up to* SEREBRYAKOV, *in agitation.* Alexander Vladimirovich, this is a very touching moment . . . Please, be kind to her and show her some tenderness. Just one kind word, the word of an honorable man, and I'll be your friend for the rest of my life. I'll even give you a team of my best horses.

SEREBRYAKOV Thank you, but I'm afarid I don't understand . . .

FYODOR I see! You don't understand! . . . One day on my way home from hunting, I saw an owl sitting on a branch right in front of me. I fired at him! Nothing happened . . . I fired again . . . Still, nothing happened. He just sat there blinking his eyes.

SEREBRYAKOV And whom are you referring to?

FYODOR The owl. *Returning to the table.*

ORLOVSKY, *listening.* Listen, everybody . . . Be quiet . . . I think I hear the fire bells.

FYODOR, *noticing the glow.* Look! There in the sky! See how red it is?

ORLOVSKY Well, what are we doing sitting here and missing it all!

DYADIN Isn't it wonderful!

FYODOR Look how bright it is! It must be near Alexeyevsk.

KHROUSCHOV No, Alexeyevsk is more to the north . . . It must be Novo-Petrovsk.

JULIA Isn't it awful! I'm so afraid of a fire.

KHROUSCHOV I'm sure it's Novo-Petrovsk.

DYADIN, *shouting.* Semyon, run and find out where the fire is.

SEMYON, *shouting.* It's the Telibeyev forest.

DYADIN What?

SEMYON The Telibeyev forest!

DYADIN Forest! . . .

A long pause.

KHROUSCHOV I've got to go . . . Good-bye, everybody . . . Forgive me, if I was rude. I've been very depressed today, but we must face up to life. Don't worry, I won't shoot myself or throw myself into the mill stream. I may not be much of a hero, but someday I'll become one! I'll grow the wings of an eagle, and no fire or devil will ever frighten me! Let the forests burn—I'll plant new ones! And if I'm not loved by one, I'll love another! *Rushing off.*

YELENA What a splendid man he is!

ORLOVSKY Indeed . . . "And if I'm not loved by one, I'll love another." I wonder what he meant by that?

SONYA Take me away from here . . . I want to go home . . .

SEREBRYAKOV Yes, it's time we go. It's terribly damp here. My blanket and overcoat must be around here somewhere.

ZHELTOUKHIN The blanket's in the carriage, and here's your coat. *Handing it to him.*

SONYA, *in violent agitation.* Take me away from here . . . Take me away. . . .

ZHELTOUKHIN I'm at your service . . .

SONYA No, I want godfather to take me home.

ORLOVSKY Why, of course, my dear, come along. *Handing her her things.*

ZHELTOUKHIN, *aside.* Damn! . . . I get nothing but insults!

FYODOR *and* JULIA *pack the picnic things into the basket.*

SEREBRYAKOV My left heel hurts . . . It must be my rheumatism. . . . That means I won't sleep again tonight.

YELENA, *buttoning up her husband's coat.* Ilya Ilyich dear, please get my hat and coat from the house!

DYADIN Certainly! *Going into the house and coming back with her hat and coat.*

ORLOVSKY Don't be afraid of the fire, my dear. It's almost out now.

JULIA Well, leave this jam for Ilya Ilyich . . . *To her brother.* Lennie, here, you take the basket.

YELENA I'm ready . . . *To her husband.* Well, statue of the commander, are you ready to take me, and go to blazes with me in your twenty-six dismal rooms! That's all I'm good for!

SEREBRYAKOV Statue of the commander! . . . I'd laugh at your simile, but the pain in my foot prevents me! . . . *To the whole company.* Good-bye, my friends! I thank you for the delightful time and for your pleasant company . . . A lovely evening, excellent tea—everything perfect; but, you must forgive me, I'll never be able to approve of your native philosophy and views on life. We must work! We must do things. . . . Yes, one must work. Good-bye! *Walking off with his wife.*

FYODOR Come on, Julia! *To his father.* Good-bye, father! *Walking off with* JULIA.

ZHELTOUKHIN, *with the basket, following them.* And I have to carry the basket. Damn it. . . . I hate these picnics . . . *Shouting behind the scene at his coachman.* Alexey, come here.

ORLOVSKY, *to* SONYA. Well, what are you waiting for? Come along, my dear . . . *Going out with* SONYA.

DYADIN, *aside.* No one said good-bye to me! . . . Oh, how delightful! *Putting out the candles.*

ORLOVSKY, *to* SONYA. What's the matter?

SONYA I can't go, godfather . . . I just can't! I'm so unhappy, godfather, so unhappy.

ORLOVSKY, *alarmed.* What's wrong? My sweet . . .

SONYA Let's stay here . . . just a little while.

ORLOVSKY First, it's take me away, then it's let's stay! . . . Why don't you make up your mind?

SONYA Today I've lost my happiness. . . . It's horrible! I can't stand it! Oh, godfather, I want to die . . . Oh, if you only knew!

ORLOVSKY Here's some water . . . Here, now, sit down . . .

DYADIN What's wrong? Sophia Alexandrovna . . . you mustn't cry, please don't, it upsets me . . . *Tearfully.* I can't stand to see anyone cry . . .

SONYA Ilya Ilyich, take me to the fire; please!

ORLOVSKY Why do you want to go to the fire? What can you do there?

SONYA Please take me to the fire. If you don't I'll walk. Oh, I'm so unhappy . . . Oh, godfather, I can't stand it! Take me to the fire.

Enter KHROUSCHOV *hurriedly.*

KHROUSCHOV, *shouting,* Ilya Ilyich!

DYADIN Here I am, what do you want?

KHROUSCHOV I can't get there fast enough; lend me your horse.

SONYA, *recognizing* KHROUSCHOV, *and crying out joyfully.* Mihail Lvovich! *Going towards him.* Mihail! *To* ORLOVSKY. Go away, godfather, I have something to say to him. *To* KHROUSCHOV. You said that you'd love another . . . *To* ORLOVSKY. Go away, godfather! *To* KHROUSCHOV. I'm different now . . . All I want is the truth . . . Nothing, nothing but the truth! I love you, I love you, I love . . .

ORLOVSKY Now I see! *Laughing.*

DYADIN This is delightful!

SONYA, *to* ORLOVSKY. Go away, godfather, please! *To* KHROUSCHOV. Yes, all I want is the truth and nothing else! . . . Well, say something . . . Why don't you speak?

KHROUSCHOV, *embracing her.* My darling!

SONYA Don't go, godfather! . . . When you told me you loved me, I was so happy but because of my silly prejudices I couldn't tell you how I really felt, just as father couldn't smile at Yelena. But now I am free!

ORLOVSKY, *laughing aloud.* Together at last! Congratulations! *Bowing low.* Such children!

DYADIN, *embracing* KHROUSCHOV. Misha, my boy, how happy you've made me!

ORLOVSKY, *embracing and kissing* SONYA. My sweet little canary!
. . . My dear little goddaughter!

SONYA *laughing aloud.*

KHROUSCHOV It's so wonderful I don't understand it. Do you
mind going away for awhile, so I can talk to her alone?

Enter FYODOR *and* JULIA.

JULIA Fyodor, you're fibbing!

ORLOVSKY Sh-sh! Quiet, that boy of mine is coming back. Let's
hide. Hurry!

ORLOVSKY, DYADIN, KHROUSCHOV, *and* SONYA *hide themselves.*

FYODOR I left my gloves here.

JULIA It's all a fib!

FYODOR Well, what of it? I don't want you to go home yet. Let's
take a little walk and then we will go . . .

JULIA You're horrible! *Clapping her hands.* And that Waffles!
Look, the table's not even cleared! Someone might have stolen
the samovar . . . He may be an old man, but he's got less sense
than a baby!

DYADIN, *aside.* Thank you.

JULIA I think I heard someone laughing . . .

FYODOR It's one of the peasants! . . . *Picking up a glove.*
There's someone's glove. . . . Why it's Sonya's . . . Today she
acted as though she were bitten by a bee. She's in love with the
Wood Demon. She's head over heels in love with him, and the
blockhead doesn't see it!

JULIA, *angrily.* Where are we going?

FYODOR To the dike . . . There isn't a prettier place around
here.

ORLOVSKY, *aside.* That's my boy. Just look at that beard.

JULIA I heard a voice.

FYODOR, *reciting.* "Here are wonders, the Wood Demon loiters,
the mermaid sits on the branches." . . . Yes, my friend! *Clapping
her on the shoulder.*

JULIA I'm not your friend.

FYODOR Let's be reasonable about this. Listen, Julia! I've been
through hell and high water . . . I'm thirty-five, and I'm just a
lieutenant in the Serbian army. I'm just hanging in the middle of
things. . . . Well, it's time I changed my mode of life, and you
see . . . do you understand, I've gotten it into my head that if I

were to marry, well, a huge change would happen in my life! . . . Will you marry me, please! There's no one else in the world . . .

JULIA, *embarrassed.* Well . . . you see . . . first of all, you'll have to reform.

FYODOR Don't beat around the bush. Yes or no?

JULIA I'm embarrassed! *Looking around.* Someone might hear us! . . . I think I can see Waffles looking out the window.

FYODOR No one's there.

JULIA, *falling on his neck.* Oh, Fedya! SONYA *laughs aloud.*

ORLOVSKY, DYADIN, KHROUSCHOV *laugh, clap their hands and shout.* Bravo! Bravo!

FYODOR My, how you frightened us! Where did you come from?

SONYA Julia, darling, congratulations! And me, too!

Laughter, kisses, noise.

DYADIN That is delightful! Just delightful!

Curtain

THE SEA GULL

CAST

IRINA NIKOLAYEVNA ARKADINA, *an actress*
KONSTANTIN GAVRILOVICH TREPLEV, *her son*
PYOTR NIKOLAYEVICH SORIN, *her brother*
NINA NIHAILOVNA ZARECHNY, *a young girl, daughter of a wealthy landowner*
ILYA AFANASYEVICH SHAMRAEV, *Sorin's steward*
POLINA ANDREYEVNA, *his wife*
MASHA, *his daughter*
BORIS ALEXEYEVICH TRIGORIN, *a famous writer*
YEVGENY SERGEYEVICH DORN, *a doctor*
SEMYON SEMYONOVICH MEDVEDENKO, *a school teacher*
YAKOV, *a worker*
COOK
HOUSEMAID

The action takes place in Sorin's house and garden.
Between the third and fourth acts two years have passed.

ACT I

The lawn of SORIN's *estate. A wide avenue of trees leads towards the lake. A roughly made stage has been erected and blocks the audience's view of the lake. Rushes surround the stage platform and there are chairs about. The sun is just setting and* YAKOV *is working on the stage behind the drawn curtain.* MASHA *and* MEDVEDENKO *enter, returning from a walk.*

MEDVEDENKO Why do you always wear black?

MASHA I'm in mourning for my life. I'm unhappy.

MEDVEDENKO Why? *Thinking.* I don't understand. I mean, your health's good, and even if your father's not rich, he's pretty well-off. My life's much harder than yours. I get only twenty-three roubles a month, before deductions, and yet I don't wear mourning.

MASHA Money isn't everything. Even a beggar can be happy.

MEDVEDENKO In theory he can, but in practice it's altogether different. For instance, I've got to support my mother, two sisters, my younger brother, and myself—all on twenty-three roubles a month. We have to eat and drink, don't we? And then we have to get tea and sugar; and what about tobacco? It isn't easy.

MASHA, *glancing at the stage.* The play will be starting soon.

MEDVEDENKO Yes. Nina's going to act, and Konstantin wrote the play. They're in love and tonight their souls will be united as they try to give expression to a work of art. But our souls aren't united. I'm in love with you. I long for you so desperately that I can't stand staying at home. Every day I walk four miles over here and four miles back, and all I ever get from you is cold indifference. Oh, I understand! I haven't any money, and I've got a large family to take care of . . . who'd want to marry a man who can't even feed himself?

MASHA Don't be silly! *Taking snuff.* I'm touched by your love, but I can't return it, that's all. *Offering him the snuff box.* Help yourself.

MEDVEDENKO No thanks. I don't feel like any right now. *Pause.*

MASHA My, how close it is! It will probably rain tonight. All you ever do is philosophize or talk about money. You think there's no greater misfortune than poverty, but I think it's a thousand times easier to wear rags and be a beggar than . . . but you wouldn't understand. . . .

Enter SORIN *and* TREPLEV.

SORIN For some reason living in the country doesn't agree with me, my boy. Obviously, I'll get accustomed to it. Last night I went to bed at ten and I got up this morning at nine feeling as though my brain were glued to my skull from sleeping so long. *Laughing.* And, then, after dinner I accidentally fell asleep again, and now I'm a wreck—like I'd had a horrible nightmare.

TREPLEV You're right, Uncle, you ought to live in town. *Noticing* MASHA *and* MEDVEDENKO. We'll call you when the play's ready to begin, my friends, but you shouldn't be here now. Please go.

SORIN, *to* MASHA Marya Ilyinishna, I wish you'd ask your father not to tie up the dog. It keeps howling all the time. It kept my sister awake again last night.

MASHA Why don't you tell him yourself? I'm not, so don't ask. *To* MEDVEDENKO. Come, let's go.

MEDVEDENKO You'll call us before the play starts, won't you? MASHA *and* MEDVEDENKO *go out.*

SORIN So the dog will howl all night again tonight. The strange thing is that I've never done anything I really wanted to do in the country. I used to come down here on my month's vacation for a rest, but no sooner had I gotten here when people began bothering me with all sorts of nonsense, and I was ready to leave almost as soon as I arrived. *Laughs.* I'm always glad when I leave. But that's the way it goes, now I'm retired and I haven't anywhere else to go. I've got to live here whether I want to or not . . .

YAKOV We're going for a swim, Konstantin Gavrilovich.

TREPLEV All right, but be sure to be back in ten minutes. *Looking at his watch.* We're going to start soon.

YAKOV Yes, sir. *Goes out.*

TREPLEV, *looking at the stage.* Now, here's a theatre for you! Nothing but a curtain and two wings. And beyond it . . . open space. No scenery, just a view of the lake and the horizon. We'll raise the curtain at eight-thirty when the moon comes up.

SORIN Wonderful!

TREPLEV But if Nina's late, then the whole effect will be ruined. She should be here by now. Her father and stepmother watch her so closely, it's almost impossible for her to get out of the house, it's like being in prison. *Straightening his Uncle's tie.* Your hair and your beard are never combed, Uncle, and you ought to have them cut or, at least, trimmed.

SORIN, *combing his beard.* That's the tragedy of my life. My appearance. . . . Why, even when I was younger I looked like I were drunk. Women have never liked me. *Sitting down.* Why's your mother in such bad humor, today?

TREPLEV She's bored, that's why! *Sitting next to* SORIN. Bored, and jealous, too! She's annoyed with me and doesn't want me to put my play on because Nina's playing the part, and she's not. Why, she hasn't even read my play, and still she hates it.

SORIN, *laughing.* Really! What an idea!

TREPLEV It makes her angry to think—even on this tiny stage—that Nina and not she will triumph. *Looking at his watch.* My mother's a real case, a psychological freak. There's no doubt about it, she's talented and intelligent; she can weep over a novel, recite all of Nekrasov's poetry by heart, and nurse the sick with the patience of an angel. But you just try praising Duse—just one word. Watch out! You can't praise anyone but her, you have to rave about her, and go into ecstasy about her wonderful performance in *Camille* or *The Fumes of Life*. But such intoxicating admiration isn't to be had here in the country, so she's bored and cross, and thinks that we're all her enemies—that it's all our fault. And she's superstitious too—afraid of three candles and the number thirteen. *And* she's stingy! She's got seventy thousand roubles in the bank—I know it for a fact—but just try to borrow some money and she'll burst into tears.

SORIN Somehow, you've gotten into your head that your mother doesn't like your play and you're upset about it. Don't worry, she worships the ground you walk on.

TREPLEV, *pulling petals from a flower.* She loves me . . . she loves me not . . . she loves me . . . loves me not . . . loves me . . . loves me not. *Laughing.* See, my mother doesn't love me.

But, then, why should she? She wants to live, have love affairs, and wear pretty clothes; and here I am—twenty-five—always reminding her that she's getting older. When I'm not around, she's thirty-two; when I am, she's forty-three . . . and she hates me for it. And she knows that I despise the theatre! She *loves* the theatre, and thinks she's serving humanity! But in my opinion our theatre's in a rut. It's nothing but clichés and shopworn conventions. When the curtain opens on those three-walled "living rooms," and I see those famous and talented actors, those high priests of that sacred art, parade about in their costumes in front of the footlights showing the way people eat, drink, make love, and walk about; when I hear them try to squeeze a moral out of commonplace phrases and meaningless events—some cliché that everyone knows and is suitable for home consumption; when they give me a thousand variations of the same old thing over and over again. . . . I have to leave! I want to run away as Maupassant ran away from the Eiffel Tower because its vulgarity was destroying him.

SORIN But we can't do without the theatre.

TREPLEV No, of course not! But [we need new forms, and if we can't have them, then it's better to have nothing at all!] I love my mother, love her very much, but she leads a meaningless kind of life, always running around with that novelist, her name always being tossed about in the newspapers. It disgusts me. And sometimes, being just an ordinary, selfish person, I resent having a famous actress for a mother, and wish she were an ordinary woman. I'd be a lot happier! Uncle, can you imagine anything more impossible, more hopeless, than to be alone—a nonentity—in a room full of celebrities, writers and actors, and know that you were being tolerated only because you were her son? Who am I? What am I? I left the University at the end of my junior year due to "circumstances," as our editors put it, "over which we have no control." I haven't any talent, no money, and I'm described on my passport as a shopkeeper from Kiev. Well, my father was a shopkeeper from Kiev, but he was a famous actor, too. So whenever all those famous artists who come to my mother's drawing room noticed me, I always knew from the looks on their faces that they thought I was an insignificant runt. I could read their thoughts and I had to suffer their humiliation. . . .

SORIN By the way, what kind of person is this writer? I can't figure him out; he never says anything.

TREPLEV Oh, I don't know. I think he's intelligent, pleasant, and a bit on the melancholy side. Really, a very decent fellow. He's well under forty, but he's already famous, and he can't complain about not having his share of everything. As for his work, well, let's say it's clever, it's charming, but after Tolstoy or Zola, you don't feel much like Trigorin.

SORIN Well, my boy, I like writers. Years ago, there were just two things I wanted more than anything else in the world. One was to get married and the other was to be a writer. I never did either one. Even at that, it must be nice to be even a minor writer.

TREPLEV, *listening*. I hear someone coming . . . *Embracing his Uncle*. I can't live without her . . . just the sound of her footsteps is beautiful . . . I'm insanely happy. *He goes quickly to meet* NINA ZARYECHNY *as she enters*. Oh, it's you, my enchantress . . . my dream. . . .

NINA, *upset*. Am I late? Oh, I hope I'm not late?

TREPLEV, *kissing her hands*. No, no, no. . . .

NINA I've been so worried all day, and so afraid! I was afraid father wouldn't let me come, but he went out with my stepmother. The sky was red and the moon was coming up, and I had to race my horse faster and faster. *She laughs*. But I'm here! Oh, I'm so happy! *She shakes* SORIN's *hand warmly*.

SORIN, *laughing*. Why you've been crying! That isn't fair, you know.

NINA It's nothing. . . . Oh, I'm so out of breath. I've got to leave in half an hour, so we'll have to hurry. I can't, I really can't, so don't ask me to stay. My father doesn't know I'm here.

TREPLEV It's time to begin, anyhow. I'll go and call everybody.

SORIN I'll go! I'll go at once! *Goes off singing* "The Two Grenadiers," *and then stops and turns back*. Once I started singing this, and the Assistant County Attorney said to me: "Your Excellency, you certainly have a powerful voice." Then he thought for a minute and said "And a bad one, too!" *Goes out laughing*.

NINA My father and stepmother won't let me come here. They say it's Bohemian . . . and they're afraid I'll go on the stage. But I feel pulled to this place, to this lake, as if I were a sea gull.

TREPLEV We're alone.

NINA I think someone's coming.

TREPLEV Nobody's there. *They kiss.*

NINA What kind of tree is this?

TREPLEV An elm.

NINA Why is it so dark?

TREPLEV It's late, everything's getting dark. Don't go early, please.

NINA I have to.

TREPLEV What if I followed you home, Nina? I'd stay in the garden all night looking up at your window.

NINA No! You mustn't! The watchman would see you and Tresor isn't used to you yet. He'd bark.

TREPLEV I love you.

NINA Ssh. . . .

TREPLEV, *hearing footsteps.* Who's there? Is that you, Yakov?

YAKOV, *behind the stage.* Yes, sir.

TREPLEV Have you got the alcohol and the sulphur? Be sure to burn the sulphur when the red eyes appear! *To* NINA. You'd better get on stage, everything's ready. Are you nervous?

NINA Yes, terribly. Your mother doesn't frighten me so much, but Trigorin terrifies me. I'm so ashamed of acting in front of him . . . a famous writer. Tell me, is he young?

TREPLEV Yes.

NINA His stories are so wonderful!

TREPLEV, *coldly.* I wouldn't know; I haven't read them.

NINA It's hard to act in your play. There aren't any living characters in it.

TREPLEV Living characters! We don't have to show life as it is, or even as it ought to be, but as we see it in our dreams!

NINA But there's hardly any action in your play—just speeches. And, then, I think there should be some love in a play.

Both go behind the stage. Enter POLINA *and* DORN.

POLINA It's getting damp out here. Please go back and put on your galoshes.

DORN I'm hot.

POLINA Why don't you take care of yourself. You're just being obstinate. You're a doctor, and you know perfectly well that the damp air is bad for you; you just want to make me worry. You stayed on the patio last night on purpose.

DORN, *hums.* "Please don't say that youth is gone". . .

POLINA You were so absorbed in your conversation with Irina, that you didn't even notice the cold. Admit it, you find her attractive.

DORN I'm fifty-five.

POLINA So! A man's not old at that age. You're still good-looking and attractive to women.

DORN Well, what am I to do about it?

POLINA You're all so anxious to worship an actress. Everyone of you!

DORN, *hums.* "Once more I stand before you". . . People always admire artists, they always have. That's why they treat them with more respect than, say, salesmen. It's a kind of idealism.

POLINA And I suppose it's idealism that makes women fall in love with you and throw themselves at you.

DORN All I can say is, that in my relationship with women there's been a great deal that was fine and good. Anyway, they liked me mostly for my skill as a doctor. You must remember that ten or fifteen years ago I was the only decent obstetrician in the whole county. And, besides, I've always been honest with people.

POLINA, *taking his arm.* Oh, you dear man.

DORN Ssh! They're coming.

Enter MADAME ARKADINA *on* SORIN'S *arm,* TRIGORIN, SHAMRAEV, MEDVEDENKO, *and* MASHA.

SHAMRAEV I remember seeing her at the Poltara Fair in '73. She was a marvelous actress! A sheer delight. Just marvelous! By the way, do you happen to know where Chadin—Pavel Semyonich Chadin—the comedian, is now? He was unmatchable as Raoplyvev, even better than Sadovsky, I can assure you, my dear lady. But where is he now?

IRINA You keep asking me about all those old fossils. How in the world should I know where he is? *She sits.*

SHAMRAEV, *sighing.* Ah, Pashka Chadin—we don't have actors like that any more. Yes, Irina Nikolayevna, the theatre's declining! Where are the mighty oaks of the past? Today we've nothing but stumps!

DORN You're right, we don't have many great actors today, but the average actor is much more competent. On the whole, the level of acting is higher.

SHAMRAEV I can't agree with you there, but that's a matter of taste, "*De gustibus aut bene aut nihil.*"

TREPLEV *enters from behind the stage.*

IRINA When's it going to start, dear?

TREPLEV In a minute. Please be patient.

IRINA, *reciting from "Hamlet."*

> Oh, Hamlet, speak no more!
> Thou turn'st mine eyes into my very soul;
> And there I see such black and grained spots
> As will not leave their tinct."

TREPLEV, *reciting from "Hamlet."*

> And let me wring thy heart, for so I shall,
> If it be made of penetrable stuff."

A horn is sounded off stage.

Ladies and gentlemen, we are ready to begin! Your attention, please! *Pause.* We'll begin! *Tapping the floor with a stick and reciting in a loud voice.* Oh, venerable shadows of olden days, ye shades that float over this lake at night, lull us to sleep and bring us dreams of what will be in two hundred thousand years. *[handwritten: play]*

SORIN There'll be nothing in two hundred thousand years!

TREPLEV Then, let the actors show us that nothing!

IRINA Yes, please do. We're almost asleep already.

The curtain opens, revealing the view of the lake, with the moon above the horizon casting its reflection on the water. *[handwritten: Treplev's play]*

NINA, *dressed in white, is sitting on a huge rock.* Men, lions, *[handwritten: white]* eagles, and partridges, horned deer, geese, spiders, and the silent fish of the deep, starfish and creatures which cannot be seen by the eye—all living things, all living things, all living things, having completed their cycle of sorrow, are now extinct. For thousands of years the earth has given birth to no living thing, and this poor moon now lights its lamp in rain. In the meadows, the cranes no longer waken with a cry, and the sound of the May beetles, humming in the lime groves, can no longer be heard. It is cold, cold, cold! Deserted, deserted, deserted! Frightening, frightening, frightening!

Pause.

All living creatures have turned to dust and the eternal matter has transformed them into rocks, water, and clouds, while the souls of all beings have been merged into one soul. This common soul of the world is I. . . . I. . . . In me is the soul of Alexander the Great, of Caesar, of Shakespeare, of Napoleon, and of the lowest form of worm. In me the consciousness of men is fused with the instincts of the animals. I remember all things, all, all, all, and in me every single life shall live anew!

Will-of-the-Wisps appear.

IRINA, *in a whisper.* This is right out of the decadent school of the symbolists.

TREPLEV, *imploring and reproaching her.* Mother!

NINA I am alone. Once in a hundred years I open my lips to speak, and then my voice echoes mournfully in the void, unheard by all. . . . You, too, pale spirits do not hear me. The stagnant marsh gives birth to you before the rising of the sun, and you wander until the day breaks . . . without thought, without will, without a tremor of life. The Prince of Darkness, the father of Eternal Matter, fearing that life should be born again in you, has created in you, as in the rocks and water, a continuum of atoms, so that your being is in constant flux. In the whole of the universe, the spirit alone remains constant and unchanged.

Pause.

Like a prisoner thrust into a deep and empty well, I know not what I am nor what lies before me. All I know is that I am destined to struggle with the Prince of Darkness, and that in that cruel and bitter battle I shall emerge victorious over the forces of matter, and then the spirit will join with matter in a triumphant harmony, and the Kingdom of the Cosmic Will will have arrived. But this must come gradually, little by little, through countless millennia when the moon, and bright Sirius, and all the earth are slowly turned to dust. Until then, only horror, horror. . . .

Pause. Two red spots appear in front of the lake.

Look! My all powerful enemy, The Prince of Darkness, is approaching. I see his terrible bloody eyes. . . .

IRINA That's the smell of sulphur, isn't it?

TREPLEV Yes.

IRINA, *laughing.* That's a good effect. Fine!

TREPLEV Mother!

NINA He is lost without Man. . . .

POLINA, *to* DORN. You've taken off your hat. Put it on again before you catch cold.

IRINA The doctor's taken his hat off to The Prince of Darkness, the Father of Eternal Matter.

TREPLEV, *flaring up angrily.* That's enough! The play's over! Curtain!

IRINA But what are you so cross about?

TREPLEV Enough! Enough, I say! Close the curtain! *Stamping his feet.* Curtain! *The curtain closes.* Forgive me! I forgot that only the elite are permitted to write plays and act in them. I've encroached on the rights of the monopoly! I . . . I mean . . . I . . . *Tries to say more, but cannot; waves his hand and goes off.*

IRINA What's wrong with him?

SORIN Irina, my dear, you must have more respect for a young man's pride!

IRINA But, what did I say?

SORIN You hurt his feelings.

IRINA He told us that it was only a joke, so that's the way I took it!

SORIN All the same. . . .

IRINA And now it seems he's written a masterpiece. Imagine that! He didn't concoct this little show and stink up the air with sulphur as a joke, but to teach us something. He wanted to show us how to write plays and what kind of plays we should act in. Really, this is getting a little tiresome! These everlasting attacks at my expense, these pinpricks; why it's enough to make a saint lose patience. Really, you must admit he's a conceited, impossible boy!

SORIN But he wanted so much to please you.

IRINA Did he really? Well, he didn't choose an ordinary play; instead he made us listen to these decadent outbursts. I'll even listen to the ravings of a madman, if it's a joke, but here we have only pretentiousness—new forms of art, a new era of creativeness! As far as I'm concerned, it's not a matter of new forms, but of bad temper.

TRIGORIN Everyone writes what he wants to write and as best he can.

IRINA Let him write whatever he likes and as he can, I don't care. Only just don't let him bother me with it. That's all I ask.

DORN Jupiter, you're angry . . .

IRINA I'm not Jupiter, I'm a woman! *Lighting a cigarette.* And I'm not angry, I'm just annoyed that the boy wastes his time that way. I certainly didn't mean to hurt his feelings.

MEDVEDENKO There's no basis for making a distinction between matter and spirit. After all the spirit is nothing more than a combination of atoms. *Excitedly to* TRIGORIN. But you know, someone ought to write a play about how teachers live. That ought to be put on the stage! Did you know we lead a very hard life?

IRINA That's true, but let's not talk of it now; or about plays or atoms either. It's such a pleasant evening. Listen! Do you hear the singing. *All listen.*

POLINA It's on the other side of the lake. *Pause.*

IRINA, *to* TRIGORIN. Sit down here beside me, my dear. You know, ten or fifteen years ago you could hear music and singing almost every night. There are six estates on the lake. Oh, and I remember such laughter, and noise, and there were shootings too—and the love affairs, love affairs all the time. . . . And the idol and favorite of all those estates, was our dear friend here. . . . *Turning to* DORN. May I present, Dr. Yevgeny Sergeyevich. He's still a charming, delightful man, but in those days he was irresistible. But my conscience is beginning to bother me. Why did I hurt the poor boy's feelings? Now, I'm all upset about it. *Calling.* Kostya! Oh, Kostya, dear!

MASHA I'll go and look for him.

IRINA Will you please, my dear.

MASHA, *going out.* Yoo-hoo! Konstantin Gavrilovich! Yoo-hoo!

NINA, *coming from behind the stage.* I guess we're not going on, so I might as well join you. Hello, everybody! *Kisses* IRINA *and* POLINA.

SORIN Bravo! Bravo!

IRINA Bravo! Bravo! You were wonderful. You know, with your good looks and lovely voice you oughtn't to stay out here in the country. It's a sin. You have real talent. Believe me, you owe it to yourself to become an actress. . . . and to the rest of us, too.

NINA Oh, that's my one and only dream! *Sighing.* But it'll never come true.

IRINA Who knows? But, forgive me, let me introduce you to Mr. Trigorin. Boris Alexeyevich Trigorin. . . .

NINA Oh, I'm so glad. . . . *Overcome with embarrassment.* I love your books. . . . I've read everything you. . . .

IRINA Here now, my dear, don't be shy. Yes, he's a famous man, but he's a gentle one, too. You notice, he's shy himself.

DORN We might as well open the curtain again, don't you think. It has a rather strange effect the way it is now.

SHAMRAEV, *shouting.* Yakov, open the curtains, will you!
The curtain opens.

NINA, *to* TRIGORIN. It's a strange play, isn't it?

TRIGORIN I didn't understand a word of it, but I enjoyed watching it. And you acted very well—with great sincerity. And the scenery was very beautiful. *Pause.* There must be a lot of fish in that lake.

NINA Yes.

TRIGORIN I love to fish. There's nothing I'd rather do than sit on the bank of a river in the evening and fish.

NINA That's so strange. I can't see how anyone who'd experienced the joy of true creation could ever find pleasure in anything else.

IRINA, *laughing.* Hush, child! When people talk like that to him, he doesn't know what to say.

SHAMRAEV I remember one night at the opera in Moscow I heard the famous Silva hit low C. By a strange coincidence, one of the basses in our church choir was in the gallery, and suddenly— to everyone's amazement—we heard from the gallery, "Bravo, Silva!" . . . But a whole octave lower. Like this: *In a deep bass.* Bravo, Silva! Why the audience was thunderstruck! You could actually hear a pin drop. *Pause.*

DORN The angel of silence has flown over us!

NINA Well, it's time for me to go. Good-bye, everyone.

IRINA Where are you off to so soon? You mustn't go!

NINA My father's expecting me.

IRINA What a man, really . . . *Embracing.* Well, if you must . . We're terribly sorry you have to go.

NINA If you only knew how much I hate to go.

IRINA Someone really ought to take you, child.

NINA, *frightened.* Oh, no, no!

Medvedenko — school teacher; always
concerned about $
this hard life

138   *THE SEA GULL*

SORIN, *to* NINA, *pleading.* Please stay.

NINA I just can't, Pyotr Nikolayevich.

SORIN Just for an hour, that's all.

NINA, *thinking a moment, and then tearfully.* I can't. *Shakes
hands with him and goes off.*

IRINA How unfortunate she is. They say her mother left her
huge fortune to her husband—every bit of it—and now the girl
has nothing, because her father married again and is leaving all
the money to his new wife. It's terrible!

DORN Yes, her father's a real beast. I grant you that.

SORIN, *rubbing his hands to keep warm.* I think we'd better go
in, too, my friends. It's awfully damp and my legs are beginning
to ache.

IRINA Oh, your poor legs! They're so stiff you can hardly walk—
just like wood. Here, let me help you, come along, my dear. *Taking
his arm.*

SHAMRAEV, *offering his arm to his wife.* Madame?

SORIN The dog's howling again. *To* SHAMRAEV. Ilya Afanasyevich,
will you be good enough to have him taken off his chain?

SHAMRAEV It's impossible, Pyotr Nikolayevich. Thieves might
break into the barn and I've just brought the grain in. *To* MED-
VEDENKO, *who's beside him.* Imagine, a whole octave lower. Bravo,
Silva! And he wasn't really a singer, he just sang in the choir.

MEDVEDENKO How much do they pay to sing in the choir?

All leave but DORN.

DORN, *alone.* I don't know, perhaps I don't know anything about
it, and maybe I'm crazy . . . but I liked that play. It's got something about it. When that girl talked about loneliness, and later
when those red eyes appeared, why I was so moved that my hands
were trembling. It was new, fresh, naïve . . . ah, but here he
comes. I must tell him lots of nice things about it.

TREPLEV, *entering.* So, they've gone already!

DORN I'm here.

TREPLEV Masha's been looking all over for me. I can't stand her!

DORN Kostya, I liked your play very much. It's a strange piece,
and of course I haven't heard it all, but it did make a deep impression on me. You're a talented man and you must go on writing.

TREPLEV *shakes his hands and embraces* DORN *impulsively.*
That's enough now. You're so nervous; and there are tears in

your eyes. . . . What I mean to say is this: You're dealing with abstract ideas, and that's good and as it should be, because a work of art must express some great idea or it will fail. Only the sublime, those things conceived with great seriousness, can ever be truly beautiful. . . . How pale you are!

TREPLEV So you think I should go on writing?

DORN Why, of course, I do. But you must only write about things that are significant and permanent. You know, my boy, I've lived a full life and had many experiences. I've enjoyed myself and I am satisfied. But if it had been my good fortune to experience the exaltation that an artist must feel at the moment of creation, I think I'd have come to despise this body of mine, and all of its pleasures, and my soul would fly off into the heights.

TREPLEV Excuse me, but where's Nina?

DORN Just one more thing. There must be a clear and definite idea in a work of art—you must know why you're writing—if not, if you walk along this enchanted highway without any definite aim, you will lose your way and your talent will ruin you.

TREPLEV, *impatiently.* Where's Nina?

DORN She's gone home.

TREPLEV What am I going to do? I've got to see her. . . . I've got to! I'm going.

Enter MASHA.

DORN, *to* TREPLEV. Calm down a bit, my friend.

TREPLEV But I'm going! I must go.

MASHA Please come in, Kostya. Your mother's terribly worried and she's waiting for you.

TREPLEV Tell her I've gone. And please, I beg of you—all of you—let me alone! Just, let me alone! Don't follow me about.

DORN Come, come, my dear boy. . . . you shouldn't carry on like this. . . . It's not right.

TREPLEV, *in tears.* Good-bye, Doctor. Thank you . . . *Leaves.*

DORN, *sighing.* Ah, youth! It always has its own way.

MASHA When people don't know what else to say, they say, "Ah, youth!" *Taking some snuff.*

DORN, *taking the snuff box from her and throwing it into the bushes.* How disgusting! *Pause.* I think I can hear them singing in the house. We'd better go in.

MASHA Wait just a minute.

DORN What is it, child?

MASHA There's something I've got to tell you again. . . . I've got to talk . . . *Very upset.* I really don't like my father, and you've always seemed more of one than he. For some reason I've always felt very close to you. Please help me. Help me, or I'll do something foolish that will mock life and ruin it. . . . I can't go on like this. . . .

DORN But what is it, my child? How can I help you?

MASHA Oh, I'm so unhappy. Nobody, nobody knows how unhappy I am. *Leaning against* DORN, *and speaking very softly.* I love Kostya.

DORN How upset everyone is! How upset! And everybody seems to be in love. . . . It must be the magic of the lake! *Tenderly.* But what can I do, my child? What can I do?

Curtain.

ACT II

A lawn on the SORIN *estate. In the background on the right a house with a large patio. On the left, a view of the lake with bright sunlight reflected in the water. It is about noon and hot. On one side of the lawn* IRINA, DORN, *and* MASHA *are sitting on a garden seat in the shade of an old lime tree.* DORN *has an open book on his lap.*

IRINA, *to* MASHA. Come, let's stand up. *Both get up.* Stand by my side. You're twenty-two and I'm nearly twice your age. Doctor, which of us looks younger?

DORN Why, you, of course.

IRINA There you see! And why is it? Because I work, I'm involved in things, I'm always on the go, while you sit in the same place all the time, you aren't really living. . . . And I make it a rule never to think about the future! And I never think of getting old, or of death. What will be, will be.

MASHA And I feel as though I'm a thousand years old, and I'm dragging my life behind me like a dress with an endless train. . . . And most of the time I don't have the slightest desire to go on living. Of course, that's all nonsense. I must pull myself out of this depression.

DORN, *humming quietly.* "Tell her, pretty flowers" . . .

IRINA And let me tell you one more thing—I am very particular about my appearance. You must never let yourself go, and that's why I'm always properly dressed and have my hair done in the latest fashion. Do you think I'd ever go out, even into the garden, in my dressing-gown or without combing my hair? Never. I've stayed young because I've never been sloppy or let myself go, as most women do . . . *Walking up and down the lawn, her hands on her hips.* There! you see? I'm as free as a bird. Why, I could play the part of a fifteen-year-old tomorrow!

DORN Well, I might as well get on with the reading. *Picking up the book.* We stopped at the place where the corn merchant and the rats . . .

IRINA Yes, the rats. Go on. *Sits down.* No, wait! Give it to me, I'll read. It's my turn. *Takes the book and is looking for the place.* The rats . . . yes, here we are. *Reads.* "And it's also true that it is as dangerous for the people in the higher circles of society to pamper and encourage novelists, as it is for corn merchants to breed rats in their granaries. And yet novelists are always pursued. Once a woman has chosen a writer whom she wishes to capture, she besieges him with compliments, flattery and favors." Well, that may be true of the French, but nothing like that goes on here. We don't plan and connive. Here a woman is usually head over heels in love with a writer long before she ever decides to capture him. You see that of course? For instance, take Trigorin and myself. . . .

SORIN *enters leaning on his stick with* NINA *walking beside him.* MEDVEDENKO *follows, wheeling an empty wheel chair.*

SORIN, *fondly, as to a child.* Indeed? So we're happy today, are we? We're feeling cheerful at last? *To his sister.* We're happy because our father and stepmother have gone to Tver, and now we're free for three whole days.

NINA, *sitting down beside* IRINA, *embraces her.* I'm so happy! Now I can be with you.

SORIN, *sitting down in his wheel chair*. Doesn't she look pretty today.

IRINA Beautifully dressed and her face is just glowing . . . She's such a fine girl . . . *Kisses her*. But we mustn't praise her too much. It's bad luck. Where's Boris Alexeyevich?

NINA He's down at the bath house . . . fishing.

IRINA I'm amazed he doesn't get bored with it! *Prepares to go on reading*.

NINA What are you reading?

IRINA Maupassant's "On the Water," darling. *Reading a few lines to herself*. Oh, well, this next bit isn't interesting. We'll skip it . . . and besides it's not true. *Closes the book*. I'm so worried. I wish somebody would tell me what's the matter with Kostya? Why is he so sullen and depressed? He's out on the lake day after day and I never see him.

MASHA His heart's troubled. *To* NINA, *shyly*. Please, Nina, won't you read us something from his play?

NINA, *shrugging her shoulders*. If you'd like, but it's so dull.

MASHA, *restraining her enthusiasm*. When he reads it, his eyes shine and his face turns pale. He has a beautiful sad voice and he looks like a poet.

SORIN *snores*.

DORIN Good night, everybody!

IRINA Petrusha!

SORIN Eh? What's that?

IRINA You've fallen asleep!

SORIN Why, I have not. *A pause*.

IRINA You're not taking your medicine. You know you should.

SORIN I'd be glad to take my medicine, but the good doctor here won't give me any.

DORN Medicine! At sixty!

SORIN Even at sixty a man wants to live.

DORN, *annoyed*. Oh, all right then, take some valerian drops.

IRINA I think it would do him a lot of good to go to the springs for a while.

DORN Well, he might go . . . Or he might not.

IRINA And what does that mean?

DORN Nothing at all. It's perfectly clear. *A pause*.

MEDVEDENKO Pyotr Nikolayevich, you ought to stop smoking.

SORIN Nonsense.

DORN Nonsense. No, it isn't nonsense. Wine and tobacco destroy one's individuality. After a cigar or a glass of vodka you're no longer just Pyotr Nikolayevich, but Pyotr Nikolayevich plus somebody else. You lose your sense of identity, and instead of seeing yourself as you are, you begin to feel like you are someone else . . . a kind of third person.

SORIN, *laughing*. It's all very well for you to talk. You've had a good life, but what about me? I've worked in the Department of Justice for twenty-eight years, but I haven't really lived, I haven't really experienced anything, I want to go on living. You've had a full life and don't care any more, that's why you can be so philosophical—but I want to live. That's why I drink sherry at dinner and smoke cigars, and all that . . . And that's that. . . .

DORN Certainly, life has to be taken seriously, but when it comes to taking cures at sixty and regretting that you didn't get enough pleasure out of life when you were young—all that, forgive me, is just a waste of time.

MASHA *gets up*. It must be almost lunch time. *Walking languidly and with an effort*. My leg's gone to sleep. *Goes out*.

DORN She'll go in and have a couple of drinks before lunch.

SORIN She's not very happy, poor girl.

DORN Oh, nonsense, your Excellency!

SORIN That's easy for you to say. You've had everything you've ever wanted.

IRINA Oh, what can be more boring than being in the country. It's so hot and muggy, and nobody does anything but sit around and philosophize. . . . Oh, it's pleasant to be here with you, my friends, I like to listen to you, but . . . how wonderful it is to sit alone in a hotel room learning a part!

NINA, *enthusiastically*. Oh, yes! I know just what you mean!

SORIN Yes, of course it's better in town. You can sit in your study, and the doorman doesn't let anyone come in unannounced and bother you, you have a telephone. . . . There are cabs on the streets, and all that sort of thing. . . .

DORN, *humming*. "Tell her, pretty flowers . . ."

SHAMRAEV *comes in, followed by* POLINA ANDREYEVNA.

SHAMRAEV Here you all are! Good morning! *Kisses* IRINA's *hand, then* NINA's. Glad to see you looking so well. *To* IRINA. My wife tells me that you're planning on going to town with her today. Am I right?

IRINA Yes, we are thinking of going.

SHAMRAEV Why, that's splendid. But—my dear lady, how do you propose to get there? We're hauling rye today, and all the men are busy. And besides, what horses are you going to use?

IRINA What horses? How should I know what horses?

SORIN Why, we'll use the carriage horses.

SHAMRAEV, *getting excited.* The carriage horses? And where am I to get harnesses for the carriage horses? Just tell me, where am I to get harnesses? You people amaze me! It is really more than I can understand! My dear lady! Please forgive me. I have the greatest respect for your talent, I'd give ten years of my life for you—but I can't let you have any horses.

IRINA But it so happens, I *have* to go! Do you understand?

SHAMRAEV My dear lady! Do you realize the problems there are in farming?

IRINA, *angrily.* The same old story! All right, then, order me some horses from the village, or else I'll walk to the station. I'm leaving for Moscow today!

SHAMRAEV, *angrily.* In that case, I resign. You can look for another manager. *Goes out.*

IRINA Every summer it's like this, every time I come here I'm insulted! I'll never set foot in this place again! *Going out in the direction of the bathhouse which is off-stage; a moment later she is seen entering the house, followed by* TRIGORIN, *who is carrying fishing rods and a pail.*

SORIN, *flaring up.* This is the limit! Such insolence! I'm sick and tired of it, once and for all! Harness every horse we've got and bring them here! This minute!

NINA, *to* POLINA To say no to Irina Nikolayevna, the famous actress! Even her slightest wish, her smallest whim, is more important than your silly old farming. It's simply incredible.

POLINA, *in despair.* But what can I do? Put yourself in my place, what can I do?

SORIN, *to* NINA. Let's go in and try to persuade my sister not to leave? *Looking in the direction in which* SHAMRAEV *has gone.* You're insufferable, man! Tyrant!

NINA, *preventing him from getting up.* Sit still, sit still. . . . We'll take you in. *She and* MEDVEDENKO *push the wheel chair.* All this is just terrible!

SORIN You're right, it is terrible! But he won't leave, I'll talk to him right away.

They go out; DORN *and* POLINA *are left alone.*

DORN People are so tiresome. Quite frankly, your husband ought to be thrown out. But of course, like always, that old woman, Pyotr Nikolayevich, and his sister will go begging his forgiveness. You'll see.

POLINA He's even sent the carriage horses out into the fields. And this sort of thing goes on every day. If you only knew how it upsets me! It makes me ill; see how I'm shaking. . . . I can't stand his rudeness. *Pleading with him.* Yevgeny, my darling, please let me come with you . . . Time is passing us by; we're not young any longer. . . . If . . . if we could only . . . at least for the rest of our lives . . . stop pretending, stop hiding the way we feel. . . .

DORN My dear, I'm fifty-five; it's too late to change now.

POLINA I know, you refuse me because you've got other women, too. You can't live with us all. I understand. Forgive me . . . you're tired of me.

NINA *appears near the house; she is picking flowers.*

DORN No, that's not so.

POLINA I'm wracked with jealousy. Of course, you're a doctor, you can't avoid women. I understand . . .

DORN, *to* NINA, *who approaches.* Well, have things quieted down in there?

NINA Irina's crying and Pyotr's had an attack of asthma.

DORN, *getting up.* I suppose I'd better go in and give them both some valerian drops.

NINA, *handing him the flowers.* For you!

DORN *"Merci bien!" Going up to the house.*

POLINA, *going with him.* Such beautiful flowers; *Near the house, in a low voice.* Give them to me! *He gives them to her and she tears them to pieces and throws them aside. Both go into the house.*

NINA, *alone.* How strange it is to see a famous actress crying . . . and over nothing! And isn't it strange that a famous writer spends all his time fishing. Here he is, a best seller, written about in all the papers, his pictures everywhere, his books translated into foreign languages, and . . . he gets all excited if he catches a couple of perch. I always thought that famous people were proud and aloof and that they despised the crowd; I thought they used their glory and fame to get revenge on people who put wealth and position above everything else. But here they are crying, and fishing, and playing cards, and laughing and getting upset like everyone else.

TREPLEV *enters, carrying a gun and a dead sea gull.* Are you all alone?

NINA Yes. TREPLEV *lays the sea gull at her feet.* What does this mean?

TREPLEV I was rotten enough to kill this sea gull today. I lay it at your feet.

NINA What's wrong with you? *Picks up the sea gull and looks at it.*

TREPLEV, *after a pause.* And soon I'm going to kill myself in the same way.

NINA What *is* wrong with you? This isn't like you at all!

TREPLEV That's true! I began to change when you did. You've changed towards me and you know it. . . . You're cold to me, and my very presence bothers you.

NINA You've been so irritable lately, and most of the time you talk in riddles and I don't understand a word you're saying. And I suppose now that this sea gull, here, is some kind of symbol too. Well, forgive me, I don't understand that either . . . *Putting the sea gull on the seat.* I'm too simple-minded to understand you.

TREPLEV It all began the night my play failed. Women never forgive failure. Well, I burnt it! Every bit of it! Oh, if you only knew how unhappy I am! And the way you've rejected me, I can't understand it! . . . It's as if I woke up one morning and found the lake suddenly drying up. You just said that you're too simple-minded to understand me. Tell me, what's there to understand? Nobody liked my play, so now you despise my talent, and think I'm ordinary and insignificant, like all the rest of them . . . *Stamping his foot*. Oh, how well I understand. How well! It's like a nail in my head . . . Oh, damn it . . . And my pride . . . sucking my life blood . . . like a snake . . . *Sees* TRIGORIN, *who enters reading*. But here comes the real genius, he walks like Hamlet himself, and with a book, too. *Mimics*. "Words, words, words." . . . The sun has hardly touched you, and already you're smiling and your eyes are melting in its rays. I won't bother you any more . . . *Goes out quickly*.

TRIGORIN, *making notes in his book*. Takes snuff and drinks vodka. Always wears black. A schoolmaster in love with her . . .

NINA Good morning, Boris Alexeyevich!

TRIGORIN Good morning. It seems that unexpectedly we're going to leave today. I don't suppose we'll meet again. I'm sorry. I don't often get a chance to meet young and interesting girls like you. I've forgotten what it feels like to be eighteen or nineteen; in fact, I can't even imagine it any more. That's why the young girls in my novels and stories usually ring false. I wish I could change places with you, just for an hour, so I could know your thoughts and the kind of person you are.

NINA And I'd like to be in your place for a while.

TRIGORIN What for?

NINA So I'd know what it feels like to be a famous, to be a talented writer. What does it feel like to be famous? What does it do to you?

TRIGORIN What does it feel like? I don't know, I've never thought about it. *After a moment's thought*. It's one of two things, I suppose: either you exaggerate my fame, or it's nothing at all.

NINA But you must read about yourself in the papers?

TRIGORIN When they praise me I'm pleased, and when they attack me I'm in bad humor for a couple of days.

NINA What a wonderful world you live in! How I envy you—if only you knew! . . . How different people's destinies are! Most people are all alike—unhappy. This obscure, tedious existence just drags on and on. And, then, there are others—like you, one in a million—who have a bright and interesting life, a life that has significance. Yours is a happy destiny.

TRIGORIN Mine! *Shrugs his shoulders*. You talk about fame and happiness, and this bright and interesting life I lead. But—to me all these fine words of yours, you must forgive me, are like great delicacies which I never eat. You are very young and very kind.

NINA Your life is beautiful.

TRIGORIN What's beautiful about it? *Looking at his watch.* I've got to go and write. Excuse me, I can't stay . . . *Laughs.* You've stepped on my favorite corn, as the saying goes, and here I'm beginning to get excited and even angry. But, let's talk. Let's talk about my bright and beautiful life. Where should we begin? *After a moment's thought.* Do you know what it is to have a compulsion? You know, when a man thinks about the same thing night and day, about . . . say, the moon. Well, I have my moon. I'm obsessed by one thought: I must write, I must write, I must . . . For some reason, no sooner have I finished one novel, when I feel I've got to start another, then another, then another . . . I write without stopping. Now, what's so bright and beautiful about that? It's absurd! Here I am with you, I'm excited, and yet I can never forget for a moment that there's an unfinished novel waiting for me. I look up and I see a cloud that looks like a grand piano . . . Immediately I think I've got to put it into a story. There's the scent of heliotrope in the air. I make a mental note: "sickly scent . . . a widow's flower . . . use it when describing a summer night." . . . I take every word, every sentence I speak, and every word you say, too, and quickly lock them up in my literary warehouse—in case they might come in handy sometime. When I finish my work, I go off to the theatre, or on a fishing trip, hoping to relax and forget myself. But no; there's a new subject rolling around in my head like a cast-iron ball. So immediately I drag myself back to my desk again, and I keep on writing and writing . . . And it's always like that, always . . . I have no rest from myself. I feel as though I'm devouring my own life, and that for the sake of the honey I give to everybody else I strip my best flowers of their pollen, tearing them up, and trampling on their roots. Do you think I'm crazy? Do you think my relatives and friends treat me like a normal person? "What are you writing down now? What's that for?" It's the same thing over and over again, until I begin to think that my friends' attention, their praise and admiration, is nothing but phony, that they're trying to fool me just as if I were insane. Sometimes I think they are going to come up to me from behind and put me into an insane asylum. And when I was younger and just starting out, then my writing was a constant torment. A minor writer, especially if he hasn't had much luck, feels clumsy, and awkward, and unnecessary. He's nervous and can't resist being around people connected with literature and the arts. But when he's with them, they don't notice him and he just wanders about afraid to look them straight in the eyes, like a passionate gambler without any money. I'd never seen any of my readers, but for some reason I always imagined them to be unfriendly and skeptical. I was frightened to death of people and public occasions, and it terrified me. Whenever a new play of mine was produced, I always felt that the dark-haired people in the audience were hostile to it, and the fair-haired ones coldly indifferent. It was awful! Such agony.

NINA But surely you have moments of happiness and exaltation —times when you feel inspired and your work's going well?

TRIGORIN Yes, while I'm writing I enjoy it. I enjoy reading the proofs, too, but . . . as soon as it's published, I can't stand it. Suddenly, I see that it wasn't what I intended, that I'd missed here, and that I should have cut there, and then I feel angry and get depressed . . . *Laughing.* And then the public reads it and says: "Yes, it's charming, very well done . . . Charming, but, of course, it's not Tolstoy." . . . Or "A fine piece, but Turgenev's *Fathers and Sons* is better." And that's the way it will be until my dying day . . . everything will be charming and well done— and nothing more. And after I'm dead my friends will pass by my grave, and say: "Here lies Trigorin. He was a good writer, but no Turgenev."

NINA Please forgive me, but I refuse to understand. You're simply spoiled by success.

TRIGORIN What success? I've never liked myself. I don't like what I write. And worst of all I live in a sort of daze, and I often don't even understand what I'm writing. I love this lake, the trees and the sky. I have an affinity for nature, it arouses a sort of passion in me, an irresistible desire to write. But, you see, I'm not just a landscape painter, I'm also a citizen. I love my country. I love its people. As a writer, I feel it's my duty to write about my people and their sufferings and their future—and about science and the rights of man, and so on, and so forth. And so I write about everything, always in a great hurry rushing to meet deadlines, having people angry with me, dashing about from one side to the other like a fox cornered by the hounds. I see science and society moving onward, while I drop further and further behind, like a peasant who's just missed his train, and finally, I come to feel that all I can do is to paint landscapes, and that everything else is false—false to the core.

NINA You've been working too hard, and you just don't want— or haven't the time—to recognize just how important you really are. You may be dissatisfied with yourself, but to the rest of us you're a great and wonderful person! If I were a writer like you, I'd give my whole life to the people, knowing that their happiness consisted in striving to rise to my level—and that they'd harness themselves to my chariot.

TRIGORIN A chariot, is it! . . . Am I an Agamemnon, or what? *Both smile.*

NINA For that kind of happiness—the happiness of being a writer or an actress—my family could disown me; I'd live in a garret with nothing to eat but rye bread; I could stand disappointment; I'd put up with the knowledge of my own weaknesses . . . But in return I'd demand fame . . . real, resounding fame . . . *Covering her face with her hands.* Oh, it makes me dizzy to even think of it.

IRINA's *voice, from the house.* Boris Alexeyevich!

TRIGORIN She's calling me . . . I've got to pack, I suppose. But I don't feel like going. *Looks round at the lake.* What a beautiful sight! How lovely it is!

NINA Do you see that house over there, with the garden?

TRIGORIN Yes.

NINA It was my mother's. I was born there and I've spent all my life on this lake. I know every island on it.

TRIGORIN It's a beautiful place! *Seeing the sea gull.* What's that?

NINA A sea gull. Kostya killed it.

TRIGORIN What a beautiful bird! Really, I don't want to go. Try to persuade Irina Nikolayevna to stay. *Writes in his notebook.*

NINA What are you writing?

TRIGORIN Just making a note . . . An idea for a story suddenly came into my head. A young girl, like you, has lived in a house on the shore of a lake since she was a little girl; she loves the lake like a sea gull, and she's as free and happy as a sea gull. Then a man comes along, sees her, and having nothing better to do, destroys her, like this sea gull here. *A pause.* IRINA *appears in the window.*

IRINA Boris Alexeyevich, where are you?

TRIGORIN I'm coming! *Goes, then looks back at* NINA. *To* IRINA *at the window.* What is it?

IRINA We're staying.

TRIGORIN *goes into the house.*

NINA *moves forward; after a few moments' meditation.* It's a dream!

Curtain.

ACT III

The dining-room in SORIN's *house. Doors right and left. A sideboard and a medicine cupboard. In the middle of the room a table. A trunk and some cardboard hat boxes indicate people are preparing to leave.* TRIGORIN *is having his breakfast while* MASHA *stands beside the table.*

MASHA I'm telling you all this because you're a writer. You can use it if you want to. Honestly, if he had seriously wounded himself, I couldn't have gone on living for another minute. But I'm getting courageous. I've just decided that I'd tear this love of mine out of my heart by the roots.

TRIGORIN How?

MASHA I'm going to marry Medvedenko.

TRIGORIN The schoolmaster?

MASHA Yes.

TRIGORIN But why?

MASHA Why love without hope, why wait years for something . . . when you can't be sure of what it is you're waiting for . . . Anyway, when I'm married there won't be any time for love, new responsibilities will take the place of . . . Anyhow, it'll be a change, you know. Let's have another.

TRIGORIN Do you think we should?

MASHA Oh, come! *Fills two glasses.* Don't look at me like that. Women drink a lot more than you think. A few of us drink openly, but most of them do it in secret. Yes. And it's always vodka or cognac. *Clinks glasses.* Well, here's to you! You're a fine man— I'm sorry you're leaving. *They drink.*

TRIGORIN I don't feel like going myself.

MASHA Why don't you ask her to stay?

TRIGORIN No, she'd never stay now. Her son is behaving very tactlessly. First he shoots himself, and now they say he's going to challenge me to a duel. What for? He sulks and groans, and preaches new art forms . . . But there's room for all kinds—new and old. Why make such a fuss about it?

MASHA He's jealous, too. But that's not my affair.

A pause. YAKOV *comes in carrying a suitcase.* NINA *comes in and stands by the window.*

My schoolteacher's not very bright and he's poor, but he's kind and very fond of me. I'm sorry for him and for his old mother, too. Well, I wish you all the best. Please remember me kindly. *Shakes his hand.* I'm grateful to you for your interest and your friendship. . . . Send me your books and be sure to inscribe them. Only don't write: "To the highly respected" and all that, just put "To Marya, who has no place and no object in life." Good-bye! *Goes out.*

NINA *holds out her hand towards* TRIGORIN, *with her fist clenched.* Odd or even?

TRIGORIN Even.

NINA, *with a sigh.* Wrong. I only had one pea in my hand. I was trying to guess my fortune—should I go into the theatre or not. If only someone would advise me!

TRIGORIN One can't give advice about that kind of thing. *A pause.*

NINA You're going to leave and . . . perhaps we'll never meet again. I want you to have this little medallion to remember me by. Please take it! I had your initials engraved on it . . . and on the back the title of your book—*Days, and Nights.*

TRIGORIN How exquisite! *Kisses the medallion.* It's a beautiful gift!

NINA Think of me sometimes.

TRIGORIN Of course, I will. I'll think of you as you were on that sunny day—do you remember?—a week ago, when you were wearing that white dress . . . we talked . . . there was a white sea gull lying on the seat.

NINA, *pensively.* Yes, a sea gull . . . *A pause.* We can't talk any more, someone's coming. Let me see you for just two minutes before you go, please . . .

Goes out. At the same time IRINA *and* SORIN *come in, the latter wearing a frock-coat with the star of an order on it.* YAKOV *follows with luggage.*

IRINA You really ought to stay here, dear. Do you think you're up to so much visiting with your rheumatism as bad as it is? *To* TRIGORIN. Who just left—Nina?

TRIGORIN Yes.

IRINA I'm sorry we disturbed you . . . *Sits down.* Well, I guess everything's packed. I'm worn out.

TRIGORIN, *reading the inscription on the medallion. Days and Nights,* page 121, lines 11 and 12.

YAKOV, *clearing the table.* Should I pack your fishing rods too, sir?

TRIGORIN Yes, I'll be wanting them again. But you can give the hooks away.

YAKOV Yes, sir.

TRIGORIN, *to himself.* Page 121, lines 11 and 12. What can they be? *To* IRINA. Are any of my books in the house?

IRINA Yes, in Pyotr's study, in the corner bookcase.

TRIGORIN Page 121 . . . *Goes out.*

IRINA Really, Petrusha, you'd better stay here.

SORIN You are going away—I couldn't stand it without you here.

IRINA But what is there to do in town?

SORIN Oh, nothing in particular, but just the same . . . *Laughs.* There'll be the laying of the cornerstone of the City Hall at Zemstvo . . . I'd like to do something! Live for a change! If only for an hour or two. For a long time now, I've felt that I've just been lying around, like an old cigarette-holder on a shelf. The horses are coming at one, so we can get started then.

IRINA, *after a pause.* You'd better stay here. Don't be bored and don't catch cold. Look after my son. Take care of him. Advise him.

A pause. Here I am going away, and I'll never know why he tried to shoot himself. Probably jealousy, so the sooner I take Trigorin away from here, the better.

SORIN That's part of it, but there were other reasons, too. It's not surprising, really. He's young, he's intelligent, but he's stuck out here in the country with no money, no position, and no future. He hasn't anything to do, really, and he's ashamed and afraid of his idleness. I am extremely fond of him, and he's fond of me too, but that doesn't change the fact that he feels he's a charity case and doesn't really belong here. After all, he does have his pride.

IRINA He's caused me a great deal of anxiety! *Pondering.* He really ought to get a job . . .

SORIN *begins to whistle, then speaks irresolutely.* I think maybe the best thing would be for you to give him some money. In the first place, he needs clothes. Just look at him, he's been wearing the same old jacket for the last three years, and he runs around without a topcoat . . . *Laughs.* Yes, and it wouldn't hurt him to have a little fun, either . . . go abroad . . . It wouldn't cost too much.

IRINA Well, I might be able to afford the suit, but as for going abroad . . . That's out of the question. As a matter of fact, right now I haven't the money for a suit. *Resolutely.* I haven't got the money. SORIN *laughs.* Well, I don't!

SORIN, *whistling.* Why, of course! Forgive me, my dear, I didn't mean to annoy you. I believe you . . . You're a generous, kind-hearted woman.

IRINA, *tearfully.* I haven't any money!

SORIN If I had any money I'd give it to him, but I haven't got a penny. *Laughs.* My manager takes every bit of my pension and spends it on the farm—buying cattle and the bees. It's just a waste of money! The cows and the bees die, and he never lets me use the horses . . .

IRINA Well, of course, I have some money, but after all, I'm an actress: my dress bill alone is enough to ruin me.

SORIN You're a fine woman, my dear . . . I respect you . . . Yes . . . But something's the matter with me again . . . *Sways.* I'm getting dizzy. *Holds on to the table.* I feel faint.

IRINA, *alarmed.* Petrusha! *Trying to support him.* Petrusha, my dear! . . . *Calling*. Help! Help! . . . TREPLEV, *with a bandage round his head, and* MEDVEDENKO *come in.* He's fainting!

SORIN It's all right, it's nothing . . . *Smiles and drinks some water.* It's better already . . .

TREPLEV, *to his mother.* Don't be frightened, Mamma, it's not serious. Uncle's been having these attacks a lot lately. *To his Uncle.* You'd better go and lie down for a while, Uncle.

SORIN Yes, for a while . . . But I'm going to town just the same. I'll lie down for a bit, then I'm going . . . That's definite. . . . *Goes out leaning on his stick.*

MEDVEDENKO, *supporting him by the arm.* Here's a riddle for you: what walks on four legs in the morning, two at noon, and three in the evening. . . .

SORIN, *laughing.* That's right. And at night on its back. I can manage alone, thank you . . .

MEDVEDENKO Come, come, let's not stand on ceremony. *Goes out with* SORIN.

IRINA How he frightened me!

TREPLEV It's not good for him to go on living out here. He gets depressed. Why don't you be generous, Mother, and lend him a couple of thousand? Then he could stay in town all year round.

IRINA I haven't any money. I'm an actress, not a banker. *A pause.*

TREPLEV Mamma, will you change my bandage for me? You do it so well.

IRINA *takes some iodine and a box of bandages out of the medicine cabinet.* The doctor's late.

TREPLEV He promised to be here by ten, and it's noon already.

IRINA Sit down. *Takes the bandage off his head.* This looks like a turban. Yesterday some stranger was asking in the kitchen what nationality you were. It's almost healed; just a tiny bit still open here. *Kisses him on the head.* Promise me you won't play with guns while I'm away?

TREPLEV I promise, Mamma. I just lost control of myself I was in such despair. It won't happen again. *Kisses her hands.* You've got such wonderful hands. I remember long ago, when you were still touring—I was a little boy then—there was a fight in our courtyard. A washerwoman was badly beaten. Do you remember?

She was unconscious . . . and you went to see her several times and took medicine to her, and bathed her children. Don't you remember?

IRINA No. *Puts on a fresh bandage.*

TREPLEV Two ballet dancers lived in the house then, too . . . They used to come and have coffee with you . . .

IRINA I remember that.

TREPLEV Weren't they pious! *A pause.* During these last few days, Mother, I've loved you as tenderly and as dearly as I used to when I was a little boy. I have no one left but you now. Only why, why, are you under the influence of that man?

IRINA You don't understand him, Konstantin. He's one of the most honorable men I've ever known. . . .

TREPLEV And yet, when he was told I was going to challenge him, his honor didn't prevent him from acting like a coward. He's leaving. Such ignominy!

IRINA What nonsense! I asked him to go myself.

TREPLEV One of the most honorable men you've ever known! Here you and I are practically quarreling over him, and at this very moment he's probably in the garden or the drawing room laughing at us . . . cultivating Nina's potential, doing his best to convince her finally that he's a genius.

IRINA You seem to enjoy saying these unpleasant things to me. I admire him, so please don't speak badly of him in my presence.

TREPLEV Well, I don't! I know. You want me to think he's a genius too, but I'm sorry, Mother. I don't like telling lies. His books make me sick.

IRINA You're jealous! Mediocrities who have grand ideas about themselves have to run down people with real talent. I hope it comforts you!

TREPLEV, *ironically.* Real talent! *Angrily.* I have more talent than any of you if it comes to that! *Tearing the bandage off his head.* It's conventional, stiff-necked people like you who've usurped the highest places in the arts today. You regard only what you do yourselves as genuine and legitimate. Everything else you stifle and suppress! I refuse to accept your authority! I refuse to accept you or him!

IRINA You decadent upstart!

TREPLEV Go on back to your precious little theatre and act in your lousy, third-rate plays!

IRINA I've never acted in lousy, third-rate plays! Let me alone! You can't even write a decent scene! You're nothing but a hack from Kiev! A parasite!

TREPLEV Miser!

IRINA Tramp! TREPLEV *sits down and weeps.* Nonentity! *Walks up and down in agitation, then stops.* Don't cry . . . You mustn't cry! . . . *Weeps.* You mustn't . . . *Kisses his forehead, then his cheeks and his head.* Please, forgive me, my darling. . . . Forgive your wicked mother. Forgive a very unhappy woman.

TREPLEV *embraces her.* Oh, Mother, if only you knew! I've lost everything. She doesn't love me, and I can't write any more . . . all my hopes are gone.

IRINA Don't despair . . . Everything will work out. He's leaving today, and then she'll love you again. *Wipes away his tears.* That's enough. We've made up now.

TREPLEV, *kissing her hands.* Yes, Mamma.

IRINA, *tenderly.* Make up with him, too. There's no need for a duel . . . Is there, really?

TREPLEV All right, Mamma, if you say so. Only I don't want to see him. It hurts too much . . . I just couldn't stand it. . . . TRIGORIN *comes in.* There he is . . . I've got to go . . . *Quickly puts away the dressings in the cupboard.* The doctor will take care of the bandage . . .

TRIGORIN, *paging through the book.* Page 121 . . . lines 11 and 12. Here it is . . . *Reads.* "If you ever need my life, come and take it." TREPLEV *picks up the bandage from the floor and goes out.*

IRINA, *glancing at her watch.* The carriage will be here soon.

TRIGORIN, *to himself.* "If you ever need my life, come and take it."

IRINA I hope you're packed!

TRIGORIN, *impatiently.* Yes, yes . . . *Musing.* Why is it I feel so sad about the plea of that dear, pure soul? Why is it that my heart aches with such pity? . . . "If ever you need my life, come and take it." *To* IRINA. Why don't we stay one more day! IRINA *shakes her head.* Please, let's stay!

IRINA Darling, I know what keeps you here. But please, try to control yourself. She's intoxicated you, but now it's time to sober up.

TRIGORIN You should try to be sober, too—be sensible, be reasonable. Try to understand this like a real friend, please, my dear . . . *Takes her hand.* You're capable of sacrifice . . . Be my friend, let me go . . .

IRINA, *very upset.* Is she that fascinating?

TRIGORIN I'm terribly drawn to her! Perhaps it is just what I need.

IRINA The love of a little country girl? Oh, how little you know yourself!

TRIGORIN Sometimes people go to sleep on their feet, and that's what's happened to me. Here I am, I'm talking to you, but all the time I'm dreaming of her. I'm possessed by sweet and wonderful dreams . . . You must let me go . . .

IRINA, *trembling.* No, no . . . what do you think I am? I'm just an ordinary woman, you can't talk to me that way . . . Don't torture me, Boris . . . I'm so afraid . . .

TRIGORIN If you wanted to, you could be so much more than that! The only thing in this life that is worth having and makes you truly happy . . . is love—a love that's young and beautiful, a love that's poetic, a love that carries you off into the world of dreams. I've never known that kind of love. When I was young I didn't have time; I was always sitting around in some editor's office, struggling to get just enough money to eat on. And suddenly, it's happened! That love has come to me . . . It calls me on and bids me to follow it. . . . How can I run away from it now . . . And why should I?

IRINA, *angrily.* You're out of your mind!

TRIGORIN And why not?

IRINA Everyone's in a conspiracy to torture me today! *Weeps.*

TRIGORIN, *taking his head with his hands.* You don't understand! You don't want to understand!

IRINA Am I really so old and ugly that you can talk to me about other women? *Embraces and kisses him.* Oh, you've gone out of your mind! My beautiful, my wonderful you. The last page of my life! *Falls on her knees.* My joy, my pride, my happiness! . . . *Embraces his knees.* If you leave me even for a single hour I won't survive it, I'll go out of my mind—my wonderful, marvelous, magnificent man, my master . . .

TRIGORIN Someone might come in. *Helps her to her feet.*

IRINA Let them, I'm not ashamed of my love for you. *Kisses his hands.* My darling reckless boy, you may want to be mad, but I won't let you, I won't let you . . . *Laughs.* You're mine . . . mine. . . . This forehead is mine, and these eyes, and this lovely silky hair. . . . All of you is mine. You're so gifted, so talented— you're the best of all the modern writers, Russia's only hope. . . . You have such sincerity, simplicity, freshness, invigorating humor. . . . With one touch you capture the essence of a character or a landscape; people in your books are alive. It's impossible to read them and not be moved. Oh, you think this is just hero-worship, that I'm flattering you! Come, look into my eyes . . . look. . . . Do I look like a liar? There, you see—I'm the only one who truly appreciates you, I'm the one person in the world who always tells you the truth, my darling, my wonderful man . . . You are coming? Yes? You won't leave me?

TRIGORIN I haven't any will of my own . . . I've never had a will of my own. Flabby, feeble, submissive—how can a woman want that kind of man? All right, take me, carry me off, but don't let me ever move a step away from you . . .

IRINA, *to herself.* He's mine! *Casually, as if nothing had happened.* But, of course, darling, you can stay if you want to. I'll go by myself, and you can come later next week, if you want. After all, there's no need for you to hurry.

TRIGORIN No, we'll go together.

IRINA Just as you like. Let's go together then . . . *A pause.*
TRIGORIN *writes in his notebook.* What are you writing?

TRIGORIN I heard a good phrase this morning—"The Maiden's Forest" . . . Might use it sometime. *Stretches.* So we're going? More trains, stations, restaurants, chops, conversations . . .

SHAMRAEV, *coming in.* It's with regret that I've come to say that everything's ready. It's time, my dear lady, that we leave for the station: the train gets in at five minutes after two. Will you do me a favor, Irina Nikolayevna? Will you find out where Suzdaltzev is now? Is he alive? Is he well? We used to drink together years ago . . . He was wonderful in *The Mail Robbery* . . . I remember at that time there was a tragedian, Izmailov, who always played with him at Elizavetgrad. . . . He was a remarkable person too. Don't rush, my dear lady, we don't have to start for another five minutes. Once they were playing the villains in some melodrama, and when they were suddenly discovered they had the line: "We're caught in a trap." But Izmalov said "We're taught in a cap." *Laughs loudly.* "Taught in a cap!"

While he's speaking, YAKOV *is busy with the suitcases; a* MAID *brings* IRINA'*s hat, coat, umbrella, and gloves, and everyone helps her to put them on. The* CHEF *looks in through the door at left, and after some hesitation enters.* POLINA, *then* SORIN *and* MEDVEDENKO *also come in.*

POLINA, *with a small basket in her hand.* Here's some fruit for the trip . . . very ripe. You might feel like having something refreshing.

IRINA You are very kind, Polina Andreyevna.

POLINA Good-bye, my dear! If everything hasn't been just as you like it, please forgive us. *Weeps.*

IRINA, *embracing her.* Everything was fine! Don't cry!

POLINA Time flies so fast!

IRINA There's nothing we can do about it.

SORIN, *wearing an overcoat with a shoulder cape and a hat, and carrying a cane, comes in from the door at left. He speaks as he walks across the room.* You'd better hurry, Sister, if you don't want to miss the train . . . I'm going to get into the carriage. *Goes out.*

MEDVEDENKO I'll walk to the station . . . to see you off. I'll be there in no time. *Goes out.*

IRINA Good-bye, everyone . . . If all goes well, we'll be here next summer . . . *The* MAID, *the* CHEF, *and* YAKOV *kiss her hand.* Don't forget me. *Gives the* CHEF *a rouble.* Here's a rouble for the three of you.

CHEF Thank you very much, madam. Have a pleasant journey. Thank you for your kindness.

YAKOV Godspeed!

SHAMRAEV Perhaps you'll write to us, it would make us very happy! Good-bye, Boris Alexeyevich.

IRINA Where is Kostya? Tell him I'm leaving. We must say good-bye. Think kindly of me. *To* YAKOV. I gave a rouble to the chef. It's for the three of you.

All go out. The stage is empty. There is the noise off-stage of people being seen off. The MAID *returns to fetch the basket of fruit from the table and goes out again.*

TRIGORIN, *returning.* I've forgotten my cane. I think I left it out here on the patio. *Walks towards the door at left and meets* NINA, *who comes in.* It's you! We're going . . .

NINA I knew we'd see each other again. *Excitedly.* Boris Alexeyevich, I've decided, the die is cast—I'm going into the theatre. I'm going tomorrow, I'm leaving my father and everything else, and I'm going to begin a new life . . . I'm going to Moscow . . . like you . . . And then I shall see you there.

TRIGORIN, *glancing behind him.* Stay at the Slavansky Bazaar. Let me know as soon as you get there . . . at Molchanovka, Groholsky House. . . . I've got to hurry . . . *A pause.*

NINA Just one minute . . .

TRIGORIN, *in an undertone.* You're so beautiful . . . Oh, how happy I am when I think that we'll be with each other soon! *She leans her head on his breast.* That I'll see these wonderful eyes again, this inexpressibly beautiful, tender smile . . . these soft features, the expression of angelic purity! My darling . . . *A prolonged kiss.*

Curtain.

Between the third and the fourth acts there is an interval of two years.

ACT IV

One of the drawing rooms in SORIN's *house, converted into a study for* KONSTANTIN TREPLEV. *Doors right and left leading to other rooms. In the middle, French doors opening on to the terrace. There is a desk in the corner on the right and a sofa by the door on the left; also a bookcase and the usual drawing room furniture. Books are lying on the window sills and on chairs. It is evening. The room is dimly lit by a shaded table lamp. There is the noise*

*of wind in the trees and the chimneys. A watchman is tapping.
Enter* MEDVEDENKO *and* MASHA.

MASHA, *calling.* Konstantin Gavrilovich! Konstantin Gavrilovich!
Looking round. No, there's no one here. The old man keeps on
asking where's Kostya, where's Kostya . . . He can't get along
without him . . .

MEDVEDENKO He's lonely. *Listening.* What horrible weather!
It's been like this for nearly two days now.

MASHA, *turning up the lamp.* And the waves on the lake are
getting bigger, too.

MEDVEDENKO And it's so dark out. By the way, we might as well
tell them to tear down that stage in the garden. It stands there like
a skeleton—naked and ugly with its curtains flapping in the wind.
You know, last night as I was walking past it, I was sure I heard
someone crying there.

MASHA What next . . . *A pause.*

MEDVEDENKO Masha, let's go home.

MASHA, *shaking her head.* No, I'm going to stay here tonight.

MEDVEDENKO, *imploringly.* Please, Masha, let's go! The baby'll
be hungry.

MASHA Nonsense! Matryona will feed him. *A pause.*

MEDVEDENKO But, I feel sorry for him. This is the third night
now, that he's been without you.

MASHA Oh, don't be so tiresome! At least you used to philosophize once in a while. Now all you ever do is talk about the
baby and home, baby and home—that's all I hear.

MEDVEDENKO Please, come, Masha!

MASHA Go by yourself.

MEDVEDENKO Your father won't give me a horse.

MASHA Yes, he will. Ask him.

MEDVEDENKO I suppose I could. . . . And you'll come home
tomorrow?

MASHA *takes snuff.* All right . . . tomorrow. Now stop pestering
me!

Enter TREPLEV *and* POLINA. TREPLEV *carries pillows and a
blanket and* POLINA *some sheets, which they put on the sofa.*
TREPLEV *then goes to his desk and sits down.* Who's this for,
Mother?

POLINA It's for Pyotr Nikolayevich. He wants to sleep in Kostya's room.

MASHA Here, let me . . . *Makes the bed.*

POLINA, *sighing.* Old people are like children . . . *Walks over to the writing desk and, leaning on her elbow, looks at a manuscript. A pause.*

MEDVEDENKO Well, I'd better go. Good-bye, Masha. *Kisses his wife's hand.* Good-bye, Mother. *Tries to kiss his mother-in-law's hand.*

POLINA, *with irritation.* Well, then go if you're going.

MEDVEDENKO Good-bye, Konstantin Gavrilovich.

TREPLEV *gives him his hand without speaking;* MEDVEDENKO *goes out.*

POLINA, *looking at the manuscript.* Who'd have guessed that you would turn out to be a real writer, Kostya? And now, thank God, the magazines are paying you for your work. *Strokes his hair.* You've gotten so handsome, too . . . Kostya, my dear, you're so good, won't you try to be kinder to Masha?

MASHA, *making the bed.* Leave him alone, Mother.

POLINA, *to* TREPLOV. She's a fine girl . . . *A pause.* All a woman wants, Kostya, is that sometimes a man give her a kind look. Believe me, I know.

TREPLEV *gets up from his desk and goes out without speaking.*

MASHA Oh, Mother, now you've made him angry! Why pester him like that?

POLINA I feel so sorry for you, Mashenka!

MASHA A lot of good that does me!

POLINA My heart aches for you. I see it all, you know . . . I understand it all.

MASHA Nonsense. Love without hope—that doesn't exist except in novels. It's nothing really. You've just got to keep a firm grip on yourself, stop yourself from hoping . . . from hoping that things will change . . . If you begin to feel love, you just forget it! Anyway, they've promised to transfer my husband to another county. As soon as we get there, I'll forget all about it . . . tear it out of my heart by the roots.

A melancholy waltz is played two rooms away.

POLINA Kostya's playing again. He must be very sad.

MASHA, *dancing two or three waltz steps.* The most important thing, Mother, is not to see him all the time. Just wait till Semyon gets his transfer . . . you'll see, I'll forget it in a month. The whole thing's nonsense.

DORN *and* MEDVEDENKO *enter, wheeling in* SORIN.

MEDVEDENKO I've got six people to take care of now, and flour's two kopecks a pound.

DORN Yes, you've got to work hard to make ends meet.

MEDVEDENKO That's easy for you to say. You've got more money than you know what to do with.

DORN Money? My friend, after thirty years of practice—thirty years of being on call night and day—all I've managed to save is two thousand roubles, and I've just spent them on my trip abroad. I haven't got anything either.

MASHA, *to her husband.* So you haven't gone yet?

MEDVEDENKO, *apologetically.* Well . . . how could I? They wouldn't give me a horse.

MASHA, *bitterly, in an undertone.* I can't stand the sight of you!

SORIN *is wheeled to the side of the room;* POLINA, MASHA *and* DORN *sit down beside him;* MEDVEDENKO, *looking depressed, stands to one side.*

DORN My, what a lot of changes you've made! You've turned this drawing room into a study.

MASHA It's more convenient for Konstantin Gavrilovich. This way he can walk out into the garden whenever he feels like it, and he can think there.

The watchman taps.

SORIN Where's my sister?

DORN She's gone to the station to meet Trigorin. She'll be back soon.

SORIN I must be very sick, if you had to send for my sister. *Pause.* It's a funny thing, here I'm very sick, and no one gives me any medicine.

DORN Well, what would you like to have? Valerian drops? Soda? Quinine?

SORIN The same old thing! Now, I suppose you're going to begin philosophizing! Oh, it's so trying! *Jerks his head in the direction of the sofa.* Is my bed ready yet?

POLINA Yes, Pyotr Nikolayevich, it's all ready.

SORIN Thank you.

DORN, *hums.* "The moon is floating in the midnight sky . . ."

SORIN You know, I'm going to give Kostya a subject for a story. I'd call it: "The Man Who Wished." *"L'homme qui a voulu."* When I was young I wanted to be a writer—and I didn't; I wanted to be a good speaker—and I spoke miserably—*Mimicking himself.* "and all that sort of thing, and all the rest of it, and so on, and so forth" . . . When I tried to sum up a case, I'd go plodding on and on until I broke out into a terrible sweat . . . I wanted to get married—and I didn't, I always wanted to live in town—and here I am finishing my life in the country, and so and so on . . .

DORN You wanted to become a state's attorney, and you did.

SORIN *laughs.* I didn't want that, it just happened.

DORN Imagine, being dissatisfied with life at sixty-two! You've got to admit, that's a bit indecent.

SORIN Won't you ever stop! Can't you understand someone wanting to live?

DORN Don't be foolish. Every life has to end—that's the law of nature.

SORIN That's talk from a man who's had everything he's ever wanted. You've had your fill, so you don't have to worry. But when death comes, you'll be afraid of it, too.

DORN The fear of death is an animal fear. You've got to overcome it. Only religious people should fear death. They believe in a future life, so they're afraid they'll be punished for their sins. You're different; first of all, you're not religious, and secondly, what sins have you committed? You served in the courts for twenty-five years . . . and that's all.

SORIN *laughs.* Twenty-eight years . . .

Enter TREPLEV, *who sits down on a stool at* SORIN's *feet.* MASHA *gazes at him continuously.*

DORN We're keeping Konstantin Gavrilovich from his work.

TREPLEV Oh, it doesn't really matter. *A pause.*

MEDVEDENKO Excuse me, Doctor, but what city did you like best?

DORN Genoa.

TREPLEV Why Genoa?

DORN Because everything's so alive. You go out of your hotel at night, and the street is crowded with people. You can go any-

where you want, and there's always that crowd. Pretty soon you
become part of it, you live with it, and before long you come to
believe that a world-soul really does exist. It's something like the
world-soul in your play, Kostya; you know, the one Nina Zarech-
naya acted in a couple of years ago. By the way, where is she
now? How is she?

TREPLEV I believe she's quite well.

DORN Someone told me she'd been leading a rather strange life.
What happened?

TREPLEV Well, it's a long story, Doctor.

DORN All right, make it short then. *A pause.*

TREPLEV Well, she ran away from home and had an affair with
Trigorin. You knew that, didn't you?

DORN Yes, that I did know.

TREPLEV She had a child and it died. Trigorin got tired of her
and went back to his old attachments, as might have been expected. Not that he'd ever given them up; for, being the spine-
less character he is, he somehow managed to make the best of
both worlds. As far as I can gather, Nina's personal life has turned
out a complete failure.

DORN And what about her career in the theatre?

TREPLEV I guess that's even worse. She began in a small
theatre at some resort near Moscow, then she went to the
provinces. At that time I never lost track of her, and for months
I followed her wherever she went. She always played big parts,
but her acting was crude and lacked taste—she tended to rant
and over-gesture. She had some good moments—when she cried
or played a death scene—that showed she had some talent, but
they were only moments.

DORN Then she has some talent, after all?

TREPLEV It's very hard to say. I suppose she must have. I saw
her of course, but she wouldn't see me, and I never got to see her
at her hotel. I knew how she felt so I didn't insist on seeing her.
A pause. Well, what else is there to say? Afterwards, when I got
back here, I had some letters from her, affectionate, intelligent letters . . . She never complaned, but I could tell that she was very
unhappy, every line showing that her nerves were on edge. And
then her mind seemed to be a little unbalanced. She always signed
herself "Sea Gull." You remember, in Pushkin's *The River Nymph*

the miller calls himself a raven. Well, in her letters, she always called herself "The Sea Gull." By the way, she's here now.

DORN How do you mean—here?

TREPLEV I mean she's staying at a hotel in town. She's been there for the last five days. I went to see her, and Masha went too, but she won't see anybody. Semyon insists that he saw her yesterday afternoon walking in the fields a mile or so from here.

MEDVEDENKO Yes, I saw her. She seemed to be walking toward town. I bowed to her and asked her why she didn't come and see us. She said she would.

TREPLEV She won't! *A pause.* Her father and stepmother won't even see her. They've got watchmen all over to see that she doesn't come to the house. *Goes with the doctor toward the writing desk.* It's so simple to be philosophical on paper, Doctor, but it's so hard in real life.

SORIN She was a charming girl.

DORN What?

SORIN I said she was a charming girl. You know, I was actually in love with her for a while.

DORN Why, you old philanderer!

Off-stage SHAMRAEV *can be heard laughing.*

POLINA I think they're back from the station . . .

TREPLEV Yes, I can hear mother.

Enter IRINA *and* TRIGORIN, *followed by* SHAMRAEV.

SHAMRAEV, *as he comes in.* We all get older and fade like leaves in winter, but you, my dear lady, you're still as young as ever . . . vivacious, graceful, a white dress.

IRINA You're still trying to bring me bad luck, aren't you, you boring old man!

TRIGORIN, *to* SORIN. How are you, Pyotr Nikolayevich? Still not feeling well, that's too bad! *Seeing* MASHA, *happily.* Ah, Marya Ilyinishna!

MASHA You remember me? *Shakes hands with him.*

TRIGORIN Of course—married?

MASHA Long ago.

TRIGORIN Happy? *Bows to* DORIN *and* MEDVEDENKO—*who bow in return*—*then hesitatingly approaches* TREPLEV. Irina Nikolayevna's told me that you've forgotten the past, and aren't angry with me any more. TREPLEV *holds out his hand.*

IRINA, *to her son.* Look, Boris Alexeyevich has brought the magazine that has your latest story in it.

TREPLEV, *taking the magazine, to* TRIGORIN. Thanks, that was kind of you.

TRIGORIN Your public sends its greetings . . . People all over Petersburg and Moscow are very much interested in your work. They keep asking me what you're like, how old you are, and what you look like. Strangely enough, they all seem to think you're an old man. And no one knows your real name! Why do you always write under a pseudonym? You're as mysterious as the Man in the Iron Mask.

TREPLEV Will you be here long?

TRIGORIN No, I've got to be back in Moscow tomorrow. I've just got to finish this novel, and then, I've promised to do something for an anthology. You know, the same as ever.

While they talk, IRINA *and* POLINA *move a card table into the middle of the room and open it.* SHAMRAEV *lights the candles and puts the chairs in place. A game of lotto is brought out of the cupboard.*

The weather's certainly given me a poor welcome. That's a bad wind. In the morning if it calms down a bit, I think I'll go fishing for a while. Besides, I want to have a look around the garden and see the place where your play was put on—you remember? I've got a good subject for a story, only I'll have to refresh my memory about the setting.

MASHA, *to her father.* Father, please let Semyon take one of the horses. He's got to get home.

SHAMRAEV, *mimics her.* He needs a horse . . . he must get home. . . . *Sternly.* You know the horses have just been to the station. They can't go out again!

MASHA But there are other horses . . . *Seeing that her father says nothing, she gestures impatiently.* Oh, you're hopeless . . .

MEDVEDENKO That's all right, Masha, I can walk.

POLINA, *with a sigh.* Walk in this weather! . . . *Sits down at the card table.* Come, everybody, let's get started.

MEDVEDENKO After all, it's only four miles . . . Good-bye . . . *Kisses his wife's hand.* Good-bye, Mother. POLINA *reluctantly holds out her hand for him to kiss.* I wouldn't have bothered you if it

weren't for the baby . . . *Bows to the group.* Good-bye . . .
Goes out guiltily.

SHAMRAEV Of course, he can walk! Who does he think he is, a
general?

POLINA, *tapping on the table.* Come along, please! Let's not
waste any time, they'll be calling us for supper soon.

SHAMRAEV, MASHA, *and* DORN *sit down at the table.*

IRINA, *to* TRIGORIN. When the long autumn evenings come, we
always play lotto when we're here. Look, this is the same set my
mother had when she played with us as children. Why don't you
play with us before supper? *Sits down at the table with* TRIGORIN.
It's a dull game, but it's not so bad when you get used to it. *Deals
three cards to everyone.*

TREPLEV, *turning over the pages of the magazine.* He's read his
own story, but he hasn't even cut the pages of mine. *Puts the magazine down on his desk and walks towards door at left. As he
passes his mother, he kisses her on the head.*

IRINA Aren't you going to play, Kostya?

TREPLEV No thanks, I don't feel like it. . . . I think I'll go for
a walk. *Exits.*

IRINA Everyone puts in ten kopecks. Put it in for me, will you,
Doctor?

DORN Certainly.

MASHA Everybody in? I'm starting. Twenty-two!

IRINA I've got it.

MASHA Three.

DORN Right!

MASHA Did you play three? Eight! Eighty-one! Ten!

SHAMRAEV Slow down.

IRINA What a reception they gave me in Karkhov! It makes me
dizzy even when I think of it.

MASHA Thirty-four!

A melancholy waltz is heard off-stage.

IRINA Why, the students gave me a regular ovation . . . Three
baskets of flowers and two wreaths, and this little brooch as well
. . . *Unfastens a brooch on her throat and tosses it on to the table.*

SHAMRAEV That's really something.

MASHA Fifty!

DORN Fifty, did you say?

IRINA And my dress was beautiful! If there's one thing I know to do, it's how to dress!

POLINA Kostya's playing the piano again. He's depressed, poor boy.

SHAMRAEV They've been attacking him quite a bit lately in the papers.

MASHA Seventy-seven!

IRINA That shouldn't bother him!

TRIGORIN It's too bad. His things never quite come off. There's something vague and mysterious about his style; it's like the ravings of a madman. And, then, none of his characters seem to have any life.

MASHA Eleven!

IRINA, *looking round at* SORIN. Petrusha, are you bored? *A pause.* He's asleep.

DORN Our great lawyer's asleep.

MASHA Seven! Ninety!

TRIGORIN If I lived in a place like this, beside a lake, I don't think I'd ever write. I'd get over this compulsion of mine and do nothing but fish.

MASHA Twenty-eight!

TRIGORIN Just to catch perch . . . how wonderful that would be!

DORN Well, I've got faith in Konstantin Gavrilovich. He's got some real talent! He thinks in images, and his stories are vivid and full of color, and personally I'm deeply moved by them. It's a pity he doesn't have a definite aim. He makes an impression and that's all, but just making an impression doesn't get you very far. Irina Nikolayevna, are you glad that your son's a writer?

IRINA Can you imagine it?—I haven't read anything he's written. It seems there's never any time.

MASHA Twenty-six!

TREPLEV *comes in quietly and walks over to his desk.*

SHAMRAEV, *to* TRIGORIN. By the way, Boris Alexeyevich, we've still got something of yours.

TRIGORIN What's that?

SHAMRAEV Konstantin Gavrilovich shot a sea gull once, and you asked me to get it stuffed for you.

TRIGORIN Did I really? *Pondering.* I don't remember it.

MASHA Sixty-six! One!

TREPLEV *opens the window and listens.* How dark it is! I can't understand why I'm feeling so restless.

IRINA Kostya, please shut the window, there's a draught!

TREPLEV *shuts the window.*

MASHA Eighty-eight!

TRIGORIN I win!

IRINA, *gaily.* Bravo, bravo!

SHAMRAEV Well done!

IRINA That man's lucky in everything! *Gets up.* Now it's time to eat. Our celebrity hasn't eaten all day. We'll play some more after supper. *To her son.* Kostya, you'd better stop writing and come and eat.

TREPLEV I don't want to, Mother, I'm not hungry.

IRINA Just as you like. *Wakes* SORIN. Petrusha, supper is ready! *Takes* SHAMRAEV's *arm.* Let me tell you about the reception they gave me at Karkhov. . . .

POLINA *blows out the candles on the table, then she and* DORN *wheel out* SORIN's *chair. Everyone goes out but* TREPLEV, *who remains alone sitting at his desk.*

TREPLEV, *getting ready to write, he reads through what he has already written.* I used to talk so much about new forms in art, and now I feel that little by little I'm getting into a rut myself. *Reads.* "The poster announced . . . A pale face framed by dark hair . . ." Announced . . . framed by dark hair . . . That's horrible! *Crosses out.* I'll begin again where the hero's awakened by the sound of the rain. I'll cut out the rest. And the description of the moonlight is no good either. Trigorin's worked out his own techniques, so it comes easily for him . . . He'd just mention the neck of a broken bottle glittering in a mill stream and the black shadow of the mill wheel—and he's got a moonlight night. But for me it's the shimmering light, the silent twinkling of the stars, and the distant sounds of a piano, dying away in the still, fragrant air . . . It's terrible! *A pause.* Yes, I'm more and more convinced that it isn't old or new forms that matter—what matters is that one should write without thinking of forms at all, and that whatever one has to say should come straight from the heart. *There is a tap on the window nearest to his desk.* What's that? *Looks through the window.* I can't see anything. . . . *Opens the French doors*

and looks out into the garden. Someone's running down the steps.
Calls. Who's there? *Goes out and is heard walking rapidly along
the patio, then returns half a minute later with* NINA. Nina! Nina!
NINA *leans her head against his breast and sobs quietly.*

TREPLEV, *deeply moved.* Nina! Nina! It's you . . . it's you . . .
I knew you'd come! All day my heart's been pounding . . . *Takes
off her cape and hat.* Oh, my darling, precious girl, you've come at
last! Don't cry, darling, don't cry!

NINA Someone's here.

TREPLEV No there isn't.

NINA Lock the doors, so no one can get in.

TREPLEV No one will come in.

NINA I know Irina Nikolayevna is here. Lock the doors.

TREPLEV *locks the door on right, then crosses to the left.* This one
doesn't have a lock, I'll have to put a chair against it. *Puts an armchair against the door.* Don't be afraid, darling, no one will come
in.

NINA *looks intently at his face.* Let me look at you for a minute.
Looking round. How nice and warm it is here! . . . Didn't this
used to be the drawing room? Have I changed a lot?

TREPLEV Yes . . . You're thinner and your eyes seem bigger.
Nina, how strange it is to be seeing you! Why wouldn't you let me
see you before? Why did you want to come here? I know you've
been in the town almost a week. . . . I've been to your hotel
every day, sometimes several times a day, and I stood under your
window like a beggar.

NINA I was afraid that you might hate me. Every night I dream
that you look at me and don't recognize me. If only you knew! Ever
since I came I've been walking round here . . . by the lake. I've
been near the house many times, but I was afraid to come in. Let's
sit down. *They sit down.* Let's just sit and talk and talk . . . It's
nice here, warm and comfortable . . . Do you hear the wind?
There's a passage in Turgenev: "Fortunate is the man who, on
stormy nights, has a roof over his head and a warm corner of his
own." I am a sea gull . . . No, that's not it. *Rubs her forehead.*
What was I saying? Yes . . . Turgenev . . . "And Heaven help
the homeless wanderers!" . . . But it doesn't matter . . . *Sobs.*

TREPLEV Nina, you're crying again! . . . Nina!

NINA Never mind, it does me good . . . I haven't cried for two

years. Yesterday, late in the evening I came into the garden to
see whether our stage was still there. It's still standing! I cried for
the first time in two years then, and it was like taking a great
weight off my heart, and I felt better. See, I'm not crying any more.
Takes his hand. So you've become a writer . . . You're a writer
and I'm an actress. We've been drawn into the whirlpool together.
I used to live here, happily as a child—I'd wake up in the morning
singing. I loved you and dreamt of fame . . . And now? Tomorrow, I leave early in the morning on a coach for Yelietz . . .
traveling with peasants; and at Yelietz, merchant lotharios will
pester me with their attentions. Life is really very ugly.

TREPLEV Why go to Yelietz?

NINA I've taken a job for the winter. It's time I went.

TREPLEV Nina, I used to curse you; I hated you, I tore up the
pictures of you and your letters, but all the time I knew that I
loved you heart and soul, and that I always would! I can't stop
loving you, Nina. Ever since I lost you, ever since I began to get
my work published, my life's been unbearable. I'm so unhappy
. . . I feel as if my youth has been suddenly torn away from me,
as if I've lived for ninety years. I call out your name, I kiss the
ground where you've walked; wherever I go I see your face, that
tender smile that brightened the days when I was happy . . .

NINA, *confused.* Why does he talk like this, why does he talk
like this?

TREPLEV I am lonely. There is no love to warm me, I feel as cold
as if I were in a dungeon—and everything I write turns out lifeless
and gloomy and bitter. Please, stay, Nina! I beg you, or else let
me come with you! NINA *quickly puts on her hat and cape.* Nina,
why—what's wrong, Nina . . . *Looks at her as she puts on her
clothes. A pause.*

NINA The horses are waiting at the gate. Don't bother to come
with me, I'll go by myself . . . *Tearfully.* Give me a glass of
water.

TREPLEV *gives her water.* Where are you going now?

NINA To town. *A pause.* Irina Nikolayevna's here, isn't she?

TREPLEV Yes . . . My uncle had an attack last Thursday, so
we wired for her to come.

NINA Why did you say you kissed the ground where I walked?
You ought to kill me. *Droops over the table.* Oh, I am so tired. I

wish I could rest . . . just rest! *Raising her head.* I'm a sea gull
. . . No, that's not it. I'm an actress. But, what difference does it
make? *She hears* IRINA *and* TRIGORIN *laughing off-stage, listens,
then runs to the door at left and looks through the keyhole.* So he is
here, too! . . . *Returning to* TREPLEV. So he is . . . it doesn't
matter . . . Yes . . . He didn't believe in the theatre, he laughed
at all my dreams, and so gradually I didn't believe them either,
and I lost faith . . And then there was the strain of love and
jealousy, and the constant worry about my baby . . . I dried up,
my acting was very bad . . . I didn't know what to do with my
hands or how to stand or how to use my voice . . . You can't
imagine what it feels like when you know that you're doing a bad
job. I'm a sea gull. No, that's not it . . . Do you remember you
shot a sea gull once? A man came along by chance, and he saw it
and destroyed it, just to pass the time . . . A subject for a short
story . . . That's not it. *Rubs her forehead.* What was I saying?
. . . Oh, yes, about the stage. I'm different now . . . I've become
a real actress. I enjoy acting! I revel in it! The stage intoxicates
me, and on it I feel very beautiful. While I've been here, I've spent
a lot of time walking and thinking . . . thinking . . . and I feel
that my spirit's growing stronger every day. I know now, Kostya,
that what matters most for us, whether we're writers or actors,
isn't fame or glamor, or any of the things I used to dream of. What
matters most is knowing how to endure, knowing how to bear your
cross and still have faith. I have faith now and I can stand my
suffering when I think of my calling, I'm not afraid of life.

TREPLEV, *sadly.* You've found your road, you know where you're
going—but I'm still floating about in a maze of dreams and images,
without knowing what it is I am to do . . . I have no faith, and
I have no calling.

NINA, *listening.* Sh-sh! . . . I'm going now. Good-bye. When I
become a great actress, come and see me act. Promise? But now
. . . *Presses his hand.* It's late. I'm so tired I can hardly stand
up . . . I'm tired and hungry . . .

TREPLEV Do stay! I'll get you some supper.

NINA No, no . . . Don't come with me, I'll go by myself . . .
My horses are close by . . . So she brought him with her? Oh,
well, it doesn't matter . . . When you see Trigorin don't say anything . . . I love him. I love him even more than before. A sub-

ject for a short story . . . Yes, I love him, I love him passionately,
I love him desperately! Do you remember how nice it used to be,
Kostya? Do you remember? How peaceful and warm, how joyous
and pure our life was then, what feelings we had? . . . like
tender, exquisite flowers . . . Do you remember? . . . *Recites.*
"Men, lions, eagles, and partridges, horned deer, geese, spiders,
and the silent fish of the deep, starfish and creatures which cannot
be seen by the eye—all living things, all living things, all living
things, having completed their cycle of sorrow, are now extinct.
For thousands of years the earth has given birth to no living thing,
and this poor moon now lights its lamp in rain. In the meadows,
the cranes no longer waken with a cry, and the sound of the May
beetles, humming in the lime groves, can no longer be heard." . . .
Impulsively embraces TREPLEV *and runs out through the French
doors.*

TREPLEV, *after a pause.* I hope no one sees her in the garden and
tells mother about it. It might upset her! *He spends the next two
minutes silently tearing up all his manuscripts and throwing them
under the table, then unlocks the door at right and goes out.*

DORN, *trying to open the door at left.* That's funny, the door
seems to be locked . . . *Comes in and puts the armchair in its
place.* What have we got here, a regular obstacle race.

Enter IRINA *and* POLINA, *followed by* YAKOV *carrying drinks,
then* MASHA, SHAMRAEV *and* TRIGORIN.

IRINA Put the red wine and the beer on the table for Boris
Alexeyvich. We'll want to drink while we play. Let's sit down,
everyone.

POLINA, *to* YAKOV. Bring the tea, too. *Lights the candles and sits
down at the card table.*

SHAMRAEV *leads* TRIGORIN *to the cupboard.* Here's the thing I
was telling you about before . . . *Takes the stuffed sea gull out
of the cupboard.* This is what you ordered.

TRIGORIN, *looking at the sea gull.* I don't remember. *Musing.* No,
I don't at all!

There is a sound of a shot off-stage on right. Everyone starts.

DORN Don't worry. Something must have gone off in my medicine case. Don't worry. *Goes out through door at right, returns in
half a minute.* Just as I thought. A bottle of ether blew up. *Hums.*
"Again I stand before you, enchanted.". . .

IRINA, *sitting down to the table*. Oh, how it frightened me! It reminded me of how . . . *Covers her face with her hands.* Everything went black for a minute.

DORN, *thumbing through a magazine, to* TRIGORIN. There was an article in here about two months ago . . . a letter from America that I wanted to ask you about . . . *Puts his arm around* TRIGORIN's *waist and leads him down-stage.* You see, I'm very much interested in this question . . . *Dropping his voice, in a lower tone.* Somehow get Irina Nikolayevna away from here. The fact is, Konstantin Gavrilovich has shot himself. . . .

Trepler

Curtain.

UNCLE VANYA

CAST

MARINA, *an old nurse*
MIHAIL LVOVICH ASTROV, *a doctor*
IVAN PETROVICH VOYNITSKY (Uncle Vanya)
ALEXANDER VLADIMIROVICH SEREBRYAKOV, *a retired pro-
    fessor*
YELENA ANDREYEVNA, *his wife*
SOFYA ALEXANDROVNA (Sonya), *his daughter by his first wife*
ILYA ILYICH TELYEGIN (Waffles), *an impoverished landowner*
MARYA VASSILYEVNA VOYNITSKAYA, *widow of a privy coun-
    cillor, mother of Uncle Vanya and the professor's first wife*
A WORKMAN

The action takes place on Serebryakov's estate.

MARINA, *pouring a cup of tea.* Here, my friend, drink a cup of tea.

ASTROV, *reluctantly taking the cup.* For some reason I don't seem to care for any.

MARINA Would you rather have some vodka?

ASTROV No, I don't drink vodka every day. And, besides, the day is too hot and stifling for it. *A pause.* Tell me, old nurse, how long have we known each other?

MARINA, *pondering and thoughtfully.* Let me see, how long is it? God only knows. You first came into these parts, let me see—when was it? Well, Sonya's mother was still alive—she died two years later; that was at least eleven years ago. . . . *Pondering.* Perhaps even longer.

ASTROV Have I changed much since then?

MARINA Oh, yes. You were young and handsome then, and now you seem like an old man. And you drink too.

ASTROV Yes. . . . Ten years have made another man of me. And why? Because I am overworked. Do you know, nurse, that I am on my feet from morning till night? I don't know what it is to rest; at night I hide in bed trembling under the blankets in the continual fear that I'll be dragged out to visit someone who is sick. Ever since I have known you, I haven't had a single day all to myself. No wonder I am growing old, how could I help it? And besides, life is tedious; it is senseless, dirty, stupid, and it just drags on and on . . . *Pause.* . . . and finally it swallows you up. *Pause.* Every one around here is commonplace, and after you live with them for a couple of years, you, too, become commonplace and queer. It's inevitable. *Twisting his mustache.* See what a long mustache I have. A foolish, long mustache. Yes, I am just as silly as all the others, nurse, just as trivial, but not as stupid; no . . . I have not grown stupid. Thank God, my brain is not muddled yet, though my feelings have grown dull. There's nothing I want, there's nothing I need, there's no one I love, except, perhaps, you. *He kisses her head.* When I was a little boy, I had a nurse just like you.

MARINA Don't you want just a little something to eat?

ASTROV No. During the third week of Lent, a typhoid epidemic broke out in the village, and I had to go. The peasants were all stretched out side by side in their huts, and the calves and the pigs were running about among the sick and the dying. How dirty and filthy it was, and the stench of the smoke, ugh, it was unbearable! I slaved among those people all day, and I didn't have a thing to eat. And then when I returned home there was still no rest for me: a switchman was carried in from the railroad; I laid him on the operating table and he died in my arms under the choloroform. And then, my feelings, which should have been deadened, awoke again; my conscience tortured me as if I had murdered the man. I sat down and closed my eyes—like this—and thought: will those who come after us two hundred years from now, those for whom we are breaking the path . . . will they remember us with grateful hearts? No, nurse, they will forget.

MARINA Man forgets, but God remembers.

ASTROV Thank you for that. You spoke the truth.

Enter Vanya from the house. He has been asleep after dinner and looks somewhat disheveled. He sits down on the bench and straightens his tie.

VANYA H'mm. Yes. *A pause.* Yes.

ASTROV Have a good nap?

VANYA Yes, very good. *He yawns.* Ever since the Professor and his wife came, our daily routine seems to have gone haywire. I sleep at the wrong time, drink too much wine, and I eat the wrong kind of food. It's no good. Sonya and I used to work together and we never had an idle moment. But now she works alone and I . . . I just eat and drink and sleep. Something is wrong.

MARINA, *shaking her head.* Such confusion in the house! The Professor gets up at twelve, the samovar has to be kept boiling all morning, and everything has to wait for him. Before they came we used to have dinner at one o'clock, like everybody else, but now we eat at seven. The Professor sits up all night writing and reading or something, and suddenly, at two o'clock, the bell rings. Heavens, what's that? The Professor wants tea! Wake up the servants, light the samovar! Lord, what disorder!

ASTROV Will they be here long?

VANYA, *whistling.* A hundred years! The Professor has decided to stay here for good.

MARINA Just look at this, for instance! The samovar has been

Telyegin — escapezoptimum

boiling away on the table for two hours now, and they've gone out for a walk!

VANYA, *calming her brusquely.* Here they are—here they are—don't get so excited.

Voices are heard. SEREBRYAKOV, YELENA, SONYA, *and* TELYEGIN *enter from the garden, returning from their walk.*

SEREBRYAKOV Superb! Superb! What glorious views!

TELYEGIN They are lovely, your excellency.

SONYA Tomorrow we shall go to the woods, shall we, father?

VANYA Ladies and Gentlemen, tea is served.

SEREBRYAKOV Won't you please send my tea into the library. I have something to do . . . ah, some work to finish.

SONYA I am sure you will love the woods, father.

YELENA, SEREBRYAKOV, *and* SONYA *go into the house.* TELYEGIN *takes a seat at the table beside* MARINA.

VANYA It is hot and humid, but our eminent scholar walks about in his overcoat and goloshes, wearing gloves and carrying an umbrella.

ASTROV Which means that he takes good care of himself.

VANYA But how lovely she is! How lovely! I have never seen a a more beautiful woman.

TELYEGIN Whether I drive through the fields or take a walk under the shady trees in the garden, or look at this table I experience a feeling of indescribable bliss! The weather is enchanting, the birds are singing; we all live in peace and harmony. . . . what else do we want? *Taking a cup of tea.* Oh, thank you.

VANYA, *dreaming.* Such eyes—a glorious woman!

ASTROV Come, Vanya, tell us something.

VANYA, *indolently.* What shall I tell you?

ASTROV Haven't you any news for us?

VANYA No, it is all old. I am the same as ever, no . . . worse, for I've become lazy. I do nothing any more but grumble like an old crow. My mother, the old magpie, is still babbling about the emancipation of women, with one eye on her grave and the other on her learned books, in which she is forever rummaging in the hopes of finding the dawn of a new life.

ASTROV And the Professor?

VANYA The Professor as usual sits in his study reading and writing from morning till night. . . .

Straining our mind, wrinkling our brow,
We write, write, write,
With no respite
Or hope of praise in the future or now.

Oh, poor unfortunate paper! He ought to write his autobiography; he would make such an excellent subject for a book! Just think, the life of a retired professor, as stale as a piece of mildewed bread, racked with gout, headaches, and rheumatism, his heart bursting with jealousy and envy, living on the estate of his first wife, although he hates it, because he can't afford to live in town. He is always whining about his hard fate, although, as a matter of fact, he is extraordinarily lucky. *Nervously.* He is the son of a common, ordinary parson and has achieved a professor's chair, has become the son-in-law of a senator, is called "your excellency," but forget it! I'll tell you something; he's been writing about art for twenty-five years, and he doesn't know the first thing about it. For twenty-five years he has been hashing over the thoughts of other men on realism, naturalism, and all the other nonsensical "isms"; for twenty-five years he has been reading and writing things that intelligent men have always known and that are stupid and boring to those who don't care; for twenty-five years he has been pouring water from one empty glass into another. Yet . . . consider the man's conceit and pretensions! He has been pensioned off . . . Not a living soul has ever heard of him. He is totally unknown. He is a nothing. That means that for twenty-five years he has been treating life as if it were a masquerade ball, and all that it has accomplished is to have kept a better man out of a job. But just look at him! He struts across the earth like a demigod!

ASTROV You know, I believe you envy him.

VANYA Yes, I do. Look at the success he's had with women! Don Juan himself was no luckier. His first wife, my sister, was beautiful, gentle, as pure as the blue sky, generous, with more suitors than the number of all his pupils put together and she loved him as only creatures of angelic purity can love those who are as pure and beautiful as they are themselves. My mother adores him to this day, and he still inspires her with a kind of worshipful awe. And now, his second wife is, as you can plainly see, a great beauty, and she is intelligent too; and yet she married him in his old age and

See p. 67

surrendered to him all the glory of her beauty and freedom. For what? . . . Why?

ASTROV Is she faithful to him?

VANYA Yes, unfortunately she is.

ASTROV Why "unfortunately"?

VANYA Because such fidelity is false and unnatural. Oh, it sounds very good, but there is no rhyme nor reason to it. It is immoral for a woman to deceive and endure an old husband whom she hates. But for her to stifle her pathetic youth, those intense longings within her heart—her feelings . . . that is not immoral!

TELYEGIN, *in a tearful voice.* Vanya, don't talk like that. Really, you know, anyone who is unfaithful to his wife or husband is a disloyal person and will betray his country, too!

VANYA, *crossly.* Oh, Waffles, dry up!

TELYEGIN No, allow me, Vanya. My wife ran away with a lover the day after our wedding, because of my . . . ah . . . rather unprepossessing appearance. Since then I have never failed to do my duty. I love her and am true to her to this day. I help her all I can and I've given my fortune to educate the children she had by her lover. I have lost my happiness, but I have kept my pride. And she? Her youth has fled, her beauty has faded according to the laws of nature, and her lover is dead. What does she have left?

YELENA *and* SONYA *enter, followed by* MARYA *carrying a book. The latter sits down and begins to read. Someone hands her a cup of tea which she drinks without looking up.*

SONYA, *hurriedly to the nurse.* Some peasants are waiting inside. Go and see what they want. I'll look after the tea.

She pours out several cups. MARINA *goes out.* YELENA *takes a cup and sits drinking in the swing.*

ASTROV, *to* YELENA. I came to see your husband. You wrote me saying he is very ill, that he has rheumatism and what not, but he seems fine, as lively as ever.

YELENA He had a fit of depression last night and complained of pains in his legs, but he seems all right again today.

ASTROV And I hurried twenty miles at breakneck speed to get here! But, never mind, it isn't the first time. However, now that I am here, I am going to stay until tomorrow; for the first time in ages I am going to sleep as long as I want.

SONYA Oh, wonderful! You spend the night with us so seldom. Have you eaten yet?

ASTROV No.

SONYA Fine, then you will have dinner with us. We don't eat until seven now. *Drinks her tea.* Oh, the tea is cold!

TELYEGIN Yes, the samovar has gone out.

YELENA Never mind, Ivan, we'll just have to drink it cold.

TELYEGIN I beg your pardon, madam, my name is not Ivan, it's Ilya, Ilya Telyegin, or Waffles, as some people call me because of my pock-marked face. I am Sonya's godfather, and his excellency, your husband, knows me very well. I now live here on this estate; perhaps, sometime you will be good enough to notice that I dine with you every day.

SONYA He is a great help to us—our right-hand man. *Tenderly.* Dear godfather, let me pour you some more tea.

MARYA Oh! Oh!

SONYA What is it, grandmother?

MARYA I forgot to tell Alexander—I must be losing my memory—I received a letter today from Paul in Kharkov. He sent me a new pamphlet.

ASTROV Is it interesting?

MARYA Yes, but it is so strange. He refutes the very theories he defended seven years ago. Isn't that queer; in fact, it's appalling.

VANYA Oh, there is nothing so appalling about it. Drink your tea, mother.

MARYA But I have something to say, I want to talk.

VANYA But that is all we have been doing for the last fifty years: talk, read a few pamphlets, and talk some more. . . . Talk. Talk. It's time to quit all that nonsense.

MARYA It seems that you never want to listen to what I have to say. If you will pardon me, Jean, you have changed so much this last year that I hardly know you. You used to be a man of strong convictions and had such an illuminating personality. . . .

VANYA Oh, yes, to be sure. I had an illuminating personality, I had elevated ideas, which illuminated or elevated no one. *A pause.* I had an illuminating personality! You couldn't say anything more cruel. I am forty-seven years old. Until last year I tried, as you still do, to blind my eyes with meaningless pedantry to the truths of life. Yes, I did it on purpose, to avoid seeing life as it

really is . . . and I thought I was doing the right thing. But now.
. . . Oh, if you only knew! If you knew how I lie awake at night,
heartsick and angry, to think how stupidly I wasted my time when
I might have been taking from life everything which is now denied
me because I am old.

SONYA Uncle Vanya, how dreary!

MARYA, *to her son.* You talk as if your former convictions were
somehow to blame, but you yourself, not they, were at fault. You
have forgotten that a conviction, in itself, is nothing but a dead
letter. You should have done something.

VANYA Done something! It isn't every man who is capable of
being a . . . a writing machine like your dear professor.

MARYA What do you mean by that?

SONYA, *imploringly.* Grandmother! Uncle Vanya! Please!

VANYA I am silent. I apologize and am silent. *A pause.*

YELENA What a fine day! Not too hot. *A pause.*

VANYA Yes, a fine day to hang oneself.

TELYEGIN *tunes his guitar.* MARINA *appears near the house, calling the chickens.*

MARINA Here chick, chick, here chick!

SONYA What did the peasants want, nurse?

MARINA The same old thing, the same old nonsense. Here chick,
chick!

SONYA Why are you calling the chickens?

MARINA The speckled hen disappeared with her chicks. I'm
afraid the hawks might get them.

TELYEGIN *plays a polka. Everyone listens in silence.* A WORKMAN
enters.

WORKMAN Is the doctor here? *To* ASTROV. Please, Dr. Astrov,
I've been sent for you.

ASTROV Where do you come from?

WORKMAN The factory.

ASTROV, *annoyed.* Thank you. I suppose I shall have to go
whether I want to or not. *Looking around him for his cap.* Damn
it, this is annoying.

SONYA Oh, yes, it is too bad. You must come back from the
factory for dinner.

ASTROV No, I shan't be able to do that. It will be too late. Now
where, where—*To the* WORKMAN. Look here, good fellow, get

me a glass of vodka, will you? *The worker goes out.* Where—where *Finds his cap.* There is a man in one of Ostrovsky's plays, with a long mustache and short wits, like me. However, let me bid you good night, ladies and gentlemen. *To* YELENA. I should be most delighted if you came to see me some day with Sonya. My place is small, but if you are interested in such things—things like terraced gardens, sapling beds, and nurseries, the likes of which you'll not find within a thousand miles of here—I'd like to show them to you. My estate is surrounded by government forests. But the old forester is always sick and complains so, that I take care of most of the work myself.

YELENA I have always heard that you were very fond of the woods. Of course you can do a great deal of good by helping to preserve them, but doesn't that work interfere with your real calling? You're a doctor, aren't you?

ASTROV God alone can know what a man's real work is.

YELENA And you find it interesting?

ASTROV Yes, very.

VANYA, *sarcastically*. Oh, extremely.

YELENA You are still young, I should say certainly not over thirty-six or seven, and I have an idea that the woods do not interest you as much as you claim. I should think that you would find them quite monotonous.

SONYA Dr. Astrov plants new forests every year, and he has been awarded a bronze medal and a diploma. He does his best to prevent the destruction of the forests. If you listen to him you will agree with him entirely. He claims that forests beautify the earth, and so teach man to understand the beautiful, and instill in him a feeling of respect and awe. Forests temper the severity of the climate. In countries where the climate is warmer, less energy is wasted on the struggle with nature and that is why man there is more gentle and loving; the people there are beautiful, supple, and sensitive, their speech is refined and their movements graceful. Art and learning flourish among them, their philosophy is not so depressing, and they treat women with refinement and nobility.

VANYA, *laughing*. Bravo, bravo! All this is charming, but not convincing and so, *To* ASTROV. I hope you'll permit me, my friend, to go on burning logs in my stove and building my barns with wood.

ASTROV You can burn peat in your stoves and build your barns of stone. Oh, I don't object, of course, to cutting wood when you have to, but why destroy the forests? The woods of Russia are trembling under the blows of the axe. Millions of trees have perished. The homes of the wild animals and the birds have been laid desolate; the rivers are shrinking, and many beautiful landscapes are gone forever. And why? Because men are too lazy and stupid to bend over and pick up their fuel from the ground. *To* YELENA. Am I wrong? Who but a senseless savage could burn so much beauty in his stove and destroy what he cannot create himself? Man has reason and creative powers so that he may increase that which has been given to him. Until now, however, he has not created, he has only destroyed. The forests are disappearing, the rivers are drying up, the game is being exterminated, the climate is spoiled, and the earth becomes poorer and more ugly every day. *To* VANYA. Oh, I read irony in your eye; you do not take seriously what I am saying; and—and—perhaps I am talking nonsense. But when I cross those peasant forests which I have saved from the axe, or hear the rustling of the young trees, which I have set out with my own hands, I feel as if I had had some small share in improving the climate, and that if mankind is happy a thousand years from now I shall have been partly responsible in my small way for their happiness. When I plant a young birch tree and see it budding and swaying in the wind, my heart swells with pride and I . . . *Sees the* WORKMAN, *who is bringing him a glass of vodka on a tray*. However. . . . *He drinks*. . . . I must be off. Probably it is all nonsense, anyhow. Good-bye.

SONYA When are you coming to see us again?

ASTROV I don't know.

SONYA In a month?

ASTROV *and* SONYA *go into the house.* YELENA *and* VANYA *walk over to the terrace.*

YELENA Vanya, you have been behaving impossibly again. What sense was there in irritating your mother with all your talk about her pamphlets and the "writing machine." And this morning you quarreled with Alexander, again. How petty and small it all is!

VANYA But suppose I hate him?

YELENA You hate Alexander without reason; he is like everyone else, and no worse than you.

VANYA If you could only see your face, your every movement and gesture! Oh, how tedious your life must be!

YELENA Yes, it is tedious, and dreary, too! All of you abuse my husband and look on me with compassion; you think, "Poor woman, she is married to an old man." How well I understand your sympathy and compassion! As Astrov said just now, see how thoughtlessly you destroy the forests, so that soon there will be nothing left on earth. In just the same way you recklessly destroy human beings, and soon, thanks to you, loyalty and purity and self-sacrifice will have vanished along with the woods. Why can't you look with calm indifference at a woman unless she belongs to you? Because . . . the doctor is right. You are all possessed by a devil of destructiveness; you have no feeling, no, not even pity, for either the woods or the birds or women, or for one another.

VANYA Would you mind stopping all this philosophizing; I don't like it. *A pause.*

YELENA That doctor has a sensitive, weary face . . . an interesting face. Sonya evidently likes him; she is in love with him, and I can understand her feeling. *Pause.* This is the third time he has been here since I have come, and I have not had a real talk with him yet or showed him much attention. He thinks I am disagreeable. Do you know, Vanya, why you and I are such friends? I think it is because we are both lonely and tiresome and unsympathetic. *Pause.* Yes, unsympathetic. *Pause.* Don't look at me that way, I don't like it.

VANYA How can I look at you in any other way since I love you? You are my joy, my life, my youth. I know that my chances of your loving me in return are infinitely small . . . no . . . they are nil, nonexistent; there are no chances, but I ask nothing of you, I want nothing. Only let me look at you, listen to you. . . .

YELENA Quiet! Someone may hear you.

VANYA Let me tell you of my love; don't drive me away. I have no other happiness.

YELENA Oh, this is agony!

Both go into the house. TELYEGIN *strums the strings of his guitar and plays a polka.* MARYA *writes something on the leaves of her pamphlet.*

Curtain.

ACT II

The dining room of SEREBRYAKOV's *house. It is night. The click of the Watchman's rattle is heard from the garden.* SEREBRYAKOV *sits dozing in an armchair by an open window and* YELENA, *likewise half asleep, is seated beside him.*

SEREBRYAKOV, *rousing himself.* Who's there? Is that you, Sonya?

YELENA It is I.

SEREBRYAKOV Oh, it's you, Lenotchka. This pain is unbearable.

YELENA Your blanket has slipped. *She wraps the blanket around his legs.* Let me shut the window.

SEREBRYAKOV No, leave it open; I am suffocating as it is. *Pause.* I just dropped off to sleep . . . and . . . I dreamt that my left leg belonged to someone else, and the pain was so agonizing that I awoke. I don't believe this is gout; it is more like rheumatism. *Pause.* What time is it?

YELENA Twenty after twelve. *Pause.*

SEREBRYAKOV I wish you'd look for Batushkov tomorrow morning; we used to have him, I remember. Oh, why do I find it so hard to breathe?

YELENA You're exhausted; this is the second night you've been unable to sleep.

SEREBRYAKOV They say that Turgenev got heart trouble from gout. I'm afraid I'm getting it, too. Oh, damn this terrible, accursed old age! Ever since I've grown old, I have been hateful to myself, and, I'm sure, hateful to all of you, too.

YELENA You talk as if we were to blame for your old age.

SEREBRYAKOV I am more hateful to you than to all the others.

YELENA *gets up, walks away from him and sits down at a distance.*

SEREBRYAKOV You are right, of course. I'm no fool; I can understand. You are young and healthy and beautiful. You want and long for life, and I am an old dotard, almost a corpse. Oh, I know it! Certainly, I see that it's foolish for me to go on living for such a long time, but wait! I shall soon set you all free. My life can't drag on too much longer.

YELENA For God's sake, be quiet! . . . You are exhausting me.

SEREBRYAKOV It seems that everybody is being exhausted, thanks to me. Everybody is miserable and depressed; everyone's youth is wasting away; only I am enjoying life in blissful triumph. Oh, yes, of course!

YELENA Be quiet! You're torturing me.

SEREBRYAKOV Why of course, I torture everybody.

YELENA, *on the verge of tears.* This is unbearable! Please, just tell me what you want me to do?

SEREBRYAKOV Nothing.

YELENA Then please be quiet.

SEREBRYAKOV It's funny that everybody listens to Vanya and his old fool of a mother, but the moment I open my mouth, you all begin to feel abused. You can't even bear the sound of my voice. Suppose I am hateful, suppose I am a selfish and egocentric tyrant, haven't I the right to be at my age? Haven't I deserved it? Haven't I, I ask you, the right to be respected, the right to be pampered and cared for . . .

YELENA No one is disputing your rights. *The window slams in the wind.* The wind is rising, I must shut the window. *She shuts it.* We shall have rain in a few minutes. *Pause.* Your rights have never been questioned by anybody.

The watchman in the garden clicks his rattle.

SEREBRYAKOV I have spent my life working for the cause of learning. I am accustomed to my study, the library and the lecture hall and to the regard and admiration of my colleagues. And, now . . . *Pause.* . . . now, I suddenly find myself in this wilderness, in this vault, condemned to see the same stupid people from morning till night and to listen to their inane talk. I want to live; I long for success and fame and the tension of an active world, and here I am in exile! Oh, it's terrible to spend every moment grieving for a past that is lost, to witness the success of others and to sit here with nothing to do but fear death. I can't stand it! It's more than I can endure. And you, you won't even forgive me for being old!

YELENA Wait; be patient; in four or five years, I shall be old too.

SONYA *comes in.*

SONYA Father, you sent for Dr. Astrov, and now you refuse to see him. It's not fair to needlessly trouble a busy man.

SEREBRYAKOV Oh, what do I care about your Astrov? He knows as much about medicine as I do about astronomy.

SONYA We can't send for famous specialists to come here to cure your gout, can we?

SEREBRYAKOV I refuse to talk to that madman.

SONYA Do as you wish then. It makes no difference to me. *She sits down.*

SEREBRYAKOV What time is it?

YELENA One o'clock.

SEREBRYAKOV It's stifling in here. . . . Sonya, hand me that bottle there on the table.

SONYA, *handing him a bottle of medicine.* Here you are.

SEREBRYAKOV, *cross and irritated.* No, not that one! Don't you ever understand? Can't I ask you to do a single thing?

SONYA Please don't be cross with me. Some people may enjoy it, but spare me, if you please, because I don't like it. Furthermore, I haven't time for it; we are planning to cut the hay tomorrow and I have to get up early.

VANYA *enters dressed in a long gown and carrying a candle.*

VANYA A thunderstorm is on its way. *The lightning flashes.* There it is! Sonya, you and Yelena had better go and get some sleep. I have come to relieve you.

SEREBRYAKOV, *frightened.* No, no, no! Don't leave me alone with him! Oh please don't. He will begin lecturing me again.

VANYA But you must let them have a little rest. They haven't slept for two nights now.

SEREBRYAKOV All right, then let them go to bed, but, please, you go away, too! Thank you. I beg of you, please go away. . . . For the sake of . . . ah . . . our former friendship, don't argue. We'll talk some other time. . . .

VANYA Our former friendship! Our former. . . .

SONYA Shh, please be quiet, Uncle Vanya!

SEREBRYAKOV, *to his wife.* My love, don't leave me alone with him. He will begin his infernal lecturing.

VANYA This is absurd.

MARINA *comes in carrying a candle.*

SONYA You must go to bed, nurse, it's late.

MARINA I haven't cleaned up the tea things. I can't go to bed yet.

SEREBRYAKOV No one can. Everyone is completely worn out. I alone enjoy perfect peace and happiness.

MARINA, *going up to* SEREBRYAKOV *and speaking tenderly.* What's the matter, little man? Does it hurt? My own legs ache, too, oh, such pain. *She arranges the blanket around his legs.* You've been sick like this for such a long time. Sonya's mother used to sit up with you night after night, too, and she wore herself out for you. She loved you dearly. *A pause.* Old people like to be pitied as much as small children, but somehow nobody cares about them. *She kisses Serebryakov's shoulder.* Come to bed, my little man, let me give you some linden-tea and warm your poor feet. I shall pray to God for you.

SEREBRYAKOV, *moved.* Let us go, Marina.

MARINA My own feet ache so badly, too, oh, so badly! *She and* SONYA *start leading* SEREBRYAKOV *out.* Sonya's mother used to wear herself out with sorrow and weeping over you. You were still a small and senseless child then, Sonya. Come along now, come along . . .

SEREBRYAKOV, MARINA, *and* SONYA *go out.*

YELENA He so completely exhausts me, that I can hardly stand up.

VANYA He has exhausted you and I have exhausted myself. I haven't had a bit of sleep for three nights now.

YELENA There's something wrong in this house. Your mother hates everything but her pamphlets and the Professor; the Professor is vexed and irritated, he won't trust me and he fears you; Sonya is angry with her father and also with me, and she hasn't spoken to me for two weeks; you hate my husband and openly sneer at your mother. I have reached the limit of my endurance . . . there is no strength left, why I've nearly burst into tears at least twenty times today. There is something wrong in this house.

VANYA Oh, why don't you stop all your speculating.

YELENA You are a cultured and intelligent man, Vanya. Certainly you must understand that the world is not destroyed by criminals and fires, but by hate and malice and all this spiteful gossiping and petty wrangling. Your duty is to make peace; your work should be to reconcile everyone and not to growl at everything.

VANYA, *seizing her hand.* My darling! First, help me to make peace with myself.

YELENA Let go! *She drags her hand away.* Go away!

VANYA The rain will soon be over, and all nature will awake refreshed. Only I am not refreshed by the storm. Night and day I am haunted by the thought that my life has been hopelessly wasted and is lost forever. My past doesn't count, because I frittered it away on trifles, and the present is so grotesque in its senselessness. What shall I do with my life and my love? What is going to become of them? This glorious passion in my heart will be lost as a ray of sunlight is lost in a dark chasm, and my life will be lost with it.

YELENA It's just as if I were benumbed when you speak to me of your love, and I don't know how to answer you. Forgive me, I have nothing to say to you. *She tries to leave.* Good night!

VANYA, *barring her way.* If you only knew how it tortures me to think that beside me in this house is another life that is being wasted and is lost forever—yours! What are you waiting for? What accursed philosophy, what damn theory, stands in your way? Oh, understand, understand. . . .

YELENA, *looking at him intently.* Ivan Petrovich, you are drunk.

VANYA Perhaps . . . perhaps.

YELENA Where is the doctor?

VANYA In there. He is going to stay with me tonight. *Pause.* Perhaps I am drunk . . . yes, perhaps I am; nothing is impossible.

YELENA Have you been drinking together? What for?

VANYA Because in that way at least I experience a semblance of life. Let me do that, Yelena!

YELENA You never used to drink and you never used to talk so much. Go to bed! You bore me!

VANYA, *falling on his knees before her.* My darling . . . my precious, beautiful one. . . .

YELENA, *angrily.* Leave me alone! Really, this has become too disgusting. *She leaves.*

VANYA, *alone.* She is gone! *A pause.* It was ten years ago that I first met her at her sister's house. She was seventeen and I thirty-seven. Why didn't I fall in love with her then and propose to her? It would have been so easy . . . then! And if I had, she would now be my wife. Yes, tonight's thunderstorm would have wakened us both. But I would have held her in my arms and whispered: "Don't be afraid! I am here." Oh, bewitching dream, so sweet that I smile when I think of it. *He laughs.* But, my God! Why are my thoughts so entangled? Why am I so old? Why won't she understand me? I despise all that rhetoric of hers, that indolent morality, that absurd talk about the destruction of the world. . . . *A pause.* Oh, how I have been deceived! For years I have worshiped and slaved for that miserable gout-ridden professor. Sonya and I have milked this estate dry for his sake. We have sold our butter and cheese and wheat like misers, and never kept a bit for ourselves, so that we could scrape together enough pennies to send to him. I was proud of him and his learning; I thought all his words and writings were inspired; he was my life . . . the very breath of my being. And now? My God. . . . Now he has retired, and what is the grand total of his life? A blank! Nothing! He is absolutely unknown, and his fame has burst like a soap-bubble. I have been deceived; I see that now, basely deceived.

ASTROV *enters. He is wearing his coat but is without waistcoat or collar and is slightly drunk.* TELYEGIN *follows him, carrying a guitar.*

ASTROV Play something!

TELYEGIN But everyone is asleep.

ASTROV Play!

TELYEGIN *begins to play softly.*

ASTROV Are you alone? No women around? *Sings with his arms akimbo.*

> The room is cold, the fire is out.
> How shall the master cure his gout?

The thunderstorm woke me. It was a torrential downpour. What time is it?

VANYA The devil only knows.

ASTROV I thought I heard Yelena's voice.

VANYA She was here a moment ago.

ASTROV What a beautiful woman! *Looking at the bottles of medicine.* Medicine, is it? What an assortment of prescriptions we have! From Moscow, from Kharkov, from Tula! Why, he has been bothering every city in Russia with his pains! Is he really sick, or simply pretending?

VANYA He is very ill. *Pause.*

ASTROV What's the matter with you tonight? You seem gloomy —so melancholic. Is it because you feel sorry for the Professor?

VANYA Leave me alone.

ASTROV Or are you in love with the Professor's wife?

VANYA She is my friend.

ASTROV Already?

VANYA What do you mean by "already"?

TELYEGIN *stops playing to listen.*

ASTROV A woman can be a man's friend only after having first been his acquaintance and then his mistress . . . then she becomes his friend.

VANYA What coarse philosophy!

ASTROV What do you mean? *Pause.* Yes, I'll admit I'm growing vulgar, but then, you see, I'm drunk. Usually I drink like this only once a month. At such times my courage and boldness know no bounds. I feel capable of anything. I attempt the most difficult operations and succeed magnificently. The most brilliant plans and ideas evolve in my brain. I'm no longer a poor simpleton of a doctor, but mankind's greatest benefactor. I work out my own system of philosophy and all of the rest of you seem to crawl insignificantly at my feet like so many worms . . . *Pause.* . . . or microbes. *To* TELYEGIN. Play, Waffles!

TELYEGIN My dear fellow, I would be delighted to, especially for you, but listen to reason; everyone in the house is asleep.

ASTROV Play!

TELYEGIN *plays softly.*

ASTROV I want a drink. Come, we still have some brandy left. Then, as soon as morning comes, you'll go home with me. All right? SONYA *enters and he catches sight of her.* I beg your pardon, I haven't got a tie on. *He departs hurriedly, followed by* TELYEGIN.

SONYA Uncle Vanya, you and the doctor have been drinking again! What a pair you two make! It's all very well for him, he's always been like that. But why must you follow his example? It's wrong at your age.

VANYA Age hasn't anything to do with it. When the realities of life are gone, or if you've never had them, then you must create illusions. That is better than nothing.

SONYA All our hay is cut and rotting in these daily rains and here you waste your time living in illusions! You are neglecting the farm completely. I've done all the work myself, until now I'm at the end of my strength . . . *Frightened.* Uncle! Your eyes are full of tears!

VANYA Tears? No . . . ah . . . Nonsense, there are no tears in my eyes. *Pause.* You looked at me then just as your dead mother used to, oh my darling child . . . *He eagerly kisses her face and hands.* My sister, my dear sister. . . . *Pause.* . . . where are you now? *Pause.* Oh, if you only knew, if you only knew!

SONYA If she only knew what, Uncle?

VANYA My heart is bursting. Oh it is dreadful . . . so useless. Never mind, though . . . maybe later on. Now, I must go. *He goes out.*

SONYA, *knocking at the door.* Mihail! Are you asleep? Please come here for a minute.

ASTROV, *behind the door.* In a moment. *He appears presently, with his collar and waistcoat on.* What do you want?

SONYA Drink as much as you please, if you don't find it disgusting, but I beg of you, don't let my uncle do it. It's bad for him.

ASTROV All right; we won't drink any more. *Pause.* I'm going home at once. That's settled. By the time the horses are harnessed, it will be dawn.

SONYA It's still raining; wait until morning.

ASTROV The storm is over. This is only the final blow. I must go. And please don't ask me to visit your father any more. I tell him he has gout, and he insists it is rheumatism. I tell him to lie down and stay in bed, and he sits up and goes about. Today he actually refused to see me.

SONYA He has been spoiled. *Looking at the sideboard.* Won't you have something to eat?

ASTROV Yes, I think I will.

SONYA I like to eat at night. I'm sure we shall find something here. *Pause.* They say he has been a great favorite with the ladies all his life and women have spoiled him. Here, have some cheese. *They stand eating by the sideboard.*

ASTROV I haven't eaten a thing all day. I must drink. *Pause.*
Your father has a very trying temper. *Taking a bottle out of the
sideboard.* May I? *Pouring himself a glass of vodka.* We are alone
here and I can speak frankly. Do you know, I couldn't bear to
live in this house—not even for a month! This atmosphere would
choke me. There is your father, wholly absorbed in his book and
his sickness; there is your uncle Vanya with his melancholy, your
grandmother, and finally your stepmother—

SONYA What about her?

ASTROV In a human being, everything ought to be beautiful:
face and dress, soul and thoughts. She is very beautiful, there's
no denying it, but, after all, all she does is eat, sleep, go for walks,
fascinate us by her beauty and—nothing more. She has no duties,
other people work for her . . . isn't that so? And an idle life
cannot be a pure one. *Pause.* And yet, perhaps I'm judging her too
harshly. I'm discontented, like your Uncle Vanya, and so both of
us are complainers.

SONYA Aren't you satisfied with life?

ASTROV I like life as life, but I hate and despise it when it
means frittering it away in a little Russian village. As far as my
personal existence is concerned . . . God! . . . it is absolutely
beyond redemption! Haven't you noticed when you cross a dense
forest in the middle of night and see a small light shining ahead
in the distance, how you forget your weariness and the darkness
and the sharp branches that lash your face? I work—as you know
—perhaps harder than anyone else around here. Fate pursues me
relentlessly; at times I suffer unbearably and I see no light ahead
of me in the distance. I have no hope; I do not care for people.
And . . . it has been a long time since I have loved any one.

SONYA You love no one?

ASTROV No one. . . . At times I feel a kind of tenderness for
your old nurse, but that's only for old time's sake. The peasants
are all alike; they are stupid, lazy, and dull. And the educated
people are difficult to get along with. I am tired of them. All our
friends are small in their ideas and small in their feelings. They
see no farther than their own noses; or perhaps, more bluntly,
they are dull and stupid. The ones who have brains and intelligence are hysterical, morbidly absorbed and consumed in intro-
spection and analysis. They whine, they hate, they find fault

everywhere. They crawl up to me secretively, leer at me and say: "That man is crazy, he's neurotic or he is fraudulent." Or, if they don't know what else to call me, if no other label fits, they say I am peculiar. I like the forests; that is peculiar. I don't eat meat; that is peculiar, too. Simple, natural, and genuine relations between man and man or between man and nature have no existence in their eyes. No, none! . . . None! *He tries to take a drink;* SONYA *prevents him.*

SONYA Please, I beg you, don't drink any more!

ASTROV Why not?

SONYA It is so debasing. You are so noble, your voice is tender, you are, more than any one I know, beautiful. Why do you wish to be like the common people who drink and play cards? Oh, don't, I beg you! You are always saying people never create anything, but only destroy what God has given them. Why, then, do you insist on destroying yourself? Oh, you must not; don't; I implore you! I entreat you!

ASTROV, *giving her his hand.* I won't drink any more.

SONYA Give me your word.

ASTROV I give you my word of honor.

SONYA, *squeezing his hand.* Thank you!

ASTROV I'm through with it. You see, I'm perfectly sober again; I've come to my senses, and I shall remain so until the end of my life. *He looks at his watch.* But as I was saying, my time is over; there is nothing for me in life; the clock has run its race and has stopped. I am old, tired, unimportant; my feelings are dead. I could never care for any one again. I don't love anyone, and I don't think I shall ever love anyone. The only thing that appeals to me is beauty. I just can't remain indifferent to it. If, for example, Yelena wanted to, she could turn my head in a day. Yet. I know that that isn't love, nor even affection . . . *He shudders and covers his face with his hands.*

SONYA What is the matter?

ASTROV Nothing. . . . During Lent one of my patients died on the operating table.

SONYA It is time to forget that. *Pause.* Tell me, Mihail, if I had a friend or a younger sister, and if you knew that she, well— that she loved you, what would you do?

ASTROV I don't know. I don't suppose I'd do anything. I'd make her understand that I could not return her love . . . and anyway, my mind cannot be bothered with such affairs now. I must start at once if I am ever to go. Good-bye, my dear girl. At this rate, we shall stand here talking till daylight. *Shaking hands with her.* If it's all right, I'll go out through the drawing room, because I'm afraid your uncle might detain me. *He goes out.*

SONYA, *alone.* And he really said nothing! His heart and soul are still hidden from me, and yet for some reason I'm strangely happy. Why? *Laughing with pleasure.* I told him that he was noble and beautiful and that his voice was tender. Was that wrong? I can still feel his voice throbbing in the air as it caresses me. *Wringing her hands.* Oh, how awful it is that I am not beautiful! How awful! And I know that I'm not beautiful. I know it, I know. Last Sunday, as people were coming out of church, I heard them talking about me, and one woman said: "She is so good and generous, what a pity she is not beautiful." Not beautiful. . . .

YELENA *enters and throws open the window.*

YELENA The storm has passed! What a refreshing breeze! *Pause.* Where is the doctor?

SONYA He's gone. *Pause.*

YELENA Sonya!

SONYA Yes?

YELENA How much longer are you going to go on brooding? We have done nothing to hurt each other. Why should we be enemies. Certainly we should be friends.

SONYA I feel this too . . . *Embracing* YELENA. Oh, let's be friends again!

YELENA With all my heart. *Both are strongly moved. Pause.*

SONYA Has father gone to bed?

YELENA No, he is sitting up in the drawing room. *Pause.* You know, it's strange. . . . I guess only the Lord knows what has kept us apart all these weeks. *Seeing the open sideboard.* Who left the sideboard open?

SONYA Mihail has just had supper.

YELENA Here is some wine. Let's drink to our friendship.

SONYA Yes, let's.

YELENA Out of one glass. *Filling a wine glass.* Now, we are friends, aren't we?

SONYA Friends. *They drink and kiss each other.* I have wished for us to be friends for so long, but somehow I was ashamed. *She weeps.*

YELENA Why do you weep?

SONYA I don't know. *Pause*. Let's forget it.

YELENA There, there, don't cry. *She weeps*. Silly! Now I am crying, too. *Pause*. You're angry with me because you think I married your father for his money, but you must not believe all the gossip you hear. I swear to you I married him for love. I was fascinated by his fame and his learning. I know now that it wasn't real love, although it seemed real enough at the time. I am innocent, and yet ever since my marriage your searching suspicious eyes have been accusing me of an imaginary crime.

SONYA Peace! Come, let's forget the past.

YELENA You mustn't look at people that way. It isn't right. You must trust and believe in people—*Pause.*—or life becomes impossible. *Pause*.

SONYA Tell me, truthfully, as a friend, are you happy?

YELENA Truthfully, no.

SONYA I knew that. One more question: would you like your husband to be young?

YELENA What a child you are! Of course I would. Go on, ask me something else.

SONYA Do you like the doctor?

YELENA Yes, very much indeed.

SONYA, *laughing*. I have a plain face, haven't I? . . . Yes, I know. He has just left, and his voice still rings in my ears; I can hear the sound of his footsteps; I can see his face in the dark window. Oh, I want so to tell you all that I have in my heart! But I cannot, I am ashamed. Words can never express our feelings. They mean and. . . . Oh, what a silly person you must think I am. *Pause*. Please talk to me about him.

YELENA What do you want me to say?

SONYA He is so wise. He understands everything and he can do anything. He can heal the sick, and plant forests, too.

YELENA It isn't a question of medicine and trees, my dear. He is a man of genius. Do you realize what that means? It means he is a man of great courage, one with deep insights and clear and far-reaching vision. He plants a tree and his mind swings a thousand years into the future and he envisions the happiness of

all mankind. Such people are rare and should be loved. What if
he does drink and use coarse language at times. In Russia, a man
of genius cannot be a saint. Think of his life. There he lives, cut
off from the world by frost and storm and trackless muddy roads,
surrounded by coarse and savage people who are crushed by
poverty and disease. His life is a continuing and endless struggle,
from which he shall never rest. How can a man live like that for
forty years and remain sober and free from all sin? *Kissing* SONYA.
With all my heart, I wish you happiness; you deserve it. *Getting
up*. As for me, I am worthless—an empty and quite pathetic
woman. I have always been futile; in music, in love, in my husband's house—in fact, in everything. If I dared even for a moment
to consider . . . Oh, Sonya, I am really very, very unhappy.
Walking excitedly back and forth. I can never achieve happiness
in this world. Never. Why do you laugh?

SONYA, *laughing and putting her hands over her face*. I am so
happy . . . *Pause*. . . . so happy!

YELENA How I should like some music at this moment. I believe
I could play once more.

SONYA Oh, do, do! *Embracing her*. I couldn't possibly go to
sleep now. Do play!

YELENA Yes, I will. Your father is still awake. Music annoys
him when he is ill, but if he says I may, then I shall play a little.
Go . . . go and ask him, Sonya.

SONYA All right. *She goes out. The sound of the Watchman's
rattle comes from the backyard.*

YELENA It's been a long time since I've had the feeling for
music. And now, I shall sit and play and cry like a small child.
Calling out of the window. Yefim, is that you out there with your
rattle?

VOICE OF WATCHMAN Yes.

YELENA Don't make so much noise. Your master is ill.

VOICE OF WATCHMAN I'm on my way. *He whistles a tune as*
YELENA *closes the window*.

SONYA, *returning*. He says "No."

Curtain.

ACT III

The drawing room of SEREBRYAKOV's *house. There are doors right, left, and center. It is early afternoon.* VANYA *and* SONYA *are seated.* YELENA *walks back and forth, deep in thought.*

VANYA His lordship, the Professor, has deigned to express the wish that we all gather in the drawing room at one o'clock. *Looking at his watch.* It is now a quarter to one. He has a message of the greatest importance to convey to the world.

YELENA It's probably a question of business.

VANYA He never has any business. He writes nonsense, grumbles and eats his heart out with jealousy; that's all he does.

SONYA, *reproachfully.* Uncle!

VANYA Very well. I beg your pardon. *Pointing to* YELENA. Look at her. Roaming up and down out of sheer idleness and boredom. A beautiful picture, I must say!

YELENA I'm surprised that it doesn't bore you to play on the same note from morning to night. *With despair.* This tedium is killing me. Oh, what am I going to do?

SONYA, *shrugging her shoulders.* There is plenty to do if you wish to.

YELENA For instance?

SONYA You could help us run the estate, teach the children, look after the sick . . . isn't that enough? Before you and father came, Uncle Vanya and I used to take the grain to market ourselves.

YELENA I know nothing about such matters, and, besides, I'm not interested in them. It's only in sentimental novels that women go out and teach and look after the sick peasants; furthermore, how could I start in doing it all of a sudden?

SONYA I don't know how you can live here and not do it. Be patient and you'll get used to it. *Embracing her.* Don't be depressed, my dear friend. *Laughing.* You feel out-of-sorts and restless, bored and idle, and unable, somehow, to fit into this life, and your restlessness and idleness is infectious. Look at Uncle Vanya, he does nothing now but follow you about like a shadow, and I have given up my work today to come here and talk with you. I'm getting lazy and losing interest in my work and I can't help it. Dr. Astrov hardly ever came here; it was all we could do to persuade him to visit us once each month, and now he has given up his forestry and forgets his patients, and comes every day. You must be a witch.

VANYA Why should you pine away here in misery and despair? *Eagerly.* Come, my darling, my sweet one, be sensible! A mermaid's blood runs in your veins. Why don't you act like one? Let yourself go for once in your life; fall head over heels in love with some other water sprite, and plunge headlong into a bottomless quarry, so that the almighty Professor and all the rest of us might be so amazed that we could escape your charms.

YELENA, *in anger.* Leave me alone! How cruel can you be! *She tries to leave.*

VANYA, *preventing her.* There, there, my darling, I apologize. Forgive me. *He kisses her hand.* Peace!

YELENA Admit that you would try the patience of a saint.

VANYA As a peace offering and as a symbol of true harmony, I am going to bring you some flowers I picked for you this morning; some autumn roses, exquisite, glorious, melancholy roses. *He leaves.*

SONYA Autumn roses, exquisite, glorious, melancholy roses. . . . *She and* YELENA *stand at the window looking out.*

YELENA It's September already! How are we ever going to live through the long winter here? *Pause.* Where is the doctor?

SONYA He's writing in Uncle Vanya's room. I'm glad Uncle Vanya left. I must talk to you about something.

YELENA About what?

SONYA About what? *She puts her head on* YELENA's *breast.*

YELENA, *carressing her hair.* There, there! Don't, Sonya.

SONYA I am not beautiful!

YELENA You have beautiful hair.

SONYA No! *Looks round so as to glance at herself in the mirror.* No! When a woman is not beautiful, she is always told: "You've got beautiful eyes, you've got beautiful hair." For six years now I have loved him; I have loved him more than one can love anyone. Every moment, I seem to hear him by my side. I feel his hand press against mine. I watch the door constantly, imagining that

I can hear his footsteps. And—don't you see?—I run to you just to talk about him. He comes here everyday now, but he never looks at me, he doesn't even notice that I am here. Yelena, my dear, it is breaking my heart and I have absolutely no hope . . . no hope. *In despair.* Oh, God! Give me strength to endure. All last night I prayed. It has gotten so that I go up to him and speak to him and look into his eyes. My pride is gone. I no longer have the strength to control myself. Yesterday I told Uncle Vanya about my love for him. I couldn't help it. And all the servants know it, too. Everyone knows that I love him.

YELENA Does he?

SONYA No, he never pays any attention to me; it is as if I didn't exist.

YELENA, *musing.* He's a strange man. Do you know what? Let me talk to him. I'll do it carefully. I'll just give him a hint. *Pause.* Now, really, how much longer do you propose to remain in uncertainty? Please! Let me do it! SONYA *nods affirmatively.* Wonderful! It will be easy to find out whether he loves you or not. Don't be ashamed, dear one, and don't worry. I shall be careful; he won't have the least suspicion. We only wish to find out whether it is yes or no, don't we? *A pause.* And if it is no, then, he must stay away from here, isn't that right? SONYA *nods.* It would be easier not to see him any more. We won't delay this another minute. He said he had some maps he wanted to show me. Go and tell him at once that I wish to see him.

SONYA, *greatly excited.* Will you tell me the whole truth?

YELENA Why certainly I will. I'm sure that whatever it is, it will be easier to endure than this uncertainty. Trust me, my dear.

SONYA Yes, yes. I shall say that you wish to see his charts. *She starts to go, but stops near the door and looks back.* No, it is better not to know with certainty . . . one has hope, at least.

YELENA What did you say?

SONYA Nothing. *She leaves.*

YELENA, *alone.* There is nothing worse than to know the secret of another human being, and to realize there's nothing you can do to help them. *In deep thought.* Obviously, he is not in love with her, But why shouldn't he marry her? To be sure, she is not beautiful, yet she is good and kind, pure of heart, and so sensible that she would make an excellent wife for a country doctor of his age. *Pause.* I can understand the poor child's feelings. Here she lives in the midst of this desperate loneliness with no one about her except these gray shadows who pass for human beings, who do nothing but eat, drink, sleep, and talk trivial commonplaces. And, then, who from time to time should appear upon the scene among them but this Dr. Astrov, so unlike the rest—so handsome, interesting, fascinating. . . . It is like seeing the moon rising, rich and full, in the darkness. Oh, to be able to surrender yourself— to forget oneself—body and soul to such a man! Yes, I too, am a little in love with him! Yes, without him I am lonely; when I think of him, I smile. Uncle Vanya says I have a mermaid's blood in my veins: "For once in your life, let yourself go!" Perhaps I should. Oh, to be free as a bird, to fly away from all those drowsy faces and their monotonous mumblings and forget that they have existed at all! Oh, to forget oneself and what one is. . . . But I am a coward; I am afraid, and tortured by my conscience. He comes here every day now. I can guess why, and already my guilt condemns me. I should like to fall on my knees at Sonya's feet and beg her to forgive me and weep . . . But. . . .

ASTROV *enters carrying a portfolio.*

ASTROV Hello, how are you this afternoon? *Shaking hands with her.* Sonya tells me that you wish to see my maps.

YELENA Yes, you promised me yesterday that you'd show me what you had been doing. Have you time now?

ASTROV Of course! *He lays the portfolio on the table, takes out a sketch and attaches it to the table with thumb tacks.* Where were you born?

YELENA, *helping him out.* In Petersburg.

ASTROV Did you go to school there, too?

YELENA Yes, at the conservatory of music.

ASTROV I don't imagine you find our way of life very interesting.

YELENA And why not? It's true I don't know the country very well, but I've read a great deal about it.

ASTROV I have my own desk there in Vanya's room. When I become so completely exhausted that I can no longer go on with my work, I abandon everything and rush over here to forget myself with my maps for an hour or two. Vanya and Sonya rattle away at their counting boards, I feel warm and peaceful, the cricket sings, and I sit near them at my table and paint. However, I usu-

ally don't indulge in such a luxury very often, certainly not more
than once a month. *Pointing to the picture.* Look! This is a survey
map of our part of the country as it was fifty years ago. Those
areas shaded in green, both light and dark, are forest lands. Half
the map, you see, is covered with them. Where the green is
stripped with red, the forests were stocked with elk and wild
goats. Here on this lake were large flocks of swans, wild geese, and
ducks; as the old men used to tell us, there was a "power" of birds
of every kind—no end of them. *Pause.* Now, they have vanished
like thin air. Here, you see, beside the towns and villages, I have
jotted down here and there the various settlements, little farms,
monasteries, and watermills. This country was rich in cattle and
horses, as you can see by this expanse of blue. For instance, see
how it deepens in this part; there were great herds here, an average of three horses to every house. *Pause.* Now, look below to the
second map. This is the country as it was twenty-five years ago. Only
a third of the map now is green with forests. The goats have disappeared and only a few elk remain. The green and blue are
lighter, and so on and so forth. Now, we come to the third drawing, our district as it is today. Still we see spots of green, but very
little. The elk, the swans, the blackcock have also disappeared.
In fact, everything is gone. On the whole, it is the picture of a
continuous and slow decline which will evidently come to completion in about ten or fifteen years. Perhaps you may object that
it is the march of progress, that the old order must give way to
the new, and you would be right if roads had been built through
these ruined forests, or if factories and schools had taken the place
of the monasteries and the watermills. Then the people would have
become better educated and healthier and richer, but as it is, and
as you can see, we, have nothing of the kind. We have the same
swamps and mosquitoes; the same disease, poverty, and misery;
typhoid, diphtheria, fires. The degradation of our country confronts
us, brought on by the human race's fierce struggle for existence.
This degeneration is due to inertia and ignorance—to a complete
lack of understanding. When a man, cold, hungry and sick, simply
to save what little there is left in life that has meaning and importance—to help his children survive—why God only knows,
he acts in desperation; he instinctively and unconsciously clutches
at anything that will fill his belly and keep him warm. Forced to

forget what all this will mean tomorrow, the devil of destruction consumes all the land. And so almost everything has been destroyed and nothing has been created to take its place. *Coldly.* But I see by your expression that all this does not interest you.

YELENA I know so little about such things!

ASTROV There's nothing to know. It simply doesn't interest you, that's all.

YELENA Frankly, my thoughts were elsewhere. Forgive me! I must ask you something, but I am embarrassed and I don't know how to begin.

ASTROV Ask me something?

YELENA Yes, a very innocent and probably not too important question. Sit down. *They both sit.* It's about a young girl I know. Let's discuss it like honest and mature people, like friends; and then, when we have finished we will forget all about it, shall we?

ASTROV All right. Whatever you say!

YELENA What I want to talk to you about is my stepdaughter, Sonya. Do you like her?

ASTROV Yes, I respect her.

YELENA But do you like her as a woman?

ASTROV, *not at once.* No.

YELENA Just one thing more and I am finished. Haven't you noticed anything?

ASTROV Nothing.

YELENA *takes him by the hand.* You don't love her, I can see it from your eyes. She is unhappy. Please understand that and . . . stop coming here.

ASTROV *gets up.* I'm afraid I'm too old for this sort of thing. And, besides, I haven't the time for it. *Shrugging his shoulders.* When indeed could I? *He is embarrassed.*

YELENA Oh, God! What a disgusting conversation. I am as breathless as if I had been running three miles uphill. Thank heaven, that's over with. Now let us forget everything that has been said. But you must leave at once. You are intelligent and sensible. You do understand, don't you? *Pause.* I am actually blushing.

ASTROV If you had spoken a month or two ago, perhaps I might have been able to consider it, but now . . . *Shrugging his shoulders.* Of course, if she is suffering . . . but wait, there is

one thing I can't understand . . . what are your reasons for bringing all this up? *Searching her face with his eyes and shaking an
admonishing finger at her.* Oh, you're a sly one!

YELENA What do you mean?

ASTROV, *laughing.* A sly one! Suppose Sonya is unhappy. I'm
ready to admit it, but what is the real meaning of your interrogation? *Preventing her from speaking, quickly.* Please, don't look so
surprised, you know perfectly well why I'm here every day. My
sweet beast of prey, don't look at me like that, I'm an old hand at
this sort of game . . . you can't deceive me.

YELENA, *perplexed.* A beast of prey? I don't understand anything.

ASTROV A beautiful, fluffy weasel. You must have your victims.
Here I've been doing nothing for a whole month, I've dropped
everything, I seek you greedily, and you're awfully pleased about
it, awfully. Well? I'm conquered, and you knew all about it
without your interrogation. *Folding his arms and bowing his head.*
I submit. Here I am . . . eat me up!

YELENA You've gone crazy!

ASTROV, *laughing ironically.* Oh, you're so shy, aren't you?

YELENA I'm more honorable than you think! I swear it! *She
tries to leave the room.*

ASTROV Wait . . . *Barring her way.* . . . I'll go away today.
I shan't come here any more. But . . . *Taking her hand and
glancing about.* . . . for the future . . . where are we going to
meet? Tell me quickly, where? Someone may come in. Tell me
quickly! . . . *Passionately.* You are so gloriously and wonderfully
beautiful! . . . Let me kiss you but once. . . . Oh, if I could kiss
your fragrant hair!

YELENA I assure you!

ASTROV Why assure me? You must not! Let's not waste words!
Ah, how lovely you are . . . what hands! *Kissing her hands.*

YELENA Stop it! Go away! *Freeing her hands.* You're forgetting
yourself!

ASTROV Tell me! Tell me! Where will we meet tomorrow?
Putting his arms around her. Don't you see! We must meet! It is
inevitable. *He kisses her.* VANYA *comes in carrying a bunch of
roses, and halts in the doorway.*

YELENA, *without seeing* VANYA. Have pity! Leave me! *She lays her head on* ASTROV's *shoulder.* Don't! *She tries to break away from him.*

ASTROV, *holding her around the waist.* Meet me in the forest arbor tomorrow at two. Yes! Oh, yes! Will you come?

YELENA, *seeing* VANYA. Let me go! *Breaking free and going to the window deeply embarrassed.* This is horrible!

VANYA, *throwing the flowers on a chair, speaking in great excitement and wiping his face with his handkerchief.* Nothing . . . yes, yes, nothing.

ASTROV, *with bravado.* It's a fine day, my dear Vanya. This morning, the sky was overcast and it looked like rain, but now the sun is shining again. After all, we've had a very fine autumn, and the wheat crop looks unusually promising. *Putting his map back into the portfolio.* But the days are growing short. *Goes out.*

YELENA, *quickly approaching* VANYA. You must do your best; you must use all the power you have to get us away from here today! Do you hear? I say, today!

VANYA, *wiping his face.* Oh! Ah! Oh! Very well! Yes, I . . . Yelena, I saw everything!

YELENA, *greatly upset.* Do you hear me? I must leave here today!

SEREBRYAKOV, SONYA, MARINA, *and* TELYEGIN *enter.*

TELYEGIN I'm not feeling very well myself, your excellency. I've been lame for two days, and my head. . . .

SEREBRYAKOV Where are the rest? I hate this house. It winds and sprawls like a labyrinth. Everyone is always scattered through its twenty-six rooms. You can never find a soul. *To* MARINA. Ask Marya and Yelena to come here!

YELENA I am here.

SEREBRYAKOV Please sit down, all of you.

SONYA, *going to* YELENA *and asking anxiously.* What did he say?

YELENA I'll tell you later.

SONYA You are upset. *Looking swiftly and with inquiry into her face.* I understand; he said he would not come here any more. *Pause.* Tell me, did he? . . . Tell me! YELENA *nods.*

SEREBRYAKOV, *to* TELYEGIN. After all, one can become reconciled to being an invalid, but not to this absurd way of life you have here in the country. I feel as if I had been cast off from this earth and dumped onto a strange planet. Please be seated, ladies and gentlemen. Sonya! *She does not hear. She stands with her head sadly bent forward.* Sonya! *A pause.* I guess she does not hear me. *To* MARINA. You sit down, too, nurse. MARINA *takes a seat and resumes knitting her stocking.* I ask your indulgence, ladies and gentlemen; uh . . . check your ears, as it were, on the hat rack of attention. *He laughs.*

VANYA, *in agitation.* Perhaps I'm not needed. . . . May I be excused?

SEREBRYAKOV No, you are needed now more than anyone else.

VANYA What do you wish?

SEREBRYAKOV You—but what makes you so angry and out of sorts? If it is anything I have done, I beg your forgiveness.

VANYA Oh, forget that and your high and mighty tone, too, and come to the point; what do you want?

MARYA *enters.*

SEREBRYAKOV Here is mother. Ladies and gentlemen, let us begin. I have asked you to gather here, my friends, to inform you that the inspector general is coming. *Laughs.* All joking aside, however, I wish to discuss a very important matter. I must ask you for your aid and advice, and realizing your unbounded kindness, I believe I can count on both. I am a scholar and bound to my library, and I am not familiar with practical affairs. I am unable, I find, to dispense with the help of well-informed people such as you, Ivan, and you, Ilya, and you, mother. The truth is, *"manet omnes una nox,"* that is to say, our lives rest in the hands of God, and as I am old and ill, I realize that the time has come for me to dispose of my property in the interests of my family. My life is nearly finished, and I am not thinking of myself, but I must consider my young wife and daughter. *A pause.* I cannot go on living in the country; we were just not meant for country life. And yet, we cannot afford to live in town on the income from this estate. We might sell the forests, but that would be an expedient to which we could not resort every year. We must work out some method of guaranteeing ourselves a permanent, and . . . ah, more or less fixed annual income. With this object in view, a plan has occurred to me which I now have the honor of proposing to you for your consideration. I shall give you only a rough outline of it, omitting all the bothersome and trivial details. Our estate does not yield, on an average, more than two percent on the investment. I propose to sell it. If then we invest our capital in bonds and

other suitable securities, it will bring us four to five percent and
we should probably have a surplus of several thousand roubles,
with which we could buy a small house in Finland. . . .

VANYA Wait a minute! Repeat what you said just now; I don't
believe I heard you quite right.

SEREBRYAKOV I said we would invest the money in bonds and
with the surplus buy a house in Finland.

VANYA No, not Finland. . . . You said something else.

SEREBRYAKOV I propose to sell this estate.

VANYA Aha! That was it! So you are going to sell the estate?
Splendid! That's a fine idea! And what do you propose to do with
my old mother and myself and with Sonya, here?

SEREBRYAKOV That will be taken care of in due course. After
all . . . uh . . . we can't do everything at once, can we?

VANYA Wait! It is clear that up to now I've never had an ounce
of sense in my head. I have always been stupid enough to think
that the estate belonged to Sonya. My late father bought it as
a wedding gift for my sister, and as our laws were made for
Russians and not for Turks, I foolishly imagined that my sister's
estate would pass on to her child.

SEREBRYAKOV Why, of course, it belongs to Sonya. Has anyone
denied it? I don't wish to sell it without Sonya's consent; on the
contrary, what I am doing is for Sonya's welfare.

VANYA This is absolutely crazy. Either I have gone insane or
. . . or . . .

MARYA Jean, don't contradict Alexander. Trust him; he knows
better than we do what is right and what is wrong.

VANYA No! Give me some water. *He drinks.* Go on! Say anything you like . . . anything!

SEREBRYAKOV I can't understand why you are so upset. I don't
pretend that my plan is ideal, and if you all object to it, I shall
not insist. *A pause.*

TELYEGIN, *looking embarrassed.* I've always had a great reverence for learning, sir, and, if I may say so, my feelings for it have
a certain family connection. I mean, sir, that my brother Gregory's
wife's brother, Konstantin Lacedaemonov, as you perhaps know,
was an M.A. . . .

VANYA Wait a minute, Waffles, we're discussing business. Wait a little . . . later . . . *To* SEREBRYAKOV. Here, ask him what he thinks; this estate was purchased from his uncle.

SEREBRYAKOV Ah! Why should I ask questions? What good would it do?

VANYA The price was ninety-five thousand roubles. My father paid seventy and left a mortgage of twenty-five. Now listen! This estate could never have been bought if I had not renounced my inheritance in favor of my sister, whom I dearly loved . . . and what is more, I worked like a slave for ten years and paid off the mortgage.

SEREBRYAKOV I regret that I ever brought the matter up.

VANYA Thanks entirely to my personal efforts, the estate is now free from debt and in good condition; and now . . . as I am getting old, you propose to kick me out!

SEREBRYAKOV I don't understand what you're talking about.

VANYA For twenty-five years I have managed this estate. I have sent you the proceeds from it like an honest servant, and you, you have never given me one single word of thanks for my efforts . . . no, not one . . . neither in my youth nor now. You gave me a meager salary of five hundred roubles a year . . . a beggar's pittance, and you have never once thought of adding a rouble to it.

SEREBRYAKOV How should I know about such things, Ivan? I am not a practical man and I don't understand them. You might have helped yourself to all you desired.

VANYA Yes, why didn't I steal? Don't you all despise me for not stealing? It would have been only fair, and I wouldn't be a poor man now.

MARYA, *sternly.* Jean!

TELYEGIN, *in agitation.* Vanya, my friend, don't talk like that. Why spoil such a pleasant relationship? Please stop!

VANYA For twenty-five years I have been sitting here with my mother buried like a mole. Every thought and hope we had was yours and yours alone. All day long we talked with pride of you and your work; and we spoke your name with respect . . . yes, almost with reverence. We wasted our evenings reading your books and articles, which I now detest to the bottom of my heart.

TELYEGIN Don't, Vanya, don't. I can't stand this sort of thing.

SEREBRYAKOV, *angrily.* What in God's name do you want, anyhow?

VANYA We used to consider you a superman, a kind of demigod, but now the scales have fallen from my eyes and I see you as you are! You write about art without knowing a thing about it. Why, those books of yours which I used to think were so wonderful aren't worth a copper kopeck. You are a fake, a fraud, a . . .

SEREBRYAKOV Can't anyone stop him? I'm leaving here immediately!

YELENA Ivan Petrovich, I command you to stop this instant! Do you hear me?

SONYA Please! Uncle Vanya!

VANYA I refuse! SEREBRYAKOV *tries to escape from the room, but* VANYA *bars the door.* Wait! I haven't finished yet! You have destroyed my life. I have never really lived. Thanks to you, my best years have gone for nothing. They have been ruined. I hate you!

TELYEGIN I can't stand it; I can't stand it. I'm going. *He leaves in great excitement.*

SEREBRYAKOV What do you want from me? What right do you have to speak to me like that? If the estate is yours, take it! I don't want it.

YELENA I'm leaving this hell right now! *Shouts.* I can't stand it any longer!

VANYA My life's ruined! I'm gifted, I'm intelligent, I'm courageous. If I'd had a normal life, I might have become a Schopenhauer, a Dostoevsky. I'm talking nonsense. I'm going insane! I'm in despair! Oh, Mother!

MARYA Do as the Professor tells you!

VANYA Mother, what am I to do? Never mind, don't tell me! I know myself what I must do! *To* SEREBRYAKOV. You will remember me! *Goes out through middle door.* MARYA *goes out after him.*

SONYA Oh, nurse, nurse!

SEREBRYAKOV This is too much! Take that madman away! I can't live under the same roof with him! He is always there. *Points to the middle door.* Let him move into town or to another house on the grounds, or I will move myself, but I cannot stay in the same house with him.

YELENA, *to her husband.* We are leaving here today; we must get ready at once.

SEREBRYAKOV What an utterly insignificant little man.

SONYA, *on her knees beside the nurse, turning to her father and speaking with emotion.* You must be merciful, Father. Uncle Vanya and I are both very unhappy! *Controlling her despair.* Have mercy on us! Remember how Uncle Vanya and grandmother used to sit up late copying and translating your books for you every night . . . every night. Uncle Vanya has worked without rest; we would never spend a penny on ourselves, but spent it all on you! We earned every mouthful of bread that we ever ate! I am not speaking as I should like to, but you must understand, Father, you must have mercy on us.

YELENA, *to her husband, much excited.* For heaven's sake, Alexander, go and talk to him . . . explain!

SEREBRYAKOV Very well, I shall talk to him. I do not accuse him of anything, and I am not angry, but you must admit that his behavior has been strange, to say the least. Very well, I shall go to him. *He leaves through the center door.*

YELENA Be gentle with him. Try to quiet him. *She follows him out.*

SONYA, *snuggling nearer to* MARINA. Nurse, oh, nurse!

MARINA It's all right, child. When the geese have cackled they will be silent again. First they cackle and then they stop.

SONYA Nurse!

MARINA, *caressing her hair.* You are trembling all over, as if you had a chill. There, there, my little child, God is merciful. A little linden tea, and it will pass. Don't cry, my sweet. *Looking angrily at the center door.* See, the geese have all gone now. The devil take them!

A shot is heard. YELENA *screams behind the scenes.* SONYA *shudders.*

MARINA What's that?

SEREBRYAKOV *runs staggering in looking terrified.* Stop him! Stop him! He's gone mad!

YELENA *and* VANYA *struggle in the doorway.*

YELENA, *trying to snatch the revolver away from him.* Give it to me! Give it to me, I tell you!

VANYA Let go of me. Let go of me, Yelena! *Freeing himself, he runs in and looks for* SEREBRYAKOV. Where is he? Ah, there he is! *Pointing the revolver at* SEREBRYAKOV. Bang! *Pause.* Missed him!

Missed him again! *Furiously.* Damn it! Damn! *Bangs the revolver a few times against the floor and sinks exhausted in a chair.*

YELENA Take me away from here! Take me away . . . kill me . . . I can't stay here, I can't.

VANYA, *in despair.* What have I done! What have I done!

SONYA, *softly.* Oh, nurse! Nurse!

Curtain.

Act IV

VANYA's *bedroom and office. Large table near window; scattered on it are ledgers, scales, and papers. Nearby* ASTROV's *table with paints and drawing materials. A map, of no use to anyone, of Africa on the wall. A large sofa covered with canvas. A door left to an inner room; door right leads to front hall. It is evening in autumn.* TELYEGIN *and* MARINA *sit facing each other, winding wool.*

TELYEGIN Hurry, Marina, or we shall have to go out to say good-bye before we've finished. They have ordered the carriage already.

MARINA, *trying to wind more rapidly.* There isn't much left to wind.

TELYEGIN They are going to live in Kharkov.

MARINA It is wise for them to go.

TELYEGIN They have been frightened. The Professor's wife refuses to stay here an hour longer. She keeps saying: "If we're going at all, let's hurry. We shall go to Kharkov and look around, and then we can send for our things." They're taking practically nothing with them. It seems, Marina, that fate has decreed that they should not live here.

MARINA And quite rightly. What a storm they raised! It was disgusting!

TELYEGIN Yes, to be sure! The scene this morning would make a fine story.

MARINA I wish I'd never laid eyes on them. *Pause.* Once more things will be as they used to be; we shall live like normal human beings again: tea at eight, dinner at one, and supper in the evening; everything in order as decent people and Christians like it. *Sighing.* It is a long time since I, poor sinner, have eaten noodles.

TELYEGIN Yes, we haven't had noodles for a great while. *Pause.* Not for ages. As I was passing through the village this morning, Marina, one of the storekeepers called after me: "Hi! you hanger-on!" I felt it bitterly.

MARINA Don't pay any attention to them, my friend; we are all dependent upon God. You, Sonya, Uncle Vanya, and myself . . . none of us sits idle; we all must work hard. All! . . . Where is Sonya?

TELYEGIN In the garden with the doctor, looking for Vanya. They are afraid he may become violent and attempt to kill himself.

MARINA Where is his gun?

TELYEGIN, *whispering.* I hid it in the cellar.

MARINA, *amused.* What goings on!

VANYA *and* ASTROV *enter.*

VANYA Let me alone! *To* MARINA *and* TELYEGIN. Go away! Get out and leave me to myself. Only for an hour! I won't have you watching me this way!

TELYEGIN, *going out on tiptoe.* Why, certainly, Vanya.

MARINA, *gathering up her wool and leaving.* The gander is cackling again; ho! ho! ho!

VANYA Let me alone!

ASTROV I would, with the greatest pleasure. I should have gone long ago, but I shan't leave you until you have returned what you took from me.

VANYA I took nothing from you.

ASTROV I'm not joking, don't delay me, I really have to go.

VANYA I took nothing of yours.

ASTROV *Both sitting down.* Oh, you didn't? All right, I shall have to stay a while longer, and if you still don't give it up, I will have to resort to force. We shall tie your hands and search you. I warn you, I mean what I say.

VANYA Do as you please. *Pause.* Oh, to think I made such a fool of myself! To shoot twice and miss him both times! I can never forgive myself.

ASTROV When you first felt the impulse to shoot someone, you would have done better to put a bullet through your own head.

VANYA, *shrugging his shoulders*. It's strange! I tried to murder a man, and they are not going to arrest me or bring me to trial. That means they think I'm insane. *Laughing bitterly*. I! I am insane, and the ones who hide their futility, their stupidity, their harsh cruelty behind a professor's mask, they . . . they are sane! Those who marry old men and then betray them before the eyes of everyone, they are sane! Yes, I saw you kiss her; I saw you in each other's arms!

ASTROV Yes, I did kiss her; which is more than you can say.

VANYA, *watching the door*. No, it is the earth that is insane, because it allows us to exist.

ASTROV That's nonsense.

VANYA Well? I am a lunatic, aren't I, and therefore irresponsible? Haven't I the right to talk nonsense?

ASTROV This is a farce! You are not insane; you are simply a ridiculous fool. I used to think every fool was out of his senses—abnormal; but now I see that lack of sense is the normal human condition, and you are perfectly normal.

VANYA, *covering his face with his hands*. Oh! If you knew how ashamed I am! There is no pain on earth greater than the bitter sense of shame. *Agonized*. I can't endure it! *Leaning against the table*. What can I do? What can I do?

ASTROV Nothing.

VANYA Tell me something! Oh, my God! I am forty-seven. I may live to be sixty; I still have thirteen years ahead of me . . . an eternity! How can I endure life for thirteen years? What shall I do? How can I fill them? Oh, don't you see? *Pressing* ASTROV's *hand convulsively*. Don't you see, if I could only live the rest of my life in some new manner! If I could only wake up some still sunny morning and feel that my life had begun all over; that the past was forgotten and had vanished like smoke. *Weeping*. Oh, to begin life anew! To start over! Tell me, tell me, how to begin!

ASTROV, *crossly*. Nonsense! What kind of a new life can we, yes both of us, you and I—look forward to? We have no hope.

VANYA None?

ASTROV None. I am convinced of that.

VANYA Please give me something to live for. *Putting his hand to his heart*. I feel such a burning pain here.

ASTROV, *shouting angrily*. Stop! *More moderately*. It may be that our posterity, despising us for our blind and stupid lives, will find some road to happiness; but we—you and I—have but one hope, the hope that perhaps, pleasant dreams will haunt us as we rest in our graves. *Sighing*. Yes, my friend, in this entire community there were only two decent and intelligent men, you and I. Ten years or so of this life of ours, this wretched life of the common-place and the trivial, have sucked us under and poisoned us with their destructive vapors, and we have become as contemptible, as petty, and as despicable as the others. *Resolutely*. But don't try to put me off! Will you give me what you took from me?

VANYA I took nothing from you.

ASTROV You took a bottle of morphine out of my medicine case. *Pause*. Listen! If you are positively determined to kill yourself, go into the woods and shoot yourself there. But give me back the morphine, or there will be a great deal of talk and suspicion; people will think I gave it to you. It will be bad enough having to perform your post-mortem. Do you think I shall find it interesting?

SONYA *enters*.

VANYA Leave me alone.

ASTROV, *to* SONYA. Sonya, your uncle has stolen a bottle of morphine from my medicine case and won't return it to me. Tell him his behavior is—well, unwise. I can't waste any more time, I must be going.

SONYA Uncle Vanya, did you take the morphine? *Pause*.

ASTROV Yes, he took it. *Pause*. I'm absolutely sure.

SONYA Give it back! Why do you wish to frighten us? *Tenderly*. Give it up, Uncle Vanya! My sorrow is perhaps even greater than yours, but I am not in despair. I endure my grief and shall go on doing so until my life comes to its natural end. You must endure yours, too. *Pause*. Give it up! *Kissing his hands*. Dear, dear, Uncle Vanya. Give it up! *Weeping*. You are so good, I am sure you'll have pity on us and give it back. You must endure your grief with patience, Uncle Vanya; you must endure it.

VANYA *takes the bottle from the table drawer and gives it to* ASTROV.

VANYA There it is! *To* SONYA. And now we must get busy at once; we must do something, or else I'll not be able to stand it.

SONYA Yes, yes, let's work! As soon as we've seen them off, we'll go to work. *Nervously she straightens out the papers on the table.* We have neglected everything!

ASTROV, *putting the bottle in the case and closing it.* Now I can go.

YELENA, *entering.* Oh, here you are, Vanya. We are leaving soon. Go to Alexander, he wishes to speak to you.

SONYA Go, Uncle Vanya. *Taking* VANYA's *arm.* Come, you and father must make peace; that is absolutely necessary for us. SONYA *and* VANYA *leave.*

YELENA I'm leaving. *Giving* ASTROV *her hand.* Good-bye.

ASTROV So soon?

YELENA The carriage is waiting.

ASTROV Good-bye.

YELENA You promised me that today you, too, would go away.

ASTROV I had forgotten. I'll go immediately. *Pause.* Were you afraid? *Taking her by the hand.* Was it so terrifying?

YELENA Yes.

ASTROV Couldn't you stay? Couldn't you? Tomorrow—in the forest arbor—

YELENA No. Everything is settled, and that is why I can look you so squarely in the eyes. Our departure is definite. One thing I must ask of you, however: don't think too harshly of me; I should like you to respect me.

ASTROV Ah! *With an impatient gesture.* Stay, I beg you! Admit there's nothing for you to do in this world. You have no object in life; nothing to occupy your attention. Sooner or later you will give in to your feelings. It is inevitable. But please not in Kharkov or in Kursk, but here, here in the lap of nature. Here, at least, it would be poetic, even beautiful. Here you have forests, Turgenev's half-ruined houses, the autumn roses . . .

YELENA How absurd you are! I am angry with you and yet I shall always remember you with pleasure. You are an interesting and different kind of man. You and I will never meet again, and so I shall tell you—why conceal it?—that I am in love with you. Come, let's shake hands and part as good friends. Please don't think badly of me.

ASTROV, *pressing her hand.* Yes, you had better go. *Thoughtfully.*
You seem sincere and good, and yet there is something strangely
restless about your whole personality. The moment you and your
husband arrived here, everyone whom you found busy and engaged in active, creative work felt compelled to drop it and give
himself up to you and your husband's gout for the entire summer.
You and your husband have infected all of us with your idleness.
I became infatuated with you and I have done nothing for a whole
month, and in the meantime people have been ill and the peasants
have been grazing their herds in my newly planted woods . . .
so that wherever you and your husband go, you bring destruction
everywhere. I am joking, of course, and yet I am strangely convinced that if you had remained here, we should have been over-
taken by the most terrible desolation and destruction. I would
have perished, and you . . . no good would have come to you
either. So go! Our little comedy is over; with a happy ending—Go!

YELENA, *snatching a pencil quickly from* ASTROV's *table.* I shall
keep this pencil as a remembrance!

ASTROV How strange it is! We meet, and then all of a sudden
it seems that we must part forever. So it is with everything in this
world. While we are still alone, before Uncle Vanya comes in with
a bouquet—allow me—to kiss you good-bye—May I? *Kissing her
on the cheek.* There! Wonderful!

YELENA I wish you every happiness. *Glancing about her.* For
once in my life. . . . *She kisses him impulsively, and they part
quickly.* I must go.

ASTROV Yes go. Since the carriage is ready, you'd better start
at once. *They stand listening.* It is finished.

VANYA, SEREBRYAKOV, MARYA *with her book,* TELYEGIN, *and*
SONYA *enter.*

SEREBRYAKOV, *to* VANYA. Woe be unto him who cannot forgive
past offences. I have passed through so much—ah, such experience
—in the last few hours that I believe I could write a whole treatise
for the benefit of all mankind on the art of living. I accept your
apology gladly, and I myself ask your forgiveness. *He kisses* VANYA
three times. Good-bye.

VANYA You will go on receiving your allowance regularly as
before. Everything will remain as it was.

YELENA *embraces* SONYA.

SEREBRYAKOV, *kissing* MARYA's *hands.* Mother!

MARYA, *kissing him.* Alexander! Have your picture taken again, and send it to me; you know how dearly I love you.

TELYEGIN Good-bye, your excellency. Don't forget us.

SEREBRYAKOV, *kissing* SONYA. Good-bye, good-bye, everyone. *Shaking hands with Astrov.* Many thanks for your pleasant company. I have a deep regard for your opinions, your enthusiasm, and your impulses, but permit an old man to add one last observation—let me give you one piece of advice: do something, my friend! Work! You must work! *They all bow.* Good luck to you all. *He goes out followed by* MARYA *and* SONYA.

VANYA, *fervently kissing* YELENA's *hand.* Good-bye . . . forgive me. We shall never meet again!

YELENA, *touched.* Good-bye, my dear Vanya. *She kisses his head lightly as he bends over her hand, and then goes out.*

ASTROV Tell them to bring my carriage around, too, Waffles.

TELYEGIN Certainly, my friend. *He goes out.*

ASTROV *and* VANYA *alone are left behind.* ASTROV *gathers together his paints and drawing materials on the table and packs them away in his bag.*

ASTROV Why don't you see them off?

VANYA Let them go! I—I can't go out there. My heart is so saddened. I must busy myself with something at once. To work! To work! *He rummages through his papers on the table. Pause. As the horses trot away, the tinkle of bells is heard.*

ASTROV They have gone! Somehow I'm sure the professor is glad to go. Nothing will tempt him to return.

MARINA, *entering.* They have gone. *She sits down in her arm chair and resumes her knitting.* SONYA *comes in drying her eyes.*

SONYA They have gone. *Wipes her eyes.* God be with them. *To* VANYA. And now, Uncle Vanya, let us do something!

VANYA To work! To work!

SONYA It has been a long, long time since you and I have sat together at this table. *Lighting a lamp on the table.* No ink! *Taking the inkstand to the cupboard and filling it from an ink bottle.* How sad it is to see them go!

MARYA, *coming in slowly.* They have gone. *She sits down and immediately becomes absorbed in her book.* SONYA *sits at the table and looks through an account book.*

SONYA First, Uncle Vanya, let us add up the bills. We have neglected them dreadfully. We received another bill today. Come. We'll both do them.

VANYA In account with . . . *Writing.* . . . in account with . . .

MARINA, *yawning.* The sandman is on his way.

ASTROV How silent it is. The pens scratch and the cricket sings; it is so warm and comfortable. You know, I hate to go.

The tinkling of bells is heard.

ASTROV Ah, but my carriage has come. All that remains is to say good-bye to you, my friends, and to my table here, and then . . . away! *He puts the map in the portfolio.*

MARINA Why be in such a hurry . . . you can stay a little while longer.

ASTROV Impossible.

VANYA, *writing.* And carry forward from the old debt two seventy-five . . .

The WORKMAN *enters.*

WORKMAN Your carriage is waiting, sir.

ASTROV All right. *He hands the* WORKMAN *his medicine case, portfolio, and box.* Be careful, don't crush the portfolio!

WORKMAN Yes, sir.

SONYA When shall we see you again?

ASTROV Probably not before next summer. Certainly not again till winter's over, at any rate. Of course, if anything happens, let me know, and I'll come at once. *Shaking hands.* Thank you for your hospitality, your kindness . . . for all you've done. *He goes to the nurse and kisses her head.* Good-bye, old nurse.

MARINA Are you going without your tea?

ASTROV I don't care for any, nurse.

MARINA Won't you have just a little vodka?

ASTROV, *hesitatingly.* Yes, I guess I might as well. MARINA *goes out. After a pause.* One of my horses has gone lame for some reason. I noticed it yesterday when Petra was watering him.

VANYA You should have him reshod.

ASTROV I shall have to stop at the blacksmith's on my way home. It can't be helped. *He stands looking up at the map of Africa on the wall.* I suppose it is terribly hot in Africa now.

VANYA Yes, I suppose it is.

MARINA *comes back carrying a tray with a glass of vodka and a slice of bread.*

MARINA There you are. ASTROV *drinks.* Your health! *Bowing deeply.* Eat your bread with it.

ASTROV No, I like it this way. And now, good-bye. *To* MARINA. You needn't come out to see me off, nurse. *He leaves.* SONYA *follows him with a candle to light him to the carriage.* MARINA *sits in her chair.*

VANYA, *writing.* On the second of February, twenty pounds of butter; on the sixteenth, twenty pounds of butter again. Buckwheat flour . . . *Pause. The tinkling of bells is heard.*

MARINA He has gone. *A pause.* SONYA *enters and sets the candlestick on the table.*

SONYA He has gone.

VANYA, *adding and writing.* Total, fifteen . . . twenty-five . . . SONYA *sits down and begins to write.*

MARINA, *yawning.* Oh, ho! The Lord have mercy on us.

TELYEGIN *enters on tiptoe, seats himself near the door, and begins to tune his guitar.*

VANYA, *to* SONYA, *caressing her hair.* My child, I feel so wretched!

SONYA What can we do? We must go on living. *Pause.* Yes, we shall live, Uncle Vanya. Shall live through the endless procession of days before us, and through all the long evenings. We shall bear patiently the burdens that fate brings to us. We shall work, without rest, for others, both now and when we are old. And, then, when our final hour comes, we shall meet it humbly, and there beyond the grave, we shall know that we have known suffering and tears . . . that our life was bitter. And God will pity us. Oh, then, dear Uncle, we shall enter into a bright and beautiful life. We shall rejoice and look back upon our grief here . . . with tenderness . . . and a smile; *Pause.* and we shall have rest. I have faith, Uncle, fervent, passionate faith. SONYA *kneels down in front of her uncle and lays her head in his hands. She speaks with a weary voice.* We shall have rest. TELYEGIN *plays softly on his guitar.* We shall have rest. We shall hear the angels sing. We shall see heaven shining in all its radiant glory. We shall see all the world's evils . . . our every pain, our suffering . . . be engulfed by God's all-pervading mercy that shall enfold the earth. Our life will be peaceful, gentle, and sweet—like a child's caress.

Oh, I have faith—*Wiping away his tears.* My poor Uncle Vanya, you are crying! *Through her tears.* You have never known joy in your life, but wait, Uncle Vanya, wait! You, too, will have rest. *Embracing him.* You, too, will rest.

   The WATCHMAN's *rattle is heard from the garden;* TELEYEGIN *plays softly;* MARYA *writes on the margin of her pamphlet;* MARINA *is knitting her stocking.* We shall rest. . . .

The Curtain slowly falls.

THE THREE SISTERS

CAST

OLGA SERGEYEVNA PROZOROV
IRINA SERGEYEVNA PROZOROV
MARYA SERGEYEVNA PROZOROV (Masha) — *Vershinin*
BARON NIKOLAI LVOVICH TUSENBACH, *an army lieutenant*
IVAN ROMANICH CHEBUTYKIN, *an army doctor*
VASSILY VASSILYEVICH SOLYONY, *an army captain*
ANFISA, *the nurse, an old woman of eighty*
FERAPONT, *an old porter from the County Council*
LIEUTENANT-COLONEL ALEXANDER IGNATYEVICH
  VERSHININ, *Battalion Commander*
ANDREY SERGEYEVICH PROZOROV
FYODOR ILYICH KULYGIN, *a high school teacher and Masha's husband*
NATALYA IVANOVNA (Natasha), *fiancée and later Andrey's wife*
ALEXEY PETROVICH FEDOTIK, *an army second-lieutenant*
VLADIMIR KARLOVICH RODÉ, *an army second-lieutenant*

The action takes place in a provincial town.

ACT I

A drawing room in the PROZOROVS' *house: It is separated from a large ballroom at the back by a row of columns. It is midday; there is a cheerful sunshine outside. In the ballroom the table is being laid for lunch.* OLGA, *wearing the regulation dark-blue dress of a secondary school teacher, is correcting her pupils' work, standing or walking about as she does so.* MASHA, *in a black dress, is sitting reading a book, her hat on her lap.* IRINA, *in white, stands lost in thought.*

OLGA Father died just a year ago today, on the fifth of May—your birthday, Irina. I remember, it was very cold and it was snowing. It seemed to me I would never live through it; and you had fainted and were lying there quite still, just as if you were dead. And now—a year's gone by, and we talk about it so easily. You're dressed in white again, and your face is positively radiant . . . *The clock strikes twelve.* The clock struck twelve then, too. *A pause.* I remember, the band was playing as they carried father to the cemetery and they fired a salute. That was because he was the general in command of the brigade. And yet there weren't many people there. Of course, it was raining hard, and there was some snow, too.

IRINA Why must we bring up all these memories?

TUSENBACH, CHEBUTYKIN, *and* SOLYONY *appear behind the columns by the table in the ballroom.*

OLGA It's so warm today that we can keep the windows wide open, but the birches haven't any leaves yet. It was eleven years ago that father got his brigade and we left Moscow. I remember so well how everything was in bloom by now; it was warm and yet I remember everything there as though we'd left it only yesterday. Why, when I woke up this morning and saw the warm sun, saw that spring was here, my heart leapt with joy. I wanted so much to go home again. Go home to Moscow!

CHEBUTYKIN, *sarcastically to* SOLYONY. A small chance of that!

TUSENBACH, *also to* SOLYONY. Of course, it's nonsense.

MASHA, *absorbed in her book, whistles part of a song softly.*

OLGA Stop whistling, Masha! How can you? *A pause.* I suppose being at school every day from morning till night gives me this constant headache. And my thoughts are as gloomy as those of an old woman. Honestly, I feel as if my strength and my youth were running out of me! Drop by drop; day by day; every day, for the last four years. . . . And one dream keeps growing stronger and stronger. . . .

IRINA Go to Moscow! Sell the house, leave everything here, and go back to Moscow.

OLGA Yes, to go back to Moscow! As soon as possible.

CHEBUTYKIN *and* TUSENBACH *laugh.*

IRINA Andrey will probably be a professor soon, anyway he won't keep on living here. The only problem is poor Masha.

OLGA Masha can come to Moscow every year and spend the whole summer with us.

MASHA *whistles a song softly.*

IRINA Everything will take care of itself with God's help. *Looking out of the window.* How beautiful it is today! I don't know why I feel so joyful. I woke up this morning and remembered it was my birthday, and suddenly I felt so happy. I thought of the time when we were children and mother was still alive. And then such wonderful thoughts came to me . . . such wonderful thoughts.

OLGA You're all aglow today—lovelier than ever. And Masha is beautiful, too. Andrey could be good-looking, too, if he hadn't put on so much weight; it doesn't suit him. As for me, I've just aged and grown a lot thinner. I suppose it's because I get so angry with the girls at school. Anyway, today I'm free, I'm home, and my head doesn't ache, and I feel so much younger than I did yesterday. After all, I'm only twenty-eight, but . . . Oh well, I suppose everything that God wills must be right and good . . . and yet, it seems to me, if I had married and stayed at home it would have been better. *A pause.* I would have loved my husband, very much.

TUSENBACH, *to* SOLYONY. Really, you talk such a lot of nonsense, I'm tired of listening to you. *Comes into the drawing room.* I forgot to tell you, Vershinin, our new battery commander, is coming to call today.

OLGA Oh really, how nice.

IRINA Is he old?

TUSENBACH No, not very. Forty, forty-five at most. He seems like a good fellow. Not a fool, that's for sure. Only he talks a lot.

IRINA Is he interesting?

TUSENBACH Yes, so-so—only he has a wife, a mother-in-law, and two little girls. What's more, she's his second wife. He goes around calling on everybody and everywhere he goes he tells people that he has a wife and two little girls. He'll tell you the same thing. It seems his wife's half crazy. She wears her hair in long braids just like a girl, and she is always philosophizing, and frequently she attempts to commit suicide, apparently to annoy her husband. I'd have left a woman like that long ago, but he puts up with her and merely complains.

SOLYONY, *entering the drawing room with* CHEBUTYKIN. With one hand I can lift only sixty pounds, but with two I can lift two hundred or even two hundred and forty pounds. From this I conclude that two men are not twice as strong as one, but three times, or even more. . . .

CHEBUTYKIN, *reading a newspaper as he comes in.* For falling hair . . . two ounces of naphthalene to half a bottle of alcohol . . . dissolve and apply daily. *Writes it down in his notebook.* Must make a note of it! No I don't want it . . . *Scratches it out.* It doesn't matter.

IRINA Ivan Romanich, dear Ivan Romanich!

CHEBUTYKIN What is it, my child, what is it?

IRINA Tell me, why is it I'm so happy today? It's just as if I were sailing along in a boat with big white sails, and above me the open, blue sky, and in the sky great white birds flying. Why is all this? Why?

CHEBUTYKIN, *kissing both her hands tenderly.* My little white bird!

IRINA You know when I woke up this morning, I suddenly felt I understood everything about the world, and I knew the way I ought to live. I know it all now, my dear Ivan Romanich. Man must work by the sweat of his brow whatever his class, for in that lies the whole meaning and purpose of his life; and his happiness and contentment, too. Oh, how good it must be to be a workman, getting up with the sun and digging ditches . . . or a farmer . . . or a teacher, teaching little children, or an engineer on a railroad. Goodness! It's better to be an ox or a horse and work, than the kind of young woman who wakes up at twelve, drinks her coffee in bed, and then takes two hours dressing . . . How dreadful! You know how you long for a cool drink when it's hot? Well, that's the way I long for work. And if I don't get up early from now on and really work, you can give me up as a friend, Ivan Romanich.

CHEBUTYKIN, *tenderly.* I will, my dear, I will . . . *[humoring her]*

OLGA Father taught us to get up at seven o'clock and so Irina always wakes up at seven—but then she stays in bed till at least nine, thinking about something or other. And with such a serious expression on her face, too! *Laughs.*

IRINA You think it's strange when I look serious because you always think of me as a little girl. I'm twenty, you know!

TUSENBACH All this longing for work . . . My God! How well I can understand it! I have never worked in my life. I was born in Petersburg, that bleak and idle city—born into a family where work and worries were simply unknown. I remember a valet pulling off my boots for me when I came home from military school . . . I grumbled at the way he did it, and my mother looked on in admiration. She was quite surprised when other people looked at me in any other way. I was protected from work! But I doubt if they have succeeded in protecting me completely . . . yes, I doubt it very much! The time has come . . . a terrific storm is coming, in fact, it's almost here. It will blow away all the laziness, the indifference, the boredom, and the prejudice against work which is ruining our society. I'm going to work, and in twenty-five or thirty years everyone will be working. Every one of us!

CHEBUTYKIN I'm not going to work.

TUSENBACH You don't count.

SOLYONY, *to* TUSENBACH. In twenty-five years you'll be dead, thank God. You'll probably die of a stroke in a year or two—or I'll lose my temper and put a bullet through your head, my friend. *Takes a phial of perfume from his pocket and sprinkles his chest and hands.*

CHEBUTYKIN, *laughing.* Really, it's quite true; I haven't done any work since I left the University, no, not a bit. I haven't even read a book, only newspapers. *Takes another newspaper out of his pocket.* For instance, here . . . I know from the paper that there was a person called Dobrolyubov, but God only knows what he wrote about. I don't know anything. *Someone knocks on the floor from downstairs.* What's that . . . they're calling me downstairs, somebody must have come to see me. I'll be back in a moment . . . *Going.* I'm coming . . . *Goes out hurriedly, stroking his beard.*

IRINA He's up to one of his little games.

TUSENBACH Yes. He looked very solemn as he left. He's obviously going to give you a present.

IRINA Oh, I wish he wouldn't.

OLGA Yes, isn't it dreadful? He's always doing something silly.

MASHA "A green oak grows by a curving shore, And round that oak hangs a golden chain". . . *Gets up as she sings under her breath.*

OLGA You're sad today, Masha.

MASHA *puts on her hat singing.*

OLGA Where are you going?

MASHA Home.

IRINA That's a strange way to act.

TUSENBACH What! Leaving your sister's birthday party?

MASHA What's the difference? I'll be back later. Good-bye, my darling. And once again, I wish you health. . . . I wish you happiness. In the old days when father was alive we used to have thirty or forty officers at our parties. What gay parties we had! And today . . . what have we got today? A man and a half, and the place is as quiet as a tomb. I'm going home. I'm depressed today, I'm sad, so don't listen to me. *Laughs through her tears.* We'll talk later on, but goodbye for now, my dear. I'll go somewhere or other . . .

IRINA, *displeased.* Really, you are such a . . .

OLGA, *tearfully.* I understand you, Masha.

SOLYONY When a man philosophizes, you'll get philosophy . . . or sophistry; but if a woman or a couple of women start philosophizing, you might as well forget it!

MASHA What do you mean by that? You're a horrible man!

SOLYONY Nothing. "He had hardly time to catch his breath Before the bear was hugging him to death." *A pause.*

MASHA, *to* OLGA, *crossly.* Do stop that crying!

Enter ANFISA *and* FERAPONT, *the latter carrying a large cake*.

ANFISA Come along, my dear, come in. Your boots are clean. *To* IRINA. A cake from Mr. Protopopov, at the Council Office. From Mihail Ivanich . . .

IRINA Thank you. Please tell him I'm very grateful. *Takes the cake*.

FERAPONT What's that, Miss?

IRINA, *louder*. Thank Mr. Protopopov.

OLGA Nurse, will you give him a piece of cake? Go along, Ferapont, they'll give you some cake.

FERAPONT What's that, Miss?

ANFISA Come along with me, my dear, come along. *Goes out with* FERAPONT.

MASHA I don't like that Protopopov, Mihail Potapich or Ivanich, or whatever it is. You shouldn't have invited him.

IRINA I didn't invite him.

MASHA Thank goodness.

Enter CHEBUTYKIN, *followed by a maid carrying a silver samovar. Murmurs of astonishment and displeasure.*

OLGA, *covering her face with her hands*. A samovar! But this is dreadful! *Goes through to the ballroom and stands by the table.*

IRINA My dear Ivan Romanich, what are you thinking of?

TUSENBACH, *laughing*. Didn't I tell you?

MASHA Ivan Romanich, you ought to be ashamed of yourself!

CHEBUTYKIN My dear, sweet girls, I've no one in the world but you. You're dearer to me than anything in the world! I'm nearly sixty, I'm an old man, a lonely, insignificant old man. The only thing that's worth anything in me is my love for you, and if it weren't for you, really I would have been dead long ago. *To* IRINA. My dear, my sweet little girl, I've known you ever since you were born—I used to carry you in my arms—I loved your mother. . . .

IRINA But why such an expensive present?

CHEBUTYKIN, *tearfully and crossly*. Expensive present! Don't talk such nonsense! *To the maid*. Take the samovar to the other room. *In a mocking tone, mimicking* IRINA. Expensive presents! *The maid takes the samovar to the ballroom.*

ANFISA, *crosses the drawing room*. Girls, a strange colonel has just arrived. He's taken off his coat and he's on his way up. Irinushka, do be nice to him, won't you. *As she goes out*. And it's time for lunch already . . . mercy on us . . .

TUSENBACH It's Vershinin, I imagine.

Enter Vershinin.

TUSENBACH Lieutenant-Colonel Vershinin!

VERSHININ, *to* MASHA *and* IRINA Allow me to introduce myself—Lieutenant-Colonel Vershinin. I'm very, very glad to be here at last. How you've changed!

IRINA Please, sit down. We're delighted to see you.

VERSHININ, *gayly*. I'm so glad to see you, so glad! But there were three little girls. I don't remember their faces, but I knew your father, Colonel Prozorov, and I remember he had three little girls. Oh, yes, I saw them myself. I remember them quite well. How time flies! My, how it flies!

TUSENBACH Alexander Ignatyevich comes from Moscow.

IRINA From Moscow? You come from Moscow?

VERSHININ Yes, from Moscow. Your father was a battery commander there, and I was an officer in his brigade. *To* MASHA. I seem to remember your face.

MASHA I don't remember you.

IRINA Olga, Olga! *Calls towards the ballroom*. Olga, come here!

OLGA *enters from the ballroom*. It seems that Lieutenant-Colonel Vershinin comes from Moscow.

VERSHININ You must be Olga Sergeyevna, the oldest. And you are Marya . . . and you are Irina, the youngest. . . .

OLGA You're from Moscow?

VERSHININ Yes. I studied in Moscow and entered the service there. I stayed there quite awhile, but then I was put in charge of a battery here—so I moved out here, you see. I don't really remember you, you know, I only remember that there were three sisters. I remember your father, though, I remember him very well. All I need to do is to close my eyes and I can see him standing there as if he were alive. I used to visit you in Moscow.

OLGA I thought I remembered everybody, and yet . . .

VERSHININ My Christian names are Alexander Ignatyevich.

IRINA Alexander Ignatyevich, and you come from Moscow! Well, what a surprise!

OLGA We're going to move there, you know.

IRINA We're going in the fall. It's our home, we were born there . . . On old Basmanaya Street. *Both laugh happily.*

MASHA Imagine, meeting someone from home so unexpectedly! *Eagerly.* I remember now. Do you remember, Olga, they used to talk of "the lovesick Major"? You were a Lieutenant then, weren't you, and you were in love with someone or other, and everyone used to tease you about it. They called you "Major" for some reason or other.

VERSHININ *laughs.* That's it, that's it . . . "The lovesick Major," that's what they called me.

MASHA In those days you only had a moustache . . . Oh, dear, how much older you look! *Tearfully.* How much older!

VERSHININ Yes, I was still a young man in the days when they called me "the lovesick Major." I was in love then. It's different now.

OLGA You've aged, yes, but you're certainly not an old man.

VERSHININ I'm going on forty-three. How long has it been since you left Moscow?

IRINA Eleven years. Now what are you crying for, Masha, you silly? *Tearfully.* You'll make me cry, too.

MASHA I'm not crying. What street did you live on?

VERSHININ On old Basmanaya.

OLGA We did, too.

VERSHININ At one time I lived on Nyemstsky Street. I used to walk from there to the Krasny Barracks, and I remember there was such a gloomy looking bridge I had to cross. I used to hear the noise of the water rushing under it. I remember how lonely and sad I felt there. *A pause.* But what a magnificently wide river you have here! It's a marvelous river!

OLGA Yes, but this is a cold place, and there are too many mosquitoes.

VERSHININ Really? I should have said you had a splendid climate here, a real Russian climate. Forests, a river . . . birch trees, too. Charming, unpretentious birch trees—I love them more than any other tree. It's nice living here. But there's one thing I can't understand: the train station is fifteen miles away, and no one knows why.

SOLYONY I know why. *Everyone looks at him.* Because if the station were nearer, it wouldn't be so far away, and since it's so far away, it can't be nearer.

An awkward silence.

TUSENBACH You like your little joke, Vassily Vassilyevich.

OLGA I'm sure I remember you now. I know I do.

VERSHININ I knew your mother.

CHEBUTYKIN She was a fine woman, God bless her!

IRINA Mother is buried in Moscow.

OLGA At the convent of Novo-Dievichye.

MASHA Would you believe it, I'm even beginning to forget what she looked like. I suppose people will not remember us either. . . . We'll be forgotten.

VERSHININ Yes, we'll all be forgotten. Such is our fate and we can't do anything about it. And what seems so very important to us now will be forgotten, and seem trivial. *A pause.* It's strange to think that we can't possibly tell what will be regarded as great and important in the future and what will be thought of as small and insignificant. Didn't the great discoveries of Copernicus—or of Columbus—appear useless and unimportant at first?—while the nonsense written by some eccentric was regarded as a revelation of a great new truth? It may well be that in time the life we live today will be considered primitive and ugly and strange, and perhaps even evil . . .

TUSENBACH Who knows? It's just as possible that future generations will think of our age as great and remember us with respect. After all, we've done away with hangings and public torture, and there haven't been any invasions, although a lot of people still suffer.

SOLYONY, *in a high-pitched voice as if calling to chickens.* Cluck, cluck, cluck! There's nothing our good Baron loves as much as philosophizing.

TUSENBACH Vassily Vassilyevich, will you let me alone? I'm getting sick of it.

SOLYONY, *as before.* Cluck, cluck, cluck! . . .

TUSENBACH, *to* VERSHININ. All the suffering we see around us—and there's a great deal—proves that our society has achieved a higher standard of morality than . . .

VERSHININ Yes, yes, of course.

CHEBUTYKIN Baron, you just said that our age will be called great; but people are small . . . *Gets up.* Look how small I am.

A violin is played off-stage.

MASHA That's our brother, Andrey, playing the violin.

IRINA He's our scholar . . . He'll probably be a professor. Father was a soldier, but his son has chosen an academic career.

OLGA We've been teasing him today. He thinks he's in love.

IRINA With a girl who lives here. She'll probably come later on.

MASHA Heavens, how she dresses! It's not that her clothes are not pretty, but she has no taste. She'll put on some weird-looking bright yellow skirt with a cheap-looking fringe, and then a red blouse to go with it. And she has such a scrubbed look. Andrey's not in love with her—I can't believe it; he's not that vulgar. I think he's playing the fool, just to annoy us. I heard yesterday that she's going to marry Protopopov, the chairman of the local board. I think that's an excellent idea. *Calls through the side door.* Andrey, come here, will you? Just for a minute.

Enter ANDREY.

OLGA This is my brother, Andrey Sergeyevich.

VERSHININ Vershinin.

ANDREY Prozorov. *Wipes the perspiration from his face.* I understand you've been appointed battery commander here?

OLGA What do you think, dear? Alexander Ignatyevich comes from Moscow.

ANDREY Do you, really? Congratulations! You'll get no peace from my sisters now.

VERSHININ I'm afraid your sisters must be bored with me already.

IRINA See what a lovely picture frame Andrey gave me for my birthday. *Shows him the frame.* He made it himself.

VERSHININ *looks at the frame, not knowing what to say.* Yes, it's . . . it's very nice. . . .

IRINA And do you see that frame on the piano? He made that, too.

ANDREY *waves his hand impatiently and walks off.*

OLGA He's a scholar, and he plays the violin, and he makes all sorts of things, too. In fact, he can do almost anything. Andrey, please, don't go. He's got such a bad habit—always walking away. Come here!

MASHA *and* IRINA *take him by the arms and lead him back, laughing.*

MASHA Now you come here!

ANDREY Leave me alone, please!

MASHA What a silly! They used to call Alexander Ignatyevich "the lovesick major," and he didn't get annoyed.

VERSHININ Not at all.

MASHA I feel like calling you a "lovesick fiddler."

IRINA Or a "lovesick professor."

OLGA He's fallen in love! Our Andriusha's in love!

IRINA, *clapping her hands.* Three cheers for Andriusha! Andriusha's in love!

CHEBUTYKIN "Nature created us for love alone." *Laughs loudly, still holding his paper in his hand.*

ANDREY That's enough, that's enough . . . *Wipes his face.* I didn't sleep all night, and I'm not feeling very well today. I read till four, and then I went to bed, but I couldn't sleep. I kept thinking about one thing and another . . . and it gets light so early; the sun just pours into my room. I'd like to translate a book from the English while I'm here during the summer.

VERSHININ You read English?

ANDREY Yes. My father—God bless him—inflicted education upon us. It sounds silly, I know, but I must confess that since he died I've begun to put on weight. It's almost as if I'd been relieved of the strain. I've gotten quite fat this past year. Yes, thanks to Father, my sisters and I know French, German, and English, and Irina here knows Italian, too. But what an effort it was!

MASHA Knowing three languages in a town like this is an unnecessary luxury. In fact, not even a luxury, just a useless encumbrance . . . like having a sixth finger. We know a lot that's just useless.

VERSHININ Really! *Laughs.* You know a lot that's useless! It seems to me that there's no place on earth, no matter how dull and depressing it may be, where intelligent and educated people aren't needed. Let's suppose that among the hundred thousand people living here, there are just three people like you—all the rest being uneducated and uncultured. Obviously, you can't hope to win out over the ignorance of the masses around you; in the course of your life, you'll have to give in little by little until you are lost in that crowd of one hundred thousand. Life will swallow you up, but not completely, for you'll have made some impression. After you've gone, perhaps there'll be six more people like you, then twelve, and so on, until finally most people will have become like you. Why, in two or three hundred years life on this earth will be wonderfully beautiful. Man longs for a life like that, and if he doesn't have it right now, he must imagine it, wait for it, dream about it, prepare for it; he must know more and see more than his father and his grandfather did. *Laughs.* And you complain because you know a lot that's useless.

MASHA *takes off her hat.* I'm staying for lunch.

IRINA, *with a sigh.* Really, someone should have written all that down.

ANDREY *has left the room unnoticed.*

TUSENBACH You say that in time to come life will be wonderfully beautiful. That's probably true. But if we're to have a part in it right now, at a distance so to speak, we've got to prepare for it and work for it.

VERSHININ *gets up.* Yes . . . Why, look at all the flowers! *Looks round.* And what a marvelous house! How I envy you! All my life I seem to have lived in a small apartment, with two chairs and a sofa and a stove which always smokes. It's the flowers that I've missed in my life, flowers like these! . . . *Rubs his hands.* But then, it's no use thinking about it.

TUSENBACH Yes, we must work. I suppose you think I'm just a sentimental German. But believe me, I'm not—I'm Russian. I don't know a word of German, and my father was a member of the Orthodox Church.

A pause.

VERSHININ *walks up and down the room.* You know, I often wonder what it would be like if we could begin our lives over again—deliberately, I mean, consciously . . . as if the life we'd already lived were just a kind of rough draft, and we could begin all over again with the final copy. If that happened, I think the thing we'd all want most would be not to repeat ourselves. We'd try at least to create a new environment, say a house like this one, for instance, with flowers and lots of light. . . . I have a wife, as you know, and two little girls; and my wife's not very well, and . . . Well, if I could begin my life all over again, I wouldn't marry. . . . No, no!

Enter KULYGIN *in the uniform of a teacher.*

KULYGIN *approaches* IRINA. Congratulations, my dear sister—from the bottom of my heart, congratulations on your birthday. I wish you the best of health and everything else a girl of your age ought to have! And allow me to give you this little book. *Hands her a book.* It's the history of our school covering the whole fifty years of its existence. I wrote it myself. It's not much, of course—I wrote it in my spare time when I had nothing better to do—but, nevertheless, I hope you'll read it. Good morning to you all! *To* VERSHININ. Allow me to introduce myself. Kulygin's the name; I'm a teacher at the high school here. *To* IRINA. You'll find a list in the book of all the pupils who have graduated from our school during the last fifty years. "*Feci quod potui, faciant meliora potentes.*" *Kisses* MASHA.

IRINA But you gave me this book last Easter!

KULYGIN *laughs.* Did I really? In that case, give it back to me—or no, better give it to the Colonel. Please take it, Colonel. Maybe you'll read it sometime when you've nothing better to do?

VERSHININ Thank you very much. *Prepares to leave.* I'm very happy to have made your acquaintance . . .

OLGA You aren't going, are you? . . . Really, you mustn't.

IRINA You must stay and have lunch with us! Please do.

OLGA Please do.

VERSHININ *bows.* It looks like I've interrupted your birthday party. I didn't know. Forgive me for not congratulating you. *Goes into the ballroom with* OLGA.

KULYGIN Today is Sunday, my friends, a day of rest; let us rest and enjoy it, each according to his age and position in life! We shall have to take up the carpets and put them away till the winter . . . And we mustn't forget to put some naphthaline on them or Persian powder . . . The Romans were a healthy people because they knew how to work *and* how to rest. They had "*mens sana in corpore sano.*" Their life had a definite shape, a form . . . The headmaster says that the most important thing about life is form. . . . A thing that loses its form is finished—that's just as true of our ordinary, everyday lives. *Takes* MASHA *by the waist and laughs.* Masha loves me. My wife loves me. Yes, and the curtains will have to be put away with the carpets, too . . . I'm happy today, very happy . . . Masha, we're invited to the headmaster's at four o'clock. A walk in the country has been arranged for the teachers and their families.

MASHA I'm not going.

KULYGIN, *distressed.* Masha, darling, why not?

MASHA I'll tell you later . . . *Crossly.* All right, I'll come, only leave me alone now . . . *Walks off.*

KULYGIN And after the walk we'll all spend the evening at the headmaster's house. In spite of his poor health, that man certainly tries to be pleasant. A fine, thoroughly enlightened man! A remarkable person! After the meeting yesterday he said to me: "I'm tired, Fyodor Ilyich. I'm tired!" *Looks at the clock, then at his watch.* Your clock is seven minutes fast. Yes, "I'm tired," he said.

The sound of the violin is heard off-stage.

OLGA Will you all come and sit down, please! Lunch is ready. There's pie.

KULYGIN Ah, Olga, my dear! Last night I worked till eleven, and I felt tired, but today I'm so happy. *Goes to the table in the ballroom.* My dear Olga!

CHEBUTYKIN *puts the newspaper in his pocket and combs his beard.* A pie? Excellent!

MASHA, *sternly to* CHEBUTYKIN. Remember, no drinking today. Do you hear? It's bad for you.

CHEBUTYKIN Never mind. I stopped that long ago! I haven't had a drink for two years. *Impatiently.* Anyway, my dear, what difference does it make?

MASHA All the same, there'll be no drinking. Don't you dare! *Crossly, but taking care that her husband does not hear.* Damn, I'll have to spend another boring evening at the headmaster's!

TUSENBACH I wouldn't go if I were you . . . It's very simple.

CHEBUTYKIN Don't go, my dear.

MASHA Oh, yes. Don't go! What a miserable life! It's intolerable . . . *Goes into the ballroom.*

CHEBUTYKIN *follows her.* Well, well! . . .

SOLYONY, *as he passes* TUSENBACH *on the way to the ballroom.* Cluck, cluck, cluck!

TUSENBACH Stop it, Vassily Vassilyevich. I've had enough . . .

SOLYONY Cluck, cluck, cluck! . . .

KULYGIN, *gayly.* Your health, Colonel! I'm a schoolteacher . . . and a member of the family. I'm Masha's husband. She has a sweet nature, such a very sweet nature!

VERSHININ I think I'll have a little of this dark vodka. *Drinks.* Your health! *To* OLGA. It feels so good to be with you all. I'm so happy.

Only IRINA *and* TUSENBACH *remain in the drawing-room.*

IRINA Masha's in a bad mood today. You know, she got married when she was eighteen, and she thought her husband was the most brilliant man in the world. It's different now. He's the kindest of men, but not the most brilliant.

OLGA, *impatiently.* Andrey, will you please come?

ANDREY, *off-stage.* I'm coming. *Enters and goes to the table.*

TUSENBACH What are you thinking about?

IRINA Oh, not much. You know, I don't like Solyony, he frightens me. He says such stupid things.

TUSENBACH He's a strange man. I'm sorry for him, even though he annoys me. In fact, I feel more sorry for him than annoyed. I think he's shy. When he's alone with me, he can be most intelligent and very friendly, but in company he's offensive and rude. Don't go yet, let them sit down first. I just want to be close to you for a moment. What are you thinking about? *A pause.* You're twenty . . . and I'm still not thirty. We've got years and years ahead of us, a whole lifetime, all full of my love for you! . . .

IRINA Don't talk to me about love, Nikolai Lvovich.

TUSENBACH, *not listening.* Oh, I long so passionately for life, to work and aspire, and all this longing is a part of my love for you, Irina. And because you are beautiful, life is beautiful for me, too! What are you thinking about?

IRINA You say that life is beautiful. Maybe it is—but what if it only seems to be beautiful? Our lives, I mean the lives of us three sisters, haven't been beautiful. The truth is that life has been stifling us, like weeds in a garden. I'm sorry I'm crying . . . I shouldn't . . . *Quickly dries her eyes and smiles.* We must work, work! The reason we feel depressed and have such a gloomy view of life is that we've never known what it is to really work. We're the children of parents who despised work. . . . *Enter* NATALYA IVANOVNA. *She is wearing a pink dress with a green belt.*

NATASHA They've gone into lunch already. . . . I'm late . . . *Glances at herself in a mirror, adjusts her dress.* Is my hair all right . . . *Catches sight of* IRINA. My dear Irina Sergeyevna, congratulations! *Gives her a vigorous and prolonged kiss.* You've got so many guests . . . I feel quite shy . . . How do you do, Baron?

OLGA *enters the drawing room.* Oh, there you are, Natalya Ivanovna! How are you, my dear? *They kiss each other.*

NATASHA Congratulations! There are so many people here, I am so afraid . . .

OLGA It's all right, they're all old friends. *Alarmed, dropping her voice.* You've got a green belt on! My dear, that must be a mistake!

NATASHA Why, is it a bad omen, or what?

OLGA No, but it just doesn't go with your dress . . . it looks so strange. . . .

NATASHA, *tearfully.* Really? But it isn't really green, it's just sort of a dull color . . . *Follows* OLGA *to the ballroom.*

All are now seated at the table; the drawing room is empty.

KULYGIN Irina, you know, I do wish you'd find yourself a good husband. It's high time you got married.

CHEBUTYKIN You ought to be getting married, too, Natalya Ivanovna.

KULYGIN Natalya Ivanovna already has a husband picked out.

MASHA *strikes her plate with her fork.* Let's have a glass of vodka! Oh, life is sweet—what the hell. . . .

KULYGIN Masha, black mark for conduct!

VERSHININ I say, this wine's very good. What's it made of?

SOLYONY Beetles!

IRINA Ugh! Ugh! How disgusting!

OLGA We're having turkey and apple pie for dinner tonight. Thank goodness, I'll be here all day today . . . tonight, too. You must all come this evening.

VERSHININ Am I invited, too?

IRINA Yes, please come.

NATASHA There are no formalities here.

CHEBUTYKIN "Nature created us for love alone . . ." *Laughs.*

ANDREY, *crossly.* Will you stop it, please? Aren't you tired of it yet?

FEDOTIK *and* RODÉ *come in with a large basket of flowers.*

FEDOTIK Look, they're eating already!

RODÉ, *in a loud voice.* Eating? So they are.

FEDOTIK Wait a minute. *Takes a snapshot.* One! Just one more!
. . . *Takes another snapshot.* Two! That's all.

*They pick up the basket and go into the ballroom where they
are greeted uproariously.*

RODÉ, *loudly.* Congratulations, Irina Sergeyevna! I wish you the
best of everything! Marvelous weather today, absolutely gorgeous.
I've been out walking with the boys all morning long. You know
I teach gym at the high school, don't you?

FEDOTIK You may move now, Irina Sergeyevna, that is, if you
want to. *Takes snapshot.* My, you look attractive today. *Takes a
top out of his pocket.* By the way, look at this top. It's got a
wonderful hum.

IRINA How lovely!

MASHA "A green oak grows by a curving shore, And round that
oak hangs a golden chain.". . . A green chain around that oak
. . . *Peevishly.* Why do I keep on saying that? Those lines have
been going through my head all day long!

KULYGIN Do you know, there are thirteen of us at the table?

RODÉ, *loudly.* You don't really believe in those old superstitions,
do you? *Laughter.*

KULYGIN When there are thirteen at the table, it means that
someone's in love. Is it you, by any chance, Ivan Romanich?

CHEBUTYKIN Oh, I'm just an old sinner. . . . But what I can't
make out is why Natalya Ivanovna looks so embarrassed.

Loud laughter. NATASHA *runs out into the drawing room.* ANDREY
follows her.

ANDREY Please, Natasha, don't pay any attention to them! Stop
. . . wait a moment. . . . Please!

NATASHA I feel so ashamed . . . I don't know what's the matter with me, and they're all laughing at me. I know it's bad
manners to leave the table like that, but I just couldn't help it
. . . I just couldn't. . . . *Covers her face with her hands.*

ANDREY My darling, please, please don't be upset. Believe me,
they aren't trying to hurt you, they're just teasing. My dearest,
darling, they're really very kind, really they are, and they love us
both. Come over here to the window, they can't see us here . . .
Looks round.

NATASHA You see, I'm not used to being with so many people.

ANDREY Oh, how young you are, Natasha, how wonderfully, beautifully young! My darling, my darling, don't be worried! Believe me, believe me . . . I'm so happy, so full of love, of joy . . . No, they won't see us! They can't see us! Why do I love you, when did I fall in love? . . . I don't understand anything. My precious, my sweet, my innocent girl, please—please marry me! I love you, I love you as I've never loved anybody . . . *Kisses her.*

Enter two officers who, seeing NATASHA *and* ANDREY *kissing, stand and stare in amazement.*

Curtain.

ACT II

The scene is the same as in Act I. It is eight o'clock in the evening. The faint sound of an accordion is heard coming from the street. The stage is unlit. Enter NATALYA IVANOVNA *in a dressing gown carrying a candle. She crosses the stage and stops by the door leading to* ANDREY's *room.*

NATASHA What are you doing, Andriusha? Reading? Oh, it's nothing. I only wanted you to know . . . *Goes to another door, opens it, looks inside and shuts it again.* No one's left a light. . . .

ANDREY *enters with a book in his hand.* What is it, Natasha?

NATASHA I was just looking to see if anyone had left any lights burning. It's carnival week, and the servants are so excited about it . . . If you don't watch them anything can happen. Last night about midnight I happened to go into the dining room and— would you believe it?—there was a candle burning on the table. I haven't found out who lit it. *Puts the candle down.* What time is it?

ANDREY *glances at his watch.* Quarter past eight.

NATASHA And Olga and Irina still out. They aren't back from work yet, poor things! Olga's still at some faculty meeting, and

Irina's at the post office. *Sighs.* This morning I said to Irina: "Darling, please take care of yourself." But she won't listen. Did you say it was a quarter past eight? I'm afraid Bobik isn't well. Why does he get so cold? Yesterday he had a fever, but today he is cold all over. . . . I'm so worried!

ANDREY It's all right, Natasha. The boy's all right.

NATASHA Still, I think he ought to have a special diet. I'm so anxious about him. Oh, by the way, they tell me that some carnival party's supposed to be coming at nine. I'd rather they didn't come, Andriusha.

ANDREY Well, I really don't know what I can do. They've been asked to come.

NATASHA This morning the little angel woke up and looked at me, and suddenly he smiled. He recognized me. "Good morning, Bobik," I said, "good morning, my darling!" And he laughed. You know, babies understand everything; they understand us perfectly well. Anyway, Andriusha, I'll tell the servants not to let that carnival party in.

ANDREY, *irresolutely.* Well . . . it's really for my sisters to decide, isn't it? It's their house, after all.

NATASHA Yes, it's their house too. I'll tell them . . . They're so kind . . . *Walks off.* I've ordered pudding for supper. The doctor says you ought to eat nothing but pudding or you'll never get any thinner. *Stops.* Bobik feels so cold. I'm afraid his room is too cold for him. He ought to be in a warmer room, at least until spring comes. For instance, Irina's room would be a perfect room for a baby: it's dry, and it's sunny all day long. I must tell her. She could share Olga's room for awhile . . . Anyway, she's never at home during the day, she just sleeps here . . . *A pause.* Andriusha, why don't you say something?

ANDREY I was thinking . . . Anyway, what's there to say . . .

NATASHA Well . . . What was it I was going to tell you? Oh, yes! Ferapont from the Council Office wants to see you about something.

ANDREY *yawns.* Tell him to come in.

NATASHA *goes out;* ANDREY, *bending over the candle which she has left behind, begins to read his book. Enter* FERAPONT *in an old shabby overcoat, his collar turned up, his ears muffled in a scarf.*

ANDREY Hello, old man! What is it?

FERAPONT The chairman's sent you these reports and a letter or something. Here! *Hands him the book and the letter.*

ANDREY Thanks. That's all. By the way, why have you come so late? It's after eight.

FERAPONT What's that?

ANDREY, *raising his voice.* I said, why have you come so late? It's after eight.

FERAPONT Yes, yes. The sun was shining when I came, but they wouldn't let me see you. The master's busy, they said. Well, if you're busy, you're busy. I'm in no hurry. *Thinking that* ANDREY *has said something.* How's that?

ANDREY Nothing. *Turns over the pages of the register.* To-morrow's Friday, there's no meeting, but I'll go to the office just the same . . . do some work. I'm so bored at home! . . . *A pause.* Yes, old man, how things change, what a fraud life is! It's strange. Why, today I picked up this notebook, I was bored and didn't have anything to do . . . Imagine, my lecture notes from the University . . . My God! Just think—I'm secretary of the local council now, and Protopopov's chairman, and the most I can ever hope for is to become a member of the council myself! I—a member of the local council! I, who dream every night that I'm a professor at the University of Moscow, a distinguished scholar, the pride of all Russia!

FERAPONT I'm sorry, I wouldn't know. I don't hear very well.

ANDREY Do you think I'd be talking to you like this if you could? I've got to talk to someone, and my wife doesn't seem to understand me, and as for my sisters . . . for some reason they frighten me. I'm afraid they'll laugh at me and I couldn't stand it . . . I don't drink and I don't like going to taverns, but how I'd enjoy just sitting at Tyestov's again, or the Great Moscow Restaurant! Just for an hour. Yes, old man, I would indeed!

FERAPONT The other day at the office a contractor was telling me about some businessmen who were eating pancakes in Moscow. One of them ate forty pancakes and died. It was either forty or fifty, I can't remember for sure.

ANDREY You can sit in some huge restaurant in Moscow and not know a soul, and no one knows you; yet somehow you feel that you belong there. . . . But here you know everybody, and everybody knows you, and yet you don't feel you belong here, no, not at all. . . . You're a stranger and all alone.

FERAPONT What's that? *Pause.* The same man told me—of course, he could have been lying—that there's a long rope stretched all the way across Moscow.

ANDREY Whatever for?

FERAPONT I'm sorry, I don't know, but that's what he said.

ANDREY Nonsense! *Reads the book.* Have you ever been to Moscow?

FERAPONT, *after a pause.* No. It wasn't God's wish. *A pause.* Shall I go now?

ANDREY Yes, you may go. Good-bye. FERAPONT *goes out.* Good-bye. *Reading.* Come in the morning, I'll have some letters for you . . . You can go now. *A pause.* He's gone. *A bell rings.* Yes, that's how it is . . . *Stretches and slowly goes to his room.*

Singing is heard off-stage; a nurse is putting a baby to sleep. Enter MASHA *and* VERSHININ. *While they talk together a maid lights a lamp and candles in the ballroom.*

MASHA I don't know. *A pause.* I don't know. Habit's a very important thing of course. For example, after Father died, it took a long time to get used to the idea of not having any orderlies around to wait on us. But even apart from habit, I think I'm perfectly justified in saying—and of course, this may be different in other places, but in this town the officers are certainly the nicest and most generous and best mannered people.

VERSHININ I'm thirsty. I'd like some tea.

MASHA *glances at her watch.* They'll bring it in soon. You see, I was married when I was eighteen. I was so afraid of my husband because he was a teacher, and I had just finished school myself. He seemed terribly brilliant then, very learned and important. But now, unfortunately, it's quite different.

VERSHININ Yes . . . I see . . .

MASHA Oh, I'm not speaking of my husband—I'm used to him now—but there are so many vulgar and unpleasant and ill-mannered people here. Rudeness upsets me, it hurts me, I actually suffer when I meet someone who lacks refinement and courtesy. When I'm with my husband's colleagues, I'm simply miserable.

VERSHININ Yes, I understand. But it seems to me it's all the same whether they are civilian or military, they are equally dull, in this town at least. It's all the same! If you talk to one of the local intelligentsia—civilian or military, he'll generally tell you that he's just worn out. It's either his wife, or his house, or his estate, or his horse, or something . . . We Russians are peculiarly given to exalted ideas—but why is it we always fall so short in life? Why is it, why?

MASHA Why?

VERSHININ Yes, why does his wife wear him out, why is he worried to death by his children? And what about *him* exhausting his wife and children?

MASHA You're really depressed today, aren't you?

VERSHININ Perhaps. I've had nothing to eat since morning. One of the girl's isn't feeling very well, and when the children are sick, I get too worried. My conscience torments me for having given them a mother like theirs. Oh, if only you could have seen her this morning! What a despicable woman! We began quarrelling at seven and at nine I finally walked out and slammed the door. *A pause.* I never talk about it. Strange, it's only to you I complain. *Kisses her hand.* Don't be angry with me. I've nobody, nobody but you . . . *A pause.*

MASHA What a noise the wind's making in the stove! Just before Father died the wind howled in the chimney. There, just like that. *Death*

VERSHININ Are you superstitious?

MASHA Yes.

VERSHININ How strange. *Kisses her hand.* You really are a wonderful creature, a marvelous woman! Wonderful, magnificent! It's dark here, but I can see your eyes shining.

MASHA *moves to another chair.* There's more light over here.

VERSHININ I love you, I love you, I love you . . . I love your eyes, love the way you move . . . I see them in my dreams. A wonderful, marvelous woman!

MASHA, *laughing softly.* When you talk to me like that, somehow I can't help laughing, although I'm frightened. Don't do it again, please. *Half-audibly.* No . . . go on. I don't mind . . . *Covers her face with her hands.* I don't mind . . . Someone's coming . . . talk about something else.

Enter IRINA *and* TUSENBACH *through the ballroom.*

TUSENBACH I have a triple-barrelled name—Baron Tusenbach-

Krone-Alschauer—but actually I'm a Russian. I was baptized in the Orthodox Church, just like yourself. There's nothing German about me, except maybe the obstinate way I keep on pestering you. Look how I bring you home every night.

IRINA How tired I am!

TUSENBACH And I'll keep bringing you home every night for the next twenty years—unless you send me away . . . *Noticing* MASHA *and* VERSHININ, *with pleasure.* Oh, it's you! How are you!

IRINA Well, here I am, home at last! *To* MASHA. A woman came into the office just as I was leaving. She wanted to send a wire to her brother in Saratov to tell him her son had just died, but she couldn't remember the address. So she sent it without an address, just to Saratov. She was crying and I was rude to her, for no reason at all. "I've no time to waste," I told her. It was stupid of me. Are the carnival people coming tonight?

MASHA Yes.

IRINA *sits down.* How nice it is to relax! I'm so tired!

TUSENBACH, *smiling.* When you get home from work, you look so young and so unhappy, somehow. *A pause.*

IRINA I'm tired. No, I don't like working at the post office, I don't like it at all.

MASHA You've gotten so much thiner . . . *Whistles.* You look younger, too, and your face is beginning to look like a little boy's.

TUSENBACH It's the way she does her hair.

IRINA I must get another job. This one doesn't suit me. It lacks all the things I long for and dream of. It's work without poetry, without meaning. *Someone knocks at the floor from below.* There's the Doctor knocking. *To* TUSENBACH. Will you answer him? I can't . . . I'm too tired. TUSENBACH *knocks on the floor.*

IRINA He'll be up in a minute. We've got to do something about all this. Andrey and the Doctor went to the club last night and lost again. They say Andrey lost two hundred roubles.

MASHA, *with indifference.* Well, what are we to do?

IRINA He lost two weeks ago, and he lost in December, too. I wish he'd just lose everything as soon as possible. Perhaps then we'd leave for Moscow. Oh dear, I dream of Moscow every night. Sometimes I feel as if I were going mad. *Laughs.* We're going back to Moscow in June. How many months are there till June? . . . February, March, April, May . . . almost half a year!

MASHA We must be careful that Natasha doesn't find out about his gambling.

IRINA I don't think she'd care.

Enter CHEBUTYKIN. *He has been resting on his bed since dinner and has only just got up. He combs his beard, then sits down at the table and takes out a newspaper.*

MASHA Here he comes. Has he paid his rent yet?

IRINA *laughs.* No. Not a penny for the last eight months. He's probably forgotten.

MASHA *laughs.* Look, how solemnly he sits there!

They all laugh. A pause.

IRINA Why are you so quiet, Alexander Ignatyevich?

VERSHININ I don't know. I just want some tea. I'd give my life for a glass of tea! I haven't eaten anything since morning . . .

CHEBUTYKIN Irina Sergeyevna!

IRINA What is it?

CHEBUTYKIN Please come here. *"Venez ici!"* IRINA *goes over to him and sits down at the table.* I can't do without you. IRINA *lays out the cards for a game of solitaire.*

VERSHININ Well, if we can't have any tea, let's philosophize a bit, anyway.

TUSENBACH Yes, fine idea. What about?

VERSHININ What about? Well . . . let's try to imagine what life will be like after we're dead, say in two or three hundred years.

TUSENBACH All right, then. . . . After we're dead, people will fly in balloons, fashions will change, the sixth sense will be discovered, and for all I know, even developed and used . . . But life itself won't be very different; it will still be mysterious, always difficult, yet filled with happiness. And in a thousand years people will still sigh and complain "How hard life is!"—and yet they'll still be afraid of death and unwilling to die, just as they are now.

VERSHININ, *after a moment's thought.* Well, you know . . . How shall I put it? I think everything is bound to change gradually—in fact, it's changing before our very eyes. In two or three hundred years, maybe it will take a thousand—how long doesn't really matter—life will be different. It will be happy. Of course, we won't be able to share it, we work and . . . yes, we suffer in order to create it. That's the purpose of our life, and you might say that's the only happiness we shall ever have.

MASHA *laughs quietly*.

TUSENBACH Why are you laughing?

MASHA I don't know. I've been laughing all day today.

VERSHININ, *to* TUSENBACH. I went to the same school as you did but I never went on to the Academy. I read a great deal, of course, but I never know what books I ought to choose, and I probably read the wrong things. And yet the longer I live the more I want to know. I'm getting older—my hair's getting gray, and yet how little I know, how little! All the same, I think I do know one thing which is not only true but also most important. I'm certain of it. Oh, if only I could convince you that there's not going to be any happiness for us and our generation, that there mustn't be and won't be . . . we must work and work. Happiness, well, that's for those who come after us, our remote descendants. *A pause.* So, even if I'll never be happy, at least my grandchildren will be.

FEDOTIK *and* RODÉ *enter the ballroom; they sit down and sing quietly, one of them playing on a guitar.*

TUSENBACH So you think it's useless to even dream of happiness! But what if I *am* happy?

VERSHININ You're not.

TUSENBACH, *flinging up his hands and laughing*. Obviously, we don't understand each other. How can I convince you?

MASHA *laughs quietly*.

TUSENBACH *holds up a finger to her*. She'll laugh at the drop of a hat! *To* VERSHININ. And life won't be any different, no, not only a couple of hundred years from now, but a million. Life doesn't change, it always goes on the same; it follows its own laws, which don't concern us and which we can't discover anyway. Think of the birds flying South in the autumn, the cranes, for instance: they just fly on and on. It doesn't matter what they're thinking, whether their heads are filled with great ideas or small ones, they just keep flying, not knowing where or why. And they'll go on flying no matter how many philosophers they happen to have flying with them. Let them philosophize as much as they like, as long as they go on flying.

MASHA Isn't there some meaning?

TUSENBACH Meaning? . . . Look there, it's snowing. What's the meaning of that? *A pause.*

MASHA But man has to have some faith, or at least he's got to seek it, otherwise his life will be empty, empty . . . How can you live and not know why the cranes fly, why children are born, why the stars shine in the sky! . . . You must either know why you live, or else . . . nothing matters . . . everything's just nonsense and waste . . . *A pause.*

VERSHININ Yes, it's sad when one's youth has gone.

MASHA "It's a bore to be alive in this world, friends," that's what Gogol says.

TUSENBACH And I say: it's impossible to argue with you, friends! Let's drop the subject.

CHEBUTYKIN *reads out of the paper.* Balzac was married in Berditchev.

IRINA *sings softly to herself.*

CHEBUTYKIN I think I'll make a note of that. *Writes.* Balzac was married in Berditchev. *Reads on.*

IRINA, *playing patience, pensively.* Balzac was married in Berditchev.

TUSENBACH Well, the die is cast. Did you know that I'd sent in my resignation, Marya Sergeyevna?

MASHA So I heard. But what good will come of it? Besides, I don't like civilians.

TUSENBACH Never mind. What kind of a soldier am I anyway? I'm not even handsome. Anyway, what difference does it make? I'll work. For once in my life, I'd like to work so hard that when I came home I'd collapse on my bed exhausted and go to sleep at once. *Goes to ballroom.* Working men must sleep well!

FEDOTIK, *to* IRINA. I bought you some crayons at Pyshikov's, on Moscow Street. And this little penknife, too . . .

IRINA You still treat me as if I were a little girl. I wish you'd realize that I've grown up. *Takes the crayons and the penknife, joyfully.* Oh, they're wonderful!

FEDOTIK Look, I bought myself a knife, too. You see, it's got another blade here, and there's another . . . this is for cleaning your ears, and this is for cutting your nails, and this is for cleaning them . . .

RODÉ, *in a loud voice.* Doctor, how old are you?

CHEBUTYKIN I? Thirty-two. *Laughter.*

FEDOTIK I'll show you another kind of solitaire. *Sets out the cards.*

The samovar is brought in, and ANFISA *attends to it. Shortly afterwards* NATASHA *comes in and begins to fuss around the table.* SOLYONY *enters, bows to the company and sits down at the table.*

VERSHININ My, what a wind there is tonight!

MASHA Yes. I'm tired of winter. I've almost forgotten what summer is like.

IRINA, *playing solitaire.* I'm going to go out. We'll get to Moscow!

FEDOTIK No, you're not. See, the eight has to go on the two of spades. *Laughs.* That means you won't go to Moscow.

CHEBUTYKIN *reads the paper.* Tsitsiker. A smallpox epidemic is raging. . . .

ANFISA *goes up to* MASHA. Masha dear, the tea's ready. *To* VERSHININ. Will you please come to the table, your excellency? Forgive me, your name's slipped my memory . . .

MASHA Bring it here, Nanny. I don't feel like getting it.

IRINA Nanny!

ANFISA I'm comi-ing!

NATASHA, *to* SOLYONY. You know, even little babies understand what we say, they can understand us completely! Why, this morning I said to Bobik, "Good morning, Bobik, good morning, my precious!"—and he looked up at me in his special way. You can say it's only a mother's imagination, but it isn't, I promise you. No, no! He is really a most unusual child!

SOLYONY If that child were mine, I'd fry him in a pan and eat him. *Picks up his glass, goes into the drawing room and sits down in a corner.*

NATASHA *covers her face with her hands.* What a rude, disgusting man!

MASHA People don't even notice whether it's summer or winter when they're happy. If I lived in Moscow I wouldn't care what the weather was like.

VERSHININ The other day I was reading the diary of some French minister—he wrote it in prison. He was convicted for his involvement in the fraud of the Panama affair. He writes with such enthusiasm and delight about the birds he can see through the prison window—the birds he never even noticed when he was a minister. Of course, now that he's released he doesn't notice them any more . . . Just as you won't notice Moscow when you live there. We're not happy and we can't be happy; we only want happiness.

TUSENBACH *picks up a box from the table.* Where's all the candy gone?

IRINA Solyony's eaten it.

TUSENBACH All of it?

ANFISA, *serving* VERSHININ *with tea.* Here's a letter for you, sir.

VERSHININ For me? *Takes the letter.* From my daughter. *Reads it.* Yes, of course . . . Forgive me, Marya Sergeyevna, I'll just slip out quietly. I won't have any tea. *Gets up, agitated.* Always the same thing . . .

MASHA What is it? Can't you tell me?

VERSHININ, *in a low voice.* My wife's tried to poison herself again. I've just got to go. I'll leave without them seeing me. How horrible all this is. *Kisses Masha's hand.* My dear, good, my sweet . . . I'll leave quietly out this way . . . *Goes out.*

ANFISA Where's he going now? And I've just poured his tea! What a strange man!

MASHA, *flaring up.* Leave me alone! Why do you keep pestering me? Why don't you leave me in peace? *Goes to the table, cup in hand.* I'm sick and tired of you, you silly old woman!

ANFISA Why . . . But I didn't mean to offend you, dear.

ANDREY'S VOICE, *off-stage.* Anfisa!

ANFISA *mimics him.* Anfisa! Sitting there in his study . . . ! *Goes out.*

MASHA *by the table in the ballroom, crossly.* Let me sit down somewhere! *Fumbles up the cards laid out on the table.* You take up the whole table with your cards! Drink your tea!

IRINA How cross you are, Masha!

MASHA Well, if I'm cross, don't talk to me, then. Just don't bother me!

CHEBUTYKIN *laughs.* Don't bother her! . . . Be careful you don't bother her!

MASHA You may be sixty, but you're always jabbering about nothing, just like a baby . . .

NATASHA *sighs.* Masha dear, must you talk that way? You know, with your good looks you'd be thought so charming, even by the best people—yes, I honestly mean it—if only you wouldn't talk that way. "*Je vous prie, pardonnez moi, Marie, mais vous avez des manières un peu grossières.*"

TUSENBACH, *with suppressed laughter*. Give me . . . will you please pass me . . . Isn't there some cognac?

NATASHA "*Il parait que mon Bobik déjà ne dort pas*" . . . I think he's crying. He hasn't been feeling well today. I must go and take care of him . . . Excuse me. *Goes out.*

IRINA Where has Alexander Ignatyevich gone?

MASHA Home. His wife's done something crazy again.

TUSENBACH *goes over to* SOLYONY *with a decanter of cognac.* You always sit alone brooding about something or other—although there's no telling what about. Come, let's make up. Let's have a drink of cognac together. *They drink.* I suppose I'll have to play the piano all night tonight—a lot of trash . . . Oh, well!

SOLYONY Why did you say "let's make up"? We haven't quarrelled.

TUSENBACH You always make me feel that something is wrong between us. You're a strange character, that you must admit.

SOLYONY *recites.* "I am strange, who isn't strange? Be not wrath, Aleko!"

TUSENBACH What's Aleko got to do with it? . . . *A pause.*

SOLYONY When I'm alone with someone I'm all right, I'm just like everybody else. But when I'm in a group of people, I get depressed and shy, and . . . I talk all sorts of nonsense. All the same, I'm a damned sight more honest than a lot of people. And I can prove it, too.

TUSENBACH You make me mad whenever you pester me when we're in company—but, you know, for some reason I still like you . . . I'm going to get drunk tonight, I don't care what happens! Let's have another drink!

SOLYONY Yes, let's. *A pause.* I've never had anything against you personally, Baron. But I have the temperament of Lermontov. *In a low voice.* I even look something like Lermontov, at least that's what they say . . . *Takes a scent bottle from his pocket and sprinkles some scent on his hands.*

TUSENBACH I have sent in my resignation! I've had enough! I've been thinking about it for five years now, and finally I've made up my mind. I'm going to work.

SOLYONY *recites*. "Be not wrath, Aleko . . . Forget, forget your dreams!"

During the conversation ANDREY *enters quietly with a book in his hand and sits down by the candle.*

TUSENBACH I'm going to work!

CHEBUTYKIN *comes into the drawing room with* IRINA. And the food was really Caucasian: onion soup, and then *"chehartma"*—that's a wonderful roast.

SOLYONY *"Chereshma"* isn't meat at all; it's a plant, like an onion.

CHEBUTYKIN No, no, my friend, *"chehartma"* isn't an onion, it's roast lamb.

SOLYONY And I tell you *"chereshma"* is a kind of onion.

CHEBUTYKIN Well, why should I argue with you about it? You've never been to the Caucasus and you've never eaten *"chehartma."*

SOLYONY I haven't eaten it because I can't stand it. *"Chereshma"* smells just like garlic.

ANDREY, *imploringly*. Stop it, my friends! Please stop it!

TUSENBACH When's the carnival party coming?

IRINA They said nine—that means any time now.

TUSENBACH *embraces* ANDREY *and sings*. "Oh, my porch, oh my beautiful new porch, my . . . "

ANDREY *dances and sings*. "With posts of maple wood . . . "

CHEBUTYKIN *dances*. "And fancy lattice-work . . . "

Laughter.

TUSENBACH *kisses* ANDREY. Let's have a drink, what the hell! Andruisha, let's drink to eternal friendship. I'll go to Moscow with you when you go back to the University.

SOLYONY Which one? There are two universities in Moscow.

ANDREY There's only one.

SOLYONY I tell you there are two.

ANDREY All right, let's make it three. The more the better.

SOLYONY There are two universities in Moscow. *Murmurs of protest and cries of "Hush!"* There are two universities in Moscow, the old one and the new one. But if you don't want to listen to me, if what I say bothers you, I'll keep quiet. In fact, I'll leave . . . *Goes out through one of the doors.*

TUSENBACH Bravo, bravo! *Laughs*. My friends, let's get started. I'll play for you. What a funny fellow that Solyony is! . . . *Sits down at the piano and plays a waltz.*

MASHA *dances alone.* The Baron is drunk, the Baron is drunk, the Baron is drunk . . .

Enter NATASHA.

NATASHA, *to* CHEBUTYKIN. Ivan Romanich! *Speaks to him, then goes out quietly.* CHEBUTYKIN *touches* TUSENBACH *on the shoulder and whispers to him.*

IRINA What is it?

CHEBUTYKIN It's time we were going.

TUSENBACH Yes, it's time we were going. Good night.

IRINA But wait . . . What about the carnival people?

ANDREY, *embarrassed.* They're not coming. You see, my dear, Natasha says that Bobik isn't feeling very well, and well . . . Anyway, I don't know . . . and I couldn't care less . . .

IRINA *shrugs her shoulders.* Bobik's not feeling well! . . .

MASHA Forget it, so what! If they kick us out, well out we go! *To* IRINA. It isn't Bobik who's sick, it's her . . . Here! . . . *Taps her forehead with her finger.* Petty "hausfrau!"

ANDREY *goes to his room on the right.* CHEBUTYKIN *follows him. The guests say good-bye in the ballroom.*

FEDOTIK What a pity! I'd counted on spending the evening, but of course, if the baby's sick . . . I'll bring him some toys tomorrow.

RODÉ, *in a loud voice.* I had a nap after lunch today on purpose, I thought I'd be dancing all night. Why, it's only nine o'clock.

MASHA Let's go outside and talk about it. We can decide what to do then.

Voices are heard saying "Good-bye! God bless you!" and TUSENBACH *is heard laughing gayly. Everyone goes out.* ANFISA *and a maid clear the table and put out the lights. The nurse sings to the baby off-stage. Enter* ANDREY, *wearing an overcoat and hat, followed by* CHEBUTYKIN. *They move quietly.*

CHEBUTYKIN I've never had time to get married, somehow . . . because my life's just flashed by like lightning, and because I was always very much in love with your mother and she was married . . .

ANDREY One shouldn't marry. One shouldn't marry, it's so boring.

CHEBUTYKIN That may be, but what about the loneliness? You can talk all you want, my boy, but loneliness is a horrible thing.

Though, as a matter of fact . . . oh well, what difference does it make! . . .

ANDREY Let's get going.

CHEBUTYKIN What's the hurry? We've plenty of time.

ANDREY I'm afraid my wife'll stop me.

CHEBUTYKIN Ah!

ANDREY I won't gamble tonight, I'll just sit and watch. You know, I don't feel very well . . . What should I do for this shortness of breath, Ivan Romanich?

CHEBUTYKIN Don't ask me. I can't remember, my boy—I really don't know.

ANDREY Let's go through the kitchen.

They go out. A bell rings. The ring is repeated, then voices and laughter are heard.

IRINA, *coming in.* Who is it?

ANFISA, *in a whisper.* The carnival party.

The bell rings again.

IRINA Tell them there's no one at home, Nanny. They'll have to excuse us.

ANFISA *goes out.* IRINA *walks up and down the room, lost in thought. She seems agitated. Enter* SOLYONY.

SOLYONY, *puzzled.* No one here . . . Where is everybody?

IRINA They've gone home.

SOLYONY That's strange! Are you alone?

IRINA Yes. *A pause.* Well . . . good night.

SOLYONY I know I behaved tactlessly before, I just lost control of myself. But you're not like the others, you're high-minded—you're pure, you can see the truth . . . You're the only one who understands me. I love you . . . I love you with a deep, with an infinite . . .

IRINA Go away, please. Good night!

SOLYONY I can't live without you. *Follows her.* Oh it's so wonderful just to look at you! *With tears.* Oh, my joy! Your glorious, marvelous, bewitching eyes—the most beautiful eyes in all the world . . .

IRINA, *coldly.* Vassily Vassilyevich, stop it!

SOLYONY I've never spoken to you of my love before . . . it's as if I were living on a different planet . . . *Rubs his forehead.* Forget it! I can't make you love me. But there will be no successful rivals . . . I swear to you by all that's sacred that if there's anyone else, I'll kill him. Oh, how wonderful, how wonderful you are!

Enter NATASHA *carrying a candle.*

NATASHA *pokes her head into one room, then into another, but passes the door leading to her husband's room.* Andrey's reading. Might as well let him. Forgive me, Vassily Vassilyevich, I didn't know you were here. I'm afraid I'm not properly dressed.

SOLYONY I don't care. Good-bye. *Goes out.*

NATASHA You must be tired, my poor girl. *Kisses* IRINA. You should go to bed earlier.

IRINA Is Bobik asleep?

NATASHA Yes, but not very quietly. By the way, dear, I keep meaning to speak to you, but then there's always been something . . . either you're not here, or I'm too busy . . . Bobik's nursery is so cold and damp . . . And your room is just perfect for a baby. Darling, I'm sure you won't mind moving in with Olga.

IRINA, *not understanding her.* Where?

The sound of bells is heard outside, as a troika is driven up to the house.

NATASHA You can share Olga's room—just for a little while—and Bobik can have your room. He is such a darling! This morning I said to him: "Bobik, you're my very own! My very own!" And he looked up at me with his sweet little eyes. *The door bell rings.* That must be Olga. How late she is! *A maid comes up to* NATASHA *and whispers in her ear.* Protopopov! What a strange man! Why, Protopopov's come to take me for a drive. In his troika. *Laughs.* How strange men are! . . . *The door bell rings again.* Somebody else's ringing. Shall I go out for a little bit? Just for a quarter of an hour? *To the maid.* Tell him I'll be right there. *The door bell rings.* There's the bell again. It must be Olga. *Goes out.*

The maid runs out; IRINA *sits lost in thought. Enter* KULYGIN *and* OLGA, *followed by* VERSHININ.

KULYGIN Well! What's going on here? You said you were going to have a party.

VERSHININ That's strange. I left not more than half an hour ago, and they were still expecting the party.

IRINA They've all gone.

KULYGIN Masha, too? Where did she go? And what's Protopopov doing outside in his troika? Who's he waiting for?

IRINA Don't ask me questions please. I'm tired.

KULYGIN You . . . spoiled child!

OLGA The faculty meeting just ended. I'm exhausted. The head-mistress is sick and I have to take her place. My head aches, oh, my head, my head . . . *Sits down.* Andrey lost again last night—two hundred roubles. The whole town's talking about it.

KULYGIN Yes, the meeting exhausted me, too. *Sits down.*

VERSHININ So now my wife's decided to frighten me. She tried to poison herself. But it's all right now, so I can relax . . . So we have to leave? Well, good night. Fyodor Ilyich, let's go some-where together? I can't go home yet, I just can't . . . Come!

KULYGIN I'm tired. I don't think I'll come. *Gets up.* I'm tired. Has my wife gone home?

IRINA She must have.

KULYGIN *kisses Irina's hand.* Good-night. We'll rest all day tomor-row and the day after tomorrow, two whole days! Well, I . . . ahh . . . *Going out.* My, I'd like some tea! I was planning on spending the evening in pleasant company, but—"*o, fallacem hominum spem*"! Accusative of exclamation.

VERSHININ Well, it looks as if I'll have to go alone. *Goes out with* KULYGIN, *whistling.*

OLGA My head aches, oh, how my head aches . . . Andrey lost at cards . . . the whole town's talking . . . I'll go and lie down. *Going out.* Tomorrow I'm free. Goodness, how pleasant that will be. Tomorrow I'm free, and the day after tomorrow I'm free . . . Oh, my head aches, my head . . .

IRINA, *alone.* They've all gone. There's no one left.

Someone is playing an accordion in the street. The nurse sings in the next room.

NATASHA *crosses the ballroom, wearing a fur coat and cap. She is followed by the maid.* I'll be back in half an hour. I'm just going for a short drive. *Goes out.*

IRINA, *alone, with intense dejection.* Oh, to go to Moscow! To Moscow! Moscow!

Curtain.

ACT III

They been pushed out

A bedroom shared by OLGA *and* IRINA. *To the left and to the right are beds, each screened off from the rest of the room. It is going on three o'clock in the morning. Off-stage a fire alarm is ringing for a fire which has been raging some time. No one in the house has gone to bed.* MASHA *lies on the couch, dressed, as usual, in black.* OLGA *and* ANFISA *enter.*

ANFISA They're sitting under the staircase. I keep telling them to come up here, but they just cry. "Where's our Daddy?" they say, "he's been burned in the fire." And then all those poor people out in the yard . . . half dressed . . . can you imagine thinking things like that!

OLGA *takes a dress out of a wardrobe.* Here, take this grey dress, Nurse . . . And this one . . . This blouse, too . . . And the skirt. Oh, Lord! what a dreadful night! It looks like all of Kirsanovsky Street's burned down . . . Take this . . . and this, too . . . *Throws the clothes into* ANFISA's *arms.* The poor Vershinins were frightened to death. Their house nearly burned down. They must spend the night here . . . we just can't let them go home. And poor Fedotik's lost everything, too, he's got nothing left. . . .

ANFISA You'll have to call Ferapont, Olyushka, I can't carry all this.

OLGA *rings.* No one answers when I ring. *Calls through the door.* Is anyone there? Please, will someone come up!

A window, red with the glow of the fire, can be seen through the open door. The sound of a passing fire engine is heard. How awful it is! And I am so tired! *Enter* FERAPONT. Take this downstairs . . . give it to the Kolotilin girls, they're under the staircase . . . and this, too . . .

FERAPONT Yes, miss. Moscow burnt down in 1812 too . . . Mercy on us! . . . Yes, the French were surprised all right.

OLGA Get along with you, take these things downstairs.

FERAPONT Yes, miss. *Goes out.*

OLGA Give them everything, Nurse dear. We don't need it, give it all away . . . I'm so tired, I can hardly stand up. We can't let the Vershinins go home. Let's see, the little girls can sleep in the drawing room, and Alexander Ignatyevich can go in with the Baron. Fedotik can too, or maybe he'd better sleep in the dining room. The Doctor's terribly drunk—you'd almost think he'd done it on purpose; he's so frightfully drunk we can't let anyone go into his room. And Vershinin's wife will have to go into the drawing room, too.

ANFISA, *wearily*. Don't send me away, Olyushka, darling! Don't send me away!

OLGA What kind of nonsense is that, Nurse! No one's going to send you away.

ANFISA *leans her head against* OLGA's *breast*. Oh, dearest! I do work, you know, I try as hard as I can . . . I suppose now that I can't do as much, they'll tell me to go. But where can I go? Where? I'm eighty years old, almost eighty-two!

OLGA Here, dear, you sit down for a bit . . . You're tired, poor thing . . . *Makes her sit down*. You just rest. How pale you look.

Enter NATASHA.

NATASHA They're saying we ought to form a society to help the victims of the fire. Well, why not? It's a fine idea! We must always try to help the poor whenever we can. Bobik and Sofotchka are sound asleep as though nothing had happened. But I wish we didn't have such a crowd of people in the house. No matter where you turn, you bump into them. You know the flu's in town . . . and I'm so afraid the children may get it.

OLGA, *without listening to her*. You can see the fire from the window, but it's quiet when the drapes are closed.

NATASHA Yes . . . Oh, my hair must be all over the place. *Stands in front of the mirror*. They say I've gotten fat, but it's not true! I haven't added a pound. Masha's asleep . . . she's so tired, poor dear . . . *Notices* ANFISA, *coldly*. How dare you sit down in my presence? Get up! Get out of here! ANFISA *goes out*. A *pause*. I can't understand why you keep that old woman around here.

OLGA, *taken aback*. Forgive my saying it, but I don't know how you . . .

NATASHA She's useless. She's just a peasant and belongs in the country. Why do you pamper her like this? I like order in any house, and there's no room for useless people. *Strokes* OLGA's *cheek*. Poor dear, you're so tired! Our headmistress is tired! You know,

Natasha is pushing Olga downstairs now

when my Sofotchka grows up and goes to school, I'll be so afraid of you.

OLGA I'm not going to be the headmistress.

NATASHA You'll be elected, Olya. Why, it's all settled.

OLGA I'll refuse. I couldn't do it . . . I haven't the strength for it. *Drinks water.* You were very rude to Nurse just now . . . You must forgive my saying it, but I just can't stand such inconsiderateness . . . I'm afraid I'm going to faint . . .

NATASHA, *agitated.* Forgive me, Olya, forgive me. I didn't mean to upset you.

MASHA *gets up, picks up a pillow and goes out angrily.*

OLGA Please try to understand . . . Perhaps we've been brought up in a strange way, but I just can't stand it. When people are treated like that, it depresses me. It makes me ill . . . It completely upsets me.

NATASHA Forgive me, dear, forgive me! . . . *Kisses her.*

OLGA Any cruel or tactless remark, even when it's not intentional, upsets me . . .

NATASHA I know I talk too much, I must be more careful—but you must admit, that she might just as well be out in the country.

OLGA She's been with us for thirty years.

NATASHA But she can't work any more, can she? Either I don't understand you, or you won't understand me. She can't work, she just sleeps and sits.

OLGA Well, let her sit.

NATASHA, *in surprise.* What do you mean, let her sit? She *is a servant, you know! Tearfully.* I just don't understand you, Olya! I have a nurse for the children and a wet nurse and we have a maid and a cook. What do we need that old woman for? What for?

The alarm is sounded again.

OLGA I've grown ten years older tonight.

NATASHA We must come to some sort of understanding, Olya. You're working at the school, and I'm working at home. You're teaching and I run the house. And if I say anything about the servants, I know what I'm talking about . . . That old thief, that old hag must get out of here tomorrow! . . . *Stamps her feet.* Do you understand! How dare you annoy me? How dare you? *Recovering her self-control.* Really, if you don't move downstairs, we'll always be quarrelling. It's terrible!

Enter KULYGIN.

KULYGIN Where's Masha? It's time to go home. They say the fire's dying down. *Stretches.* Only one block burned, but at first it looked as if the whole town was going to be set on fire by the wind. *Sits down.* I'm so tired, Olya, my dear. You know, I've often thought that if I hadn't married Masha, I'd have married you, Olya. You're such a good person. I'm worn out. *Listens.*

OLGA What's that?

KULYGIN The Doctor's drunk just as if he'd done it on purpose. Drunk out of his mind . . . As if he'd done it on purpose. *Gets up.* I think he's coming up here . . . Hear him? Yes, here he comes. *Laughs.* What a man, really! . . . I'm going to hide. *Goes to the wardrobe and stands between it and the wall.* What a scoundrel!

OLGA He hasn't had a drink for two years, and suddenly now he gets drunk. *Goes with* NATASHA *behind one of the screens.*

CHEBUTYKIN *enters; without staggering, as if he were sober, he crosses the room, stops, looks around, then goes to the washstand and begins to wash his hands.*

CHEBUTYKIN, *glumly.* The devil take them all . . . the whole lot of them! They think I can cure anything just because I'm a doctor, but I don't know anything . . . nothing at all. I've forgotten everything I ever knew. I don't remember anything, absolutely nothing . . . OLGA *and* NATASHA *come out from behind the screen and leave the room without his noticing.* The hell with them! Last Wednesday I treated a woman at Zasyp. She died, and it's all my fault that she died. Yes . . . I knew something twenty-five years ago, but I don't remember anything now. Not a thing! Perhaps I'm not even a man at all, but just imagine that I've got hands and feet and a head. Perhaps I don't exist at all, and I only imagine that I walk and eat and sleep. *Weeps.* Oh, if only I didn't exist! *Stops crying, glumly.* God knows . . . The other day they were talking about Shakespeare and Voltaire at the club . . . I hadn't read them, never read a single line, but I pretended that I had. The others did the same thing. How small we all are! How disgusting! And then all of a sudden I remembered that woman I killed on Wednesday. Everything came back to me, and I felt such a disgust, so sick of myself that I went and got drunk . . .

Enter IRINA, VERSHININ, *and* TUSENBACH. TUSENBACH *is wearing a fashionable new civilian suit.*

IRINA Let's sit here. No one will come in here.

VERSHININ The whole town would have burned if it hadn't been for the soldiers. They're a fine bunch of men! *Rubs his hands with pleasure.* Excellent men! Yes, a splendid group!

KULYGIN *approaches them.* What time is it?

TUSENBACH It's after three. As a matter of fact, it's getting light.

IRINA Everyone's sitting in the dining room and no one seems to think of going. That Solyony is there, too . . . *To* CHEBUTYKIN. You should be in bed, Doctor.

CHEBUTYKIN I'm all right . . . Thanks . . . *Combs his beard.*

KULYGIN *laughs.* You're pretty far gone, Ivan Romanich! *Slaps him on the shoulder.* You're a fine one! *"In vino veritas"* as the Romans used to say.

TUSENBACH I've been asked to arrange a benefit concert for the victims of the fire.

IRINA But, who . . .

TUSENBACH It could be arranged if we tried. In my opinion, Marya Sergeyevna plays the piano beautifully.

KULYGIN Oh, yes, she does play very well.

IRINA But she's forgotten how. It's been at least three, maybe four, years since she's played.

TUSENBACH In this town nobody understands music, not a soul. But I, I do understand it—and believe me, Marya Sergeyevna plays magnificently, almost like a concert pianist.

KULYGIN You're right, Baron. I'm very fond of Masha. She's such a nice girl.

TUSENBACH Just imagine, being able to play so well, and to know all the time that there is no one to appreciate it—no one!

KULYGIN *sighs.* Yes . . . But would it be proper for her to take part in a concert? *A pause.* Of course, I know nothing about such matters. It may be quite all right. But you know, although our headmaster is a good man, a very fine man indeed, a most intelligent man, I know he has certain opinions . . . Of course, it's none of his business, but I'll ask him about it, just the same, if you like.

CHEBUTYKIN *picks up a china clock and examines it.*

VERSHININ I've gotten my clothes all dirty helping with the fire, I must look terrible. *A pause.* They were saying yesterday that our brigade might be transferred to somewhere a long ways away from here. Some said to Poland, and others thought it would be to Northern Siberia, near Cheeta.

TUSENBACH I heard that, too. The town will really be empty then.

IRINA And we're going away, too!

CHEBUTYKIN *drops the clock and breaks it.* Smashed to smithereens!

A pause. Everyone looks upset and embarrassed.

KULYGIN *picks up the pieces.* Imagine breaking such a valuable thing! Ah, Ivan Romanich, Ivan Romanich! Black mark for conduct!

IRINA It was mother's clock.

CHEBUTYKIN Well, so it was. If it was your mother's clock, then it was your mother's. Perhaps I didn't break it but it just seems as though I did. Perhaps we only imagine that we exist, but we don't really exist at all. Perhaps I don't know anything, no one knows anything. *Stops at the door.* Why are you staring at me? Natasha's having a disgusting affair with Protopopov, and you don't see it. You sit here seeing nothing, and all the time Natasha's having a pleasant little affair with Protopopov . . . *Sings.* "Won't you accept this little present from me?" . . . Strange. *Goes out.*

VERSHININ So . . . *Laughs.* How strange it all is, really! A *pause.* When the fire started, I ran home as fast as I could. When I got to the house, I saw that it was all right and out of danger, but my two little girls were standing in the doorway in their pajamas. Their mother was gone. People were rushing about, horses, dogs, and in the children's faces I saw terror and anxiety, the most helpless look, I don't know what! . . . When I saw their faces, my heart sank. My God, I thought, what will these children have to go through for the rest of their lives? I grabbed them and ran back here, and all the time I kept thinking one thing: What else will they have to live through? *The alarm is sounded. A pause.* When I got here, my wife was already here . . . shouting and angry. *Enter* MASHA *carrying a pillow.* And while my little girls were standing there in the doorway with nothing on but their pajamas, and the street was red with the fire and full of terrible noises, I suddenly realized that this is what it must have been like years ago, when armies used to make sudden raids, plundering and burning . . . Anyway, is there really any difference between things as they used to be and the way they are now? And you know, it won't be very long, say another two or three hundred years, before people will look at our way of life with horror and scorn, just as we look at the past now. Everything about our life will seem uncouth to them, boring and awkward and strange . . . Oh, what a great life that will be! What a life! *Laughs*. Forgive me I'm philosophizing again . . . but may I go on, please? I have a great desire to talk about the future. *A pause*. It looks like everyone's gone to sleep. As I was saying: How wonderful life will be then! Just imagine . . . Today there are only three people like you in this town, but in the future there will be more and more people like you. At last the time will come when everything will be just as you'd want it to be. People will begin to live their lives in your way, in fact, they may even make improvements, and a new group will emerge even better than you are . . . *Laughs*. I'm in a very strange mood today. I have such a tremendous longing for life . . . *Sings*. "To Love all ages are in fee, The passion's good for you and me" . . . *Laughs*.

MASHA *sings*. Tara-ta-tum . . .

VERSHININ Tum-tum . . .

MASHA Tara-tara-tara . . .

VERSHININ Tum-tum, tum-tum . . . *Laughs*.

Enter FEDOTIK.

FEDOTIK, *dancing about*. Burnt, burnt to the ground! Everything I had in the world—burnt!

All laugh.

IRINA What kind of joke is that? Is everything gone?

FEDOTIK *laughs*. Everything. Nothing's left. My guitar, my camera, all my letters, why even the little notebook I was going to give you has been burnt.

Enter SOLYONY.

IRINA No, please go away, Vassily Vassilyevich. You can't come in here.

SOLYONY Can't I? But why can the Baron come in here if I can't?

VERSHININ We've really got to go, all of us. How's the fire?

SOLYONY They say it's dying down. But I can't understand why the Baron can come in here, and I can't. *Takes a scent bottle from his pocket and sprinkles himself with scent*.

VERSHININ Tara-tara.

MASHA Tum-tum, tum-tum.

VERSHININ *laughs*; *to* SOLYONY. Let's go into the dining room.

SOLYONY Very well, but I'll make a note of it. "I hardly need to make my moral clear: That might be teasing geese, I fear!" *Looks at* TUSENBACH. Cluck, cluck, cluck! *Goes out with* VERSHININ *and* FEDOTIK.

IRINA That Solyony has filled the room with smoke . . . *Puzzled.* The Baron's asleep. Baron! Baron!

TUSENBACH, *waking out of his doze.* I must be tired. The brick-yard, and . . . No, I'm not talking in my sleep. I really am going to the brickyard and will start working there soon . . . I've talked to the manager. *To* IRINA, *tenderly.* You are so pale, so beautiful, so bewitching . . . It seems to me your paleness brightens the darkness around you like light, somehow . . . You're sad, you're dissatisfied with life . . . Oh, come away with me, we can work together!

MASHA Nikolai Lvovich, I wish you'd go away.

TUSENBACH *laughs.* Are you here? I didn't see you. *Kisses* IRINA's *hand.* Good-bye, I'm going. You know, as I look at you now, I keep thinking of the day—it seems like such a long time ago on your birthday—when you talked about the joy of work . . . You were so gay and confident then . . . And what a happy life I imagined for us! Where is it all now? *Kisses her hand.* There are tears in your eyes. Go to bed, it's getting light . . . it's almost morning . . . Oh, if only I could give my life for you!

MASHA Nikolai Lvovich, please leave! Really now . . .

TUSENBACH I'm going. *Goes out.*

MASHA *lies down.* Are you asleep, Fyodor?

KULYGIN Eh?

MASHA Why don't you go home?

KULYGIN My darling Masha, my dear Masha . . .

IRINA She's tired. Let her rest awhile, Fedya.

KULYGIN I'll go in a minute. My wife, my dear, good wife! How I love you! . . . Only you!

MASHA, *crossly.* "Amo, amas, amat, amamus, amatis, amant!"

KULYGIN *laughs.* Really, what an amazing woman she is!—I've been married to you for seven years, but it seems as if we were *now Natasha in control*

married only yesterday. Honest, it does! You really are wonderful! Oh, I'm so happy, happy, happy!

MASHA And I'm so bored, bored, bored! *Sits up.* I can't get it out of my head . . . It's so annoying. It sticks in my head like a nail . . . I've just got to say something. It's about Andrey . . . He's actually mortgaged the house to the bank, and his wife's taken all the money—but the house doesn't belong to him, but to the four of us! He must know that, if he has any decency at all.

KULYGIN Why talk about it, Masha? Why think of it now? Andriusha owes money to everyone . . . Let him alone.

MASHA Anyway, it's revolting. *Lies down.*

KULYGIN At any rate, we aren't poor, Masha. I've got work, I teach at the high school, and I tutor in my spare time . . . I'm just a simple, honest man . . . *"Omnia mea mecum porto,"* as they say.

MASHA I'm not asking for anything, I just don't like injustice. *A pause.* Why don't you go home, Fyodor?

KULYGIN *kisses her.* You're tired. Just rest here for a while . . . I'll wait for you . . . Go to sleep. *Goes to the door.* I'm happy, happy, happy! *Goes out.*

IRINA As a matter of fact, Andrey has become awfully dull. He's getting old and since he's been living with that woman he's lost all his ambition! He used to work for his professorship and just yesterday he was buzzing about getting elected to the County Council. Imagine him a member, with Protopopov as chairman! The whole town's laughing at him, and he's the only one who doesn't know or see anything. Here everyone's rushing off to the fire and he just sits in his study playing his violin. He hasn't even noticed it. *Agitated.* Oh, it's awful, just awful, awful! I can't take it any more, I can't, I really can't! . . .

Enter OLGA. *She starts arranging things on her bedside table.*

IRINA *sobs loudly.* Turn me out! You must turn me out of here! I can't stand it anymore!

OLGA, *alarmed.* What is it? What is it, my darling?

IRINA, *sobbing.* Where . . . Where has it all gone? Where is it? Oh, God! I've forgotten . . . I've forgotten everything . . . Everything's so confused . . . I don't remember the Italian for "window" or for "ceiling" . . . Every day I'm forgetting more and more, and life's slipping by, and it will never, never return . . . We'll never go to Moscow . . . I just know we'll never go . . .

OLGA Don't, dear, don't . . .

IRINA, *trying to control herself* I'm miserable. *Pause.* I've had enough, enough. I can't, I won't, I will not work! . . . First I worked at the post office, now I'm a secretary at the Council office, and I hate and despise it all. I'm nearly twenty-four, and all I've done is work, my brain's drying up. I know I'm getting thinner and uglier and older, and there's nothing, nothing I can look forward to, no satisfaction in life that I can hope for, none at all. Time is flying past . . . and I feel as if I'm moving from any hope of a genuine fine life, and I seem to be getting further and further away from real life, from a life that is beautiful. I feel that I am heading for some horrible disaster. I'm in despair and I don't know why I go on living, why I haven't killed myself . . .

OLGA Don't cry, my child, don't cry . . .

IRINA I'm not crying—I'm not crying. I've stopped now, see? I'm not crying any more. I've stopped. I've stopped . . .

OLGA Darling, let me tell you something . . . as your sister, as your friend . . . if you'll take my advice . . . you'll marry the Baron. IRINA *weeps quietly.* You do respect him don't you? You think highly of him . . . It's true, he's not handsome, but he's such an honest, decent man . . . After all, people don't marry for love, but to fulfill their duty. At least, I think so, and I'd marry even if I weren't in love. I'd marry anyone that proposed to me, as long as he was a decent man. I'd even marry an old man.

IRINA I've been waiting all this time, expecting that we'd be moving to Moscow, and that there I'd meet the man I'm meant for. I've dreamt about him and I've loved him in my dreams . . . But it's all turned out to be nothing . . . nothing . . .

OLGA, *embracing her.* My darling sister, I think I understand everything. When the Baron resigned his commission and came to see us dressed in his civilian clothes, I thought he looked so ugly that I actually started to cry . . . He asked me why I was crying . . . How could I tell him? But, if it were God's will that he should marry you, I'd be happy about it. That's a different thing, you know, quite different!

NATASHA, *carrying a candle, comes out of the door on the right, crosses the stage and goes out through the door on the left without saying anything.*

MASHA *sits up.* She walks around looking as if she'd set the town on fire herself.

OLGA You're silly, Masha. You're the silliest person in our family. You must forgive me for saying it. *A pause.*

MASHA My dear sisters, I've got something to confess to you. I have to tell someone, I need to . . . I'll confess it to the two of you, and then never again, never to anybody! NO! Right now. *In a low voice.* It's a secret, but you must know everything. I can't keep silent any longer. *A pause.* I'm in love, in love . . . I love that man . . . You just saw him . . . Oh, what's the use? . . . I love Vershinin . . .

OLGA *goes behind her screen* Don't say it. I don't want to hear it.

MASHA But, what am I to do? *Holding her head.* At first I thought him very strange, then I felt sorry for him and—and then I fell in love with him . . . love everything about him—his voice, his words, his troubles, his two little girls . . .

OLGA I don't want to hear it. You can talk as much nonsense as you like, I'm not listening.

MASHA Don't be silly, Olya! If I love him, well—that's my fate! That's my destiny. And he loves me. It's frightening, isn't it? Is it wrong? *Takes* IRINA *by the hand and draws her to her.* Oh, my darling! . . . How are we going to live through the rest of our lives? What's to become of us? When you read a novel, everything in it seems too trite and obvious. It's so understandable—but when you fall in love yourself, you suddenly discover that no one really knows anything, and you've got to make your own choices . . . My dear sisters, my dear sisters! . . . I've confessed to you, and now I'll be silent . . . Like Gogol's madman—silence . . . silence! . . .

Enter ANDREY *followed by* FERAPONT.

ANDREY, *crossly.* What do you want? I don't understand.

FERAPONT, *stopping in the doorway, impatiently.* I've told you ten times already, Andrey Sergeyevitch.

ANDREY In the first place, I'm not Andrey Sergeyevitch—you're to call me "Your Honor."

FERAPONT Your Honor, the firemen want to go through the garden to go to the river. They've been taking the long way round and it's been a terrible nuisance!

ANDREY All right. Tell them it's all right. FERAPONT *goes out.* Why do they keep on bothering me? Where's Olga? OLGA *comes from behind the screen.* I've come to get the key to the cupboard; I've lost mine. You know the one I mean, the little one . . .

OLGA *silently hands him the key.* IRINA *goes behind the screen on her side of the room.*

ANDREY What a wonderful fire! It's dying down though. Ferapont made me lose my temper, damn him! That was stupid of me . . . Telling him to call me "Your Honor"! . . . *A pause.* Why don't you say something, Olya? *A pause.* Let's stop this foolishness . . . There's no reason to sulk . . . You here, Masha? And Irina, too. Good! Let's have it out once and for all. What have you got against me? What is it?

OLGA Forget it for now, Andriusha. We'll talk about it to-morrow. *Agitated.* What a horrible night!

ANDREY, *in great embarrassment.* Don't get upset. I'm asking you calmly, what have you got against me? Tell me frankly.

VERSHININ'S VOICE, *off-stage.* Tum-tum-tum!

MASHA, *in a loud voice, getting up.* Tara-tara-tara! *To* OLGA. Good-night, Olya, God bless you! *Goes behind the screen and kisses* IRINA. Sleep well . . . Good night, Andrey. I'd go away now, they're tired . . . talk about it tomorrow . . . *Goes out.*

OLGA Yes, really, Andriusha, let's wait until tomorrow . . . *Goes behind the screen on her side of the room.* It's time we were in bed.

ANDREY I only want to say one thing, then I'll go, as soon as . . . First of all, you've got something against my wife, against Natasha. I've noticed it from the day we got married. Natasha is a very fine woman, she's honest and straightforward and . . . that's my opinion. I love and respect my wife. Do you understand? I respect her, and I expect others to respect her, too. I repeat; she's an honest, honorable person, and all your complaints against her—and I must say this—are all in your imagination, and nothing more . . . *A pause.* Second, you seem disappointed in me for not being a professor, because I've stopped studying. But I'm working; I'm a member of the Council, and I feel my work there is just as important as any academic work I might do. I'm a member of the Council, and if you want to know, I'm proud of it! *A pause.* Third . . . there's something else I must tell you . . . I know I mortgaged the house without asking your permission . . . That was wrong, I admit it, and I ask you to forgive me . . . I had to because of my debts . . . thirty-five thousand roubles, but I don't gamble any more, I gave that up long ago . . . The only thing I can say in my defense, is that all of you get an annuity, while I don't get anything . . . no salary, I mean . . . *A pause.*

KULYGIN, *calling through the door.* Is Masha there? She's not? *Alarmed.* Where can she be then? That's strange . . . *Goes away.*

ANDREY So you won't listen? Natasha, I tell you, is a fine, honest woman. *Walks up and down the stage, then stops.* When we got married I was sure we'd be happy, all of us . . . But . . . Oh, my God! . . . *Weeps.* My dear sisters, my dear, good sisters, don't believe what I've been saying, don't believe it . . . *Goes out.*

KULYGIN, *through the door, agitated.* Where's Masha? Isn't Masha here? How strange. *Goes away.*

The alarm is heard again. The stage is empty.

IRINA, *speaking from behind the screen.* Olya! Who's that knocking on the floor?

OLGA It's the Doctor, Ivan Romanich. He's drunk.

IRINA It's been one catastrophe after another all night. *A pause.* Olya! *Peeps out from behind the screen.* Have you heard? The brigade is leaving . . . they're being transferred to someplace far away.

OLGA That's only a rumor.

IRINA Then we shall be alone . . . Olya!

OLGA Well?

IRINA Olya, darling, I respect the Baron . . . I think a great deal of him, he's a very good man . . . I'll marry him, Olya, I'll agree to marry him, if only we can go to Moscow! Let's go, please let's go! There's no place in the world like Moscow. Let's go, Olya! Let's go!

Curtain.

ACT IV

An old garden in front of the PROZOROVS' *house. A river is seen at the end of a long avenue of fir trees, and on the other side of the river a forest. To the right, a terrace with a table on which champagne bottles and glasses have been left. It is noon. Occasionally people from the street pass through the garden to get to the river. Five or six soldiers march through quickly.* CHEBUTYKIN, *in an affable mood which does not leave him throughout the act, is sitting in a chair in the garden waiting to be called. He is wearing his army cap and is holding a walking stick.* KULYGIN, *with a decoration round his neck and with his moustache shaved off,* TUSENBACH *and* IRINA *are standing on the terrace saying good-bye to* FEDOTIK *and* RODÉ, *who are coming down the steps. Both officers are in dress uniform.*

TUSENBACH, *embracing* FEDOTIK. You're a fine fellow, Fedotik; we've been good friends! *Embraces* RODÉ. Once more, then . . . Good-bye, my friends!

IRINA Au revoir!

FEDOTIK No, it's not au revoir—It's good-bye. We'll never meet again!

KULYGIN Who knows? *Wipes his eyes, smiling.* There, I'm beginning to cry, too.

IRINA We'll meet some day.

FEDOTIK In ten or fifteen years maybe. But by then we'll hardly know each other . . . We'll just meet and say very coldly, "How are you?". . . *Takes a picture.* Stand still . . . Just one more, for the last time.

RODÉ *embraces* TUSENBACH. We probably won't meet again . . . *Kisses* IRINA'*s hand.* Thank you for everything . . . everything!

FEDOTIK, *annoyed.* Just wait a second!

TUSENBACH I hope we do, and we will meet again if it's our fate. But write to us. Be sure to write.

RODÉ, *glancing around the garden.* Good-bye, trees! *Shouts.* Halloo! *A pause.* Good-bye, echo!

KULYGIN It wouldn't surprise me if you got married in Poland

. . . You'll get some Polish wife, and she'll put her arms round you and say: *"Kohane"! Laughs.*

FEDOTIK *glances at his watch.* We leave in less than an hour. Solyony is the only one from the battery who's going on the barge. Everyone else is marching with the division. Three batteries are leaving today and the other three tomorrow—then the town will have peace and quiet.

TUSENBACH Yes, and dreadful boredom, too.

RODÉ By the way, where's Marya Sergeyevna?

KULYGIN She's somewhere in the garden.

FEDOTIK We must say good-bye to her.

RODÉ Good-bye. I really must go, or I'll start crying. *Quickly embraces* TUSENBACH *and* KULYGIN, *kisses* IRINA's *hand.* We've had a wonderful time here . . .

FEDOTIK, *to* KULYGIN. Here's a souvenir for you—a notebook and pencil . . . We'll go down to the river this way. *They go off, glancing back.*

RODÉ, *shouts.* Halloo!

KULYGIN *shouts* Good-bye!

At the back of the stage FEDOTIK *and* RODÉ *meet* MASHA, *and say good-bye to her; she goes off with them.*

IRINA They've gone . . . *Sits down on the bottom step of the terrace.*

CHEBUTYKIN They forgot to say good-bye to me.

IRINA Well, what about you?

CHEBUTYKIN That's true, I forgot, too. Oh well, I'll be seeing them again soon. I leave tomorrow. Yes . . . only one more day. And then, in a year I'll retire. I'll come back and spend the rest of my life with you. Just one more year and then I get my pension . . . *Puts a newspaper in his pocket and takes out another.* I'll come back here and lead a reformed life. I'll become a nice, quiet, respectable little man.

IRINA Yes, it's about time you reformed, Ivan Romanich. You ought to lead a better kind of life.

CHEBUTYKIN Yes . . . I think so, too. *Sings quietly.* "Tarara-boom-di-ay . . . I'm sitting on a tomb-di-ay" . . .

KULYGIN You're incorrigible, Ivan Romanich! Absolutely incorrigible!

CHEBUTYKIN Yes, if only you had taken me in hand. You'd have reformed me!

IRINA Fyodor's shaved his moustache off. I can't bear to look at him.

KULYGIN Why not?

CHEBUTYKIN If I could only tell you what your face looks like now—but I'd better not.

KULYGIN Well! It's the fashion now! The *"modus vivendi,"* you know. The headmaster shaved his moustache off, so when I became the principal, I shaved mine off, too. No one likes it, but I don't care. I'm content. Whether I've got a moustache or not, it's all the same to me. *Sits down.*

ANDREY *passes across the back of the stage pushing a baby carriage with a child asleep in it.*

IRINA Ivan Romanich, my dear friend, I'm terribly worried about something. You were in town last night—tell me what happened?

CHEBUTYKIN What happened? Nothing. Just a trifle. *Reads his paper.* It doesn't matter anyway.

KULYGIN They say that Solyony and the Baron met outside the theatre last night and . . .

TUSENBACH Stop it, please! What's the good? . . . *Waves his hand at him deprecatingly and goes into the house.*

KULYGIN It was outside the theatre . . . Solyony started insulting the Baron, and the Baron lost his temper and insulted him.

CHEBUTYKIN I don't know anything about it. It's all nonsense.

KULYGIN A teacher once wrote "nonsense" on one of his student's papers, and the student couldn't figure it out. He thought it was a Latin word. *Laughs.* Isn't that funny? They say that Solyony's in love with Irina and that he hates the Baron . . . Well, that's understandable. Irina's a very sweet girl. She's a lot like Masha, all wrapped up in her own thoughts. *To* IRINA. But you have a gentler disposition than Masha. And yet Masha has a very pleasant disposition, too. I love my Masha, I love her.

From the back of the stage comes a shout: "Halloo!"

IRINA *starts.* Everything seems to frighten me today. *A pause.* Well, all my things are ready. I'm sending the luggage off after lunch. The Baron and I are going to get married tomorrow, and then we're moving to the brickyard, and the next day I begin work at the school. So, God willing, our new life will begin. When I passed my exams, I felt so happy that I cried with a feeling of pure bliss . . . *A pause.* They will be coming for my things in a minute . . .

KULYGIN That's all very well, but it doesn't seem serious. Nothing but ideas and theories, nothing really serious. Anyway, I wish you the best of luck.

CHEBUTYKIN, *moved.* My precious little girl, my dear child! You've gone on so far ahead of me, I'll never catch up with you now. I've been left behind like a bird that's too old and can't keep up with the rest of the flock. Fly away, my dear, fly away, and God bless you! *A pause.* It's a shame you've shaved your moustache off, Fyodor Ilyich.

KULYGIN Don't keep that up, please. *Sighs.* Well, the soldiers are leaving today, and then everything will be as it used to. I don't care what they say, Masha is a fine, loyal wife and I love her very much and I'm grateful for what God has given me. Fate treats people so differently. For instance, there's a clerk in the tax office called Kozyrev. We went to school together and he was expelled in his fifth year because he just couldn't understand the "*ut consecutivum.*" He's terribly poor now; and in bad health, too, and whenever I meet him, I say to him: "Hello, '*ut consecutivum!*'" "Yes," he says, "that's just the trouble—'*consecutivum*'" . . . and he begins to cough. And here I am—I've always been successful. I'm happy. Why, I've even been awarded the order of Saint Stanislav, second class—and now I'm teaching the students the same old "*ut consecutivum.*" Of course, I'm clever, cleverer than most people, but happiness doesn't consist of being clever . . .

In the house someone plays "The Maiden's Prayer" on the piano.

IRINA After tomorrow I won't have to listen to "The Maiden's Prayer." I won't have to meet Protopopov. . . *A pause.* By the way, he's in the drawing room. He's here again today.

KULYGIN Hasn't the headmistress come yet?

IRINA No, we've sent for her. If you only knew how hard it's been for me to live here by myself, without Olya! Now that she's the headmistress and lives at school and is busy all day long and I'm here alone, I'm bored, I've nothing to do, and I hate the *accepts it more than the others* (handwritten annotation)

room I live in. ~~So I've decided that~~ if I'm not going to live in Moscow, then it just can't be helped. It's my fate and there's nothing to be done about it. It's God's will, everything that happens, there's no doubt about it. Nikolai Lvovich proposed to me . . . Well, I thought it over, and I just decided. He's a good man, it's really amazing how kind he is . . . And then suddenly I felt as though my soul had grown wings. I was more cheerful and I longed to work again. To work! . . . Except something happened yesterday, and now there's a mystery hanging over me . . .

CHEBUTYKIN Nonsense!

NATASHA, *speaking through the window.* Our headmistress!

KULYGIN Our headmistress has come! Let's go in. *Goes indoors with* IRINA.

CHEBUTYKIN *reads his paper and sings quietly to himself.* "Tarara-boom-di-ay . . . I'm sitting on a tomb-di-ay . . ."

MASHA *walks up to him;* ANDREY *passes across the back of the stage pushing the baby carriage.*

MASHA You look comfortable . . .

CHEBUTYKIN Well, why not? Anything happening?

MASHA *sits down.* No, nothing. *A pause.* Tell me something. Were you in love with my mother?

CHEBUTYKIN Yes, very much in love.

MASHA Did she love you?

CHEBUTYKIN, *after a pause.* I can't remember any more.

MASHA Is my man here? Our cook Marfa always used to call her policeman "my man." Is he here?

CHEBUTYKIN Not yet.

MASHA When you have to take your happiness in bits and snatches, and then you lose it, as I have, you can't help but get hardened and bitter. *Points at her breast.* I'm seething inside as if I'll boil over. *Looking at* ANDREY, *who again crosses the stage with the carriage.* And there's our Andrey . . . All our hopes are shattered. It's the same as when thousands of men raise a huge bell up into a tower. A lot of work and money is spent on it, and then suddenly it falls and gets smashed. Suddenly, for no reason at all. That is Andrey . . .

ANDREY When will they be quiet in the house? There is so much noise.

CHEBUTYKIN Soon. *Looks at his watch.* You know, this is a very

old watch: it strikes . . . *Wind his watch which then strikes.*
The first, second and fifth batteries are going at one o'clock. *A
pause.* And I am going tomorrow.

ANDREY For good?

CHEBUTYKIN I don't know. Perhaps I'll come back next year.
Although, God knows . . . it doesn't matter one way or the other.
The sounds of a harp and a violin are heard.

ANDREY The town will be empty. Just as if life were snuffed out
like a candle. *A pause.* Something happened yesterday at the
theatre; everybody's talking about it. But I don't know anything
about it.

CHEBUTYKIN It was nothing. Just a lot of nonsense. Solyony
started bothering the Baron again, and the Baron lost his temper
and insulted him, and so Solyony had to challenge him to a duel.
Looks at his watch. It's about time to go . . . At half-past twelve,
in the forest, on the other side of the river . . . Bang-bang!
Laughs. Solyony thinks he's Lermontov. Why he even writes
poetry. But, all kidding aside, this is his third duel.

MASHA Whose?

CHEBUTYKIN Solyony's.

MASHA What about the Baron?

CHEBUTYKIN Well, what about him? *A pause.*

MASHA My thoughts are all confused. Anyway you shouldn't
let them fight. He might wound the Baron or even kill him.

CHEBUTYKIN The Baron's a fine man, but what does it really
matter if there's one Baron more or less in the world? What difference does it make? *The shouts of "Yoo-hoo!" and "Halloo!" are
heard from beyond the garden.* That's Skvortsov, the second,
shouting from the boat. Let him wait.

ANDREY Frankly, I think it's downright immoral to fight a duel,
or even to be present at one as a doctor.

CHEBUTYKIN It only seems that way . . . We don't really exist,
nothing does, we only think so. . . And anyway, what difference
does it make?

MASHA Talk, talk, talk, nothing but talk all day long! . . . *Starts
to go.* To have to live in this terrible climate with the snow
threatening to fall all the time, and then to have to listen to all
this talk . . . *Stops.* I'm not going into the house, I can't stand
going in there . . . Will you let me know when Vershinin

comes? . . . *Walks off along the avenue.* Look, the birds are beginning to fly away already! *Looks up.* Swans or geese . . . Lovely birds, happy birds . . . *Goes off.*

ANDREY The house will seem awfully empty. The officers are leaving, you're going, my sister's getting married, and I'll be left alone in the house.

CHEBUTYKIN What about your wife?

Enter FERAPONT *with some papers.*

ANDREY My wife is my wife. She's a good, decent woman . . . and she's really very kind, but there's something about her that reduces her to the level of some petty, blind, hairy animal. Anyway, she's not a human being. I'm telling you this as a friend, the only person I can really talk to. I do love Natasha, but sometimes she seems so completely vulgar, that I don't know what to think, and then I can't understand why I love her—or, why I ever did love her . . .

CHEBUTYKIN *gets up.* Well, my boy, I'm leaving tomorrow and I might never see you again. So I'll give you a piece of advice. Put on your hat, take a walking stick, and go away . . . Go away, and don't ever look back. And the further you go, the better. *Pause.* But do as you like! What difference does it make?

SOLYONY *passes across the back of the stage accompanied by two officers. Seeing* CHEBUTYKIN, *he turns towards him, while the officers walk on.*

SOLYONY It's time, Doctor. Twelve-thirty already. *Shakes hands with* ANDREY.

CHEBUTYKIN Just a minute. Oh, I'm so sick of you all. *To* ANDREY. Andriusha, if anyone asks for me, tell them I'll be back. *Sighs.* Oh-ho-ho!

SOLYONY "He had hardly time to catch his breath / Before the bear was hugging him to death." *Walks off with him.* What are you grumbling about, old man?

CHEBUTYKIN Oh, well!

SOLYONY How do you feel?

CHEBUTYKIN, *crossly.* Fit as a fiddle.

SOLYONY There's nothing to be so upset about, old man. I shan't go too far, I'll just touch his wings a little, like a snipe. *Takes out a perfume bottle and sprinkles perfume over his hands.* I've used up a whole bottle today, but my hands still smell . . . like a corpse. *A pause.* By the way . . . Do you remember that poem of Lermontov's? "And he, rebellious, seeks a storm, / As if in storms there were tranquility". . .

CHEBUTYKIN Yes. "He had hardly time to catch his breath / Before the bear was hugging him to death." *Goes out with* SOLYONY. *Shouts of "Halloo! Yoo-hoo!" are heard.*

FERAPONT Will you sign these, please?

ANDREY, *with irritation.* Let me alone. Let me alone, please. *Goes off with the carriage.*

FERAPONT That's what papers are for—to be signed. *Goes to back of stage.*

Enter IRINA *and* TUSENBACH, *wearing a straw hat.* KULYGIN *crosses the stage, calling: "Yoo-hoo! Masha! Yoo-hoo!"*

TUSENBACH He's probably the only person in town who's glad the officers are leaving.

IRINA That's understandable, I guess. *A pause.* The town will be quite empty now.

TUSENBACH Darling, I'll be back in just a minute.

IRINA Where are you going?

TUSENBACH I've got to go to town, and then . . . I want to see some of my comrades off.

IRINA It's not true . . . Nikolai, why are you so absent-minded today? *A pause.* What happened last night at the theatre?

TUSENBACH, *with a gesture of impatience.* I'll be back in an hour . . . back with you again. *Kisses her hands.* My beautiful one . . . *Gazes into her eyes.* I've loved you now for five years and still I can't get used to it. You seem more beautiful every day. What marvelous, lovely hair! What wonderful eyes! I'll take you away tomorrow. We'll work, we'll be rich and my dreams will come true. And you'll be happy! But—there's only one thing, only one—you don't love me!

IRINA I can't help that! I'll be your wife, I'll be faithful and loyal to you, but I can't love you . . . We can't do anything about it. *Weeps.* I've never really loved anyone in my life. Oh, I've dreamt about being in love! I've been dreaming about it for years and years, day and night . . . but somehow my soul is like an expensive grand piano that someone has locked and the key's been lost. *A pause.* What's wrong?

TUSENBACH I didn't sleep last night. Not that there's anything

I'm afraid of. It's just that the thought of that lost key torments me and I can't sleep. Say something to me . . . *A pause.* Say something!

IRINA What? What am I to say? What?

TUSENBACH Anything.

IRINA Don't, my dear, don't, please . . . *A pause.*

TUSENBACH It's strange how little things—trifles sometimes become so important in our lives, for no reason at all. You laugh at them, just as you always have done, you still regard them as trifles, and yet you suddenly find they're controlling you, and you haven't the power to stop them. But let's not talk about that! Really, I feel fine. I feel as if I were seeing those pine trees and maples and birches for the first time in my life. They all seem to be looking at me, waiting for something. What beautiful trees— and when you think of it, how beautiful life ought to be when there are trees like these! *Shouts of "Halloo!" are heard.* I've got to go . . . Look at that tree, it's dead, but it goes on swaying in the wind with the others. And it seems to me that in the same way, if I die, I'll still have a part in life, one way or another. Good-bye, my darling . . . *Kisses her hands.* The papers you gave me, are on my desk, under the calendar.

IRINA I'm coming with you.

TUSENBACH, *alarmed.* No, no! *Goes off quickly, then stops in the avenue.* Irina!

IRINA What?

TUSENBACH, *not knowing what to say.* I didn't have any coffee this morning. Will you tell them to make me some? *Goes off quickly.*

IRINA *stands, lost in thought, then goes to the back of the stage and sits down on a swing. Enter* ANDREY *with the carriage;* FERAPONT *appears.*

FERAPONT Andrey Sergeyevich, the papers aren't mine, you know; they're official. I didn't invent them.

ANDREY Oh, where has it gone?—What's become of my past when I was young and gay and clever, when I had beautiful dreams and was full of ideas, and the present and the future were bright with hope? Why do you become so dull, so ordinary, so uninteresting almost before we've begun to live? . . . This town's been here for two hundred years; a hundred thousand people live in it, but we're all the same! There's never been a scholar or an artist or a saint in this place, not one man remarkable enough to make you feel envy or want to imitate him. They only eat, drink and sleep . . . Then they die and others take their places, and they eat, drink and sleep, too—and as if for variety, just to avoid being bored to death, they gossip, drink vodka, gamble and cheat. The wives deceive their husbands, and the husbands lie to their wives, and pretend they don't see or hear anything . . . And it's this overwhelming vulgarity that crushes our children and destroys any talent they might have, so that they become miserable and more dead than alive, all alike and just like their parents . . . *To* FERAPONT, *crossly.* What do you want?

FERAPONT What? Here are the papers to sign.

ANDREY What a nuisance you are!

FERAPONT *hands him the papers.* The janitor at the tax office was saying that last winter they had two hundred degrees of frost in Petersburg.

ANDREY I hate my life as I am living it now, but oh! the sense of elation when I think of the future! Then I feel so light-hearted, have such a sense of release! I seem to see a bright light in the distance, light and freedom. I'll be free, and my children, too,—free from idleness, free from kvass, free from those meals of goose and cabbage, from after-dinner naps, and from all this degrading parasitism! . . .

FERAPONT And he said two thousand people were frozen to death and that everyone was frightened to death. It was either in Petersburg or in Moscow, I don't remember for sure.

ANDREY, *with sudden emotion, tenderly.* My dear sisters, my wonderful sisters! *Tearfully.* Masha, my dear sister! . . .

NATASHA, *through the window.* Who's talking so loudly out there? Is that you, Andryusha? You'll wake Sofotchka. *"Il ne faut pas faire du bruit, la* Sophie *est dormie déjà. Vous êtes un ours."* *Getting angry.* If you want to talk, give the carriage to someone else. Ferapont, take the carriage from the master.

FERAPONT Yes, Ma'am. *Takes the carriage.*

ANDREY, *embarrassed.* I was talking quietly.

NATASHA, *in the window, caressing her small son.* Bobik! Naughty Bobik! You naughty boy, you!

ANDREY, *glancing through the papers.* All right, I'll go through these. You can take them back to the office later. *Goes into the house, reading the papers.*

FERAPONT *wheels the carriage into the garden.*

NATASHA, *in the window.* What's Mommy's name, Bobik? You little angel! And who's that? Auntie Olya. Say: "Hello, Auntie Olya."

Two wandering musicians, a man and a girl, enter and play a violin and a harp. VERSHININ, OLGA, *and* ANFISA *come out of the house and listen in silence for a few moments; then* IRINA *approaches them.*

OLGA Our garden's like a city park; everybody goes through it. Nurse, give this to the musicians.

ANFISA, *giving them money.* Get along with you and God bless you! Poor souls! *The musicians bow and go away. To* IRINA. How are you, Irinushka? *Kisses her.* Ah, my child, what a time I'm having! Living in a big apartment at the school with Olyushka— and no rent to pay, either! The Lord's been good to me in my old age. I've never lived so well in my life, old sinner that I am! A big apartment, and a whole room to myself with my own bed, and no rent to pay. When I wake up in the night, why then—Oh, Lord! Oh, Holy Mother of God! Oh, I'm the happiest person in the world!

VERSHININ *glances at his watch.* They'll be leaving soon, Olga Sergeyevna. It's time I left, too. *A pause.* I wish you all the happiness in the world . . . only the best . . . Where's Marya Sergeyevna?

IRINA She's somewhere in the garden. I'll go and look for her.

VERSHININ Would you please? I've really got to hurry.

ANFISA I'll come and help you. *Calls out.* Mashenka, yoo-hoo, yoo-hoo!

VERSHININ Everything comes to an end. Well, here we are—and it's time to say "good-bye." *Looks at his watch.* There was a lunch for us at the city hall, and we drank champagne and the mayor made a speech. I ate and listened, but my heart was with all of you here . . . *Glances round the garden.* I've grown so . . . so accustomed to you.

OLGA Do you think we'll ever meet again?

VERSHININ Probably not! *A pause.* My wife and two little girls will be staying on for another month or so. Please, if anything happens, if they need anything . . .

OLGA Yes, yes, of course. Don't worry about it. *A pause.* To-morrow there won't be a single soldier left in town . . . Everything will be just a memory, and a new life will begin for us here . . . *A pause.* Nothing has turned out as we expected. I didn't want to be headmistress, but I've become one, which means that I shall never go to Moscow . . .

VERSHININ Well . . . Thank you for everything. Forgive me if ever I've done anything wrong . . . I've talked a lot, far too much, I'm afraid . . . Forgive me for that, too.

OLGA *wipes her eyes.* Oh . . . Why doesn't Masha come?

VERSHININ What else can I say now it's time to say "good-bye"? What shall I philosophize about now? . . . *Laughs.* Yes, life is hard. It seems quite hopeless for most of us, just a blank . . . And yet you must admit that it is gradually getting easier and more hopeful, and there's no doubt about it that the time isn't far off when happiness will be everywhere. *Looks at his watch.* It's time for me to go . . . In the old days men were always at war, our life was filled with nothing but campaigns, invasions, retreats, victories . . . All that's out of date now, and in its place there's a great void which can't be filled. Humanity is passionately search-ing for something to fill that void, and, of course, it will find something some day. Oh! If only it would happen soon! *A pause.* If only we could make working people aware of culture and make our cultured people work . . . *Looks at his watch.* I really must go . . .

OLGA Here she comes!

Enter MASHA.

VERSHININ I've come to say good-bye . . .

OLGA *walks off and stands a little to one side so they can say good-bye.*

MASHA, *looking into his face.* Good-bye. *A long kiss.*

OLGA All right, that'll do.

MASHA *sobs loudly.*

VERSHININ Write to me . . . Don't forget me! Let me go now . . . It's time. Olga Sergeyevna, please take her . . . I must go

. . . I'm late as it is . . . *Deeply moved, he kisses* OLGA's *hands, then embraces* MASHA *once more and goes out quickly.*

OLGA Please, Masha! Don't my dear, don't . . .

Enter KULYGIN.

KULYGIN, *embarrassed.* Never mind, let her cry, let her . . . My good Masha, my dear, sweet Masha . . . You're my wife, and I'm happy in spite of everything . . . I'm not complaining, I won't blame you—Olga is my witness . . . We'll start our life over again just like it used to be, and I won't say a word . . . Not a word . . .

MASHA, *suppressing her sobs.* "A green oak grows by a curving shore, And round that oak hangs a golden chain.". . . "A golden chain round that oak.". . . Oh, I'm going mad . . . By a curving shore . . . a green oak . . .

OLGA Quiet, Masha, calm yourself . . . Give her some water.

MASHA I'm not crying any more . . .

KULYGIN She's stopped crying . . . she's such a good girl.

The hollow sound of a gunshot is heard in the distance.

MASHA "A green oak grows by a curving shore, And round that oak hangs a golden chain." A green cat . . . a green oak . . . I've got it all mixed up . . . *Drinks water.* My life's mixed up . . . I don't want anything now . . . I'll be quiet in a minute . . . It doesn't matter . . . What *is* "the curving shore"? Why does it keep coming into my head all the time? Why does it haunt me? My thoughts are all mixed up.

Enter IRINA.

OLGA Calm down, Masha. That's right . . . good girl! . . . Let's go inside.

MASHA, *irritably.* I'm not going in there! *Sobs, but immediately checks herself.* I am not going into that house ever again!

IRINA Let's all just sit here for a minute, and not say anything. I'm leaving tomorrow, you know . . . *A pause.*

KULYGIN Yesterday I took this beard away from one of the boys. I've got it here. *Puts it on.* Do I look just like the German teacher? . . . *Laughs.* I do, don't I? Those boys are funny.

MASHA Yes, you do look like that German of yours.

OLGA *laughs.* Yes, he does.

MASHA *cries.*

andrey - now is being pushed out

IRINA Stop it, Masha!

KULYGIN Yes, a great deal like him, I think!

NATASHA, *to the maid.* What? Oh, yes. Mr. Protopopov is going to watch Sofotchka, and Andrey Sergeyevich is going to take Bobik out in the carriage. Children are such a bother! . . . *To* IRINA. So you're really leaving tomorrow, Irina? What a shame! Why don't you stay another week? *Seeing* KULYGIN, *shrieks; he laughs and takes off the false beard.* Why look at you! How you frightened me! *To* IRINA. I've gotten so used to your being here . . . You mustn't think it's going to be easy for me after you're gone. I'll put Andrey and his old violin into your room: there he can saw away at it as much as he likes. And then we'll put Sofotchka into his study. She's such a darling child, really! Really a wonderful child! This morning she looked at me with her big eyes and said: "Mommie!"

KULYGIN That's true, she is a beautiful child.

NATASHA So tomorrow I'll be alone here. *Sighs.* First, I'll have these firs cut down, then that maple tree. It's so ugly in the evening . . . *To* IRINA. My dear, that sash doesn't suit you at all. It's such bad taste. You ought to get something bright and shiny . . . I'll tell them to put flowers everywhere, lots of flowers, and there'll be such a lovely scent . . . *Sternly.* What's this fork doing on the table? *Going into the house, to the maid.* Why was that fork left? *Shouts.* Answer me!

KULYGIN She's started again!

A band plays a military march off-stage; all listen.

OLGA They're going.

Enter CHEBUTYKIN.

MASHA The soldiers are going. Well . . . happy journey to them! *To her husband.* We must go home . . . where are my hat and cape? . . .

KULYGIN I took them into the house. I'll get them.

OLGA Yes, we can go home now. It's time.

CHEBUTYKIN Olga Sergeyevna!

OLGA What is it? *A pause.* What?

CHEBUTYKIN Nothing . . . I don't know quite how to tell you . . . *Whispers into her ear.*

OLGA, *frightened.* It can't be!

CHEBUTYKIN Yes . . . it's too bad . . . I'm so tired . . . worn out . . . I don't want to say another word . . . *With annoyance.* Anyway, nothing matters!

MASHA What happened?

OLGA *puts her arms round* IRINA. This is a terrible day! . . . I don't know how to tell you dear . . .

IRINA What is it? Tell me quickly, what is it? For God's sake! . . . *Cries.*

CHEBUTYKIN The Baron's just been killed in a duel.

IRINA *cries quietly.* I knew it, I knew it . . .

CHEBUTYKIN *goes to the table and sits down.* I'm tired . . . *Takes a newspaper out of his pocket.* Let them cry . . . *Sings quietly to himself.* "Tarara-boom-di-ay, I'm sitting on a tomb-di-ay" . . . What difference does it make?

The three sisters stand huddled together.

MASHA Oh, listen to the music! They're leaving us . . . one has already gone, gone for good . . . forever! And now we're left alone . . . to start our lives all over again. We must go on living . . . we must go on living . . .

IRINA *puts her head on* OLGA's *breast.* Some day people will know why such things happen, and what the purpose of all this suffering is . . . Then there won't be any more mysteries . . . Meanwhile we must go on living . . . we must work. To work! Tomorrow I'll go away alone and teach in a school somewhere; I'll give my life to people who need it . . . It's autumn now, it will be winter soon, and everything will be covered with snow . . . But I'll go on working . . . I will work . . .

OLGA *puts her arms round both her sisters.* How happy the music is . . . I almost feel as if I wanted to live! Oh, God! The years will pass, and we shall all be gone. We shall be forgotten . . . Our faces, our voices will be forgotten and people will even forget that there were once three of us here . . . But our sufferings will mean happiness for those who come after us . . . Then peace and happiness will reign on earth, and we shall be remembered kindly and blessed. No, my dear sisters, our lives aren't finished yet. We shall live! The band is playing and soon we shall know why we live, why we suffer . . . Oh, if we only knew, if only we knew!

The music grows fainter and fainter. KULYGIN, *smiling cheer-*

fully, brings out the hat and the cape. ANDREY *enters pushing the carriage with Bobik in it.*

CHEBUTYKIN *sings quietly to himself.* "Tarara-boom-di-ay . . . I'm sitting on a tomb-di-ay" *Reads the paper.* It doesn't matter. Nothing matters!

OLGA If only we knew, if only we knew! . . .

Curtain.

THE CHERRY ORCHARD

A Comedy in Four Acts

CAST

LYUBOV ANDREYEVNA RANEVSKY, *owner of the cherry orchard*

ANYA, *her daughter, age 17*

VARYA, *her adopted daughter, age 24*

LEONID ANDREYEVICH GAEV, *Lyubov's brother*

YERMOLAY ALEXEYEVICH LOPAHIN, *a business man*

PYOTR SERGEYEVICH TROFIMOV, *a student*

BORIS BORISOVICH SEMYONOV-PISHCHIK, *a landowner*

CHARLOTTA IVANOVNA, *a governess*

SEMYON PANTALEYEVICH EPIHODOV, *a clerk on the Ranevsky estate*

DUNYASHA, *a maid*

FEERS, *an old servant, age 87*

YASHA, *a young servant*

A TRAMP

THE STATION MASTER

A POST-OFFICE CLERK

GUESTS *and* SERVANTS

The action takes place on the estate of Madame Ranevsky.

ACT I

*A room which used to be the children's room and is still called
the nursery. Several doors, one leading into* ANYA's *room. It is early
in the morning and the sun is rising. It is early in May, but there
is a morning frost. The windows are closed but through them can
be seen the blossoming cherry trees. Enter* DUNYASHA, *carrying a
candle, and* LOPAHIN *with a book in his hand.*

LOPAHIN The train's arrived, thank God. What time is it?

DUNYASHA It's nearly two. *Blows out the candle.* It's daylight
already.

LOPAHIN The train must have been at least two hours late.
Yawns and stretches. And what a fool I am! I make a special trip
out here to meet them at the station, and then I fall asleep. . . .
Just sat down in the chair and dropped off. What a nuisance. Why
didn't you wake me up?

DUNYASHA I thought you'd gone. *Listens.* I think they're coming.

LOPAHIN *also listens.* No . . . I should've been there to help
them with their luggage and other things . . . *Pause.* Lyubov
Andreyevna has been abroad for five years. I wonder what she's
like now. She used to be such a kind and good person. So easy to
get along with and always considerate. Why, I remember when I
was fifteen, my father—he had a store in town then—hit me in
the face and it made my nose bleed. . . . We'd come out here for
something or other, and he was drunk. Oh, I remember it as if it
happened yesterday. . . . She was so young and beautiful . . .
Lyubov Andreyevna brought me into this very room—the nursery,
and she fixed my nose and she said to me, "Don't cry, little peasant,
it'll be better by the time you get married". . . . *Pause.* "Little
peasant" . . . She was right, my father was a peasant. And look
at me now—going about in a white waistcoat and brown shoes,
like a crown in peacock's feathers. Oh, I am rich all right, I've got
lots of money, but when you think about it, I'm still just a peasant.
Turning over pages of the book. Here, I've been reading this book,
and couldn't understand a word of it. Fell asleep reading it. *Pause.*

DUNYASHA The dogs have been awake all night: they know their mistress is coming.

LOPAHIN Why, what's the matter with you, Dunyasha?

DUNYASHA My hands are shaking. I think I'm going to faint.

LOPAHIN You've become too delicate and refined, Dunyasha. You get yourself all dressed up like a lady, and you fix your hair like one, too. You shouldn't do that, you know. You must remember your place.

Enter EPIHODOV *with a bouquet of flowers; he wears a jacket and brightly polished high boots which squeak loudly. As he enters he drops the flowers.*

EPIHODOV *picks up the flowers.* The gardener sent these. He says they're to go in the dining room. *Hands the flowers to* DUNYASHA.

LOPAHIN And bring me some kvass.

DUNYASHA All right.

EPIHODOV It's chilly outside this morning, three degrees of frost, and here the cherry trees are all in bloom. I can't say much for this climate of ours, you know. *Sighs.* No, I really can't. It doesn't contribute to—well, you know, things . . . And what do you think, Yermolay Alexeyevich, the day before yesterday I bought myself a pair of boots and they squeak so much . . . well, I mean to say, they're impossible. . . . What can I use to fix them?

LOPAHIN Oh, be quiet! And don't bother me!

EPIHODOV Every day something unpleasant happens to me. But I don't complain; I'm used to it, why I even laugh. *Enter* DUNYASHA: *she serves* LOPAHIN *with kvass.* Well, I have to be going. *Bumps into a chair which falls over.* There, you see! *Triumphantly.* You can see for yourself what I mean, you see . . . so to speak . . . It's absolutely amazing! *Goes out.*

DUNYASHA I must tell you a secret, Yermolay Alexeyevich. Epihodov proposed to me.

LOPAHIN Really!

DUNYASHA I don't know what to do. . . . He's a quiet man, but then sometimes he starts talking, and then you can't understand a word he says. It sounds nice, and he says it with so much feeling, but it doesn't make any sense. I think I like him a little, and he's madly in love with me. But the poor man, he's sort of unlucky! Do you know, something unpleasant seems to happen to him every day. That's why they tease him and call him "two-and-twenty mis-fortunes."

LOPAHIN *listens*. I think I hear them coming. . . .

DUNYASHA Coming! . . . Oh, what's the matter with me. . . . I feel cold all over.

LOPAHIN Yes, they're really coming! Let's go and meet them at the door. I wonder if she'll recognize me? We haven't seen each other for five years.

DUNYASHA, *agitated*. I'm going to faint . . . Oh, I'm going to faint! . . .

The sound of two carriages driving up to the house can be heard. LOPAHIN *and* DUNYASHA *hurry out. The stage is empty. Then there are sounds of people arriving in the next room.* FEERS, *who has gone to meet the train, enters the room leaning on a cane. He crosses the stage as rapidly as he can. He is dressed in an old-fashioned livery coat and a top hat and is muttering to himself, though it is impossible to make out what he is saying. The noises off-stage become louder.*

VOICE, *off-stage*. Let's go through here.

Enter LYUBOV ANDREYEVNA, ANYA, *and* CHARLOTTA IVANOVNA, *leading a small dog, all in traveling clothes,* VARYA, *wearing an overcoat and a kerchief over her head,* GAEV, SEMYONOV-PISHCHIK, LOPAHIN, DUNYASHA, *carrying a bundle and parasol and other servants with luggage.*

ANYA Let's go through here. Do you remember what room this is, Mamma?

LYUBOV, *joyfully, through her tears*. The nursery!

VARYA How cold it is! My hands are numb. *To* LYUBOV. Your rooms are the same as always, Mamma dear, the white one, and the lavender one.

LYUBOV The nursery, my dear, beautiful room! . . . I used to sleep here when I was little. *Cries*. And here I am again, like a little child . . . *She kisses her brother, then* VARYA, *then her brother again*. And Varya hasn't changed a bit, looking like a nun. And I recognized Dunyasha, too. *Kisses* DUNYASHA.

GAEV The train was two hours late. Just think of it! Such efficiency!

CHARLOTTA, *to* PISHCHIK. And my dog eats nuts, too.

PISHCHIK, *astonished.* Think of that!

They all go out except ANYA *and* DUNYASHA.

DUNYASHA We've waited and waited for you . . . *Helps* ANYA *to take off her hat and coat.*

ANYA I haven't slept for four nights . . . I'm freezing.

DUNYASHA It was Lent when you left, and it was snowing and freezing; but it's spring now. Darling! *She laughs and kisses her.* Oh, how I've missed you! I could hardly stand it. My pet, my precious . . . But I must tell you . . . I can't wait another minute . . .

ANYA, *without enthusiasm.* What time is it? . . .

DUNYASHA Epihodov, the clerk, proposed to me right after Easter.

ANYA You never talk about anything else . . . *Tidies her hair.* I've lost all my hairpins. . . . *She's so tired she can hardly keep on her feet.*

DUNYASHA I really don't know what to think. He loves me . . . he loves me very much!

ANYA, *looking through the door into her room, tenderly.* My own room, my own windows, just as if I'd never left them! I'm home again! Tomorrow I'm going to get up and run right to the garden! Oh, if only I could fall asleep! I couldn't sleep all the way back, I've been so worried.

DUNYASHA Pyotr Sergeyevich came the day before yesterday.

ANYA, *joyfully.* Pyeta!

DUNYASHA We put him in the bathhouse, he's probably asleep now. He said he didn't want to inconvenience you. *Looks at her watch.* I should have gotten him up, but Varya told me not to. "Don't you dare get him up," she said.

Enter VARYA *with a bunch of keys at her waist.*

VARYA Dunyasha, get some coffee, and hurry! Mamma wants some.

DUNYASHA I'll get it right away. *Goes out.*

VARYA Thank God, you're back! You're home again. *Embracing her.* My little darling's come home! How are you, my precious?

ANYA If you only knew what I've had to put up with!

VARYA I can just imagine . . .

ANYA You remember, I left just before Easter and it was cold then. And Charlotta never stopped talking the whole time, talking and those silly tricks of hers. Why did you make me take Charlotta?

VARYA But you couldn't go all alone, darling. At seventeen!

ANYA When we got to Paris it was cold and snowing. My French was terrible. Mamma was living on the fifth floor, and the place was filled with people—some French ladies, and an old priest with a little book, and the room was full of cigarette smoke. It was so unpleasant. All of a sudden I felt so sorry for Mamma that I put my arms around her neck and hugged her and wouldn't let go I was so upset. Later Mamma cried and was very kind.

VARYA, *tearfully*. I can't stand to hear it! . . .

ANYA She had already sold her villa at Mentone, and she had nothing left, not a thing. And I didn't have any money left either, not a penny. In fact, I barely had enough to get to Paris. And Mamma didn't understand it at all. On the way, we'd eat at the best restaurants and she'd order the most expensive dishes and tip the waiters a rouble each. Charlotta's the same way. And Yasha expected a full-course dinner for himself; it was horrible. You know, Yasha is Mamma's valet, now, we brought him with us.

VARYA Yes, I've seen the scoundrel.

ANYA Well, how's everything here? Have you paid the interest on the mortgage?

VARYA With what?

ANYA Oh dear! Oh dear!

VARYA The time runs out in August, and then it will be up for sale.

ANYA Oh dear!

LOPAHIN *puts his head through the door and moos like a cow*. Moo-o. . . . *Disappears*.

VARYA, *tearfully*. I'd like to hit him . . . *Clenches her fist*.

ANYA, *her arms round* VARYA, *dropping her voice*. Varya, has he proposed to you? VARYA *shakes her head*. But he loves you. . . . Why don't you talk to him, what are you waiting for?

VARYA Nothing will come of it. He's too busy to have time to think of me . . . He doesn't notice me at all. It's easier when he isn't around, it makes me miserable just to see him. Everybody talks of our wedding and congratulates me, but in fact there's nothing to it, it's all a dream. *In a different tone*. You've got a new pin, it looks like a bee.

ANYA, *sadly.* Mamma bought it for me. *She goes into her room and then with childlike gaiety.* Did you know that in Paris I went up in a balloon?

VARYA My darling's home again! My precious one's home. DUN-YASHA *returns with a coffeepot and prepares coffee. Standing by* ANYA*'s door.* You know, all day long, as I go about the house doing my work, I'm always dreaming. If only we could marry you to some rich man, I'd be more at peace. Then they could go away; first I'd go to the cloisters, and then I'd go on a pilgrimage to Kiev, and then Moscow . . . I'd spend my life just walking from one holy place to another. On and on. Oh, what a wonderful life that would be!

ANYA The birds are singing in the garden. What time is it?

VARYA It must be nearly three. Time you went to bed, darling. *Goes into* ANYA*'s room.* Oh, what a wonderful life!

Enter YASHA, *with a blanket and a small bag.*

YASHA, *crossing the stage, in an affectedly genteel voice.* May I go through here?

DUNYASHA My, how you've changed since you've been abroad, Yasha. I hardly recognized you.

YASHA Hm! And who are you?

DUNYASHA When you went away, I was no bigger than this . . . *Shows her height from the floor.* I'm Dunyasha, Fyodor's daughter. You don't remember me!

YASHA Hm! You're quite a little peach! *Looks around and embraces her; she screams and drops a saucer.* YASHA *goes out quickly.*

VARYA, *in the doorway, crossly.* What's happening in here?

DUNYASHA, *tearfully.* I've broken a saucer.

VARYA That's good luck.

ANYA, *coming out of her room.* We ought to warn Mamma that Petya's here.

VARYA I gave strict orders not to wake him up.

ANYA, *pensively.* Six years ago father died, and then a month later Grisha was drowned in the river. He was such a beautiful little boy—and only seven! Mamma couldn't stand it so she went away . . . and never looked back. *Shivers.* How well I understand her! If she only knew! *Pause.* And, Petya was Grisha's tutor, he might remind her . . .

Enter FEERS, *wearing a jacket and a white waistcoat.*

FEERS *goes over and is busy with the samovar.* The mistress will have her coffee in here. *Puts on white gloves.* Is it ready? *To* DUNYASHA, *severely.* Where's the cream?

DUNYASHA Oh, I forgot! *Goes out quickly.*

FEERS, *fussing around the coffeepot.* That girl's hopeless. . . . *Mutters.* They've come from Paris . . . Years ago the master used to go to Paris . . . Used to go by carriage . . . *Laughs.*

VARYA Feers, what are you laughing at?

FEERS What would you like? *Happily.* The mistress has come home! Home at last! I don't mind if I die now . . . *Weeps with joy.*

Enter LYUBOV, LOPAHIN, GAEV *and* SEMYONOV-PISHCHIK, *the latter in a long peasant coat of fine cloth and full trousers tucked inside high boots.* GAEV, *as he comes in, moves his arms and body as if he were playing billiards.*

LYUBOV How does it go now? Let me think . . . The red off the side and into the middle pocket!

GAEV That's right! Then I put the white into the corner pocket! . . . Years ago we used to sleep in this room, and now I'm fifty-one, strange as it may seem.

LOPAHIN Yes, time flies.

GAEV What?

LOPAHIN Time flies, I say.

GAEV This place smells of patchouli . . .

ANYA I'm going to bed. Goodnight, Mamma. *Kisses her.*

LYUBOV My precious child! *Kisses her hands.* Are you glad you're home? I still can't get used to it.

ANYA Goodnight, Uncle.

GAEV *kisses her face and hands.* God bless you. You're so much like your mother! *To his sister.* You looked exactly like her at her age, Lyuba.

ANYA *shakes hands with* LOPAHIN *and* PISHCHIK, *goes out and shuts the door after her.*

LYUBOV She's very tired.

PISHCHIK It's been a long trip for her.

VARYA, *to* LOPAHIN *and* PISHCHIK. Well, gentlemen? It's nearly three o'clock, time to say good-bye.

LYUBOV *laughs.* You haven't changed a bit, Varya. *Draws* VARYA *to her and kisses her.* Let me have some coffee, then we'll all turn in.

FEERS *places a cushion under her feet.* Thank you, my dear. I've got into the habit of drinking coffee. I drink it day and night. Thank you, my dear old friend. *Kisses* FEERS.

VARYA I'd better see if they brought all the luggage in. *Goes out.*

LYUBOV Is it really me sitting here? *Laughing.* I'd like to dance and wave my arms about. *Covering her face with her hands.* But am I just dreaming? God, how I love it here—my own country! Oh, I love it so much, I could hardly see anything from the train, I was crying so hard. *Through tears.* Here, but I must drink my coffee. Thank you, Feers, thank you, my dear old friend. I'm so glad you're still alive.

FEERS The day before yesterday.

GAEV He doesn't hear very well.

LOPAHIN I've got to leave for Kharkov a little after four. What a nuisance! It's so good just to see you, and I want to talk with you . . . You look as lovely as ever.

PISHCHIK, *breathing heavily.* Prettier. In her fancy Parisian clothes . . . She's simply ravishing!

LOPAHIN Your brother here—Leonid Andreyevich—says that I'm nothing but a hick from the country, a tight-fisted peasant, but it doesn't bother me. Let him say what he likes. All I want is that you trust me as you always have. Merciful God! My father was your father's serf, and your grandfather's, too, but you've done so much for me that I've forgotten all that. I love you as if you were my own sister . . . more than that even.

LYUBOV I just can't sit still, I can't for the life of me! *She jumps up and walks about in great excitement.* I'm so happy, it's too much for me. It's all right, you can laugh at me. I know I'm being silly . . . My wonderful old bookcase! *Kisses bookcase.* And my little table!

GAEV You know, the old Nurse died while you were away.

LYUBOV *sits down and drinks coffee.* Yes, you wrote to me about it. May she rest in peace.

GAEV Anastasy died, too. And Petrushka quit and is working in town for the chief of police. *Takes a box of gumdrops out of his pocket and puts one in his mouth.*

PISHCHIK My daughter, Dashenka, sends you her greetings.

LOPAHIN I feel like telling you some good news, something to cheer you up. *Looks at his watch.* I'll have to leave in a minute, so there's not much time to talk. But briefly it's this. As you know, the cherry orchard is going to be sold to pay your debts. They've set August 22nd as the date for the auction, but you can sleep in peace and not worry about it; there's a way out. Here's my plan, so please pay close attention. Your estate is only twenty miles from town, and the railroad is close by. Now, if the cherry orchard and the land along the river were subdivided and leased for the building of summer cottages, you'd have a yearly income of at least twenty-five thousand roubles.

GAEV Such nonsense!

LYUBOV I'm afraid I don't quite understand, Yermolay Alexeyevich.

LOPAHIN You'd divide the land into one acre lots and rent them for at least twenty-five roubles a year. I'll bet you, that if you advertise it now there won't be a lot left by the fall; they'll be snapped up almost at once. You see, you're saved! And really, I must congratulate you; it's a perfect setup. The location is marvelous and the river's deep enough for swimming. Of course, the land will have to be cleared and cleaned up a bit. For instance, all those old buildings will have to be torn down . . . And this house, too . . . but then it's not really good for anything any more. . . . And then, the old cherry orchard will have to be cut down . . .

LYUBOV Cut down? My good man, forgive me, but you don't seem to understand. If there's one thing that's interesting and really valuable in this whole part of the country, it's our cherry orchard.

LOPAHIN The only valuable thing about it is that it's very large. It only produces a crop every other year and then who wants to buy it?

GAEV Why, this orchard is even mentioned in the Encyclopedia.

LOPAHIN, *looking at his watch.* If you don't decide now, and do something about it before August, the cherry orchard as well as the estate will be auctioned off. So make up your minds! There's no other way out, I promise you. There's no other way.

FEERS In the old days, forty or fifty years ago, the cherries were dried, preserved, pickled, made into jam, and sometimes. . . .

GAEV Be quiet, Feers.

FEERS And sometimes, whole wagon-loads of dried cherries were shipped to Moscow and Kharkov. We used to make a lot of money on them then! And the dried cherries used to be soft, juicy, sweet, and very good . . . They knew how to do it then . . . they had a way of cooking them . . .

LYUBOV And where is that recipe now?

FEERS They've forgotten it. Nobody can remember it.

PISHCHIK, *to* LYUBOV. What's it like in Paris? Did you eat frogs?

LYUBOV I ate crocodiles.

PISHCHIK Well, will you imagine that!

LOPAHIN Until recently only rich people and peasants lived in the country, but now lots of people come out for the summer. Almost every town, even the small ones, is surrounded with summer places. And probably within the next twenty years there'll be more and more of these people. Right now, all they do is sit on the porch and drink tea, but later on they might begin to grow a few things, and then your cherry orchard would be full of life again . . . rich and prosperous.

GAEV, *indignantly*. Such a lot of nonsense!

Enter VARYA *and* YASHA.

VARYA There were two telegrams for you, Mamma dear. *Takes out the keys and opens the old bookcase, making a great deal of noise.* Here they are.

LYUBOV They're from Paris. *Tears them up without reading them.* I'm through with Paris.

GAEV Do you know, Lyuba, how old this bookcase is? Last week I pulled out the bottom drawer, and I found the date it was made burned in the wood. Just think, it's exactly a hundred years old. What do you think of that, eh? We ought to celebrate its anniversary. I know it's an inanimate object, but still—it's a bookcase!

PISHCHIK, *astonished*. A hundred years! Can you imagine that!

GAEV Yes . . . That's quite something. *Feeling round the bookcase with his hands.* Dear, most honored bookcase! I salute you! For one hundred years you have served the highest ideals of goodness and justice. For one hundred years you have made us aware of the need for creative work; several generations of our family have had their courage sustained and their faith in a brighter future fortified by your silent call; you have fostered in us the ideals of public service and social consciousness. *Pause.*

LOPAHIN Yes . . .

LYUBOV You haven't changed a bit, Leonia.

GAEV, *slightly embarrassed*. I shoot it off the corner into the middle pocket! . . .

LOPAHIN *looks at his watch*. Well, I've got to go.

YASHA *brings medicine to* LYUBOV. Would you like to take your pills now; it's time.

PISHCHIK You shouldn't take medicine, my dear . . . they don't do you any good . . . or harm either. Let me have them. *Takes the box from her, pours the pills into the palm of his hand, blows on them, puts them all into his mouth and drinks them down with kvass.* There!

LYUBOV, *alarmed*. You're out of your mind!

PISHCHIK I took all the pills.

LOPAHIN What a stomach! *All laugh.*

FEERS His honor was here during Holy Week, and he ate half a bucket of pickles. *Mutters.*

LYUBOV What's he saying?

VARYA He's been muttering like that for three years now. We're used to it.

YASHA It's his age. . . .

CHARLOTTA IVANOVNA, *very thin, and tightly laced in a white dress, with a lorgnette at her waist, passes across the stage.*

LOPAHIN Excuse me, Charlotta Ivanovna, for not greeting you. I didn't have a chance. *Tries to kiss her hand.*

CHARLOTTA, *withdrawing her hand*. If I let you kiss my hand, then you'd want to kiss my elbow next, and then my shoulder.

LOPAHIN This just isn't my lucky day. *All laugh.* Charlotta Ivanovna, do a trick for us.

CHARLOTTA Not now. I want to go to bed. *Goes out.*

LOPAHIN I'll be back in three weeks. *Kisses* LYUBOV's *hand*. It's time I'm going so I'll say good-bye. *To* GAEV. Au revoir. *Embraces* PISHCHIK. Au revoir. *Shakes hands with* VARYA, *then with* FEERS *and* YASHA. I don't want to go, really. *To* LYUBOV. Think over the idea of the summer cottages and if you decide anything, let me know, and I'll get you a loan of at least fifty thousand. So think it over seriously.

VARYA, *crossly*. Won't you ever go?

LOPAHIN I'm going, I'm going. *Goes out.*

GAEV What a boor! I beg your pardon . . . Varya's going to marry him, he's Varya's fiancé.

VARYA Please don't talk like that, Uncle.

LYUBOV Well, Varya, I'd be delighted. He's a good man.

PISHCHIK He's a man . . . you have to say that . . . a most worthy fellow . . . My Dashenka says so too . . . she says all sorts of things. . . . *He drops asleep and snores, but wakes up again at once.* By the way, my dear, will you lend me two hundred and forty roubles? I've got to pay the interest on the mortgage tomorrow . . .

VARYA, *in alarm.* We haven't got it, really we haven't!

LYUBOV It's true, I haven't got a thing.

PISHCHIK It'll turn up. *Laughs.* I never lose hope. There are times when I think everything's lost, I'm ruined, and then—suddenly!—a railroad is built across my land, and they pay me for it! Something's bound to happen, if not today, then tomorrow, or the next day. Perhaps Dashenka will win two hundred thousand—she's got a lottery ticket.

LYUBOV Well, we've finished our coffee; now we can go to bed.

FEERS, *brushing* GAEV, *admonishing him.* You've got on those trousers again! What am I going to do with you?

VARYA, *in a low voice.* Anya's asleep. *Quietly opens a window.* The sun's rising and see how wonderful the trees are! And the air smells so fragrant! The birds are beginning to sing.

GAEV, *coming to the window.* The orchard is all white. You haven't forgotten, Lyuba? How straight that lane is . . . just like a ribbon. And how it shines on moonlight nights. Do you remember? You haven't forgotten, have you?

LYUBOV *looks through the window at the orchard.* Oh, my childhood, my innocent childhood! I used to sleep here, and I'd look out at the orchard and every morning when I woke up I was so happy. The orchard was exactly the same, nothing's changed. *Laughs happily.* All, all white! Oh, my orchard! After the dark, gloomy autumn and the cold winter, you are young again and full of joy; the angels have not deserted you! If only this burden could be taken from me, if only I could forget my past!

GAEV Yes, and now the orchard's going to be sold to pay our debts, how strange it all is.

LYUBOV Look, there's Mother walking through the orchard . . . dressed all in white! *Laughs happily.* It is Mother!

GAEV Where?

VARYA Oh, please, Mamma dear!

LYUBOV You're right, it's no one, I only imagined it. Over there, you see, on the right, by the path that goes to the arbor, there's a small white tree that's bending so it looks just like a woman.

Enter TROFIMOV. *He is dressed in a shabby student's uniform, and wears glasses.*

What a wonderful orchard! Masses of white blossems, the blue sky . . .

TROFIMOV Lyubov Andreyevna! *She turns to him.* I'll just say hello and leave at once. *Kisses her hand warmly.* They told me to wait until morning, but I couldn't wait any longer. LYUBOV *looks at him, puzzled.*

VARYA, *through tears.* This is Petya Trofimov.

TROFIMOV Petya Trofimov, I was Grisha's tutor. Have I changed that much?

LYUBOV *puts her arms round him and weeps quietly.*

GAEV, *embarrassed.* Now, now, Lyuba . . .

VARYA *weeps.* Didn't I tell you to wait until tomorrow, Petya?

LYUBOV My Grisha . . . my little boy . . . Oh, Grisha . . . my son . . .

VARYA Don't cry, Mamma darling. There's nothing we can do, it was God's will.

TROFIMOV, *gently, with emotion.* Don't, don't . . . please.

LYUBOV, *weeping quietly.* My little boy was lost . . . drowned . . . Why? Why, my friend? *More quietly.* Anya's asleep in there, and here I'm crying and making a scene. But tell me, Petya, what's happened to your good looks? You've aged so.

TROFIMOV A peasant woman on the train called me "that moth-eaten man."

LYUBOV You used to be such an attractive boy, a typical young student. But now your hair is thin and you wear glasses. Are you still a student? *She walks to the door.*

TROFIMOV I expect I'll be a student as long as I live.

LYUBOV *kisses her brother, then* VARYA. Well, go to bed now. You have aged, too, Leonid.

PISHCHIK, *following her.* Yes, I suppose it's time to get to bed.

Oh, my gout! I'd better spend the night here, and in the morning, Lyubov Andreyevna, my dear, I'd like to borrow the two hundred and forty roubles.

GAEV Don't you ever stop?

PISHCHIK Just two hundred and forty roubles . . . To pay the interest on my mortgage.

LYUBOV I haven't any money, my friend.

PISHCHIK Oh, I'll pay you back, my dear. It's not much, after all.

LYUBOV Oh, all right. Leonid will give it to you. You give him the money, Leonid.

GAEV Why, of course; glad to. As much as he wants!

LYUBOV What else can we do? He needs it. He'll pay it back.

LYUBOV, TROFIMOV, PISHCHIK *and* FEERS *go out.* GAEV, VARYA *and* YASHA *remain.*

GAEV My sister hasn't lost her habit of throwing money away. *To* YASHA. Get out of the way, you smell like a barnyard.

YASHA, *with a sneer.* And you haven't changed either, have you Leonid Andreyevich?

GAEV What's that? *To* VARYA. What did he say?

VARYA, *to* YASHA. Your mother came out from town yesterday to see you, and she's been waiting out in the servant's quarters ever since.

YASHA I wish she wouldn't bother me.

VARYA Oh, you ought to be ashamed of yourself.

YASHA What's she in such a hurry for? She could have come tomorrow. YASHA *goes out.*

VARYA Mamma hasn't changed a bit. She'd give away everything we had, if she could.

GAEV Yes . . . You know, when many things are prescribed to cure a disease, that means it's incurable. I've been wracking my brains to find an answer, and I've come up with several solutions, plenty of them—which means there aren't any. It would be wonderful if we could inherit some money, or if our Anya were to marry some very rich man, or if one of us went to Yaroslavl and tried our luck with our old aunt, the Countess. You know she's very rich.

VARYA, *weeping.* If only God would help us.

GAEV Oh, stop blubbering! The Countess is very rich, but she doesn't like us . . . To begin with, my sister married a lawyer, and not a nobleman . . . ANYA *appears in the doorway*. She married a commoner . . . and since then no one can say she's behaved in the most virtuous way possible. She's good, kind, and lovable, and I love her very much, but no matter how much you may allow for extenuating circumstances, you've got to admit that her morals have not been beyond reproach. You can sense it in everything she does . . .

VARYA, *in a whisper*. Anya's standing in the doorway.

GAEV What? *A pause.* Isn't that strange, something's gotten into my right eye . . . I'm having a terrible time seeing. And last Thursday, when I was in the District Court . . . ANYA *comes in*.

VARYA Anya, why aren't you asleep?

ANYA I don't feel like sleeping. I just can't.

GAEV My dear little girl! *Kisses* ANYA's *face and hands.* My child! *Tearfully.* You're not just my niece, you're an angel, my whole world. Please believe me, believe . . .

ANYA I believe you, Uncle. Everyone loves you, respects you . . . but, dear Uncle, you shouldn't talk so much, just try to keep quiet. What were you saying just now about mother, about your own sister? What made you say that?

GAEV Yes, yes! *He takes her hand and puts it over his face.* You're quite right, it was a horrible thing to say! My God! My God! And that speech I made to the bookcase . . . so stupid! As soon as I finished it, I realized how stupid it was.

VARYA It's true, Uncle dear, you oughtn't to talk so much. Just keep quiet, that's all.

ANYA If you keep quiet, you'll find life is more peaceful.

GAEV I'll be quiet. *Kisses* ANYA's *and* VARYA's *hands.* I'll be quiet. But I must tell you something about all this business, it's important. Last Thursday I went to the District Court, and I got talking with some friends, and from what they said it looks as if it might be possible to get a second mortgage so we can pay the interest to the bank.

VARYA If only God would help us!

GAEV I'm going again on Tuesday to talk with them some more. *To* VARYA. Oh, stop crying. *to* ANYA. Your mother's going to talk with Lopahin, and he certainly won't refuse her. And after you've had a little rest, you can go to Yaroslavl to see your grandmother, the Countess. You see, we'll attack the problem from three sides, and—it's as good as solved! We'll pay the interest, I'm sure of it. *He eats a gumdrop.* On my honor, on anything you like, I swear the estate'll not be sold! *Excited.* I'll bet my happiness on it! Here's my hand, you can call me a worthless liar if I allow the auction to take place. I swear it with all my soul!

ANYA, *calmer, with an air of happiness.* How good you are, Uncle, and how sensible! *Embracing him.* I'm not afraid anymore. I feel so happy and at peace.

Enter FEERS.

FEERS, *reproachfully.* Leonid Andreyevich, aren't you ashamed of yourself? When are you going to bed?

GAEV In a minute. Now you go away, Feers. I can get ready for bed myself. Come along, children, time for bed. We'll talk about it some more tomorrow, you must go to bed now. *Kisses* ANYA *and* VARYA. You know, I'm a man of the 'eighties. People don't think much of that period these days, but still I can say that I've suffered a great deal in my lifetime because of my convictions. There's a reason why the peasants love me. You have to know the peasants! You have to know . . .

ANYA You're beginning again, Uncle!

VARYA Yes, you'd better keep quiet, Uncle dear.

FEERS, *sternly.* Leonid Andreyevich!

GAEV I'm coming, I'm coming! Go to bed now! Bank the white into the side pocket. There's a shot for you . . . *Goes out;* FEERS *hobbles after him.*

ANYA I feel better now, although I don't want to go to Yaroslavl, I don't like the Countess at all, but then, thanks to Uncle, we really don't have to worry at all. *She sits down.*

VARYA I've got to get some sleep. I'm going. Oh, by the way, we had a terrible scene while you were gone. You know, there are only a few old servants left out in the servants' quarters: just Yefmushka, Polya, Yevstignay, and Karp. Well, they let some tramp sleep out there, and at first I didn't say anything about it. But then later, I heard people saying that I had given orders to feed them nothing but beans. Because I was stingy, you see . . . Yevstignay was the cause of it all. "Well," I think to myself, "if that's how things are, just you wait!" So I called Yevstignay in. *Yawns.* So he came. "What's all this, Yevstignay," I said to him, "you're such a fool." *She walks up to* ANYA. Anichka! *A pause.* She's asleep! . . . *Takes her arm.* Let's go to bed! Come! *Leads her away.* My darling's fallen asleep! Come . . . *They go towards the door. The sound of a shepherd's pipe is heard from far away, beyond the orchard.* TROFIMOV *crosses the stage, but, seeing* VARYA *and* ANYA, *stops.* Sh-sh! She's asleep . . . asleep . . . Come along, come along.

ANYA, *softly, half-asleep.* I'm so tired. . . . I can hear the bells ringing all the time . . . Uncle . . . dear . . . Mamma and Uncle. . . .

VARYA Come, darling, come. . . . *They go into* ANYA's *room.*

TROFIMOV, *deeply moved.* Oh, Anya . . . my sunshine! My spring!

Curtain.

ACT II

An old abandoned chapel in a field. Beside it are a well, an old bench, and some tombstones. A road leads to the Ranevsky estate. On one side a row of poplars casts a shadow; at that point the cherry orchard begins. In the distance, a line of telegraph poles can be seen, and beyond them, on the horizon is the outline of a large town, visible only in very clear weather. It's nearly sunset. CHARLOTTA, YASHA *and* DUNYASHA *are sitting on the bench;* EPIHODOV *is standing near by, playing a guitar; everyone is lost in thought.* CHARLOTTA *is wearing an old hunting cap; she has taken a shotgun off her shoulder and is adjusting the buckle on the strap.*

CHARLOTTA, *thoughtfully.* I don't know how old I am. For you see, I haven't got a passport . . . but I keep pretending that I'm still very young. When I was a little girl, my father and mother traveled from fair to fair giving performances—oh, very good ones. And I used to do the "*salto-mortale*" and all sorts of other tricks, too. When Papa and Mamma died, a German lady took me to live with her and sent me to school. So when I grew up I became a governess. But where I come from and who I am, I don't know.

Who my parents were—perhaps they weren't even married—I don't know. *Taking a cucumber from her pocket and beginning to eat it.* I don't know anything. *Pause.* I'm longing to talk to someone, but there isn't anybody. I haven't anybody . . .

EPIHODOV *plays the guitar and sings.* "What care I for the noisy world? . . . What care I for friends and foes?" How pleasant it is to play the mandolin!

DUNYASHA That's a guitar, not a mandolin. *She looks at herself in a little mirror and powders her face.*

EPIHODOV To a man who's madly in love this is a mandolin. *Sings quietly.* "If only my heart were warmed by the fire of love requited.". . . YASHA *joins in.*

CHARLOTTA How dreadfully these people sing! . . . Ach! Like a bunch of jackals.

DUNYASHA, *to* YASHA You're so lucky to have been abroad!

YASHA Of course I am. Naturally. *Yawns, then lights a cigar.*

EPIHODOV Stands to reason. Abroad everything's reached its maturity . . . I mean to say, everything's been going on for such a long time.

YASHA Obviously.

EPIHODOV Now, I'm a cultured man, I read all kinds of extraordinary books, you know, but somehow I can't seem to figure out where I'm going, what it is I really want, I mean to say—whether to live or to shoot myself. Nevertheless, I always carry a revolver on me. Here it is. *Shows the revolver.*

CHARLOTTA That's finished, so now I'm going. *Slips the strap of the gun over her shoulder.* Yes, Epihodov, you are a very clever man, and frightening, too; the women must be wild about you! Brrr! *Walks off.* All these clever people are so stupid, I haven't anyone to talk to. I'm so lonely, always alone, I have nobody and . . . and who I am and what I'm here for, nobody knows . . . *Wanders out.*

EPIHODOV Frankly, and I want to keep to the point, I have to admit that Fate, so to speak, treats me absolutely without mercy, like a small ship is buffeted by the storm, as it were. I mean to say, suppose I'm mistaken, then why for instance should I wake up this morning and suddenly see a gigantic spider sitting on my chest? Like this . . . *Showing the size with both hands.* Or if I pick up a jug to have a drink of kvass, there's sure to be something horrible, like a cockroach, inside it. *Pause.* Have you read Buckle? *Pause.* May I trouble you for a moment, Dunyasha? I'd like to speak with you.

DUNYASHA Well, go ahead.

EPIHODOV I'd very much like to speak with you alone. *Sighs.*

DUNYASHA, *embarrassed*. Oh, all right . . . But first bring me my little cape . . . It's hanging by the cupboard. It's getting terribly chilly . . .

EPIHODOV Very well, I'll get it. . . . Now I know what to do with my revolver. *Takes his guitar and goes off playing it.*

YASHA Two-and-twenty misfortunes! Just between you and me, he's a stupid fool. *Yawns.*

DUNYASHA I hope to God he doesn't shoot himself. *Pause.* He makes me so nervous and I'm always worrying about him. I came to live here when I was still a little girl. Now I no longer know how to live a simple life, and my hands are as white . . . as white as a lady's. I've become such a delicate and sensitive creature. I'm afraid of everything . . . so frightened. If you deceive me, Yasha, I don't know what will happen to my nerves.

YASHA *kisses her*. You sweet little peach! Just remember, a girl must always control herself. Personally I thing nothing is worse than a girl who doesn't behave herself.

DUNYASHA I love you so much, so passionately! You're so intelligent, you can talk about anything. *Pause.*

YASHA *yawns*. Yes, I suppose so . . . In my opinion, it's like this: if a girl loves someone it means she's immoral. *Pause.* I enjoy smoking a cigar in the fresh air . . . *Listens.* Someone's coming. It's the ladies and gentlemen. . . . DUNYASHA *impulsively embraces him*. Go to the house now, as though you'd been swimming down at the river. No, this way or they'll see you. I wouldn't want them to think I was interested in you.

DUNYASHA, *coughing softly*. That cigar has given me such a headache . . . *Goes out.*

YASHA *remains sitting by the shrine*. Enter LYUBOV, GAEV *and* LOPAHIN.

LOPAHIN You've got to make up your minds once and for all; there's no time to lose. After all, it's a simple matter. Will you lease your land for the cottages, or won't you? You can answer in one word: yes or no? Just one word!

LYUBOV Who's been smoking such wretched cigars? *Sits down.*

GAEV How very convenient everything is with the railroad nearby. *Sits down.* Well, here we are—we've been to town, had lunch and we're home already. I put the red into the middle pocket! I'd like to go in . . . just for one game. . . .

LYUBOV You've got lots of time.

LOPAHIN Just one word! *Beseechingly.* Please give me an answer!

GAEV *yawns.* What did you say?

LYUBOV, *looking into her purse.* Yesterday I had lots of money, but today there's practically none left. My poor Varya feeds us all milk soups to economize; the old servants in the kitchen have nothing but dried peas, and here I am wasting money senselessly, I just don't understand it. . . . *She drops her purse, scattering gold coins.* Now I've dropped it again. . . . *Annoyed.*

YASHA Allow me, madam, I'll pick them right up. *Picks up the money.*

LYUBOV Thank you, Yasha . . . And why did we go out for lunch today? And that restaurant of yours . . . the food was vile, the music ghastly, and the tablecloths smelled of soap. And Leonia, why do you drink so much? And eat so much? And talk so much? Today at the restaurant you were at it again, and it was all so pointless. About the seventies, and the decadents. And to whom? Really, talking to the waiters about the decadents!

LOPAHIN Yes, that's too much.

GAEV, *waving his hand.* I know I'm hopeless. *To* YASHA, *irritably.* Why are you always bustling about in front of me?

YASHA *laughs.* The minute you open your mouth I start laughing.

GAEV, *to his sister.* Either he goes, or I do. . . .

LYUBOV Get along, Yasha, you'd better leave us now.

YASHA *hands the purse to* LYUBOV. I'm going. *He can hardly restrain his laughter.* Right this minute. . . . *Goes out.*

LOPAHIN You know, that rich merchant Deriganov is thinking of buying your estate. They say he's coming to the auction himself.

LYUBOV Where did you hear that?

LOPAHIN That's what they say in town.

GAEV Our Aunt in Yaroslavl has promised to send us some money, but when and how much we don't know.

LOPAHIN How much will she send? A hundred thousand? Two hundred?

LYUBOV Well, hardly . . . Ten or fifteen thousand, perhaps. And we should be thankful for that.

LOPAHIN Forgive me for saying it, but really, in my whole life I've never met such unrealistic, unbusinesslike, queer people as you. You're told in plain language that your estate's going to be sold, and you don't seem to understand it at all.

LYUBOV But what are we to do? Please, tell us.

LOPAHIN I keep on telling you. Every day I tell you the same thing. You must lease the cherry orchard and the rest of the land for summer cottages, and you must do it now, as quickly as possible. It's almost time for the auction. Please, try to understand! Once you definitely decide to lease it for the cottages, you'll be able to borrow as much money as you like, and you'll be saved.

LYUBOV Summer cottages and vacationers! Forgive me, but it's so vulgar.

GAEV I agree with you entirely.

LOPAHIN Honestly, I'm going to burst into tears, or scream, or faint. I can't stand it any more! It's more than I can take! *To* GAEV. And you're an old woman!

GAEV What did you say?

LOPAHIN I said, you're an old woman!

LYUBOV, *alarmed.* No, don't go, please stay. I beg you! Perhaps we can think of something.

LOPAHIN What's there to think of?

LYUBOV Please don't go! I feel so much more cheerful when you're here. *Pause.* I keep expecting something horrible to happen . . . as though the house were going to collapse on top of us.

GAEV, *in deep thought.* I bank it off the cushions, and then into the middle pocket. . . .

LYUBOV We've sinned too much. . . .

LOPAHIN Sinned! What sins have you . . .

GAEV, *putting a gumdrop into his mouth.* They say I've eaten up my fortune in gumdrops. *Laughs.*

LYUBOV Oh, my sins! Look at the way I've always wasted money. It's madness. And then I married a man who had nothing but debts.

And he was a terrible drinker . . . Champagne killed him! And then, as if I hadn't enough misery, I fell in love with someone else. We went off together, and just at that time—it was my first punishment, a blow that broke my heart—my little boy was drowned right here in this river . . . so I went abroad. I went away for good, never to return, never to see this river again . . . I just shut my eyes and ran away in a frenzy of grief, but *he* . . . he followed me. It was so cruel and brutal of him! I bought a villa near Mentone because he fell ill there, and for three years, day and night, I never had any rest. He was very sick, and he completely exhausted me; my soul dried up completely. Then, last year when the villa had to be sold to pay the debts, I went to Paris, and there he robbed me of everything I had and left me for another woman. . . . I tried to poison myself. . . . It was all so stupid, so shameful! And then suddenly I felt an urge to come back to Russia, to my own country, to my little girl . . . *Dries her tears.* Oh, Lord, Lord, be merciful, forgive my sins! Don't punish me any more! *Takes a telegram out of her pocket.* This came from Paris today. He's asking my forgiveness, he's begging me to return. *Tears up the telegram.* Sounds like music somewhere. *Listens.*

GAEV That's our famous Jewish orchestra. Don't you remember, four violins, a flute, and a bass?

LYUBOV Are they still playing? Sometime we should have a dance and they could play for us.

LOPAHIN *listens.* I can't hear anything . . . *Sings quietly.* "And the Germans, if you pay, will turn Russians into Frenchmen, so they say". . . *Laughs.* I saw a wonderful play last night. It was so funny.

LYUBOV It probably wasn't funny at all. Instead of going to plays, you should take a good look at yourself. Just think how dull your life is, and how much nonsense you talk!

LOPAHIN That's true, I admit it! Our lives are stupid . . . *Pause.* My father was a peasant, an idiot. He knew nothing and he taught me nothing. He only beat me when he was drunk, and always with a stick. And as a matter of fact, I'm just as much an idiot myself. I don't know anything and my handwriting's awful, I'm ashamed for people to see it—it's like a pig's.

LYUBOV You ought to get married, my friend.

LOPAHIN Yes . . . That's true.

LYUBOV You ought to marry our Varya. She's a fine girl.

LOPAHIN Yes.

LYUBOV She comes from simple people, and she works hard all day long without stopping. But the main thing is she loves you, and you've liked her for a long time yourself.

LOPAHIN Well. . . . I think it's a fine idea . . . She's a nice girl. *Pause*.

GAEV I've been offered a job at the bank. Six thousand a year. Did I tell you?

LYUBOV Yes, you did. You'd better stay where you are.

FEERS *enters, bringing an overcoat.*

FEERS, *to* GAEV. Please put it on, sir, you might catch cold.

GAEV *puts on the overcoat.* Oh, you *are* a nuisance.

FEERS You must stop this! You went off this morning without letting me know. *Looks him over.*

LYUBOV How you've aged, Feers!

FEERS What can I do for you, Madam?

LOPAHIN She says you've aged a lot.

FEERS I've lived for a long time. They were planning to marry me before your father was born. *Laughs.* Why, I was already head butler at the time of the emancipation, but I wouldn't take my freedom, I stayed on with the master and mistress. . . . *Pause.* I remember everyone was happy at the time, but what they were happy about, they didn't know themselves.

LOPAHIN That was the good life all right! All the peasants were flogged!

FEERS, *not having heard him.* That's right! The peasants belonged to their masters, and the masters belonged to the peasants; but now everything's all confused, and people don't know what to make of it.

GAEV Be quiet, Feers. Tomorrow I've got to go to town. I've been promised an introduction to some general or other who might lend us some money for the mortgage.

LOPAHIN Nothing will come of it. And how would you pay the interest, anyway?

LYUBOV He's talking nonsense again. There aren't any generals. *Enter* TROFIMOV, ANYA *and* VARYA.

GAEV Here come the children.

ANYA There's Mamma.

LYUBOV Come here, my dears. Oh, my darling children. . . . *Embraces* ANYA *and* VARYA. If you only knew how much I love you! Here now, sit down beside me. *All sit down.*

LOPAHIN Our perennial student is always with the girls.

TROFIMOV It's none of your business.

LOPAHIN He'll soon be fifty, and he's still a student.

TROFIMOV Oh, stop your stupid jokes.

LOPAHIN What's bothering you? My, you *are* a strange fellow!

TROFIMOV Why do you keep pestering me?

LOPAHIN *laughs.* Just let me ask you one question: what's your opinion of me?

TROFIMOV My opinion of you, Yermolay Alexeyevich, is this: you're a rich man, and soon you'll be a millionaire. For the same reason that wild beasts are necessary to maintain nature's economic laws, you are necessary, too—each of you devours everything that gets in his way. *Everybody laughs.*

VARYA You'd better talk about the planets, Petya.

LYUBOV No, let's go on with the conversation we had yesterday.

TROFIMOV What was that?

GAEV About pride.

TROFIMOV We talked for a long time yesterday, but we didn't agree on anything. The proud man, the way you use the word, has some mysterious quality about him. Perhaps you're right in a way, but if we look at it simply, without trying to be too subtle, you have to ask yourself why should we be proud at all? Why be proud when you realize that Man, as a species, is poorly constructed physiologically, and is usually coarse, stupid, and profoundly unhappy, too? We ought to put an end to such vanity and just go to work. That's right, we ought to work.

GAEV You'll die just the same, no matter what you do.

TROFIMOV Who knows? And anyway, what does it mean—to die? It could be that man has a hundred senses, and when he dies only the five that are known perish, while the other ninety-five go on living.

LYUBOV How clever you are, Petya!

LOPAHIN, *ironically.* Oh, very clever!

TROFIMOV Humanity is continually advancing, is continually seeking to perfect its powers. Someday all the things which we can't understand now, will be made clear. But if this is to happen, we've got to work, work with all our might to help those who are searching for truth. Up until now, here in Russia only a few have begun to work. Nearly all of the intelligentsia that I know have no commitment, they don't do anything, and are as yet incapable of work. They call themselves "the intelligentsia," but they still run roughshod over their servants, and they treat the peasants like animals, they study without achieving anything, they read only childish drivel, and they don't do a thing. As for their knowledge of science, it's only jargon, and they have no appreciation of art either. They are all so serious, and they go about with solemn looks on their faces; they philosophize and talk about important matters; and yet before our very eyes our workers are poorly fed, they live in the worst kind of squalor, sleeping not on beds, but on the floor thirty to forty in a room—with roaches, odors, dampness, and depravity everywhere. It's perfectly clear that all our moralizing is intended to deceive not only ourselves, but others as well. Tell me, where are the nursery schools we're always talking about, where are the libraries? We only write about them in novels, but in actuality there aren't any. There's nothing but dirt, vulgarity, and decadent Orientalism. . . . I'm afraid of those serious faces, I don't like them; I'm afraid of serious talk. It would be better if we'd just keep quiet.

LOPAHIN Well, let me tell you that *I'm* up before five every morning, and I work from morning till night. I always have money, my own and other people's, and I have lots of opportunities to see what the people around me are like. You only have to start doing something to realize how few honest, decent people there are. Sometimes, when I can't sleep, I start thinking about it. God's given us immense forests, and wide-open fields, and unlimited horizons—living in such a world we ought to be giants!

LYUBOV But why do you want giants? They're all right in fairy tales, anywhere else they're terrifying.

EPIHODOV *crosses the stage in the background, playing his guitar.*

LYUBOV, *pensively.* There goes Epihodov. . . .

ANYA, *pensively.* There goes Epihodov. . . .

GAEV The sun's gone down, my friends.

TROFIMOV Yes.

GAEV, *in a subdued voice, as if reciting a poem.* Oh, glorious Nature, shining with eternal light, so beautiful, yet so indifferent

to our fate . . . you, whom we call Mother, the wellspring of
Life and Death, you live and you destroy. . . .

VARYA, *imploringly.* Uncle, please!

ANYA You're doing it again, Uncle!

TROFIMOV You'd better bank the red into middle pocket.

GAEV All right, I'll keep quiet.

*They all sit deep in thought; the only thing that can be heard
is the muttering of* FEERS. *Suddenly there is a sound in the distance, as if out of the sky, like the sound of a harp string breaking,
gradually and sadly dying away.*

LYUBOV What was that?

LOPAHIN I don't know. Sounded like a cable broke in one of
the mines. But it must've been a long way off.

GAEV Perhaps it was a bird . . . a heron, maybe.

TROFIMOV Or an owl. . . .

LYUBOV *shudders.* Whatever it was, it sounded unpleasant . . .
A pause.

FEERS It was the same way before the disaster: the owl hooted
and the samovar was humming.

GAEV What disaster?

FEERS Before they freed us. *A pause.*

LYUBOV We'd better get started, my friends. It's getting dark
and we should get home. *To* ANYA. You're crying, my darling!
What's wrong? *She embraces her.*

ANYA Nothing, Mamma. It's nothing.

TROFIMOV Someone's coming.

Enter A TRAMP *in a battered white hunting cap and an overcoat; he's slightly drunk.*

TRAMP Excuse me, but can I get to the station through here?

GAEV Yes, just follow the road.

TRAMP Much obliged to you, sir. *Coughs.* It's a beautiful day
today. *Declaiming.* "Oh, my brother, my suffering brother! . . .
Come to the Volga, whose groans . . ." *To* VARYA. Mademoiselle,
could a poor starving Russian trouble you for just enough to . . .

VARYA *cries out, frightened.*

LOPAHIN, *angrily.* Really, this is too much!

LYUBOV, *at a loss what to do.* Here, take this . . . here you are.
Looks in her purse. I haven't any silver . . . but that's all right,
here's a gold one. . . .

TRAMP Thank you very much! *Goes off. Laughter.*

VARYA, *frightened.* I'm going. . . . I'm going . . . Oh, Mamma, you know there's not even enough to eat in the house, and you gave him all that!

LYUBOV Well, what can you do with a silly woman like me? I'll give you everything I've got as soon as we get home. Yermolay Alexeyevich, you'll lend me some more, won't you?

LOPAHIN Why of course I will.

LYUBOV Come, it's time to go now. By the way, Varya, we've just about arranged your marriage. Congratulations!

VARYA, *through her tears.* Don't joke about things like that, Mother!

LOPAHIN Go to a nunnery, Okhmelia! . . .

GAEV Look at how my hands are trembling: I haven't had a game for so long.

LOPAHIN Okhmelia, nymph, remember me in your prayers!

LYUBOV Come along, everybody. It's almost supper time.

VARYA That man frightened me so. My heart's still pounding.

LOPAHIN My friends, just one thing, please just a word: the cherry orchard's to be sold on the 22nd of August. Remember that! Think of what. . . .

All go out except TROFIMOV *and* ANYA.

ANYA *laughs.* We can thank the tramp for a chance to be alone! He frightened Varya so.

TROFIMOV Varya's afraid—she's afraid we might fall in love—so she follows us about all day long. She's so narrow-minded, she can't understand that we're above falling in love. To free ourselves of all that's petty and ephemeral, all that prevents us from being free and happy, that's the whole aim and meaning of our life. Forward! We march forward irresistibly towards that bright star shining there in the distance! Forward! Don't fall behind, friends!

ANYA, *raising her hands.* How beautifully you talk! *A pause.* It's wonderful here today.

TROFIMOV Yes, the weather's marvelous.

ANYA What have you done to me, Petya? Why don't I love the cherry orchard like I used to? I used to love it so very much I used to think that there wasn't a better place in all the world than our orchard.

TROFIMOV The whole of Russia is our orchard. The earth is

great and beautiful and there are many wonderful places in it.
A pause. Just think, Anya: Your grandfather, and your great grandfather, and all your ancestors were serf owners—they owned living
souls. Don't you see human beings staring at you from every tree
in the orchard, from every leaf and every trunk? Don't you hear
their voices? . . . They owned living souls—and it has made you
all different persons, those who came before you, and you who
are living now, so that your mother, your uncle and you yourself
don't even notice that you're living on credit, at the expense of
other people, people you don't admit any further than your kitchen.
We're at least two hundred years behind the times; we have no
real values, no sense of our past, we just philosophize and complain
of how depressed we feel, and drink vodka. Yet it's obvious that
if we're ever to live in the present, we must first atone for our past
and make a clean break with it, and we can only atone for it by
suffering, by extraordinary, unceasing work. You've got to understand that, Anya.

ANYA The house we live in hasn't really been ours for a long
time. I'll leave it, I promise you.

TROFIMOV Yes, leave it, and throw away the keys. Be free as
the wind.

ANYA, *in rapture.* How beautifully you say things.

TROFIMOV You must believe me, Anya, you must. I'm not thirty
yet, I'm young, and I'm still a student, but I've suffered so much
already. As soon as winter comes, I'll be hungry and sick and
nervous, poor as a beggar. Fate has driven me everywhere! And
yet, my soul is always—every moment of every day and every
night—it's always full of such marvelous hopes and visions. I
have a premonition of happiness, Anya, I can sense it's coming. . . .

ANYA, *pensively.* The moon's coming up.

EPIHODOV *is heard playing the same melancholy tune on his
guitar. The moon comes up. Somewhere near the poplars* VARYA *is
looking for* ANYA *and calling.*

VARYA, *off-stage.* Anya! Where are you?

TROFIMOV Yes, the moon is rising. *A pause.* There it is—happiness—it's coming nearer and nearer. Already, I can hear its footsteps. And if we never see it, if we never know it, what does it
matter? Others will see it!

VARYA's *voice*. Anya! Where are you?

TROFIMOV It's Varya again! *Angrily*. It's disgusting!

ANYA Well? Let's go to the river. It's lovely there.

TROFIMOV Yes, let's. TROFIMOV *and* ANYA *go out*.

VARYA's *voice*. Anya! Anya!

Curtain.

ACT III

The drawing room separated by an arch from the ballroom. The same Jewish orchestra that was mentioned in Act II, is playing off-stage. The chandelier is lighted. It is evening. In the ballroom they are dancing the Grand-rond. SEMYONOV-PISHCHIK *is heard calling:* "Promenade à une paire!" *Then they all enter the drawing room.* PISHCHIK *and* CHARLOTTA IVANOVNA *are the first couple, followed by* TROFIMOV *and* LYUBOV, ANYA *and a* POST-OFFICE CLERK, VARYA *and* THE STATION MASTER, *etc.* VARYA *is crying softly and wipes away her tears as she dances.* DUNYASHA *is in the last couple.* PISHCHIK *shouts:* "Grand-rond balancez!" *and* "Les cavaliers à genoux et remerciez vos dames!" FEERS, *wearing a dress coat, crosses the room with soda water on a tray.* PISHCHIK *and* TROFIMOV *come back into the drawing room.*

PISHCHIK I've got this high blood-pressure—I've had two strokes already, you know—and it makes dancing hard work for me; but, as they say, if you're one of a pack, you wag your tail, whether you bark or not. Actually I'm as strong as a horse. My dear father —may he rest in peace—had a little joke. He used to say that the ancient line of Semyonov-Pishchik was descended from the very same horse that Caligula made a member of the Senate. *Sitting down*. But my trouble is, I haven't any money. A starving dog can think of nothing but food . . . *Starts to snore, but wakes up almost at once*. That's just like me—I can't think of anything but money . . .

TROFIMOV You know, you're right, there *is* something horsy about you.

PISHCHIK Well, a horse is a fine animal, you can sell a horse. . . .

The sound of someone playing billiards is heard in the next room. VARYA *appears under the arch to the ballroom.*

TROFIMOV, *teasing her.* Madame Lopahin! Madame Lopahin!

VARYA, *angrily.* The "moth-eaten man"!

TROFIMOV Yes, I am a moth-eaten man, and I'm proud of it.

VARYA, *thinking bitterly.* Now we've hired an orchestra—but how are we going to pay for it? *Goes out.*

TROFIMOV, *to* PISHCHIK. If all the energy you've spent during your life looking for money to pay the interest on your debts had been used for something useful, you'd have probably turned the world upside down by now.

PISHCHIK The philosopher Nietzsche, the greatest, the most famous—a man of the greatest intelligence, in fact—says its quite all right to counterfeit.

TROFIMOV Oh, you've read Nietzsche?

PISHCHIK Of course not, Dashenka told me. But right now I'm in such an impossible position that I could forge a few notes. The day after tomorrow I've got to pay 310 roubles. I've borrowed 130 already. . . . *Feels in his pockets, in alarm.* The money's gone! I've lost the money. *Tearfully.* Where's the money? *Joyfully.* Oh, here it is, inside the lining! I'm so upset, I'm sweating all over! . . . *Enter* LYUBOV *and* CHARLOTTA.

LYUBOV, *humming the "Lezginka."* What's taking Leonid so long? What's he doing in town? *To* DUNYASHA. Dunyasha, offer the musicians some tea.

TROFIMOV The auction was probably postponed.

LYUBOV The orchestra came at the wrong time, and the party started at the wrong time . . . Oh, well . . . never mind . . . *She sits down and hums quietly.*

CHARLOTTA *hands a deck of cards to* PISHCHIK. Here's a deck of cards—think of any card.

PISHCHIK I've thought of one.

CHARLOTTA Now shuffle the deck. That's right. Now give it to me, my dear Monsieur Pishchik. "*Ein, zwei, drei!*" Why look! There it is, in your coat pocket.

PISHCHIK *takes the card out of his coat pocket*. The eight of spades, that's right! *In astonishment*. Isn't that amazing!

CHARLOTTA, *holding the deck of cards on the palm of her hand, to* TROFIMOV. Quickly, which card's on the top?

TROFIMOV Well . . . ahh . . . the queen of spades.

CHARLOTTA You're right, here it is! Now, which card?

PISHCHIK The ace of hearts.

CHARLOTTA Right again! *She claps her hand over the pack of cards, which disappears*. What beautiful weather we're having today! *A woman's voice, as if coming from underneath the floor, answers her*.

VOICE Oh yes, indeed, the weather's perfectly marvelous!

CHARLOTTA, *addressing the voice*. How charming you are! I'm fond of you!

VOICE And I like you very much, too.

STATION MASTER, *applauding*. Bravo, Madame ventriloquist! Bravo!

PISHCHIK, *astonished*. Isn't that amazing! Charlotta Ivanovna, you're absolutely wonderful! I'm completely in love with you!

CHARLOTTA, *shrugging her shoulders*. In love? What do you know about love? "*Guter Mensch, aber schlechter Musikant.*"

TROFIMOV *slaps* PISHCHIK *on the shoulder*. He's just an old horse, he is!

CHARLOTTA Your attention please! Here's one more trick. *She takes a shawl from a chair*. Now there's this very nice shawl . . . *Shakes it out*. Who'd like to buy it?

PISHCHIK, *amazed*. Imagine that!

CHARLOTTA "*Ein, zwei, drei!*"

She lifts up the shawl and ANYA *is standing behind it;* ANYA *curtsies, runs to her mother, gives her a hug, and runs back to the ballroom. Everybody's delighted*.

LYUBOV, *clapping*. Bravo, bravo!

CHARLOTTA Once more. "*Ein, zwei, drei!*"

Lifts the shawl again; behind it is VARYA, *who bows*.

PISHCHIK, *amazed*. Isn't that amazing!

CHARLOTTA It's all over! *She throws the shawl over* PISHCHIK, *curtsies, and runs into the ballroom*.

PISHCHIK, *going after her*. You little rascal! . . . Have you ever seen anything like her? What a girl . . . *Goes out*.

LYUBOV Leonid's still not here. I can't understand what's keeping him all this time in town. Anyway, by now everything's been settled; either the estate's been sold or the auction didn't take place. Why does he wait so long to let us know?

VARYA, *trying to comfort her.* Uncle's bought it, I'm sure he did.

TROFIMOV, *sarcastically.* Why of course he did!

VARYA Our great-aunt sent him power of attorney to buy it in her name, and transfer the mortgage to her. She's done it for Anya's sake . . . God will look after us, I'm sure of it—Uncle will buy the estate.

LYUBOV Your great-aunt sent us fifteen thousand to buy the estate in her name—she doesn't trust us—but that's not enough to even pay the interest. *She covers her face with her hands.* My fate is being decided today, my fate. . . .

TROFIMOV, *to* VARYA, *teasingly.* Madame Lopahin!

VARYA, *crossly.* The perpetual student! Why, you've been thrown out of the University twice already!

LYUBOV But why get so cross, Varya? He's only teasing you about Lopahin, there's no harm in that, is there? If you want to, why don't you marry him; he's a fine man, and he's interesting, too. Of course, if you don't want to, don't. No one's trying to force you, darling.

VARYA I'm very serious about this, Mother . . . and I want to be frank with you . . . he's a good man and I like him.

LYUBOV Then marry him. What are you waiting for? I don't understand you at all.

VARYA But, Mother, I can't propose to him myself, can I? It's been two years now since everybody began talking to me about him, and everybody's talking, but he doesn't say a word, or when he does, he just jokes with me. I understand, of course. He's getting rich and his mind's busy with other things, and he hasn't any time for me. If only I had some money, even a little, just a hundred roubles, I'd leave everything and go away, the farther the better. I'd go into a convent.

TROFIMOV How beautiful!

VARYA, *to* TROFIMOV. Of course, a student like you has to be so intelligent! *Quietly and tearfully.* How ugly you've become, Petya, how much older you look! *To* LYUBOV, *her tearfulness gone.* The only thing I can't stand, Mother, is not having any work to do. I've got to stay busy.

Enter YASHA.

YASHA, *with difficulty restraining his laughter.* Epihodov's broken a cue! . . . *Goes out.*

VARYA But what's Epihodov doing here? Who let him play billiards? I don't understand these people. . . . *Goes out.*

LYUBOV Please don't tease her, Petya. Don't you see she's upset already?

TROFIMOV Oh, she's such a busy-body—always sticking her nose into other people's business. She hasn't left Anya and me alone all summer. She's afraid we might fall in love. What difference should it make to her? Besides, I didn't give her any reason to think so. I don't believe in such trivialities. We're above love!

LYUBOV And I suppose I'm below love. *Uneasily.* Why isn't Leonid back? If only I knew whether the estate's been sold or not. It's such an incredible calamity that for some reason I don't know what to think, I feel so helpless. I think I'm going to scream this very minute . . . I'll do something silly. Help me, Petya. Talk to me, say something!

TROFIMOV What difference does it make whether the estate's sold today or not? It was gone a long time ago. You can't turn back, the path's lost. You mustn't worry, and above all you mustn't deceive yourself. For once in your life you must look the truth straight in the face.

LYUBOV What truth? *You* know what truth is and what it isn't, but I've lost such visionary powers. I don't see anything. You're able to solve all your problems so decisively—but, tell me, my dear boy, isn't that because you're young, because life is still hidden from your young eyes, because you can't believe anything horrible will ever happen to you and you don't expect it to? Oh, yes, you're more courageous and honest and serious than we are, but put yourself in our position, try to be generous—if only a little bit—and have pity on me. I was born here, you know, and my father and mother lived here, and my grandfather, too, and I love this house—I can't conceive of life without the cherry orchard, and if it really has to be sold, then sell me with it . . . *Embraces* TROFIMOV, *kisses him on the forehead.* You know, my little boy was drowned here. . . . *Weeps.* Have pity on me, my dear, kind friend.

TROFIMOV You know that I sympathize with you from the bottom of my heart.

LYUBOV But you should say it differently . . . differently. *Takes out her handkerchief and a telegram falls on to the floor.* There's so much on my mind today, you can't imagine. It's so noisy around here that my soul trembles with every sound, and I'm shaking all over—yet I can't go to my room because the silence of being alone frightens me. . . . Don't blame me, Petya. . . . I love you as if you were my own son. I'd gladly let Anya marry you, honestly I would, but, my dear boy, you must study, you've got to graduate. You don't do anything, Fate tosses you from one place to another —it's so strange—Well, it is, isn't it? Isn't it? And you should do something about your beard, make it grow somehow. . . . *Laughs.* You look so funny!

TROFIMOV *picks up the telegram.* I don't care how I look. That's so superficial.

LYUBOV This telegram's from Paris. I get one every day . . . Yesterday, today. That beast is sick again, and everything's going wrong for him. . . . He wants me to forgive him, he begs me to return, and, really, I suppose I should go to Paris and stay with him for a while. You're looking very stern, Petya, but what am I to do, my dear boy, what am I to do? He's sick, and lonely, and unhappy, and who'll take care of him, who'll stop him from making a fool of himself, and give him his medicine at the right time? And anyway, why should I hide it, or keep quiet about it? I love him; yes, I love him. I do, I do. . . . He's a stone around my neck, and I'm sinking to the bottom with him—but I love him and I can't live without him. *She presses* TROFIMOV'S *hand.* Don't think I'm evil, Petya, don't say anything, please don't. . . .

TROFIMOV, *with strong emotion.* Please—forgive my frankness, but that man's swindling you!

LYUBOV No, no, no, you mustn't talk like that. . . . *Puts her hands over her ears.*

TROFIMOV But he's a scoundrel, and you're the only one who doesn't know it! He's a despicable, worthless scoundrel. . . .

LYUBOV, *angry, but in control of herself.* You're twenty-six or twenty-seven years old, but you're talking like a schoolboy!

TROFIMOV Say whatever you want!

LYUBOV You should be a man at your age, you ought to understand what it means to be in love. And you should be in love. . . . Tell me, why haven't you fallen in love! *Angrily.* Yes, yes! Oh, you're not so "pure," your purity is a perversion, you're nothing but a ridiculous prude, a freak. . . .

TROFIMOV, *horrified.* What is she saying?

LYUBOV "I'm above love!" You're not above love, you're useless, as Feers would say. Imagine not having a mistress at your age! . . .

TROFIMOV, *horrified.* This is terrible! What's she saying? *Goes quickly towards the ballroom, clutching his head between his hands.* This is dreadful. . . . I can't stand it, I'm going. . . . *Goes out, but returns at once.* Everything's over between us! *Goes out through the door into the hall.*

LYUBOV *calls after him.* Petya, wait! You funny boy, I was only joking! Petya!

Someone can be heard running quickly downstairs and suddenly falling down with a crash. ANYA *and* VARYA *scream, and then begin laughing.*

What's happened?

ANYA *runs in.*

ANYA, *laughing.* Petya fell down the stairs. *Runs out.*

LYUBOV What a strange boy he is!

The STATION MASTER *stands in the middle of the ballroom and begins to recite "The Sinner" by Alexey Tolstoy. The others listen to him, but he's hardly had time to recite more than a little bit when a waltz is played, and he stops. Everyone dances.* TROFIMOV, ANYA, VARYA *come in from the hall.*

Poor Petya . . . there, my dear boy . . . Please forgive me . . . Come, let's dance . . . *She dances with* PETYA. ANYA *and* VARYA *dance. Enter* FEERS, *then* YASHA. FEERS *leans on his cane by the side door.* YASHA *looks at the dancers from the drawing room.*

YASHA How are you, old boy?

FEERS Not too well . . . We used to have generals, barons, and admirals at our parties . . . long ago, but now we send for the post-office clerk and the station master, and even they don't want to come it seems. I seem to be getting weaker somehow . . .

My old master, the mistress' grandfather, used to make everyone take sealing wax no matter what was wrong with them. I've been taking it every day for the last twenty years, maybe even longer. Perhaps that's why I'm still alive.

YASHA How you bore me, old man! *Yawns.* Why don't you just go away and die . . . It's about time.

FEERS Eh, you! . . . You're useless . . . *Mutters.*

TROFIMOV *and* LYUBOV *dancing, come into the drawing room.*

LYUBOV Thank you. I think I'll sit down for a bit. *Sits down.* I'm tired.

Enter ANYA.

ANYA, *agitated.* There's a man in the kitchen who's been saying that the cherry orchard was sold today.

LYUBOV Sold? To whom?

ANYA He didn't say. He's gone.

She and TROFIMOV *dance into the ballroom.*

YASHA There was some old man gossiping there. A stranger.

FEERS Leonid Andreyevich isn't back yet, he hasn't come yet. And he's only got his light overcoat on; he'll probably catch a cold. Oh, these youngsters!

LYUBOV I've got to know, or I think I'll die. Yasha, go and find out who bought it.

YASHA But the old guy went away a long time ago. *Laughs.*

LYUBOV, *with a touch of annoyance.* What are you laughing at? What's so humorous?

YASHA Epihodov's so funny—he's so stupid. Two-and-twenty misfortunes!

LYUBOV Feers, if the estate's sold, where will you go?

FEERS I'll go wherever you tell me to go.

LYUBOV Why are you looking like that? Aren't you well? You ought to be in bed.

FEERS Yes . . . *With a faint smile.* But if I went to bed, who'd take care of the guests and keep things going? There's no one in the house but me.

YASHA, *to* LYUBOV Lyubov Andreyevna! I want to ask you something! If you go back to Paris, will you please take me with you? I couldn't stand staying here. *Looking round and speaking in a low voice.* I don't have to say it, you can see for yourself how un-civilized everything is here. The people are immoral, it's frightfully dull, and the food is terrible. And then there's that Feers walking about the place and muttering all sorts of stupid things. Take me with you, please!

Enter PISHCHIK.

PISHCHIK May I have this dance, beautiful lady . . . LYUBOV *gets up to dance.* I'll have that 180 roubles from you yet, you enchantress . . . Yes, I will . . . *Dances.* Just 180 roubles, that's all . . . *They go into the ballroom.*

YASHA *sings quietly.* "Don't you understand the passion in my soul? . . ."

In the ballroom a woman in a grey top hat and check trousers starts jumping and throwing her arms about; shouts of: "Bravo, Charlotta Ivanovna!"

DUNYASHA *stops to powder her face.* Anya told me to dance: there are so many men and not enough ladies; but I get so dizzy from dancing and it makes my heart beat so fast. Feers Nikolaye-vich, the post-office clerk said something to me just now that completely took my breath away. *The music stops.*

FEERS What did he say?

DUNYASHA You're like a flower, he said.

YASHA *yawns* What ignorance! . . . *Goes out.*

DUNYASHA Like a flower . . . I'm so sensitive, I love it when people say beautiful things to me.

FEERS You'll be having your head turned if you're not careful. *Enter* EPIHODOV.

EPIHODOV Avdotya Fyodorovna, you act as if you don't want to see me . . . as if I were some kind of insect. *Sighs.* Such is life!

DUNYASHA What do you want?

EPIHODOV But then, you may be right. *Sighs.* Of course, if one looks at it from a certain point of view—if I may so express my-self, and please excuse my frankness, you've driven me into such a state . . . Oh, I know what my fate is; every day some mis-fortune's sure to happen to me, but I've long since been accus-tomed to that, so I look at life with a smile. You gave me your word, and though I . . .

DUNYASHA Please, let's talk later, just let me alone now. I'm lost in a dream. *Plays with her fan.*

EPIHODOV Some misfortune happens to me every day, but I— how should I put it—I just smile, I even laugh.

VARYA *enters from the ballroom.*

VARYA Are you still here, Semyon? Your manners are abominable, really! *To* DUNYASHA. You'd better go now, Dunyasha. *To* EPIHODOV. First you play billiards and break a cue, and now you're going about the drawing room, like one of the guests.

EPIHODOV Permit me to inform you, but you have no right to attack me like this.

VARYA I'm not attacking, I'm telling you. You just wander from one place to another, instead of doing your work. We've hired a clerk, but why no one knows.

EPIHODOV, *offended.* Whether I work, wander, eat, or play billiards, the only people who are entitled to judge my actions are those who are older than me and have some idea of what they're talking about.

VARYA How dare you say that to me? *Beside herself in anger.* You dare to say that? Are you suggesting that I don't know what I'm talking about? Get out of here! Right now!

EPIHODOV, *cowed.* I wish you'd express yourself more delicately.

VARYA, *beside herself.* Get out this minute! Get out! *He goes to the door, she follows him.* Two-and-twenty misfortunes! Get out of here! I don't want ever to see you again!

EPIHODOV *goes out; his voice is heard from outside the door.* I'm going to complain.

VARYA Oh, you're coming back, are you? *She seizes the stick which* FEERS *left by the door.* Well, come along, come in . . . I'll show you! So, you're coming back . . . are you? There, take that . . . *Swings the stick, and at that moment* LOPAHIN *comes in.*

LOPAHIN, *whom the stick did not, in fact, touch.* Thank you very much!

VARYA, *angry and ironically.* I'm sorry!

LOPAHIN Don't mention it. I'm much obliged to you for the kind reception.

VARYA That's quite all right. *Walks away and then looks around and asks gently.* I haven't hurt you, have I?

LOPAHIN No, not at all. . . . But there's going to be a huge bump, though.

VOICES, *in the ballroom.* Lopahin's here! Yermolay Alexeyevich!

PISHCHIK There he is! You can see him, do you hear him? . . .

Embraces LOPAHIN. You smell of cognac, my good fellow! . . . Well we're having a party here, too.

Enter LYUBOV.

LYUBOV It's you, Yermolay Alexeyevich? What's taken you so long? Where's Leonid?

LOPAHIN Leonid Andreyevich's here, he'll be along in a minute.

LYUBOV, *agitated.* Well, what happened? Was there an auction? Tell me!

LOPAHIN, *embarrassed, afraid of betraying his joy.* The auction was over by four o'clock . . . We missed our train and had to wait until nine-thirty. *Sighs heavily.* Ugh! I feel a little dizzy . . .

Enter GAEV; *he carries packages in his right hand and wipes away his tears with his left.*

LYUBOV Leonia, what happened? Leonia? *Impatiently, with tears.* Tell me quickly, for God's sake! . . .

GAEV *doesn't answer, but waves his hand. To* FEERS, *crying.* Here, take these . . . it's some anchovies and Kerch herrings . . . I haven't eaten all day . . . What I've been through!

Through the open door leading to the ballroom a game of billiards can be heard and YASHA's *voice is heard.*

YASHA Seven and eighteen.

GAEV, *his expression changes and he stops crying.* I'm very tired. Come, Feers, I want to change my things. *Goes out through the ballroom, followed by* FEERS.

PISHCHIK Well, what happened at the auction? Come on, tell us!

LYUBOV Has the cherry orchard been sold?

LOPAHIN It has.

LYUBOV Who bought it?

LOPAHIN I did.

A pause. LYUBOV *is overcome; only the fact that she is standing beside a table and a chair keeps her from falling.* VARYA *takes the keys from her belt, throws them on the floor in the middle of the room and goes out.*

I bought it. Wait a moment, ladies and gentlemen, please. I'm so mixed up, I don't quite know what to say . . . *Laughs.* When we got to the auction, Deriganov was already there. Leonid had only fifteen thousand roubles, and immediately Deriganov bid thirty thousand over and above the mortgage. I saw how things were, so I stepped in and raised it to forty. He bid forty-five, I went to fifty-five; he kept on raising five thousand and I raised it ten thousand. Well, finally it ended—I bid ninety thousand over and above the mortgage, and it went to me. The cherry orchard's mine now! All right, tell me I'm drunk, tell me I'm crazy and that I'm just imagining all this. . . . *Stamps his feet.* Don't laugh at me! If only my father and grandfather could rise from their graves and see all that's happened . . . how their Yermolay, their ignorant, beaten Yermolay, the little boy that ran around in his bare feet in the winter . . . if only they could see that he's bought this estate, the most beautiful place in the world! Yes, he's bought the very estate where his father and grandfather were slaves and where they weren't even admitted to the kitchen! I must be asleep, I'm dreaming, it only seems to be true . . . it's all just my imagination, my imagination must be confused . . . *Picks up the keys, smiling gently.* She threw these down because she wanted to show that she's not the mistress here anymore. *Jingles the keys.* Well, never mind. *The orchestra is heard tuning up.* Hey there! you musicians, play something for us! I want some music! My friends, come along and soon you'll see Yermolay Lopahin take an axe to the cherry orchard, you'll see the trees come crashing to the ground! We're going to build hundreds of summer cottages, and our children and our grandchildren will see a whole new world growing up here . . . So play, let's have some music!

The band plays. LYUBOV *has sunk into a chair and is crying bitterly. Reproachfully.*

Why, why didn't you listen to me? My poor, dear lady, you'll never get it back now. *With tears.* Oh, if only all this could be over soon, if only we could change this unhappy and disjointed life of ours somehow!

PISHCHIK, *taking his arm, in a low voice.* She's crying. Come into the ballroom, let her be by herself . . . Come on . . . *Takes his arm and leads him away to the ballroom.*

LOPAHIN What's the matter! Where's the music? Come on, play! Play! Everything will be as *I* want it now. *Ironically.* Here comes the new owner, here comes the owner of the cherry orchard! *He tips over a little table accidentally and nearly upsets the candelabra.* Don't worry about it, I can pay for everything! *Goes out with* PISHCHIK. *There is no one left in the ballroom or drawing room, but* LYUBOV, *who sits huddled up in a chair, crying bitterly. The orchestra continues to play quietly.* ANYA *and* TROFIMOV *enter quickly;* ANYA *goes up to her mother and kneels beside her,* TROFIMOV *remains at the entrance to the ballroom.*

ANYA Mamma! . . . Mamma, you're crying. Dear, kind, good Mamma, my precious one, I love you! God bless you, Mamma! The cherry orchard's sold, that's true, it's gone, but don't cry, Mamma, you still have your life ahead of you, you still have your good, innocent heart. You must come with me, Mamma, away from here! We'll plant a new orchard, even more wonderful than this one—and when you see it, you'll understand everything, and your heart will be filled with joy, like the sun in the evening; and then you'll smile again, Mamma! Come, dearest one, come with me! . . .

Curtain.

ACT IV

The same setting as for Act I. There are no pictures on the walls or curtains at the windows; most of the furniture is gone and the few remaining pieces are stacked in a corner, as if for sale. There is a sense of desolation. Beside the door, suitcases and other luggage have been piled together. The voices of VARYA *and* ANYA *can be heard through the door on the left, which is open.* LOPAHIN *stands waiting;* YASHA *is holding a tray with glasses of champagne. In the hall* EPIHODOV *is tying up a large box. Off-stage there is a low hum of voices; the peasants have called to say good-bye.* GAEV'S *voice from off-stage.*

GAEV Thank you, friends, thank you.

YASHA The peasants have come to say good-bye. In my opinion, Yermolay Alexeyevich, they're good people, but they don't know much.

The hum subsides. LYUBOV *and* GAEV *enter from the hall;* LYUBOV *is not crying but her face is pale and it quivers. She is unable to speak.*

GAEV You gave them everything you had, Lyuba. You shouldn't have done that. You really shouldn't.

LYUBOV I couldn't help it! I couldn't help it! *Both go out.*

LOPAHIN *calls after them through the door.* Please, have some champagne, please do! Just a little glass before you go. I didn't think to bring some from town, and at the station I could find only this one bottle. Please have some. *A pause.* You don't want any, my friends? *Walks away from the door.* If I'd known that, I wouldn't have brought it. . . . Well, then I won't have any either. YASHA *carefully puts the tray on a chair.* Have a drink, Yasha, nobody else wants any.

YASHA To the travelers! And to those staying behind. *Drinks.* This champagne isn't the real thing, believe me.

LOPAHIN What do you mean, eight roubles a bottle. *A pause.* God, it's cold in here.

YASHA The stoves weren't lit today. What difference does it make since we're leaving? *Laughs.*

LOPAHIN Why are you laughing?

YASHA Because I feel good.

LOPAHIN It's October already, but it's still sunny and clear, just like summer. Good building weather. *Looks at his watch, then at the door.* Ladies and gentlemen, the train leaves in forty-seven minutes. We've got to start in twenty minutes. So hurry up.

TROFIMOV, *wearing an overcoat, comes in from outdoors.*

TROFIMOV It's time we get started. The horses are ready. God knows where my goloshes are, they've disappeared. *Calls through the door.* Anya, my goloshes aren't here; I can't find them.

LOPAHIN I've got to go to Kharkov. I'm taking the same train. I'll be spending the winter in Kharkov: I've stayed around here too long, and it drives me crazy having nothing to do. I can't be without work: I just don't know what to do with my hands; they hang there, as if they didn't belong to me.

TROFIMOV We'll be gone soon, then you can start making money again.

LOPAHIN Have a drink.

TROFIMOV No, thanks.

LOPAHIN So, you're going to Moscow?

TROFIMOV Yes, I'll go with them to town, and then, tomorrow I'll leave for Moscow.

LOPAHIN I suppose the professors are waiting for you to come before they begin classes.

TROFIMOV That's none of your business.

LOPAHIN How many years have you been studying at the university?

TROFIMOV Can't you say something new for a change, that's getting pretty old. *Looks for his goloshes.* By the way, since we probably won't see each other again, let me give you a bit of advice, as we say good-bye: stop waving your arms! Try to get rid of that habit of making wide, sweeping gestures. And another thing, all this talk about building estates, these calculations about summer tourists that are going to buy property, all these predictions —they're all sweeping gestures, too. . . . You know, in spite of everything, I like you. You've got beautiful delicate fingers, like an artist's, you've a fine, sensitive soul. . . .

LOPAHIN *embraces him.* Good-bye, my friend. Thanks for everything. I can give you some money for your trip, if you need it.

TROFIMOV What for? I don't need it.

LOPAHIN But you haven't got any!

TROFIMOV Yes, I have, thank you. I got some money for a translation. Here it is, in my pocket. *Anxiously.* But I can't find my goloshes.

VARYA, *from the other room.* Here, take the nasty things! *She throws a pair of rubber goloshes into the room.*

TROFIMOV What are you so angry about, Varya? Hm . . . but these aren't my goloshes!

LOPAHIN I sowed three thousand acres of poppies last spring, and I've made forty thousand on it. And when they were in bloom, what a picture it was! What I mean to say is that I've made the forty thousand, so now I can lend you some money. Why be so stuck up? So I'm a peasant . . . I speak right out.

TROFIMOV Your father was a peasant, mine was a druggist. What's that got to do with it? LOPAHIN *takes out his wallet.* Forget it, put it away . . . Even if you offered me two hundred thousand, I wouldn't take it. I'm a free man. And all that you rich men—and poor men too—all that you value so highly doesn't have the slightest power over me—it's all just so much fluff floating about in the air. I'm strong and I'm proud! I can get along without you, I can pass you by. Humanity is advancing towards the highest truth, the greatest happiness that it's possible to achieve on earth, and I'm one of the avant-garde!

LOPAHIN Will you get there?

TROFIMOV Yes. *A pause.* I'll get there myself, or show others the way to get there.

The sound of an axe hitting a tree is heard in the distance.

LOPAHIN Well, my friend, it's time to go. Good-bye. We show off in front of one another, and all the time life is slipping by. When I work all day long, without resting, I'm happier and sometimes I even think I know why I exist. But how many people there are in Russia, my friend, who exist for no reason at all. But, never mind, it doesn't matter. They say Leonid Andreyevich has a job at the bank, at six thousand a year. That won't last long; he's too lazy. . . .

ANYA, *in the doorway.* Mamma begs you not to let them cut down the orchard until we've left.

TROFIMOV Really, haven't you got any tact? *Goes out through the hall.*

LOPAHIN All right, I'll take care of it. . . . These people! *Follows* TROFIMOV.

ANYA Has Feers been taken to the hospital?

YASHA I told them to take him this morning. He's gone, I think.

ANYA, *to* EPIHODOV, *who passes through the ballroom.* Semyon Pantaleyevich, will you please find out whether Feers has been taken to the hospital?

YASHA, *offended.* I told Yegor this morning. Why ask a dozen times?

EPIHODOV That old Feers—frankly speaking, I mean—he's beyond repair, it's time he joined his ancestors. As for me, I can only envy him. *He places a suitcase on top of a cardboard hatbox and squashes it.* There you are, you see! . . . I might have known it! *Goes out.*

YASHA, *sardonically.* Two-and-twenty misfortunes!

VARYA, *from behind the door.* Has Feers been taken to the hospital?

ANYA Yes.

VARYA Why wasn't the letter to the doctor taken then?

ANYA I'll send someone after them with it . . . *Goes out.*

VARYA, *from the adjoining room.* Where's Yasha? Tell him his mother is here and wants to say good-bye to him.

YASHA *waves his hand.* This is too much! I'll lose my patience.

While the foregoing action has been taking place, DUNYASHA *has been busy with the luggage; now that* YASHA *is alone, she comes up to him.*

DUNYASHA If only you'd look at me just once, Yasha! You're going . . . you're leaving me! . . . *She cries and throws her arms around his neck.*

YASHA What are you crying for? *Drinks champagne.* In a week I'll be in Paris again. Tomorrow we'll get on the train—and off we'll go—gone! I can't believe it. *"Vive la France!"* I can't stand it here and could never live here—nothing ever happens. I've seen enough of all this ignorance. I've had enough of it. *Drinks.* What are you crying for? Behave yourself properly, then you won't cry.

DUNYASHA, *looking into a handmirror and powdering her nose.* Please, write to me from Paris. You know how much I've loved you, Yasha. Oh, I've loved you so much! I'm very sensitive, Yasha!

YASHA Sshh, someone's coming. *Pretends to be busy with a suitcase, humming quietly.*

Enter LYUBOV ANDREYEVNA, GAEV, ANYA *and* CHARLOTTA IVANOVNA.

GAEV We've got to leave soon. There isn't much time left. *Looks at* YASHA. What a smell! Who's been eating herring?

LYUBOV We'll have to leave in the carriage in ten minutes. *Looks about the room.* Good-bye, dear house, the home of our fathers. Winter will pass and spring will come again, and then you won't be here any more, you'll be torn down. How much these walls have seen! *Kisses her daughter passionately.* My little treasure, how radiant you look, your eyes are shining like diamonds. Are you glad? Very glad?

ANYA Oh, yes, very glad, Mamma! Our new life is just beginning!

GAEV, *gaily.* Really, everything's all right now. Before the cherry orchard was sold we were all worried and upset, but as soon as things were settled once and for all, we all calmed down and even felt quite cheerful. I'm working in a bank now, a real financier. . . . The red into the side pocket . . . And say what you like, Lyuba, you're looking much better. No doubt about it.

LYUBOV Yes, that's true, my nerves are better. *Someone helps her on with her hat and coat.* I'm sleeping better, too. Take out my things, Yasha, it's time. *To* ANYA. My little darling, we'll be seeing each other again soon. I'm going to Paris—I'll live on the money which your Grandmother sent us to buy the estate—God bless Grandmamma!—but that money won't last very long either.

ANYA You'll come back soon, Mamma . . . won't you? I'll study and pass my exams and then I'll work and help you. We'll read together, Mamma . . . all sorts of things . . . won't we? *She kisses her mother's hands.* We'll read during the long autumn evenings. We'll read lots of books, and a new wonderful world will open up before us . . . *Dreamily.* Mamma, come back soon . . .

LYUBOV I'll come back, my precious. *Embraces her.*

Enter LOPAHIN. CHARLOTTA *quietly sings to herself.*

GAEV Happy Charlotta! She's singing.

CHARLOTTA *picks up a bundle that looks like a baby in a blanket.* Bye-bye, little baby. *A sound like a baby crying is heard.* Hush, be quiet, my darling, be a good little boy. *The "crying" continues.* Oh, my baby, you poor thing! *Throws the bundle down.* Are you going to find me another job? If you don't mind, I've got to have one.

LOPAHIN We'll find you one, Charlotta Ivanovna, don't worry.

GAEV Everybody's leaving us, Varya's going away . . . all of a sudden nobody wants us.

CHARLOTTA There's no place for me to live in town. I'll have to go. *Hums.* Oh, well, what do I care. *Enter* PISHCHIK.

LOPAHIN Look what's here!

PISHCHIK, *gasping for breath.* Oohhh, let me get my breath . . . I'm worn out . . . My good friends. . . . Give me some water . . .

GAEV I suppose you want to borrow some money? I'm going . . . Excuse me . . . *Goes out.*

PISHCHIK I haven't seen you for a long time . . . my beautiful lady . . . *To* LOPAHIN. You're here, too . . . glad to see you . . . you're a man of great intelligence . . . here . . . take this . . . *Gives money to* LOPAHIN. Four hundred roubles . . . I still owe you eight hundred and forty. . . .

LOPAHIN, *shrugging his shoulders in amazement.* It's like a dream. . . . Where did you get it?

PISHCHIK Wait a minute . . . I'm so hot . . . A most extraordinary thing happened. Some Englishman came along and discovered some kind of white clay on my land. . . . *To* LYUBOV. Here's four hundred for you also, my dear . . . enchantress . . . *Gives her the money.* You'll get the rest later. *Takes a drink of water.* A young man on the train was just telling me that some great philosopher advises people to jump off roofs. You just jump off, he says, and that settles the whole problem. *Amazed at what he has just said.* Imagine that! More water, please.

LOPAHIN What Englishmen?

PISHCHIK I leased the land to them for twenty-four years. . . . And now you must excuse me, I'm in a hurry and have to get on. I'm going to Znoikov's, then to Kardamonov's . . . I owe them all money. *Drinks.* Your health. I'll come again on Thursday . . .

LYUBOV We're just leaving for town, and tomorrow I'm going abroad.

PISHCHIK What's that? *In agitation.* Why to town? Oh, I see . . . this furniture and the suitcases. . . . Well, never mind . . . *Tearfully.* What difference does it make. . . . These Englishmen, you know, they're very intelligent . . . Never mind. . . . I wish you all the best, God bless you. Never mind, everything comes to an end eventually. *Kisses* LYUBOV's *hand.* And when you hear that my end has come, just think of a horse, and say: "There used to be a man like that once. . . his name was Semyonov-Pishchik— God bless him!" Wonderful weather we're having. Yes . . . *Goes out embarrassed, but returns at once and stands in the doorway.* Dashenka sends her greetings. *Goes out.*

LYUBOV Well, we can get started now. I'm leaving with two worries on my mind. One is Feers—he's sick. *Glances at her watch.* We've still got five minutes. . . .

ANYA Mamma, Feers has been taken to the hospital. Yasha sent him his morning.

LYUBOV The other is Varya. She's used to getting up early and working, and now, with nothing to do, she's like a fish out of water. She's gotten so thin and pale, and she cries a lot, the poor dear. *A pause.* You know very well, Yermolay Alexeyevich, that I've been hoping you two would get married . . . and everything pointed to it. *Whispers to* ANYA *and motions to* CHARLOTTA, *and they both go out.* She loves you, and you're fond of her, too . . . I just don't know, I don't know why you seem to avoid each other. I don't understand it.

LOPAHIN Neither do I, I admit it. The whole thing's so strange. . . . If there's still time, I'm ready to. . . . Let's settle it at once—and get it over with! Without you here, I don't feel I'll ever propose to her.

LYUBOV That's an excellent idea! You won't need more than a minute. I'll call her at once.

LOPAHIN And there's champagne here, too, we'll celebrate. *Looks at the glasses.* They're empty, someone's drunk it all. YASHA *coughs.* They must have poured it down.

LYUBOV, *with animation.* Oh, I'm so glad. I'll call her, and we'll leave you alone. Yasha, *"allez!" Through the door.* Varya, come here for a minute, leave what you're doing and come here! Varya! *Goes out with* YASHA.

LOPAHIN, *looking at his watch.* Yes. . . .

A pause. Whispering and suppressed laughter are heard behind the door, then VARYA *comes in and starts fussing with the luggage. At last she says:*

VARYA That's strange, I can't find it. . . .

LOPAHIN What are you looking for?

VARYA I packed it myself, and I can't remember . . . *A pause.*

LOPAHIN Where are you going to now, Varvara Mihailovna?

VARYA I? To the Rogulins. I've taken a job as their housekeeper.

LOPAHIN That's in Yashnevo, isn't it? Almost seventy miles from here. *A pause.* So this is the end of life in this house. . . .

VARYA, *still fussing with the luggage.* Where could it be? Perhaps I put it in the trunk? Yes, life in this house has come to an end . . . there won't be any more. . . .

LOPAHIN And I'm going to Kharkov. . . . On the next train. I've got a lot of work to do there. I'm leaving Epihodov here. . . . I've hired him.

VARYA Really! . . .

LOPAHIN Remember, last year at this time it was snowing already, but now it's still so bright and sunny. Though it's cold . . . Three degrees of frost.

VARYA I haven't looked. *A pause*. Besides, our thermometer's broken. . . .

A pause. A voice is heard from outside the door.

VOICE Yermolay Alexeyevich!

LOPAHIN, *as if he had been waiting for it*. I'm coming! Right away! *Goes out quickly*.

VARYA *sits on the floor, with her head on a bundle of clothes, crying quietly. The door opens*, LYUBOV *enters hesitantly*.

LYUBOV Well? *A pause*. We must be going.

VARYA *stops crying and wipes her eyes*. Yes, Mamma, it's time we got started. I'll just have time to get to the Rogulins today, if we don't miss the train.

LYUBOV *calls through the door*. Anya, put your things on.

Enter ANYA, *followed by* GAEV *and* CHARLOTTA. GAEV *wears a heavy overcoat with a hood. Servants and coachmen come into the room.* EPIHODOV *is picking up the luggage*. Now we can begin our journey!

ANYA, *joyfully*. Our journey!

GAEV My friends, my dear, beloved friends! As I leave this house forever, how can I be silent, how can I refrain from expressing to you, as I say good-bye for the last time, the feelings which now overwhelm me. . . .

ANYA, *begging*. Uncle!

VARYA Uncle, please don't!

GAEV, *downcast*. I put the red into the corner and then . . . I'll keep quiet.

Enter TROFIMOV *and* LOPAHIN.

TROFIMOV Well, ladies and gentlemen, it's time we get started.

LOPAHIN Epihodov, my coat!

LYUBOV I'll just stay for one more minute. It seems as if I'd never seen the walls and ceilings of this house before, and now I look at them with such longing, such love. . . .

GAEV I remember when I was six—it was Trinity Sunday . . . I was sitting here at this window watching father on his way to church. . . .

LYUBOV Have they taken everything out?

LOPAHIN It looks like it. *To* EPIHODOV, *as he puts on his coat*. Be sure to take care of everything, Epihodov.

EPIHODOV, *in a husky voice.* Don't worry, Yermolay Alexeyevich!

LOPAHIN What is wrong with your voice?

EPIHODOV I just had some water, and it went down the wrong throat.

YASHA, *with contempt.* What a fool!

LYUBOV After we leave, there won't be a soul here. . . .

LOPAHIN Not until spring.

VARYA *pulls an umbrella from a bundle of clothes;* LOPAHIN *pretends to be afraid.* What are you doing that for? . . . I didn't mean to. . . .

TROFIMOV Ladies and gentlemen, hurry up, it's time. The train will be here soon.

VARYA Pyeta, here are your goloshes beside the suitcase. *Tearfully.* How dirty and old they are! . . .

TROFIMOV *puts them on.* Hurry up, ladies and gentlemen!

GAEV, *greatly embarrassed, afraid of breaking into tears.* The train, the station . . . The red off the white into the middle pocket. . . .

LYUBOV Let us go!

LOPAHIN Are we all here? No one left? *Locks the door on the left.* There are some things stored in there, best to keep it locked up. Come along!

ANYA Good-bye, old house! Good-bye, old life!

TROFIMOV Welcome to the new life! . . . *Goes out with* ANYA.

VARYA *looks around the room and goes out slowly.* YASHA *and* CHARLOTTA, *with her little dog, follow.*

LOPAHIN And so, until the spring. Come, my friends. . . . Au revoir! *Goes out.*

LYUBOV *and* GAEV *alone. They seem to have been waiting for this moment, and now they embrace each other and cry quietly, with restraint, so as not to be heard.*

GAEV, *in despair.* Sister, my sister. . . .

LYUBOV Oh, my orchard, my beloved, my beautiful orchard! My life, my youth, my happiness . . . good-bye! . . . Good-bye!

ANYA, *off-stage, calling gaily.* Mama! . . .

TROFIMOV, *off-stage, gaily and excitedly.* Yoo-hoo! . . .

LYUBOV Just one last time—to look at these walls, these windows. . . . Mother loved to walk in this room. . . .

GAEV Sister, my sister . . .

ANYA, *off-stage*. Mamma!

TROFIMOV, *off-stage*. Yoo-hoo!

LYUBOV We're coming . . . *They go out.*

The stage is empty. The sound of doors being locked and then of carriages driving off. Silence. In the stillness the dull sounds of an axe striking on a tree can be heard. They sound mournful and sad. Footsteps are heard and from the door on the right FEERS *enters. He is dressed, as usual, in a coat and white waistcoat, and is wearing slippers. He is ill.*

FEERS *walks up to the middle door and tries the handle.* Locked. They've gone . . . *Sits down on a sofa.* They've forgotten me. Never mind. . . . I'll sit here for a bit. I don't suppose Leonid Andreyevich put on his fur coat, he probably wore his light one. *Sighs, preoccupied.* I didn't take care of it . . . These young people! . . . *Mutters something unintelligible.* My life's slipped by as if I'd never lived. . . . *Lies down.* I'll lie down a bit. You haven't got any strength left, nothing's left, nothing. . . . Oh, you . . . you old good-for-nothing! . . . *Lies motionless.*

A distant sound that seems to come out of the sky, like a break-ing harp, slowly and sadly dying away. Then all is silent, except for the sound of an axe striking a tree in the orchard far away.

Curtain.

Rinehart Editions